BEHAVIOR MODIFICATION
AND
FAMILIES

Behavior Modification and Families

Edited by

ERIC J. MASH, Ph.D.
Associate Professor of Psychology
The University of Calgary

LEO A. HAMERLYNCK, Ed.D.
Coordinator, Mental Health/Mental Retardation
State of Montana

and

LEE C. HANDY, Ph.D.
Associate Professor of Educational Psychology
The University of Calgary

BRUNNER/MAZEL, *Publishers*   New York

Published by
BRUNNER/MAZEL, INC.
64 University Place, New York, N. Y. 10003

Library of Congress Cataloging in Publication Data

Banff International Conference on Behavior Modification, 6th, 1974.
   Behavior modification and families.

   Proceedings of the conference held in March 1974 in Banff.
   Includes bibliographies and index.
   1. Behavior modification—Congresses.   2. Child psychology—Congresses.   3.
Parent and child—Congresses.   I. Mash, Eric J., 1943-   II. Hamerlynck, Leo A.,
1929-   III. Handy, Lee C., 1939-   IV. Title.   [DNLM:1. Behavior therapy
—Congresses.   2. Family therapy—Congresses.
W3 BA203 1974b / WM420 B215 1974b]
BF637.B4B34   1974   618.9'28'915   75-37733
ISBN 0-87630-118-9

PREFACE

This volume is part of a continuing series of publications sponsored by the Banff International Conferences on Behavior Modification. The conferences are held each spring in Banff, Alberta, Canada, and serve the purpose of bringing together outstanding behavioral scientists to discuss and present data related to emergent issues and topics in the field of what is now termed Behavior Modification. Thus, the International Conferences, as a continuing event, have served as an expressive "early indicator" of the developing nature and composition of behavioristic science and scientific application.

Distances, schedules, and the restricted audiences preclude wide attendances at the conferences. Consequently, this series of publications has equal status with the conference proper. Past conference topics and faculty were:

1969: I. IDEAL MENTAL HEALTH SERVICES

Nathan Azrin	Gerald Patterson	Richard B. Stuart
Ogden Lindsley	Todd Risley	

1970: II. SERVICES AND PROGRAMS FOR EXCEPTIONAL CHILDREN AND YOUTH

Loren and Margaret Acker	David R. Evans	Nancy J. Reynolds
Wesley C. Becker	Leo A. Hamerlynck	James A. Sherman
Nancy Buckley	Ogden Lindsley	Richard B. Stuart
Donald Cameron	Patrick McGinley	Walter Zwirner
L. Richard Crozier		

1971: III. IMPLEMENTING BEHAVIORAL PROGRAMS FOR SCHOOLS AND CLINICS

Joe A. Cobb	Hugh McKenzie	Ernest G. Poser
Rodney Copeland	Garry L. Martin	Roberta S. Ray
R. Vance Hall	Jack L. Michael	Richard B. Stuart
Ogden Lindsley	Gerald R. Patterson	Carl E. Thoresen

1972: IV. BEHAVIOR CHANGE: METHODOLOGY, CONCEPTS, AND PRACTICE

Eric J. Mash	G. C. Davison	H. M. Walker and H. Hops
S. M. Johnson and	G. R. Patterson	J. LoPiccolo and W. C. Lobitz
O. D. Bolstad	H. Hops and J. A. Cobb	D. L. Fixsen, M. M. Wolf and
K. D. O'Leary and R. Kent	J. B. Reid and	E. L. Phillips
K. Skindrud	A. F. C. J. Hendriks	R. L. Weiss, H. Hops, and
R. R. Jones	R. B. Stuart	G. R. Patterson
L. A. Hamerlynck	Lee C. Handy	

v

1973: V. Evaluation of Behavioral Programs

James R. Barclay
Peter Bates
Michael F. Cataldo
William W. Cooley
William J. DeRisi
Thad A. Eckman
Robert P. Hawkins
Siegfried S. Hiebert
Srinika Jayaratne
Richard R. Jones
Robert L. Kahn
Larry W. King
Carl H. Koenig
Gaea Leinhardt
Robert Paul Liberman

Peter D. McLean
William B. Neenan
Aldred H. Neufeldt
H. S. Pennypacker
Todd R. Risley
Rosemary C. Sarri
W. H. Seaver
Elaine Selo
Bryan C. Smith
Richard B. Stuart
Tony Tripodi
Charles Windle
David Wood
Steven H. Zarit

Many people have donated their energies and talents to maintain the annual role of the Banff International Conference on Behavior Modification as a medium for behavioral scientists and applied professionals. Foremost, certainly, must be the guest faculty who develop, present, and discuss the topics found in this volume.

It is gratefully noted that the material support and technical guidance of The University of Calgary's Division of Continuing Education has again been of a typically high order. Ms. Donna Fraser has been the person responsible for making this extraordinary service an everyday occurrence. Dr. David Leighton and the staff of the Banff Centre insured that the physical environment for the conference was enjoyable and facilitative. Dr. W. R. N. Blair again contributed his support and enthusiasm for the concept of the conferences.

Other members of the editorial board and conference planning committee deserve to be singled out for their substantial help and guidance. They are Dr. Frank W. Clark, Social Work, The University of Calgary; Dr. Richard Stuart, Psychiatry, and Dr. Park D. Davidson, Psychology, The University of British Columbia.

It is impossible to conclude our acknowledgments without thanking our colleagues and the conference participants who guided our efforts by their feedback, and our families, who have continually refreshed our endeavors.

E.J.M.
L.A.H.
L.C.H.

The University of Calgary, Alberta, Canada.

FOREWORD
Cyril M. Franks

There was a time, not so very long ago, when behavior modification was a simple, cut and dried affair. All that was needed was a working knowledge of the well-established principles of classical and operant conditioning as they applied to the individual, a small reservoir of techniques, and an unswerving belief that the therapist knew best. Family units, social organizations, societal and ethical issues—all these were of little or no concern; events directly within the person were as of little relevance as those far away. Unlike Gertrude Stein, we knew both question and answer and, like the good doctor in Voltaire's "Candide," we knew that, behaviorally speaking, we are living in the best of all possible worlds. In those halcyon days, our thinking and our behavior were unfettered by complications or doubts; for us, stimuli and responses were straightforward, direct, mostly immediate, one to one, and generally unhampered by nuances or complicating factors. In a word, we and our behavioral model were simplistic.

This, of course, was a virtually inevitable and probably even desirable stage in the evolution of our burgeoning new science. All theoretical and conceptual models are over-simplifications, especially in their early stages, and if it were otherwise we could not possibly develop a viable system. Sophistication comes with experience; behavior therapy is no exception to this observation. It is within this context that we should assess contemporary developments within behavior therapy. Little less than a decade ago, behavior therapists were concerned primarily with the individual and his immediate stimulus-response systems. On the one hand, intrapsychic processes were viewed as unacceptable carry-overs from an alien psychoanalytic tradition. On the other hand, behavior therapists had, as yet, developed neither the awareness of the need nor the necessary techniques for meaningful interpersonal intervention. For example, behavior therapy in groups—e.g., group desensitization—was well developed, but group behavior therapy, in which group processes per se were utilized, did not exist.

To appreciate the present scene in all its complexities, it is also necessary to take into account behavior therapy's many and richly diverse technical and conceptual roots. However, it is neither appropriate nor feasible to unravel and delineate these many strands here. Suffice it to note that contemporary behavior therapy is broad and far reaching, by no means monolithic in either strategy or origins, probing deep within the individual and far outside the boundaries uncharted as recently as a year ago. Within the individual, biofeedback, imagery and other cognitive processes are now very much part of the contemporary scene. Beyond the physical confines of the person, such seemingly diverse disciplines as systems analysis, ecology, geoplanning and socio-political structures are all potentially germane to the ever expanding canvas of behavior therapy.

Throughout this seeming turmoil a number of intriguing signs are beginning to emerge. Objectivity and tolerance are replacing polemics, factionalism is yielding to a willingness to consider virtually any data-oriented proposal regardless of its allegiance to conventional learning theory. As behavior therapy broadens its perspectives, so the possibility increases that, in so doing, we may lose our identity. When the model was a simple S-R one, it was easy to see what was and what was not behavior therapy and how we should proceed. Now, with the canvas assuming Joycean proportions, almost any scientifically bona fide strategy becomes legitimate for the behavior therapist to explore. The questions then arise as to what is to be included under the rubric of behavior therapy and what is not, what is to be our definition of behavior therapy and how does behavior therapy differ from other therapeutic approaches. If we become too narrow and too simplistic, then we cannot possibly incorporate all the complexities of socio-biological 1975 man into our framework. And if we are too broad, then we may lose that unique identity that we once rightly claimed to possess. Of course, one might well argue with conviction that, if a paradigm shift is really occurring, then the latter possibility is no great loss in the total scheme of things. It is probably true to say that, if behavior therapy has not yet developed a philosophy or image of man in the way that certain other great schools of therapeutic endeavor have, the glimmerings of such an ethos are beginning to emerge. It is also possible that we are witnessing both a broadening of behavior therapy *and* a paradigm shift.

Whatever the validity of such speculation, there is undoubtedly a pattern, a continuity to emerging trends. One way to spotlight, evaluate and place this pattern in perspective is by an ongoing, integrated series of planned scrutinies. The Banff International Conferences on Behavior Modification serve just such a purpose, and are rapidly and deservedly becoming a tradition. Over the years we have learned to look at the Banff Conference as a sensitive barometer of the climate of change in our field. Each year, the carefully planned and coordinated contributions of the distinguished participants serve to chronicle and appraise the evolving nature of our science on an ongoing basis. The 1974 Conference, dedicated to the twin themes of families and parenting, continues manifestly in this honorable tradition, and these published Proceedings make it possible for those who were unable to be present at Banff in person to participate meaningfully and constructively in the deliberations, nevertheless.

Under the experienced and penetrating direction of the three dedicated editors, the present volume devotes itself exclusively to behavior modification and families. The major issues of concern focal to the mid-70's and the changing nature of the family unit in our equally changing society are skillfully incorporated into their thoughtful Introduction, and we are well prepared for the intellectual feast that is to follow. One by one, the contributors present their evidence and marshall their points, and it is evident from a careful reading of the rich fare that is contained in these pages that we have indeed come a long way from the simplistic era of the 1960s. If we have not as yet achieved a behavioral theory and philosophy of man, it is deliberations such as these which point the way. Whether these developments reflect a broadening of the model within the behavioral framework, or the birth of a paradigm shift in the sense that Kuhn uses this term, remains to be seen. It may well be that what we are witnessing is the breakdown of existing, circumscribed ways of ordering our phenomenal world, and the emergence of new ways of approaching these data which entail a major conceptual restructuring. It is books such as this which place the present in perspective and serve to shape the future.

The information contained in these pages is timely, the Commentaries by Mash, Hamerlynck and Handy superb, the range of problems tackled and issues considered wide and far-reaching, the presentations searching, and the conclusions valid and significant. All concerned with this worthy endeavor are to be congratulated and, hopefully, the Banff tradition will continue to flourish and expand in the years to come.

CONTENTS

EDITORS' INTRODUCTION

The promulgation of particular goals for the conduct of family affairs has had a long and extensive history. So, too, has advice-giving related to how these goals might be achieved through the application of specific procedures. Such advice-giving has received its impetus from both formal and informal institutions of society—religion, education, medicine, welfare, the local community, and members of the immediate family. The areas of family living targeted for advice have ranged from marital relations to management of economic affairs. However, nowhere has advice-giving been more predominant than in matters relating to child rearing. While touching on all of these areas, the selections in this volume reflect this proportionate emphasis.

The precedent for information-giving in relation to parenting is pervasive and irrefutable. From the standpoint of insuring the biological survival of the developing fetus and neonate, the giving of advice has been a long-standing and necessary component of human existence. Such advice has been represented by grandmotherly participation, midwives, and more recently by the provision of prenatal classes for expectant parents and courses in family living offered at primary levels in our educational system. Formal avenues for giving advice relating to the social, educational, and emotional development of the child have probably had a briefer history, but unquestionably still a long and extensive one. Child-rearing advice is very much a part of the fabric of our society and has always been so. Today, such advice comes through most of the sources of mass media. There are magazines, radio and television programs, and numerous pamphlets and books that in sum have something to say about every facet of child rearing. The focus of such advice ranges from promoting normal development to dealing with behavior which is labeled as aberrant. Implicit in every theory of child development, whether it be predominantly a maturational or environmentally based approach, are guidelines for raising children. The degree to which such implicit guidelines have been made explicit and popularized has varied from theory to theory, yet they have generally been quite pervasive. Contributions are similar from most theories of abnormal behavior which project and sanction styles of parenting that have both contributed to, and may be used to alter the course of, problematic child behavior.

Within the context of this extensive system for giving advice on family living, the systematic application of the principles and procedures of behavior modification to the family is a relatively recent arrival on the scene, in spite of the fact that there are numerous isolated reports of the informal application of child-rearing procedures which would seem to reflect very closely the principles of behavioral analysis. It is somewhat paradoxical that while the application of behavior modification to the family is relatively recent from an historical perspective, it is relatively old in relation to the life span of behavior modification.

Family intervention has permeated research and practice throughout the developing stages of behavior modification and has probably served as a focal point for much of this development. This concomitant and parallel development most likely relates to the fact that family intervention directly reflects and highlights some of the broader defining characteristics of behavioral analysis. These characteristics include, among other things, the emphasis on intervention in the natural environment (Tharp and Wetzel, 1969), which nowhere has been more evident than in applications with families. This emphasis is based on the assumption that behavior is maintained by contemporaneous events in the natural environment, and it is through the alteration of these events that behavior change is achieved. This assumption leads directly to the utilization of family members in mediating behavior change, and has served as the basis for the multitudinous number of "parent training" programs which have developed (Berkowitz and Graziano, 1972; Johnson and Katz, 1973; O'Dell, 1974).

Another defining characteristic of behavioral approaches has been a concern for the efficiency of treatment (Baer et al., 1968). Again, family intervention which attempts to utilize agents in the natural environment possesses the potential for less costly intervention, from the standpoint of both program maintenance and reduction in the professional resources needed (Patterson, 1974).

This book is organized into three broad areas of work and study attempting to develop the technology of applied behavioral analysis for the family. In general, the content of each section describes the historical and current status of the science and art, with conclusions predicting directions for future trends, developments, and problems. The three areas are:

I. *Directions and Developments* in Family Life and Child Rearing;
II. The *Generalization and Maintenance* of Healthy Family Behavior;
III. *Problems and Perspectives* in the Conduct of Research and Intervention.

In order to establish a "set" for this examination of behavior modification in the family, a number of predominant emphases which have characterized previous behavior modification work with families are outlined. In many ways, these characteristics have served as an impetus for many of the issues raised in this volume, and for some of the newer areas of development. *First,* behavior modification work with families has been predominantly concerned with families in which there is an identified problem. Although it has been frequently noted that "family education" is something everybody should have, and repeatedly stated that family intervention before problems emerge provides a strong prevention base, the focus for research and practice has nevertheless been primarily on family disturbance. A dissatisfaction with such an emphasis is reflected in many of the selections in this volume which attempt to develop and stimulate the application of behavioral analysis with non-deviant populations.

A *second* characteristic of previous behavioral work with families has been a focus on the child as the individual whose behavior is targeted for change. Again, while lip service has been paid to the notion that the entire family must be involved, the involvement of the family has typically been in terms of providing a context for the occurrence and subsequent modification of the child's behavior. The very notion of "parent training" implies that the parent will be taught how to change the child's behavior. Presumably the parent's behavior will also change in the process; however, this change is placed in a role subordinate to the major one of influencing what the child is doing. The selections in this volume reflect a growing concern for dealing with the family as a system of reciprocal influence.

A *third* characteristic of behavior modification work with families has been the emphasis on teaching contingency management rather than stimulus control and/or self-controlling strategies. This emphasis is reflected in the numerous case studies which have modified single child behaviors through the provision of reward systems. Such programs have attempted to alter child behavior by having the parent serve as mediator for the contingent application of material, token, and social rewards, and have ranged from early demonstrations involving simple alterations of parental responses (e.g., ignoring tantrums, Williams, 1959) to more complex arrangements based upon the use of formal contracts for regulating the exchange of rewards (DeRisi and Butz, 1975). In contrast to these approaches, the selections in this volume reflect an increasing recognition of the possibilities for promoting adaptive family functioning through the implementation of social-ecological engineering and strategies of self-control, rather than through approaches based predominantly on the management of contingencies.

A *fourth* characteristic of behavior modification work with families has been a primary concern with intervention in relatively intact families and in what may be described as traditional family situations. The technology for behavior change which has developed parent training, for example, has given little attention to what might be referred to as "special" family situations; yet such situations are becoming increasingly more frequent within our society. Included here are families in which there is only one parent; families in which a large proportion of the child's time may be spent in day-care facilities because parent(s) are working; families participating in group or communal living arrangements; families in which parents are older; child abusing families; families in which parents are handicapped; etc. The existing behavioral approaches to the family have in many instances been insensitive to these types of situations. Many of the selections in this volume adapt and extend the application of behavioral analysis in order to reflect some of the trends in our society involving alternative family systems.

It can be seen from the foregoing statements that behavioral approaches to the family have neglected a number of important areas. This is not to imply that the previous work in this area was, and is, not a necessary part of the development of an emerging conceptual base and technology for working with families. What we are suggesting is that there is a need to consider behavior modification family research and applications in relation to a number of broader conceptual and research issues, rather than solely within the narrow formulation of training parents to be therapists for specific problem behaviors that their children are exhibiting.

The papers in this volume highlight a number of recent conceptual and research developments. Specifically, a major section deals with questions relating to the general area of parenting and considers the relationships between behavioral and non-behavioral approaches to the family, as well as intervention programs for populations and situations that have frequently been overlooked. Among these are single-parent families, group living situations, and "normal" families. Another important area of discussion centers on what the goals for family intervention should be.

A further subject of concern for behavioral intervention strategies in the family has been the question of generalization of treatment effects across situations, behaviors, and time. Such questions are essential for considering the efficiency of any applied efforts. A major section of this volume is devoted to this question.

In considering any behavior change program a key question relates to the base rate of various behaviors. This knowledge is essential for developments which attempt to foster positive behaviors in non-deviant populations, as well as in evaluating the effectiveness of programs for deviant populations. In effect, the question here is basically one of behavioral norms. The normative question in a behavioral approach attempts to relate behavioral occurrence to specific situations. A number of papers in this volume make comparisons between children's behavior in various situations and across various populations.

The reader will find a detailed discussion of a growing concern for consideration of the family system as involving reciprocal influence, and a deemphasis of programs which attempt to change the child's behavior without considering the overall family context and the child's influence on the parents.

Although the papers in this volume point to a number of new directions for behavioral researchers and practitioners concerned with the family, it should be recognized that they also maintain and retain the features of behavioral analysis which have served as major strengths. These include the use of procedures and principles that are empirically based, and an evaluation of program effectiveness by means of an objective description of procedures, careful measurement, and an interest in efficiency.

REFERENCES

BAER, D. M., WOLF, M. M., and RISLEY, T. R.: Some current dimensions of applied behavior analysis. *J. Appl. Behav. Anal.*, 1, 91-97, 1968.

BERKOWITZ, B., and GRAZIANO, A.: Training parents as behavioral therapists: A review. *Behav. Res. and Ther.*, 10, 297-317, 1972.

DERISI W. J., and BUTZ, G.: *Writing Behavioral Contracts: A Case Stimulation Practice Manual.* Champaign, Ill.: Research Press, 1975.

JOHNSON, C., and KATZ, R. C.: Using parents as change agents for their children: A review. *J. Child Psychol. and Psychiat.*, 14, 181-200, 1973.

O'DELL, S.: Training parents in behavior modification: A review. *Psychol. Bull.*, 81, 418-433, 1974.

PATTERSON, G. R.: Interventions for boys with conduct problems: Multiple settings, treatments and criteria. *J. Consult. and Clin. Psychol.*, 42, 471-481, 1974.

THARP, R. G., and WETZEL, R.: *Behavior Modification in the Natural Environment.* New York: Academic Press, 1969.

WILLIAMS, C. D.: The elimination of tantrum behaviors by extinction procedures. *J. Abnorm. and Soc. Psych.*, 59, 269, 1959.

CONTRIBUTORS

VICTOR A. BENASSI
*California State University,
Long Beach*

MARTHA E. BERNAL
University of Denver

ELAINE A. BLECHMAN
Yale University

ORIN D. BOLSTAD
University of Oregon

BRADLEY D. BUCHER
University of Western Ontario

MICHAEL F. CATALDO
*John F. Kennedy Institute
Baltimore, Maryland*

HEWITT B. CLARK
University of Kansas

JOHN B. CONWAY
University of Saskatchewan

JOHN A. CORSON
McGill University

LEO F. DELFINI
University of Denver

RICHARD FEALLOCK
University of Kansas

ANN M. GARNER
*University of Oregon Medical
School*

FRANCES DEGEN HOROWITZ
University of Kansas

RUSSELL H. JACKSON
*University of Oregon Medical
School*

SANDRA JOHANSSON
*Family Guidance Clinic
Medina, Ohio*

STEPHEN M. JOHNSON
University of Oregon

SUSAN L. KREUTZER
University of Denver

KATHRYN M. LARSON
*California State University,
Long Beach*

ALICE LIES
University of Kansas

GRETCHEN K. LOBITZ
University of Oregon

MARTHA MANNING
Yale University

SANDER MARTIN
University of Houston

L. KEITH MILLER
University of Kansas

JUEL ANN NORTH
University of Denver

GERALD R. PATTERSON
*University of Oregon and Oregon
Research Institute*

DAN L. PETERSEN
University of Kansas

ROBERT F. PETERSON
University of Nevada, Reno

TODD R. RISLEY
University of Kansas

PAUL M. ROSEN
University of Denver

LEIF TERDAL
*University of Oregon Medical
School*

GAIL WAHL
University of Oregon

Section I

DIRECTIONS AND DEVELOPMENTS

Commentary

The papers in this section are somewhat unique in their emphasis on examining the principles and technologies of behavioral analysis within the broader context of social goals and values. They relate not only to what *can* be done with respect to enhancing the family situation, but also to issues concerned with both the implementation and acceptance of the technology, and the end to which technology is being applied.

The first paper, by Horowitz, provides an excellent overview of the area of parenting, which includes what we presently know about parental influence and how this information can be utilized. Beginning with the premise that there is growing empirical support for the possibility of a technology of control within the family, Horowitz examines both historical and contemporary reactions to such control. She goes on to discuss some of the objections to behavioral analysis frequently raised by professionals and nonprofessionals—including that it is too cold, too mechanistic, or too simplistic—and compares parenting approaches based upon the management of rewards and punishment to those based upon the pervasive dimension of "parental warmth."

As part of the broader question of possible goals for programs of parent education, Horowitz examines several areas in which there is empirical support for the role of parenting in affecting child behavior—intellectual development and the shaping of cognitive styles, social adjustment, and physical development. In all of these areas the reciprocal nature of the parent-child interaction is emphasized, a theme which is developed extensively in the last section of this volume (for example, by Patterson).

Horowitz recommends the development of parenting courses within our existing educational system and of community-based parent-child research stations as vehicles for exploring the possibilities of creating

1

more effective parents within our present social structure. At the same time she acknowledges the need for exploration of alternative parenting systems, and recommends setting up different types of short-term experimental communities as a way of understanding alternate approaches. These latter points serve as transition for the subsequent papers in this section.

As indicated in the introduction, behavioral approaches to the family have most frequently been concerned with the management of problematic behavior. The next paper in this section, by Risley, Clark, and Cataldo, represents a significant shift away from this "band-aid" approach to family problems, towards one which emphasizes the utilization of behavioral technology for "normal" families and for everyday types of problematic situations with which they are confronted. Implicit in this approach is a positive emphasis on and concern for the enhancement of the general quality of life for significant numbers of people, and a strong commitment to a preventive approach to family disturbance.

Initially, Risley et al. make the point that in order to prepare for types of situations which families are likely to be faced with in the future, it is essential to consider current societal trends such as smaller families, more inexperienced parents, and working parents. These trends are considered in terms of their practical outcomes, which are likely to reflect an increasing need for daily child care and assistance with child rearing of the kind that is no longer being provided by the extended family.

In relation to the quality of child care, Risley et al. describe a number of systematic programs which have been developed and are developing for day care of infants, toddlers and preschoolers, and older children and youths. In these programs there is an increasing emphasis on teaching and guidance as the child gets older, as well as a focus on the antecedent physical and social stimulus control of behavior through the use of architecture and interior design, organization of materials and activities, and prepackaged programs for staff training. In part, this emphasis reflects a growing concern for the efficiency of procedures and the need to reduce costs while optimizing gains.

Risley et al. also consider the need for developing programs of family advice which, rather than providing a general child-rearing attitude or principles for dealing with a variety of child behaviors, give the parents specific skills for solving everyday child-rearing problems. In keeping with an emphasis on stimulus control and prevention, they point out that the types of situations that frequently cause problems must be identified and predicted. Such an approach not only permits the more efficient and efficacious management of behavior but also presents the possibility of behavioral enhancement and problem circumvention through prestructuring such situations. The paper clearly reflects the view that "a comprehensive system of child-rearing assistance for families is needed," and that serious attention must be given to the development, packaging, and dissemination of such assistance. The broad, comprehensive, and highly empirical approach being advocated by Risley et al. represents a potential solution to some of the persistent problems which have characterized purely remediational behavioral approaches to the family, including the pervasive problem of generalization of treatment effects, which is discussed in the next section of this volume.

The points made by Risley et al. in relation to working or single-parent families are developed and expanded upon in the next paper, by Blechman and Manning, which considers both primary prevention and intervention strategies specifically in relation to the unique needs of single-parent families.

Blechman and Manning first review evidence of the increasing incidence of single-parent families within our society. They point out that there has been little systematic attention to the development of intervention strategies for this population; that family roles in many traditional theories of personality development and deviancy create a negative bias against single-parent families; and that a behavioral approach, which views single-parent family characteristics as setting events that lead to selective exposure of the individuals involved to certain classes of situations and reinforcers, may serve to dispel this bias. Here again, as was the case in the Risley et al. paper, the importance of identifying "critical" situations and their stimulus-controlling properties as a remediational and preventive strategy is stressed.

Blechman and Manning then identify a number of setting events characteristically associated with single-parent families. They also make the point that such families represent a heterogeneous group and that there are a number of factors which can contribute to diversity among them, such as the sex of the single parent, the cause of parental absence, and the way in which family functions were carried out before the loss of one of the parents in single-parent families which were initially intact.

In addition to events creating diversity, they identify a number of factors that serve to contribute to uniformity within the population of single-parent families. Among these are the increase in time demands placed upon the single parent, the tendency to use the two-parent family as a reference group, and the likelihood that some imbalance in behavioral control will result in the reciprocal relationships between parent and children.

Finally, Blechman and Manning make a number of recommendations for the development of behavior change programs for the single-parent family. These recommendations are based upon the interplay between the empirical data base of behavior analysis and the specified characteristics unique to single-parent families. The identification of persistent and recurrent problems in this type of family situation provides a strong basis for the development of preventive programs as well.

In the final paper in this section Miller, Lies, Peterson, and Feallock present a number of the points which have been stressed throughout the initial part of this volume. Miller et al. recognize that principles for the control of behavior are available and that, while most applications have been directed at the modification of abnormal behavior, the possibilities for using behavioral technology in normal family situations are numerous. The position taken by Miller et al. is similar to that advocated by Horowitz and represents an implementation of this viewpoint. The viewpoint is that, rather than attempt to design a "utopian" family system at the present point in time, it might be more fruitful to explore the possibilities by designing experimental communities which represent successive approximations to some of the alternative family situations that might develop. Such experimental communities provide the necessary empirical base from which decisions about possible alternate family styles may be made.

The project described by Miller et al. is an engineered group-living situation for unmarried university students. This particular alternate family system was considered to be appropriate as it requires a minimum amount of dissuasion away from existing family patterns. The engineered group-living situation was designed to reflect a number of goals, including the creation of an efficient worksharing system, and the development of a "behavioral culture" and a "positive behavioral community." The specific steps for attempting to meet each of these objectives, as well as procedures for the evaluation of program effectiveness, are described in some detail. In conclusion, Miller et al. make a number of projections for future directions involving developments with other populations such as married individuals and individuals with children.

In summary, the papers presented in this section provide a number of new directions and developments for behavior modification approaches to the family. Probably the most recurrent theme is that behavioral analysis may have some of its greatest applicability to populations, situations, and problems that are essentially of a nondeviant nature.

1

Directions for Parenting

FRANCES DEGEN HOROWITZ

When I accepted the invitation to participate in this conference almost nine months ago, I did not anticipate that writing this paper would be as difficult a task as it turned out to be. I took the assigned title *very* seriously. I made numerous attempts to begin the paper only to repeatedly discard one beginning draft after another. In fact, on three different evenings, as I began to write, the lights all suddenly went out—victims of one of the many storms in what was an unusually severe winter for Israel and the Middle East where I have been these last ten months. And, having already absorbed some of the culture of the Middle East, where superstition and signs are ancient guides, I began to think there was a possibly important omen in the coincident darkness—either predicting an unworthy outcome for my efforts or indicating that the project should be abandoned. But the long years of socialized rational training persisted—as did I, leaving omens behind for the social reinforcers of audience response. Nevertheless, for once I decided it did seem easier to do something about parenting than to talk about it. All of which may be a sign, in its own right, that we have come past the corner of philosophizing to action, partially as a result of the obvious and increasingly successful technology of behavioral science.

Such a state of affairs, if it does indeed exist, would have warmed the heart of a courageous Iowa lady who has been immortalized in the memories of the students of what was the Iowa Child Welfare Research

The author wrote this paper in Rehovot, Israel, while on sabbatical leave from the University of Kansas. In addition to sabbatical leave support from the University of Kansas, funds from the Grant Foundation also provided support during the time this paper was written.

Station. Her story,* though it took place almost 60 years ago, is worth retelling, not only for its historical interest but for its recurrent relevance to our present situation. This lady was as fertile—having produced a brood of children in the course of several marriages—as she was wealthy. Encountering difficulties in raising her children, she made the apt analogy that Iowa farmers having problems raising their corn and hogs had access to advice from a series of agricultural research stations. Why, she reasoned, ought not parents to have similar resources for growing their children? With this, she offered a considerable endowment to the University to establish a child research station, only to be told by an indulgent and rather uninterested president that the University really needed a bell tower and they would name it after her if she would, instead, donate her sums to such a project. Not deterred by his lack of discernment as to the significance of her original proposal, she persisted until the matter came before the Iowa legislature. To this elected body she put the proposition that the state establish a child research station for the express purpose of doing research on child development, training people to work with children and parents, and advising parents about the process of growing children—or, in more modern parlance, of parenting. And, the story goes, her offer, generous and well reasoned as it was, was turned down. One of the telling arguments of the time— this being the year 1916—was that growing children and parenting was an essentially private affair for which the government had no business providing resources lest the line between government and family life be blurred. But she was not a lady easily deflected from her purposes, and in 1919 the matter again came before the Iowa legislators. This time she won—and the legislation to establish the famous Iowa Child Welfare Research Station (a curious name for those of us who were students there in the 1950's) was passed.

Though only three years had elapsed between her first and her final assault upon the governmental decision makers, time was not the measure of the change that had occurred which permitted a different outcome. What had intervened was the first World War, with its national draft and the results of the assessments of the young men called up to army service. As all of you well know, there is nothing like data to help effect a change in attitudes, and the data from these national assessments destroyed the myth that American young men were fit in all respects.

---

* Boyd R. McCandless regularly told this story to graduate students at the Iowa Child Welfare Research Station. Any inaccuracies that may have crept in are a function of the author's memory of the details.

The percentage who could not be accepted for army service because of physical and psychological problems shocked many and made them more receptive to the argument that the state and government did, indeed, have a stake in that most private of all affairs—the process of raising a family. Thus was born an era of child development—of research, training, and teaching about children and family relations—an era not peculiar to the state of Iowa, but one which, during the 1920's, came to characterize many newly established child development settings in the United States, Canada, and elsewhere in the Western World.

In these last 55 years, the vision of the generous Iowa lady has not been fully realized, though the outpouring of research is testimony enough to the validity of her concern. Perhaps the whole matter of aiding parents in growing children is more complex than aiding farmers in growing corn and hogs. Perhaps, too, the agricultural research station can dispense advice with greater ease and success because the knowledge base from which that advice springs is greater and more certain than the knowledge base in the behavioral domain. I do not wish to belabor this analogy too far, but just a bit more of it may prove useful to the kinds of analyses and issues for discussion that I would like to raise. There is a certain attraction to the simplicity of aiding farmers that some of us can envy. When the district advisor tells his agricultural field representatives that the quantity and quality of the yield in corn in their areas can be increased by the addition of nitrogen to the soil, he is not likely to have anyone in his audience who will challenge him as to just what he means by nitrogen, or who will accuse him of being mechanistic and manipulative, and of ignoring the "dynamic aspects" of the interaction of the seed and the soil. Not only is the functional relationship accepted, but the basic terminology and facts are well established. It is true, as we have come to realize, sometimes painfully, that successful technology cannot be isolated from values and social goals. One may legitimately argue about the issue of chemical enrichment of the soil and its long-term consequences, both for the human who consumes food grown in such soil and for the availability of resources. But no one doubts that there is a variable of nitrogen and no one doubts the immediate effects that can be produced by its application.

Perhaps it is to the credit of the human organism that even *before* the basic controlling phenomena of behavior are well documented, objections to the possible harmful effects of implementing them systematically have been raised. Indeed, the arguments and issues have sometimes been raised so sharply and heatedly that the basic facts to be discovered were often obscured. But slowly, despite this, and for possibly unrelated reasons, the knowledge base about the variables that function to produce, control, maintain, and change behavior has become more surely identified and understood. If the hallmark of most science is the reproducibility as well as the predictability of its phenomena, then the behavioral account of the human organism, under sometimes complex and "noisy" conditions, is becoming increasingly more impressive. And the use of behavior modification techniques to change and maintain behavior in family units is evidence that the application of our knowledge can succeed in just those settings where psychiatrically oriented professionals have for so long met with only minimal success.

However, the application of what knowledge we have is not always easy. The diversity of points of view, vocabulary, and style sometimes seriously interferes with the entire process of communicating about behavioral phenomena. A few months ago I had the opportunity to talk to a group of school psychologists about assessment of the behavior repertoire of normal infants. I discussed the possibility that some infants, at birth, already had a more readily available repertoire than others of behaviors which were more reinforcing for the behavior of their mothers. After the discussion had proceeded along these lines for several minutes, a woman in the audience said: "But, when you talk like that, aren't you ignoring the dynamic aspects of the mother-infant relationship? How can you talk about the mother and her infant like that? What about warmth, and love, and security?"

"Well," I answered, "maybe it would help if we would talk about what is meant by terms like warmth, and love, and security. Perhaps there is more of a semantic problem here than one of basic disagreement."

But this communicative effort was not to succeed, for my interrogator replied by saying: "I don't want to get us off on *that*. These are *very, very* deep issues, *very, very serious philosophical* matters."

Thus the interchange was closed—as if, instead of a matter of dialogue, were about to embark on an obviously too costly and time-consuming expedition of drilling for oil at the very plumbed depths of the earth.

Why is it possible for a discussion between two psychologists to end by one declaring that the phenomenon under consideration is just too deep to be pursued? Can you imagine two physicists or two chemists coming to the same impasse about chemical or other natural phenomena? I believe that the nature of much psychological inquiry has contributed to some of this. Perhaps because of the same fears and concerns that the Iowa legislators expressed over 50 years ago, perhaps because of the complexity of the phenomenon of parent-child interactions, certainly because of the issues of privacy, much of the early inquiry involved parental reports and attitude measurement. Out of such research, general dimensions of parental behavior were labeled and correlated with either child behavior or labels given to various groups of children based upon some behavioral observations. Thus came some of the categories which are now so much a part of the professional and popular belief systems: "warmth" and "acceptance" in parent attitudes correlated with children judged to be "adjusted" and "pro-social," while "hostility" and "rejection" were correlated with children judged to be "maladjusted" and "antisocial." The quest was an earnest and serious one, and to *some* extent a productive one.

The attitudinal line of inquiry led to a constant search for the improved assessment of attitudes—trying to get closer and closer to a congruence between what parents said and what they did. Perhaps the height of this strategy was reflected in the high hopes for one of the more carefully developed attitude assessment procedures during the late '50's and early '60's—an instrument known as the PARI, the Parent Attitude Research Instrument (Schaefer and Bell, 1958).

I think one needs to understand the history of this literature and to know the substance of its findings in order to understand the wellsprings that feed the objections to and rejections of the application of such techniques as one finds in behavior modification approaches to parent-child relations. In 1964, in the first volume of the *Review of Child Development Research* (Hoffman and Hoffman, 1964), Wesley Becker (1964) attempted to take stock of what was then over 30 years of research on parenting—a period of investigation that started not long after the hopeful establishment of child development research centers, many of which had the expressed or ultimate purpose of helping parents. Interestingly, of the 88 references cited by Becker, 34 were dated between the years 1960 and 1963. The chapter, entitled "Consequences of parental discipline," concluded with three observations—one summarizing the dimensions of parent behavior that appeared to have emerged out of the research, one regarding what the next step might be, and the third reflecting on what had, after all, been accomplished. Becker noted that parental warmth and hostility appeared to be related to the effects of parenting. In respect to the future, Becker's statement is almost an outline of what, in fact, happened in the next ten years:

Next, where the disciplinary approach to the child does not seem
to be producing the desired effects, this review suggests that it
might be profitable to give attention to a detailed analysis of what
the parent is rewarding and punishing, the timing of the punishment in relation to what the child does, the degree of frustration
involved, the clarity with which expectations are communicated to
the child, the consistency of reinforcement within and between parents, and the types of models for the child implied by the parents'
behavior. In many instances it is possible that making the parent
more aware of how his or her behavior is having an impact on the
child can motivate a change in the parent's handling of the child.
(Becker, 1964, p. 204)

As an aside, Becker added: ". . . it should be pointed out that the
effectiveness of various educational procedures in modifying parent behavior has not been adequately researched."

Becker said, finally, that from the point of view of time and history in
any field of science, the gains in the 30 years of the research he reviewed
could be viewed as impressive, but from the point of view of those
trying to help families in trouble, the "gains must seem trivial."

The professional worker attempting to help families could well learn
from the literature that parental acceptance and warmth were related
to desired child behaviors, while hostility and rejection were not. The
well-trained professional's thinking, shaped by a good knowledge of the
research literature, would understandably center around love, acceptance,
warmth, and security. And he or she would try to use this perspective in
helping families.

Now, a short ten years after the publication of Becker's review, another and a splendid chapter has been written that specifically updates
Becker's. Entitled simply "Parent-child relations," it has been published in
the fourth volume of the *Review of Child Development Research* (Horowitz, et al., 1975). The author, Barclay Martin, has included some 256
references, more than 200 of which are dated from 1960 onward. In
seven separate summaries on topics such as attachment and dependency,
aggression, achievement, and withdrawn and neurotic behavior, there is
a heartening consistency to the findings suggesting not only a considerable advance in our knowledge, but also, if one is willing to translate
across different approaches, a convergence of the results from the experimental literature and the attitudinal assessment literature. On the one
hand the contingent uses of reward and punishment are almost like
recurrent musical themes, while on the other hand the "one-sided summary variable," as Martin calls it, of "parental warmth" continues to be

identified as an attitudinal dimension and, from some of the experimental literature, as a behavioral class, in producing well-socialized children.

As Martin notes, these two dominant threads are strongly reflected in the popular literature. Implementing the reinforcement or social learning approach are *Living with Children* by Patterson and Gullion (1968), *Parents Are Teachers* by Becker (1971), and *Parents/Children/Discipline* by Madsen and Madsen (1972); conveying the point of view supported by the "warmth and acceptance" approach is *Between Parent and Child* by the late Haim Ginott (1965). While those who are adamantly in one or the other of the two supposed camps enjoy thinking of how opposed they are one to the other, in fact, except for the specificity of the language it might be hard for one not socialized to the argument to say from which of the two camps comes this early frame in Patterson and Guillion:

> Food and money are not the only important rewards. Other kinds of reinforcers are far more effective. One of the most powerful reinforcers for a child is the love, interest, and attention of his mother and his father. Listening to the child, hugging him, smiling at him or talking to him are all reinforcers, the kind that are given thousands of times every day to most children.

If, in fact, the sweet reasonableness of the reinforcement-and-social-learning approach is not inimical or antithetical to the parental-warmth-and-acceptance approach, why then can one elicit such hostility or rejection when talking in reinforcement terminology? Perhaps training has not caught up with knowledge; perhaps, too, those in the social sciences—so long bedeviled by the enormously complex nature of the phenomena with which they have had to deal, and by the emotional dimensions of human interactions—are suspicious of the possibility that an approach so specific in its language, and sometimes so seemingly simple, can be a true account of what is happening.

How often one encounters the reaction, "It sounds so cold, so mechanistic." Or, if one talks about a particular parent behavior increasing or decreasing the frequency of a child behavior, one often elicits the response, "But aren't you being simplistic? After all, parent-child interactions are very, very complex—one cannot only think of the present, but one must also take into consideration the history of the relationship and its future course." By implication, and sometimes not even by implication, the targeting of specific behaviors is considered both simpleminded and naive.

However, as theory has turned to fact, and as these facts have become realistic bases for applied programs of remediation and help, it is no longer an academic argument. There is a variety of responses one can make in such discussions. Suppose you don't like to hear me say: "When you smile at your child after he has done something of which you approve, there is a greater possibility that your child will repeat that behavior under similar circumstances." What are your alternatives? You could walk away in disgust and rejection; you could regard the remark as obscene and ask me never to repeat it in your presence. These would probably have the desired effect—I would not make the statement to you again; but, if the statement is true, it would not affect its truth. You could challenge the statement by saying, "No, it isn't true," in which case one could resort to data and let the argument rest on facts. You could, however, take a leap of sophistication and say, "It is not so simple." This reveals the difference between you and me—I am simple-minded and you are not. It also has the effect, if I bite, of changing the subject from one that is about a lawful relationship to issues about the complexity or simplicity of human behavior. While these are valid issues for discussion, they are not a refutation, necessarily, of a statement of fact. Finally, you could choose to respond, "That may or may not be true, but if it is true, I don't like or want to hear it, for it implies a point of view which I do not find to be emotionally compatible." This is, in many ways, a very honest, sincere response, for it reveals the dilemma of many people in regard to their own thinking about human behavior and especially about parent-child relationships.

The clear implication of such a fundamental statement about parental smiling and child behavior is that the nature of the behavioral repertoire acquired by the child is under control of the parent or caretaker. This is, of course, an assumption, but it is an assumption that frightens many people. It raises the spectre of *Brave New World* (Huxley, 1946) and *1984* (Orwell, 1949), not to mention *Beyond Freedom and Dignity* (Skinner, 1971) or *Walden II* (Skinner, 1948).

In scientific fact, however, we are really dealing with an empirical question. How much and what parts of the child's behavior repertoire are influenced by parental behavior? How extensively do environmental events shape the behavioral repertoire? What aspects of the repertoire are shapable? Of the environmental events that are functional, what proportion involve parenting behaviors? These are among the questions that form the rationale for much of the current basic research on human behavior. The topics of responsibility and control are central to any consideration about future directions in parenting behavior, and I would like to return to them later in the context of alternatives.

I believe that most people can accept a statement about a lawful inter-action among behavioral phenomena and that this is not a denial of being human; in fact, most people act as if they do believe human behavior is lawful and not capricious. This is a position with the Freud-ians were among the first to champion and fight for. And now there is an increasing cadre of applied behavioral scientists who know how to minimize jargon and who can talk to parents and teachers in basic every-day language, so as to reduce the emotional level of those who have been socialized into a less specific behavioral vocabulary and approach.

A second issue raised by those critical of reinforcement and behavior management approaches concerns the attention to single behaviors or single classes of behaviors. There is a valid, as well as an invalid, basis to this criticism. The invalid basis is a hangover from the many years where applied behavioral science could point to only minimal successes or none at all, where more often than not the success of an individual therapist or counselor lay in the personal art of his or her technique rather than in the applications of known and specified principles. Given situations with families who were in trouble and had multiple problems, however, even the well intentioned and artful proved inadequate. The repetition of such genuine disappointments produces a rule of its own: The problems are complex; complex problems are not solvable given our present base of knowledge and techniques; when we know more we will be able to help solve these complex problems. This has, indeed, led to a kind of a malaise in many quarters of the helping professions such as social work, guidance, and counseling. Many workers in these groups almost know before they attempt a new case that their chances of basic and long-lasting effects are low. Not only are the techniques of treatment they bring to the problems often minimally effective, but what successes are achieved are frequently fragile and ephemeral—giving way to the massive impact of environmental circumstances of poverty, neighborhood disintegration, bureaucracy, and red tape. The "system" and the com-plexity of the problems to be solved become convenient scapegoats for failures to succeed, and they reinforce some of the unbelievably low levels of morale among sincere and hardworking professionals.

Even when those massive environmental variables are absent, a sense of effective competence among the helping professions is not often exuded—partly, perhaps, because what success they have goes unmeas-ured and unrewarded. But where success has obviously *not* been achieved, the complexity of the problem becomes an explanatory variable. A consistent educational history of thinking about complex problems as complex probably produces a set which makes the advocates who analyze complex problems into less complex components seem simpleminded. The identification of the component problems that produce, in aggregate, the complex situation does not necessarily deny that the entire matter under consideration is very complicated and often convoluted. But it becomes an empirical question: Does analysis into simpler components increase the chance of successful treatment? By itself, possibly not. But if analysis into simpler components is accompanied by a treatment procedure aimed at those components, one by one, with some measure of effectiveness available before one moves on, then possibly yes—as the increasing contributions to the literature demonstrate.

Complexity in and of itself is not a cause of failure or of a low rate of success. On the other hand, success with simple components of complicated problems does not always solve the larger problems. Does this mean that if one can help a family with some of its difficulties, but not all of them, one shouldn't go ahead and apply techniques that can provide limited success? Obviously not—and very few people maintain a different position, whatever their theoretical orientation. Perhaps, however, the difference is that the behavior modifier specifies the particular behaviors to be remedied while the non-behavior modifier says, "Of course, we do what we can and we try to help the family." The ironic part of this is that a good traditional social worker and a good behavior modifier might indeed have similar effects—except that the latter can more easily specify what those effects are and will talk about them in terms of particular behavior changes. It makes it seem as if the behavior modifier is naive, because in speaking about specific behavioral changes it sometimes appears that he or she has no appreciation of the extent of the problems that were not solved or aided. This is partly the verbal style and partly the enthusiasm of early novitiates to behavior modification—both of which are remediable problems. One question, of course, is whether giving a family some success in producing behavioral changes in a limited area does not give them a sense of competence that has something of a ripple effect on other aspects of their problem. Jerry Patterson's data (Chapter 11 of this volume) suggest this kind of outcome. Further documentation of this kind would, I think, prove to be very helpful in perhaps identifying the set of competencies that permit families to be weaned from the aid of professionals.

Although there are, obviously, many questions about the development of the child still to be answered, the evidence to date does not seriously challenge the notion that parental behavior has an effect upon child behavior. Further, the evidence points to the consistency, timing, nature, and frequency of parental reinforcement and punishment as being important though not necessarily sole agents in shaping the behavioral repertoire of the child. A careful reading of the literature summarized by Martin (1975) even produces a sense of optimism that an area which has seemed to so defy any orderliness is coming into something of a scientific focus. Such scientific focus in many ways reflects an article of faith long held by parent educators, utopian dreamers, and reformers of all kinds. For, if it is true that parental behavior—or the socialization experiences of the child provided by the parent or other caretakers— does affect the development of the child, then the key to improving our world lies in either influencing the behavior of parents or in supplementing or supplanting the parent. When Lucile Paden and I were gathering the material for a chapter reviewing environmental intervention programs, Dr. Paden found an expression of such hope in the rationale offered by a Strassbourg pastor in the year 1769. He proposed opening an infant school because he thought that by getting at the children so young he could *form* them and thereby save himself the trouble of having to *reform* them as adults (Horowitz and Paden, 1973).

Taking the optimistic point of view for the moment, one can consider a variety of alternatives that range from basically "helping" parents to be better parents, by their own definitions, to applying the known principles with such different outcomes in development as to, in fact, produce a different society. I'd like to take up several topics and explore each of them in terms of this range of alternatives. The topics are, in a sense, like textbook headings—and I apologize for the cliché-like character of their enumeration, but perhaps they have endured for so long because of their basic utility in thinking about development. They include intellectual development, social development, and physical development. These are areas of child behavior and development which are possibly affected by parenting behavior, though in each area there has been controversy over the role of genetic and biological factors.

Intellectual Development: The role of genetic factors in intellectual development is still unknown. Despite the extensive recent controversy in this area, our basic knowledge has not advanced very far (Cancro, 1971; Horowitz and Paden, 1973; Scarr-Salapatek, 1971, 1975). Nevertheless, hardly anyone would maintain the argument that it is an "either-or" proposition, even though some of the participants in the controversy

sometimes act as if it were. Not even the most convinced environmental-
ist would deny the role of genetic and biological factors in development,
but the question is to what extent they exist and to what extent environmental factors can be or are brought into play. It is quite possible, for
instance, that some of the forms of intellectual behavior, as described
by Piaget, are biologically determined in the sequencing of their appear-
ance during development. But this is not incompatible with the notion
that the level of competency attained within each biologically outlined
form is environmentally controlled. Or, to put it in another way—biological factors may determine what are the most likely behavioral chains
in development, but environmental factors determine, at one extreme,
whether the normal chain develops or, at a less extreme position, some
of the quality and perhaps quantity of behavior that occurs at different
points along the chain. If this is the case, then there is a further qualification that needs to be considered. How many of the environmental
events that affect intellectual development are inanimate and how many
are animate or mediated by animate elements—parents, caretakers,
siblings, and others?

Where does the evidence stand on the role of environmental factors
in intellectual development? There is the extensive literature on "social
class" to indicate that variables associated with this envelope concept
do affect performance in traditional schools and on traditional achievement tests. Exactly what behaviors are performed by parents and caretakers in different social class groups that are responsible for the differential outcomes is not clear. However, teaching styles and amount of
interaction as well as contingency factors are repeatedly implicated in
the current literature (Hess and Shipman, 1965; Kagan and Tulkin,
1971; Martin, 1975). The constellation of results points to the conclusion that these naturally occurring variations are of the kind which are
amenable to being harnessed for systematic variation. What comes
through the differences in terminology, style, theory, and practice is the
strong probability that the principles of contingency management are, in
fact, widely applied for shaping some cognitive styles as well as influencing the level and kind of intellectual development attained by children.
While biological and constitutional factors are surely not irrelevant, the
more likely manipulability of environmentally arranged contingencies
than of biological factors makes environmental intervention the most
plausible alternative available at present for affecting the intellectual
development of the child.

So—let us assume that influencing parenting behaviors and the parental arrangement of the environment could affect intellectual development of the child. At the most democratic or laissez faire level one could say—good, let's tell parents about this and they will surely apply the principles into which they have been educated. This, of course, assumes that all would-be and current parents would be reached by such education and that such education would be effective. Certainly, the spate of books advising parents how to raise the IQ of their children is part of this optimism. And, certainly, if the net effect of such education were to eliminate the necessity for remedial education, reduce the prevalence of borderline normal development, and allow each child to develop at least at the average and, in many cases, at the above average level of intelligence (which would, of course, statistically produce a higher "average"), one could hardly say the result was modest. Indeed, the central hope of most early intervention programs was no less, and millions of dollars have been spent in pursuit of such a goal (Horowitz and Paden, 1973). Is it realistic? I think so. But only if one defines "realistic" in terms of possibility and not probability. I think it is realistic, given what we know, to conceive of providing for each child born into this world a minimally supportive environment where, in the absence of gross physiological problems, normal intellectual development can be achieved. I believe it is even possible, by the radical alteration of that environment, to systematically produce individuals who differ in intellectual competencies and to realize both the hopes and fears of behavioral utopians. But I do not believe our largest payoff will come by starting with utopian conceptions, and so perhaps our hopes and fears in their most exaggerated sense are still far from realization. At the present time, I believe we could offer parents some skills and techniques that could *prevent* problems in intellectual development.

Social Development: I include in this general category both personality patterns and the repertoire of behaviors defined as social. Here, I believe, the same arguments apply with regard to genetic and environmental factors, with the possibility that both personality and social behaviors can take a wider variety of forms than we find in behaviors assigned to the domain of intellectual development. Part of the assignment to intellectual or social is, admittedly, arbitrary. But it does seem that the social forms of behavior found over a range of cultures are more varied than the behaviors labeled intellectual.

Analogous to books advising parents how to raise their children's IQs, we have the books advising parents how to raise their children so that they are socially well adjusted and relatively pleasant—or at least not obnoxious. (However, it is an interesting, if casual, observation that there are an awful lot of obnoxious children who do turn out to be quite fine adults. There is either a discontinuity in development or a relational thread and intervention of variables of which we are presently unaware.) That there are techniques available for helping parents to produce socially acceptable child behavior has already been amply demonstrated. The greatest deterrents to the application of these techniques are prejudice against the techniques, ignorance of them, and lack of motivation.

What is interesting about the naturally occurring variations that produce differences in social and personality development is the strong interrelationship between ideological factors and social development factors. As cultural anthropology has well documented, the entire fabric of social ethics, values, and customs combine to produce different repertoires of social behavior defined as acceptable in different cultures. What is even more interesting is that serious recipes for social change often involve drastic changes in economic systems, and changed economic systems may be the most influential systems for bringing about either voluntary or involuntary changes in parenting practices. These typically have the avowed purpose of breaking the cycles of each generation reproducing itself in terms of social values. Thus, in the alternatives for affecting the developmental outcome of children in social development, one can range from the modest goals of producing well-adjusted and happy children to that of producing children whose behavioral repertoires are significantly different from those of their parents—often in the context of radically different economic systems.

Physical Development: While this area is in some ways the most beholden to biological factors, it is probably also the most dramatically illustrative of the influence of environmental factors as they are mediated by parenting behavior interacting with medical and other resources. In large part, physical stature is biologically determined but, in an analogy that is perhaps parallel to periods in intellectual development, environmental factors such as nutrition, eating habits, access to medical care and consultation, and opportunities for physical exercise significantly influence the quality and quantity of the expressed biological form of development. Again, cultural and physical anthropology has revealed some interesting effects of environmental influence—the role of imitation by one generation of another in the area of food habits; the effects of breakdown of family patterns on disrupting the imitative repertoire, and the subsequent physical and behavioral effects; and the difficulty of supplanting the natural opportunities for imitative learning with both informal and formal educational programs. As far as expanding the possibilities for development is concerned, one only has to look at the effects of improved regimes of training on athletic performance.

Thus, it seems to me that one can say that in all areas of development where we have a possible interest in influencing outcome, the role of environmental factors, and especially the role of primary caretakers, can be identified as significant. As our understanding of the exact function of the role grows, so grows our ability to systematically apply our knowledge to produce specific outcomes. Typically our concern has been for the future outcome of the development of the child, seeing, as have reformers and dreamers before us, the sweet utopia of the happy, well-adjusted, creative, productive, etc., etc., child become adult. But such utopian dreaming is self-defeating if it focuses only upon the child and not upon the parents or caretakers who must, most often, implement the environmental engineering. Unless one can build into a system of environmental engineering a concern for the reinforcement of parenting behavior itself, the success of the utopia is probably limited.

There has been a recent growing interest in looking at parenting behavior not only as an interaction between caretaker and child, but also in terms of how fully the interaction reinforces the repertoire of parenting behavior. I have already mentioned some of the interesting notions about infant behavior where some infants appear to have a repertoire of behavior that is more reinforcing for mothering behavior than others. Except for Erik Erikson's theoretical discussions about periods of development through middle and old age (Erikson, 1950), there has been very little concern for the development of the behavioral repertoire of adults in terms of its potential in a developmental sense. Yet I suspect that there are large payoffs from influencing parenting behaviors in the effects on the parents themselves—a matter coming up recurrently in the papers in this volume. In fact, in many cases, parents seeking help for their children are motivated to seek such help because of their own behavior, which they perceive as unsatisfying. It is interesting to note that radical alternative systems of parenting are concerned with influencing the behavior of the parents as much as the children.

While the fullest conception of a utopia would, obviously, concern itself with parents as well as with children, there is a more compelling reason to shun the temptation to be utopian in talking about directions for parenting. As any good social programmer knows, "utopia" is the last frame in the program—almost by definition. While the specification of the last frame may serve as the ultimate behavioral objective and the dream of its attainment may be somewhat self-reinforcing, I think that it encourages one to bypass the beginning and intermediate frames for obtaining the behavioral objective. And since it is the specification of the first and not the last steps that is necessary to start the process at all, focusing so strongly upon the last frame of the future distracts one from the immediate, and sometimes difficult, implementation of the early frames.

There is another reason why I think it is counterproductive to be seriously utopian at this point in our scientific understanding of behavior. This last frame of social dreams is, ultimately, a grandiose and arbitrary proposal. What is fitted into the conception of the last frame is a matter of values and social philosophy, and typically must include untested propositions. It generates arguments and discussions about what is and is not included in an utopian conception and, while this is often intellectually stimulating, the investment of the same time and energy in discussing and trying the first frames might have more immediate results. I have come to believe that there is no single utopia of which one can dream that will be universally satisfactory. If one is going to engage in realistic utopian thinking, it requires a very clear understanding of the varieties of culturally defined social values which, in concert with an empirically derived set of principles and practices of social organization, would generate different kinds of societies, each aimed at producing the maximal level of satisfaction and productivity among its members, as defined by those members. For the present and the immediate future, however, I think there are several very practical courses of action which have some hope of implementation and some possibility of measurable effects.

The first area for action concerns individual education. The history of education for parenting is long and honorable and filled with dedicated people whose efforts were arduous, if not necessarily effective. In the absence of serious problems requiring intensive remediational efforts, the only permissible avenues of influence are reading materials, voluntary parent education programs, and all forms of socially acceptable exhortations. This seemingly disorganized and somewhat laissez faire enterprise is widely thought to have had its effects in changing both the belief systems about the role of parents and some parenting behaviors. Benjamin Spock recently offered a public apology for the possibly harmful effects that the voluntary adoption of his advice might have produced. I think, however, that we have now come to the point where we ought to vigorously campaign for the adoption of behavioral science as a required subject in elementary and high school curricula. Our knowledge base about simple behavioral phenomena is at least as solid as our knowledge base about the fundamental aspects of simple phenomena in the non-behavioral areas, and there is no reason why the basic principles of such topics as reinforcement should not become part of common educational knowledge. One need not even be theoretically partisan in the matter. There is no serious psychological theory which denies the simple phenomenon of reinforcement. As for the real issues of disagreement in the field, these can be left for advanced courses. Chemistry, at the beginning level, does not concern itself with its current major theoretical controversies. We in behavioral science seem to be very quick to keep our disputes at the beginning of our courses instead of letting our knowledge base come first.

It has long been the position of the parent education movement and, I should add, the field of home economics, that the one most likely role for which all young people are destined is parenthood—and it is the role for which people are the least prepared by educational curricula. Perhaps this is again a manifestation of the notions about the sanctity of family behavior. But there is ample room for recognition of variables of cultural patterns and social values while high school students are being provided with the basic principles of behavioral science and behavioral management.

In addition, there is a vast reservoir of time and service that could be put to use in any community for practical application of behavioral management techniques. Why, for instance, shouldn't there be a basic course on *Behavior and Development,* in which not only the academic presentation of subject matter but the practical application in child care settings would be as routine as basic chemistry or driver education? There are two important possible ripple effects from such a program. The first is the development of a set of skills which one might translate as a sense of competence in relating to and working with children. The second is that we could at least begin to combat the enormous ignorance about behavior and development. If people were as ignorant about basic principles of electricity as they are about behavior, there would be many more accidental deaths.

I believe that it is now possible to incorporate in the educational curriculum a program on behavioral science. It could increase the general level of competency in behavioral management among potential parents as well as provide the first steps in preventive treatment of early development problems by teaching techniques of early stimulation and facts about early development. There are, however, two important cautions.

The first has to do with values—a topic raised repeatedly in this volume. As pointed out in the paper by Risley et al., techniques and principles of science are amoral. That is, contingencies have nothing to do with what is good or bad, or valued or not valued. Choosing to care about whether children pick up their clothes from the floor is a personal value. I think this point is important because any suggestion that behavioral management be introduced into the curriculum will inevitably raise these value issues. It is incumbent upon those who advocate inclusion of behavior management in curricula to understand clearly the division between principles being taught and the behaviors to which those principles might be applied.

The second caution has to do with limiting the claims of what can and cannot be taught, or what constitutes competency. A student who has had a course in principles of engineering is not an engineer, and that is clearly understood by all concerned. Someone who has had just a course in principles of behavior modification is not a behavior modifier, but that is not understood by all concerned. The dilution of the label to encompass a broad range of knowledge and competencies will inevitably weaken the confidence in that label. This is one reason why jargon is so dangerous—because jargon is an easy behavior to acquire. To glibly explain everything as being a function of a history of reinforcement is not unlike explaining everything as being related to the forces of ego and id. At the university level we already see the bandwagon effect, with people whose skill levels in the area are very minimal claiming to be in behavior modification and to explain all in terms of reinforcement. Indiscriminate proselytizing and uncontrolled initiation rites inevitably weaken the principal strength of a position, and the dangers of this happening in applied behavior science—be it in behavior modification, T groups, or open education—are readily apparent.

Despite these cautions, the inclusion of a serious course or set of courses in behavioral science and child care for both male and female students in public school systems has many implications for influencing parenting behavior, if such courses emphasize what is known about principles of behavior, minimize the theoretical controversies that preoccupy the field of social science, and require *performance* competency in order to pass the course. I think one could aim for such a goal and document the effects.

The second area of action has to do with the development of resources at the community level. I think it is time to seriously consider the possibility of Parent-Child Research Stations and to thus revive the original aims of the determined lady from Iowa. I chose the title of these centers carefully so as to model upon the Agricultural Research Station—a resource that is used frequently and automatically by farmers without taint of failure, social class, or inadequacy. The term "research" is an important element in the title because it implies that a problem brought to the station, for which there is not available an immediately applicable answer, becomes a problem for investigation by both the family and the station. It puts the solution of the problem squarely in the province of data.

I think that Parent-Child Research Stations could systematically alert parents to behaviors they might choose to shape at especially important or sensitive periods in development—much as farmers receive continuous advice from agricultural stations. For instance, soon after language has developed and children begin to be expected to be quiet in certain settings, it is one of my pet hunches that an important behavior parents can teach a very young child is how to whisper.

Another role such stations could play would be to provide settings whereby parents could practice changing behavior control strategies across different developmental periods. I think the further possibilities and operation of such stations are almost obvious and the practical implications could be very exciting. But their success depends upon many things: the care with which the behavioral objectives of such a setting are defined; the competencies of the personnel who staff such stations; and the reinforcement for parents who utilize the services of the stations. Membership and successful implementation of advice could be reinforced by social activities, free bowling, free baby sitting, or even, in some communities, tax credits. This last is not a bizarre suggestion if a community comes to realize the value of successful parenting.

However, in this age of quick and political social action programs, the field of social science should have learned a very hard lesson. Acquiescing to standards that are below what one knows to be a minimum level necessary for success is not only to risk failure of the particular enterprise in question, but to discredit an entire field. Those of us who contributed to the politically expedient establishment of the Head Start program in the United States, as well as to several other anti-poverty programs, know only too well the consequences of such cooperation against our own best judgments. In medicine no one would agree to a proposition that if we don't have enough vaccine to go around we should just dilute the minimum dosage. Yet in social science action programs, partly because we do not have enough faith in our own competencies, we agree to such propositions all the time.

Given the appropriate staffing and the realistic goals based upon our knowledge, I think Parent-Child Research Stations could make a significant contribution to the prevention of problems and to the treatment of problems before they become so convoluted as to defy our current level of abilities to remediate difficulties. The initial establishment and acceptance of such a resource model would require careful preparation, but it is, I think, a practical possibility—one for which we could provide the necessary trained personnel and one which could be implemented under present conditions.

The ultimate acceptance of such stations requires that parenting become a more "open," perhaps public, system so that seeking advice is a normal and natural practice. Western culture has developed the most elaborate and acceptable systems for seeking advice and increasing competence for a wide variety of trivial and non-trivial behaviors—you can get help to improve your bridge game, grow nicer roses, or learn fancier knitting—all without taint of failure or disgrace. Is not parenting important enough to be serviced by similar easy access systems? But interestingly, playing better bridge, growing nicer roses, and making fancier sweaters are all heavily reinforced by social praise, public display, or even money. Parenting behavior, except for the mother-of-the-year award that you'd never win anyway, is on the leanest schedule possible.

You might at this point ask how proposals for high school curriculum development or Parent-Child Research Stations relate to directions for parenting. They are hardly radical proposals and they do not necessarily imply the development of alternative life-styles or "new looks" in parenting possibilities. True enough—and intentionally so. The reason is that without major economic and social philosophy changes providing an underpinning to life-style and parenting-behavior alternatives, it is not likely that radical changes in parenting styles can occur successfully. But, given the advances in behavioral technology, it is, I believe, realistic to suggest that an attainable goal in the field of parenting is to develop the motivations, conditions, and resources to make parents in our present social structure more successful in fostering maximal development in their children. At the same time, such success may reinforce parental behavior in such a way as to liberate the energies previously spent in less satisfying parent-child interactions for fostering the development of both the individuals who are parents and the children involved. There may be a much more elastic set of possibilities with regard to developmental outcomes for individual children than we typically envisage. Thus, the level of cognitive development, the degree of social sensitivity, the capacities for personal aesthetic satisfaction, and abilities in creativity, leadership, and productivity which can potentially be fostered within the framework of largely positive parent-child interactions may be such as to bring a generation of children to adulthood who achieve a kind of developmental outcome which one could indeed say was an improvement over the generation that preceded it. If parenting behaviors can be moved in this direction, the accomplishment will have been significant.

Finally, however, there is the whole area of trying alternative parenting systems. The discussion of parenting has so far assumed that the basic model of family life is that of a nuclear or slightly extended family, where the responsibility for decisions about socialization training rests with the biological parents and whomever they choose to include in their decision-making process. Even when such families turn over the care of their children to baby-sitters or day-care centers, it is assumed either that the surrogate caretakers share the same values and goals or that those hired will accede to the right of the parents to have the major role in decisions regarding the upbringing of their children. Even in societies which have more extended family arrangements, the responsibility for socializing the child may only be more distributed in terms of how much of the socializing role is shared with other members of the family. But the basic responsibility for the decisions to be made remain with the family—as long as those decisions conform to the basic values of the larger society of which the family is a part. Developmental outcomes in terms of personality characteristics and cognitive styles do seem to have some systematic cultural variations, but the specific parenting behaviors or socializing forces responsible for these differences have yet to be identified (Glick, 1975).

Social reformers, revolutionaries, and utopian dreamers have, however, always viewed changing the socialization of the child as a key to making a permanently better society—usually in concert with economic changes. At the present time, there are numerous countries where economic revolutions have been accompanied by changes in the systems of child care which essentially remove from the biological parents the full responsibility for the care and socialization of the child. However, except for such descriptive and personal observations as that of Russia by Bronfenbrenner (1970) and a monograph series describing early child care in 12 different countries, including a number of communist nations, there has been very little general access to objective descriptions of the effects of such systems upon the developmental outcome of children.

The one alternative system which *has* been subjected to a variety of research, as well as descriptive probes, is that of the collective child care practices in the kibbutzim found in Israel (Amir, 1969; Bettelheim, 1969; Gewirtz and Gewirtz, 1969; Marcus, 1971; Shapiro and Madsen, 1969; Talmon, 1972). As a voluntary association of people in some 250 settlements, encompassing more than 90,000 people in these settlements that have existed in some cases for as long as 60 years (Marcus, 1971), the kibbutzim are the most enduring purposeful alternative system to the traditional nuclear or extended family system for child-rearing. An important and immediate qualification is that there is no single description which fits all kibbutzim. Not only are there small variations from settlement to settlement, but each kibbutz is a member of one of four kibbutz movement organizations that differ on political, social, religious and economic dimensions. Nevertheless, as Marcus (1971) has noted, "there is a communality in the kibbutz experience." This communality is probably most evident in the arrangements for collective child rearing in which, while the family is not eliminated as a social unit, its functions are radically reduced with regard to both the physical care and the socialization of the child.

Sociologically it has been frequently noted that kibbutz members are disproportionately represented in political leadership roles in Israel. However, because of the self-selection factor determining the first-generation membership in the kibbutzim, it is difficult to credit the kibbutz experience itself as the functional agent. But, if one looks at the research on the effects of kibbutz rearing on the children born to kibbutz parents, there is a growing consistency in the facts. First, there do not seem to be adverse effects in the standard areas of child development—be they physical, intellectual, or social (Gewirtz and Gewirtz, 1969; Maccoby and Feldman, 1972; Marcus, 1971). Second, some of the developmental outcomes, while not harmful, are different. For instance, in a rather intriguing study. Shapiro and Madsen (1969) demonstrated that kibbutz-reared children in Israel were more successful in abandoning non-functional competitive behavior and adopting cooperative behavior patterns than were urban-reared Israeli children. Exactly what aspects of the kibbutz child-rearing systems account for such differences cannot presently be specified. But it is interesting to note that Bruno Bettelheim's descriptive report in his book, *Children of the Dream* (1969), though written from a psychoanalytic point of view, can be read as a description of the extensive and consistent reinforcement of the children's group and cooperative behavior.

To what extent the kibbutz is an exportable social model is presently unknown. Kibbutz-like communal attempts in the United States have typically been short-lived and economically non-viable. None have endured long enough to provide a second generation. Whether there is a special constellation of unusual factors which allowed the kibbutz in Israel to become a real alternative life-style is difficult to say. A rather interesting sociological analysis by Yonina Talmon (1972) clearly documents that the kibbutz is not only non-monolithic, but a constantly evolving social structure. I understand that the kibbutz model is now being seriously copied in Japan, and this may be an interesting test of the reproducibility of the model in an entirely different cultural setting.

Whether there are really viable and potentially durable alternative systems for parenting without concomitant changes in the economic system is questionable. There are many alternative parenting systems within any given economic system, but these typically do not exist for the *purpose* of producing different developmental outcomes. They are basically variations on an agreed-upon theme with regard to socialization of the child and the transmission of cultural values—day-care facilities, in-home care, neighborhood cooperatives, and so on. Though there are many opinions about what is and is not good for children, there is very little documentation of the effects of these different child-care arrangements on the development of children or on the parents themselves.

When it comes to discussions of directions for parenting, speculation becomes a high-frequency behavior, partly because there are so few sources of data to guide the discussions. Until there are more reliable data sources, speculation will remain as a dominant behavior. Obviously, voluntary experimental communities committed to data collection would be ideal. But experimental and different-life-style communities in the United States have a high rate of failure in that they do not last long enough to determine any outcomes. Possibly a more empirical short-term approach in terms of successive waves would prove successful. By this I mean that experimental communities could be established which have timed, self-destruct mechanisms. People would agree to join for a period of up to five years. At the end of five years, data having been collected on specified aspects of the community, the experiment and the community would end. Based upon what was learned, a new experimental community would be started, the limited time again imposed, and the process repeated. This would, I think, help break the failure cycle which has so plagued experimental communities since Robert Owen's time and perhaps before. Individuals would not have to make a life-commitment to an unknown life-style, and the predetermined breakup of the community, its mission accomplished, would reinforce not only the individuals who participated, but also the idea of limited-duration experimental communities. Applied social experimentation with regard to parenting cannot occur in isolation. But, since we do not know what the complex setting ought to look like in order to produce particular effects, this should become the experimental question. One does not begin a program by approximating the last frame.

There are a number of other topics that one might include in thinking about directions for parenting. I have not dealt at all with the ecology of environments and the kinds of manipulation possible which might change some aspects of parenting behavior, but the work of Risley, Cataldo, and the Living Environments Group is, as Patterson points out, moving into this area. Nor have I discussed the growing literature on individual differences in children which elicit different parenting behaviors. There is also the theoretical and empirical consideration of how latent learning and imitation aid one generation of parents in adopting the behaviors of a previous generation of parents. But I am mindful that this has been a long discussion—longer than I thought it would be when I began—so let me summarize the main points I have tried to make.

1. Research on parenting behavior has come to have an encouraging consistency. Whether one chooses to talk about parental warmth and acceptance or reinforcement and contingency management, it is clear that parenting behaviors which seem to most approximate the characteristics of good teaching tend to produce children whose behavioral repertoires are seen as desirable and functional for their own development.

2. Behavior modification analysis of these data often elicits strong objections, but these objections, dealt with systematically and patiently, need not be obstacles to communication—especially if one can translate across semantic systems and if one appreciates the limits of what we now know.

3. Our basic knowledge of behavioral phenomena is such that we may be able to influence the acquisition of parenting behavior by the serious

introduction of behavioral science into the educational curriculum of the public schools.

4. Our basic knowledge and our ability to train personnel are also sufficient to entertain the possibility of establishing easily available resource stations for helping parents and for preventing developmental difficulties.

5. Radically different systems of child care exist, but the functional aspects of the systems for producing different developmental outcomes have not been clearly identified.

6. Progress in understanding how to establish such alternatives and what to include in them might be best served by limited, self-destruct experimental communities rather than the immediate establishment of larger scale experimental societies.

In thinking seriously about the future, I've felt a periodically gnawing discomfort about the importance of the behaviors repeatedly targeted for change. Many societies and communities are today deeply troubled—many, possibly, in a lull before another set of storms. We could, I believe, encourage a lot of successful parenting that achieved having socks picked up off the floor, beds made, and no sassing, creating relatively neat, nice, and happy homes, but the net effect of it all would not change our society one whit. In many environments in which children grow up, social ills, poverty, discrimination, and the use and distribution of resources are totally irrelevant to being happy, having fun, and maximizing the backup reinforcers of the good life. Training for moral and social responsibility has fallen into the domain of simplistic and ineffective preaching, glib clichés, or seasonal songs. Our concern for shaping pro-social behaviors is, more often than not, in terms of developing skills in executing social protocol—being nice and polite, saying hello and good-bye, and keeping up a decent rate of smiling without much concern for content or commitment. What will the sum outcome of more effective parenting be if it contributes little to the solution of problems that threaten to rip apart the fabric of society as we know it?

I apologize for concluding on this somewhat somber note. Perhaps one reason why this paper was so difficult to write is that, sitting as I was in the Middle East, one felt close to the edge of the meaning of the words survival and vulnerability—and it was sometimes difficult to think about understanding the behaviors of parents and children, when the physical forces of nature had been so well understood as to provide for the possibility of our own cataclysmic self-destruction. One felt impelled to come up with some grand scheme, employing behavioral technology in yet another utopian service. Attractive as that was for one's fantasy life, it was, I decided, ultimately not helpful. The need to talk about things that could realistically be accomplished seemed much more useful. Still, one periodically faces the feeling that we may yet overwhelm ourselves with our physical powers before our behavioral knowledge and application can succeed in saving us from ourselves. As none of us can know for sure what the future will bring, the two behaviors that may be the most important for our collective survival are the expression of a clear sense of irony and the practice of a good sense of humor.

REFERENCES

AMIR, Y.: The effectiveness of the kibbutz-born soldier in the Israel defense forces. *Human Relations,* 22, 333-334, 1969.

BECKER, W. C.: Consequences of parental discipline. In: M. S. Hoffman and L. W. Hoffman (Eds.), *Review of Child Development Research,* Vol. 1. New York: Russell Sage Foundation, 1964.

BECKER, W. C.: *Parents Are Teachers: A Child Management Program.* Champaign, Ill.: Research Press, 1971.

BETTELHEIM, B.: *The Children of the Dream.* New York: Macmillan, 1969.

BRONFENBRENNER, U.: *Two Worlds of Childhood: U.S. and U.S.S.R.* New York: Russell Sage Foundation, 1970.

CANCRO, R. C.: *Intelligence: Genetic and Environmental Influences.* New York: Grune and Stratton, 1971.

ERIKSON, E.: *Childhood and Society.* New York: Norton, 1950.

GEWIRTZ, H. B., and GEWIRTZ, J. L.: Caretaking settings, background events, and behavior differences in four Israeli child-rearing environments: Some preliminary trends. In: B. M. Foss (Ed.), *Determinants of Infant Behavior.* Vol. IV. London: Methuen, 1969.

GINOTT, H.: *Between Parent and Child.* New York: Macmillan, 1965.

GLICK, J.: Cognitive development in cross-cultural perspective. In: F. D. Horowitz (Ed.), *Review of Child Development Research,* Vol. 4. Chicago: U. of Chicago Press, 1975.

HESS, R. D., and SHIPMAN, V.: Early experience and the socialization of cognitive modes in children. *Child Devel.,* 36, 869-886, 1965.

HOFFMAN, M. L., and HOFFMAN, L. W.: *Review of Child Development Research,* Vol. 1. New York: Russell Sage Foundation, 1964.

HOROWITZ, F. D. (Ed.), and HETHERINGTON, M., SCARR-SALAPATEK, S., and SIEGEL, G. (Assoc. Eds.): *Review of Child Development Research,* Vol. 4. Chicago: U. of Chicago Press, 1975.

HOROWITZ, F. D., and PADEN, L. Y.: The effectiveness of environmental intervention programs. In: B. M. Caldwell and H. Ricciuti (Eds.), *Review of Child Development Research,* Vol. 3. Chicago: U. of Chicago Press, 1973. Pp. 331-402.

HUXLEY, A.: *Brave New World.* New York: Harper & Brothers, 1946.

KAGAN, J., and TULKIN, S. R.: Social class differences in child rearing during the first year. In: H. R. Schaffer (Ed.), *The Origins of Human Social Relations.* New York: Academic Press, 1971. Pp. 165-186.

MACCOBY, E. E., and FELDMAN, S. S.: Mother-attachment and stranger-reactions in the third year of life. *Monographs of the Society for Research in Child Development,* 37. No. 1, 1972.

MADSEN, C. K., and MADSEN, C. H.: *Parents/Children/Discipline*. Boston: Allyn and Bacon, 1972.

MARCUS, J.: Early child development in kibbutz group care. *Early Child Devel. and Care*, 1, 67-98, 1971.

MARTIN, B.: Parent-child relations. In: F. D. Horowitz (Ed.), *Review of Child Development Research*, Vol. 4. Chicago: U. of Chicago Press, 1975.

ORWELL, G.: *1984*. New York: Harcourt, Brace, 1949.

PATTERSON, G. R., and GULLION, M. E.: *Living with Children*. Champaign, Ill.: Research Press, 1968.

SCARR-SALAPATEK, S.: Race, social class, and IQ. *Science*, 174, 1285-1295, 1971.

SCARR-SALAPATEK, S. Genetics and the development of intelligence. In: F. D. Horowitz (Ed.), *Review of Child Development Research*, Vol. 4. Chicago: U. of Chicago Press, 1975.

SCHAEFER, E., and BELL, R. Q.: Development of a parental attitude research instrument. *Child Devel.*, 29, 339-361, 1958.

SHAPIRO, A. and MADSEN, M. C.: Cooperative and competitive behavior of kibbutz and urban children in Israel. *Child Devel.*, 40, 609-617, 1969.

SKINNER, B. F.: *Beyond Freedom and Dignity*. New York: Knopf, 1971.

SKINNER, B. F.: *Walden II*. New York: Macmillan, 1948.

TALMON, Y. *Family and Community in the Kibbutz*. Cambridge: Harvard U. Press, 1972.

2

Behavioral Technology for the Normal Middle-Class Family

TODD R. RISLEY, HEWITT B. CLARK,
and MICHAEL F. CATALDO

Increasingly, the focus of applied behavioral research is turning away from finding solutions to severe and unusual problems and toward investigating ways of helping normal people deal with troublesome everyday situations. For this work to have its maximum social impact, we must look further than the immediate problems people bring to us. We must try to predict and prepare for the types of problems that can be expected to trouble families in the future. Our first step must therefore be to take a close look at significant societal trends that have the effect of placing additional pressures on families.

As could be predicted from the well publicized decrease in birthrate, indications are that the average family size in the United States is in the midst of a fairly rapid decline, from a mean of approximately 6.8 in 1810 to the 1970 average number of children per family of 2.3 (Commission on Population Growth and the American Future, 1972). As is shown in Figure 1, throughout the past 150 years the number of children per family has decreased with some consistency, but two deviations from the gradual decline, both in the last 50 years, have occurred. These two "bulges"—one representing a decrease in births during the 1920's and the other the post-World-War-II "baby boom"—have ramifications that extend throughout society. One of the most pervasive is the alteration in our current age distribution. (Figure 2 clearly shows this effect.)

This paper reports on one in a series of projects by the Living Environments Group at the University of Kansas under the direction of Todd R. Risley and in conjunction with the Johnny Cake Child Study Center, directed by Hewitt B. Clark.

NUMBER OF CHILDREN PER FAMILY

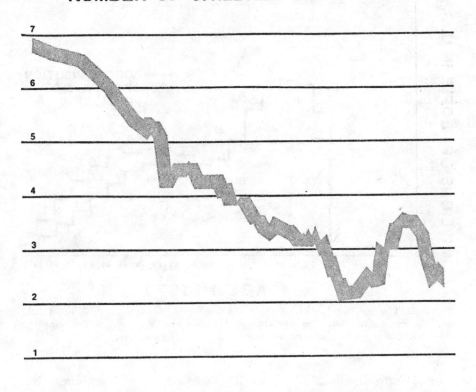

FIGURE 1: The number of children per family in the United States from 1810 to 1970. (Statistics from *Population Growth and the American Future*, 1972.)

At the same time as the number of dependent children and young adults (ages 5-25) is exceedingly high, the size of the age class that tends to be most productive and responsible (ages 30-45) is proportionately lower than it has been in the past (Commission on Population Growth and the American Future, 1972). Also shown in Figure 2 is the age distribution of a population which has stabilized. Since the total fertility rate has remained at or below the family "replacement" rate of 2.11 for the past four years, we can expect such an age distribution in the

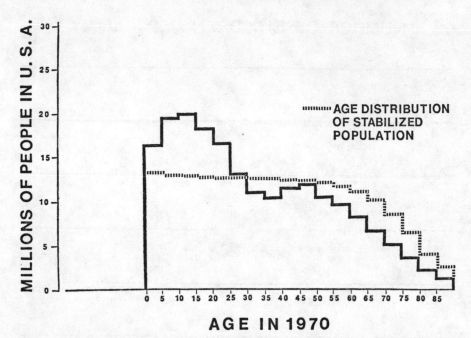

AGE IN 1970

FIGURE 2: The age distribution of the United States population in 1970 (solid line) and the age distribution of a hypothetical population which has stabilized (broken line). (Statistics from *Population Growth and the American Future*, 1972.)

United States in the 21st century if this low birthrate continues (National Center for Health Statistics, 1974).

A likely result of the current unusual age distribution has been the rise in crime. Statistics indicate that half of the crime wave occurring in the past 15 years can be accounted for simply by the increase in the number of people in the 14 to 24 age group—the age in which criminal and delinquent acts have always been more prevalent (Figure 3) (Graham and Gurr, 1969). Perhaps even more significant than total numbers, however, is the shift in the ratio of mature adults to youth that occurred during this time. We've seen a change in this ratio in the years between 1955, when there were three adults to every youth, and 1970, when there were only two mature adults to every youth. It has been observed that half the marked increase in crimes during the past 15 years can be explained by the numerical increase in people in this "high crime" age. The other half might be a function of the decreasing social influence exerted over youth and young adults by the proportionately fewer ma-

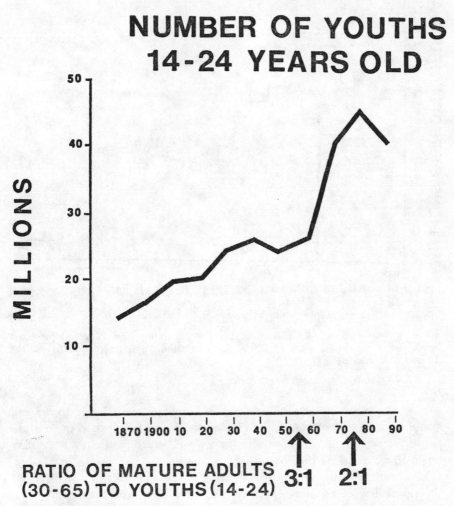

**NUMBER OF YOUTHS
14-24 YEARS OLD**

RATIO OF MATURE ADULTS 3:1   2:1
(30-65) TO YOUTHS (14-24)

FIGURE 3: The number of persons 14-24 years of age in the United States from 1870 to the present, with projections to 1990, and the ratio of mature adults to youths in 1955 and 1970. (Statistics from *Population Growth and the American Future*, 1972.)

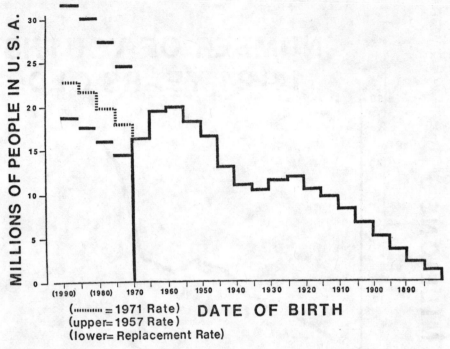

FIGURE 4: The 1970 age distribution of the United States population and projected number of births per 5 years to 1990. (Statistics from *Population Growth and the American Future,* 1972.)

ture adults in our society. Therefore, as the population bulge moves on, and the current large number of youths and young adults become mature adults, it would appear that the "crisis" of juvenile delinquency may begin to abate of its own accord.

However, despite the decline in number of children per family and the possibility of maintaining a replacement birthrate, the actual number of children born each year will not decrease significantly for some time as the population bulge reaches child-bearing age (Figure 4). Rather, the children will be spread out over a greater number of families with the result that more children than in the past will be raised by inexperienced parents. Therefore, there will be a large number of adults able to shoulder the financial and social responsibility of educating children and exerting social influence over youth.

Another social change that is profoundly affecting the American fam-

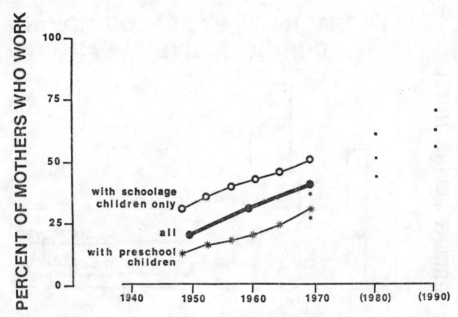

FIGURE 5: The percentage of mothers in the labor force, projected to 1990. (Statistics from *Profiles of Children*, White House Conference on Children, 1970.)

ily is the increasing frequency of working mothers (Morris, 1974; Linden, 1973). While in 1950 fewer than 25% of all mothers held outside jobs, in 1970 more than 40% were employed away from home (Figure 5). If this trend continues as expected, by 1990 more than 60% of all mothers, including 55% of mothers with preschool children and nearly 75% of mothers with school-age children, will be working. Obviously, these families have an urgent and continuing need for extra-family child care and youth supervision (Commission on Population Growth and the American Future, 1972; Emlen et al., 1971). And, largely because of their double incomes, many of these families can afford to pay for child-care services (Linden, 1973; White House Conference on Children, 1970).

Young families with children are subject to another form of stress: frequent moves. One family in five moves each year and, as can be seen in Figure 6, the 20-30 age range, the prime time for family growth, is also prime time for moving (U.S. Bureau of the Census, 1970; Commission on Population Growth and the American Future, 1972). In contrast to much pre-World-War-II mobility, which involved migration

PROBABILITY, BY AGE, OF MOVING
DURING A GIVEN YEAR

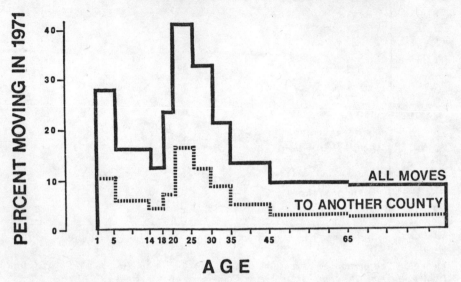

FIGURE 6: The probability that a person in a particular age group will move in a given year. (Statistics from U.S. Bureau of the Census.)

from rural areas to cities, the current trend is for families to move out of urban areas to suburbia. Since suburbs tend to concentrate particular age categories of people, most families who move are relocating in new neighborhoods filled with strangers who closely resemble themselves in age and income. As a result, inexperienced parents are surrounded by other inexperienced parents and are usually cut off from the child-rearing advice and support that traditionally was offered by grandparents, aunts and uncles, and close friends. Thus these families need not only organized daily child care but also assistance with all aspects of child rearing.

Our brief glance at population and family trends clearly shows that these problems will not diminish but instead are likely to increase substantially in the near future. If we are to avert a child-rearing crisis, therefore, it is essential that we begin to look seriously at solutions to the problems of young families headed by inexperienced parents, both of whom work outside the home and who are living in an environment that offers them little opportunity to share the responsibility for raising their children. Not only must we develop solutions, but we must begin to investigate means of disseminating and presenting our solutions so that all parents may take advantage of the developing technology in handling their problems.

The following two sections of this chapter suggest some ways of dealing with the normal family's child-rearing problems, both through development of community child-care systems and through dissemination of advice for enhancing family life.

FUTURE CONCERNS FOR COMMUNITY CENTERED CHILD-CARE PROGRAMS

The demographic data presented in the previous section clearly indicate that quality child care is a consistent and increasing need in our society.

One of the most serious problems in delivering quality child care is that keeping costs low requires salary scales to be low. Thus many caregiver positions go to unskilled persons. As a result of the low salaries, heavy responsibilities, and lack of professional status, the average stay of employment of these child-care workers is only about six months.

The transient nature of day-care staff makes traditional training approaches cumbersome and expensive, yet efficient systems for staff training and program evaluation to ensure quality child care are almost nonexistent. What is needed are clear guidelines and procedures for: (a) well specified, efficient child-care routines designed to handle such common problems as diapering or toileting, meals, and movement of children from one setting to another; (b) assignment of staff responsibilities so as to ensure both adequate child care and a high frequency of staff-child play and educational interaction; (c) packaged staff training and evaluation materials that will establish and maintain quality child care through on-the-job training. Without this technology, the majority of both staff and child time in day care will be consumed in an inadequate and inefficient manner. In the absence of efficient routines a disproportionate amount of time is spent handling crises, leaving little time for fun and educational interactions between the staff and children.

For the past several years we have been developing Community Center Systems that provide a technology for reliable care of young children, and for guidance and protection of pre-adolescents and teenagers. This technology includes day-care programs for infants, toddlers, and pre-schoolers, and after-school recreation for youth. Each program has been designed to function efficiently with staff who, except for the supervisor, are low-paid, transient, and not specifically nor extensively trained in working with children. In order to insure quality programs with such staff we have been attentive to many non-staff variables, including architecture, interior design, materials selection, activity organization, development of simple "packaged" staff training procedures, self-corrective monitoring, and program evaluation techniques. In short, we have carefully considered environmental and organizational variables in order to help staff conduct quality child-care programs. The result is a series of programs for all the children and youth of a community, from the youngest infant through the oldest teenager, and a technology for implementing these programs with relatively unskilled staff. This environmental and organizational approach to child care is part of all our Community Center Systems programs, but is perhaps best depicted through the example of the Infant Day Care Center.

Infant Day Care

The Infant Day Care Center model (Cataldo and Risley, 1974) is designed to provide care for up to nine hours each day, Monday through Friday, for a maximum of 20 children four weeks to twelve months of age with the equivalent of five full-time staff members. The center is based on an open-environment design which facilitates both child supervision and monitoring of staff, and is divided by low, movable partitions into a series of activity areas for diapering, feeding, play, sleep and receiving/departing (Twardosz, Cataldo, and Risley, 1974a).

Because previous research (LeLaurin and Risley, 1972; Doke and Risley, 1972) has shown that children can be more continuously engaged with their environment when staff are assigned responsibility for specific activity areas rather than specific children, staff assignments in the infant center are defined by areas of activity; that is, one staff member acts as the supervisor, and the others are assigned on a rotating basis to specific activity areas: diapering, feeding, and play. The sleep area does not require the constant supervision of a full-time staff member because the physical design of the center permits this area to be monitored from any point; thus, responsibility for the sleep area can be easily assigned to the person in charge of diapering or to the supervisor. The supervisor manages the receiving/departing area as well as overseeing the operation of all other areas.

In each activity area, the arrangement of the area and the staff procedures are designed to facilitate reliable child care by full- or part-time staff who have not previously been trained. For example, the diapering area is arranged for maximum safety and efficiency. Each child's diapers, powders, and ointments are stored in the child's individual diaper bin. Taped to each child's bin are instructions from the parents on diapering and for the use of any special medication for diaper rash. Other materials needed (paper towels, tissues) are arranged conveniently on or near the diapering table so no child is ever left unattended. A diapering/bathing table which is secured in a bathtub with suction cups on side braces has been designed. A solid top for diapering is attached with hinges and can be raised to expose a bathing surface of nylon netting which cradles the child and allows the water to run through the netting without requiring staff to carry or support a slippery child.

In addition to the organization of the area and the necessary materials, simple "packaged" staff routines are also crucial for effective child care. The staff procedure for the diapering area provides an example: When a child at the infant center needs a change, the staff member in charge of the diapering area first sets out the necessary materials from the child's diaper bin. When everything is within easy reach, the infant is brought into the diapering area. Because of efficient planning there is time for adult-child social interaction and play. After the child is changed and placed in another area, the diapering area is cleaned and a record of why and when the child was changed is made for both the center and the parents. Each step in this routine has been described in writing, and checklists have been prepared for use in training new staff members and for regular monitoring of performance levels.

This attention to staff routines and materials design is part of all areas in the infant center. For example, cribs are bolted on top of crib stands which also serve as storage shelves for children's blankets, favorite crib toys, and pacifiers. Thus, all materials are easily accessible at nap time. The cribs have collapsible sides for convenience in placing and removing the child. Further, the cribs are at adult eye level for maximum eye contact, and children are removed after naps when they make a social response such as eye contact or vocalization. In the play area, materials and activities have been selected which both engage infants in activities and promote adult-child interaction, and the environment has been designed to allow maximum exploration with a minimum of danger. Because of this attention to organization, design, materials selection, and simple staff procedures, this infant center model provides quality care for children regardless of staff experience or previous training.

Our approach to developing this infant center technology has been to describe those procedures and designs which, independent of staff, best facilitate reliable child care. While some aspects of this technology are explicit and just plain common sense, others required experimental investigation to determine the most useful procedure. For example, while the diapering area routine and design of necessary materials are straightforward and the monitoring of staff performance of the routine uncomplicated, efficient organization of diapering involves more than just replacing wet with dry. We found that the average staff member assigned to diapering spent more than a quarter of his or her time just checking diapers to determine whether the well-considered and efficient diapering procedures needed to be put into effect. A study was therefore designed to determine how the diaper-checking procedure could be made more efficient without significantly altering the frequency of diaper changes. As a result of this study, we can recommend checking diapers each time children are transferred from one activity area to another, such as from play to feeding, and a supplemental check every hour for those children who have not changed activity areas during the hour (LeLaurin, 1973).

Similarly, we have conducted research demonstrations in other areas of the center to substantiate particular elements of our procedures and design. In the sleep area, for example, we have shown that the recommended "open environment" design, with no walls or visual partitions between areas, does not hinder children's sleep even though their cribs are open to the sights and sounds of the rest of the center (Twardosz, Cataldo, and Risley, 1974a). Another study in this area showed that when toys are present in cribs children do play with them, but that neither the onset nor the duration of sleep is affected by the additional stimulation (Twardosz, Cataldo, and Risley, 1974b).

In a study in the feeding area we found that children's individual schedules are more closely adhered to, even by new and substitute staff, when a large feeding schedule board is displayed within view of the entire infant center (LeLaurin, Cataldo, and Risley, in press). Thus, a simple architectural device which publicly displays each child's schedule and his status vis-à-vis that schedule may enable children to effectively receive individual care in group settings. In another feeding area study, we compared the procedure of holding children while feeding with that of having children eat while seated in high chairs or infant seats.

Since no difference was found in the amount children eat or the time spent eating, it can be recommended that children be fed in infant seats or high chairs, a procedure which makes possible feeding several children at the same time, often a necessary procedure for insuring that all children are fed at their scheduled time (Valdivieso-Cedeno, 1972).

A primary concern of infant day care is providing a high level of adult-child social interaction. At first it might be thought that increasing the number of staff, although expensive both in terms of using paid staff or valuable volunteer time, would be effective in increasing social interaction. However, our observations, substantiated by our research demonstrations (Cataldo and Risley, 1972; Haskins, 1974), indicate that an increase in staff actually decreases each person's level of interaction with the children. Our technology therefore recommends an alternative method for increasing staff-child interaction: assigning staff responsibility for conducting specific play area activities.

Once the infant center technology was developed, the descriptions of materials, simple staff routines, and environmental design were developed into a series of training manuals suitable for use by persons with less than a high school education (Herbert-Jackson et al., 1974). Tests with these manuals have shown that a high degree of accuracy in performing staff routines could be achieved simply by training staff through the use of the manuals and that this high level of adherence to routines was not lost over successive "generations" of staff turnover, as is often the case when training is conducted verbally (Sheppard, 1974).

Toddler and Preschool Care

Similar considerations as in the infant center have been applied to the design and operation of day-care programs for toddler-age children (1 and 2 years) and preschoolers (3 to 5 years). While in the selection of materials and components of environmental design the infant center model had to be altered to suit the age and developmental level of toddlers and preschoolers, the requirement of developing a technology to be implemented by a relatively small number of nonprofessional staff remained the same.

The toddler center technology employs an open environment design, similar in concept to that employed in the infant center, because it provides for efficient use of both space and personnel without interfering with children's sleep or small group activities (Twardosz, Cataldo, and Risley, 1974a). As in the infant center, toddler center staff responsibilities are organized by areas of activity, and again we found that increasing the number of staff was not as effective in increasing personal attention to children as was the provision of specified activity assignments (Cataldo and Risley, 1972).

Since children of toddler age are expected to gain certain skills (e.g., self-toileting, self-feeding, and following adult instructions), these must be considered in providing a group care technology for one- and two-year-olds. However, day-care staff can only attend to these issues in the context of efficient daily operation. For example, regardless of whether children can or cannot feed themselves, or are in the process of learning to do so, food must be prepared and set out for the children, children must be gathered in a feeding area for their meal, they must eat, and, finally, the area must be cleaned after the meal. While many approaches to self-feeding are known to be successful, only a procedure which can be incorporated into the normal sequence of mealtime and which can be implemented by staff not highly skilled or experienced in training children is appropriate in a day-care setting.

To help make mealtime successful, we used a simple food weighing procedure to establish a set of menus made up of nutritious foods that toddlers will eat (Twardosz, Cataldo, and Risley, 1975). At the same time, we found that certain of the preferred foods, because they are "mushy," tend to promote spoon use. Therefore, our recommended procedure for training self-feeding relies heavily on the selection of nutritious, preferred foods which promote spoon use so that relatively untrained staff need employ only simple prompting and, on occasion, contingent attention procedures. The supervisor, who is well trained, can then vary menus, depending upon the level of skill of the children.

In our work with preschoolers we have found that some ecological variables which are very easy to implement have significant effect on children's play behavior and can be used to reduce disruptions in group settings. For example, we found that when a group of children are evenly spaced around the teacher who is reading a story or demonstrating the use of materials, their visual attention is markedly higher than when the children follow the more usual procedure of crowding around the teacher (Krantz and Risley, 1972). Likewise, inappropriate behavior can be effectively reduced through activity scheduling that avoids following an active play period with a sedentary one; instead, the intermediary step of relatively inactive play before sedentary activities produces fewer disruptions and a higher rate of attention during the sedentary period (Krantz and Risley, 1972).

Another example is our studies of how the type of play materials presented and the way they are presented affect children's play. Children provided with the type of toys that are commonly played with by one child at a time ('isolate''' toys) show much lower rates of social play than do children presented with the type of toys commonly used in groups ("social" toys), thereby suggesting that the encouragement of social learning through play must be accompanied by the provision of appropriate toys (Quilitch and Risley, 1973). Storage of toys—whether scrambled in toy boxes or arranged on shelves—can also significantly affect children's play, and when children need to request one toy at a time from a teacher, rather than having direct access to materials, the number of interactions that can be used by preschool teachers as learning situations is increased (Montes and Risley, in press).

Our efforts to build into the environment procedures to develop children's spontaneous working language we have called "incidental teaching." When play materials are placed out of child reach, the child must initiate interaction with an adult by asking for a particular toy. This is an ideal situation for teaching because the child is indicating that his or her attention is focused on the desired object, and language is the method that must be used to obtain the object. Thus the teacher can use the situation to require a simple additional language response from the child. Such a procedure has been used to teach such language skills as labeling (Hart and Risley, 1974), elaboration of language (Hart and Risley, 1975), and letter and word matching and identification (Montes, 1973), and could be used for a wide variety of other teachings.

Programs for Older Children and Youth

As children grow older they no longer need care; instead, they need guidance in establishing the skills necessary for successful and appropriate adult behavior, and they need protection from serious effects of official consequences for their occasional acts of social deviance. We have considered two technologies for achieving these goals. One, suitable for pre-adolescents who are more readily amenable to adult direction than are teenagers, is "survival training" in academic, achievement, and job-related skills. The second is a "safe passage" program to provide older youth with an alternative to the activities of the street and of irresponsible peers, and to increase adolescents' contacts with and socialization to responsible adults. The focus for both programs is recreation, which can provide both consequences for youths' activity and maximum contact with responsible adults.

In designing a technology for the safe and trouble-free operation of a recreation center as an environment free from social deviance, we have developed toy and activity evaluation procedures to insure that the center's programs are attractive and engaging for youth. Further, we have developed a technology which uses these recreation activities as consequences for youths' behavior. As with our other programs, these technologies can be implemented by nonprofessional, low-paid, transient staff. Our recreation technology can best be described by two examples of research demonstrations: one, which is particularly important to the safe passage program, dealing with a method for increasing youth participation in center activities and socialization to adults, and a second describing a method of efficiently employing community staff resources.

Crucial to the success of recreation-center-based youth programs are attendance and contacts with adults that involve cooperation rather than confrontation. We found that new members could be recruited by providing additional access to recreation activities for those youths who bring new members to the center (Pierce and Risley, 1974a). Many recreation centers have a high level of fights, broken equipment, and littered floors, which create recurrent cost, safety, and health problems requiring immediate action. Frequently recreation center staff deal with such disruptions by trying to determine and confront the individual responsible for maintaining order. However, we have found that disruptive behavior can be reduced without confrontation by using peer-established rules and sanctions enforced by a youth or adult supervisor on a group contingency basis. In a research demonstration, when rules were enforced by the supervisor's closing the center 1 or 15 minutes earlier per infraction depending upon the severity of the offense, disruptive behavior was effectively decreased (Pierce and Risley, 1974a).

Once the technology for operating a good recreation program is available, recreation center directors still need some method for insuring that their staff actually employ the technology. In many youth programs, which are partially subsidized by federal, state, or local funds, staff pay is not contingent on employees' job performance but rather upon their physical presence, a situation which is not conducive to high performance levels. In an effort to increase the job performance of seven Neighborhood Youth Corps workers being paid an hourly wage for serving as aides in an urban recreation program, we first drew up thorough job descriptions and then threatened termination of employment, but neither was sufficient to maintain adequate job performance. However, when the hourly wage (required by the Neighborhood Youth Corps program) was made contingent on job performance by crediting the workers with working time proportional to their rating on a simple checklist of job performance, their job performance was maintained at near perfect levels. Thus, while this simple semantic shift in emphasis—from *"hours worked"* to "hours *worked"*—was still interpreted as meeting the Neighborhood Youth Corps requirements for hourly pay, its behavioral effects were substantial (Pierce and Risley, 1974b).

Packaging

Much of the technology for the extra-family child-rearing support needed by many young parents has been developed over the past several years as we have worked to develop quality infant, toddler, preschool, and after-school day care and recreation programs. The primary work that remains is to make this technology readily available through comprehensive training, management, and monitoring software, including quality control procedures.

The Infant Day Care Center program represents the most complete example of how these latter steps may be successfully undertaken. Software packages on tested staff training procedures, detailed management plans, environmental design, and monitoring procedures have been completed. The specified quality control procedures which are included can be used by state licensing and other regulatory bodies or funding agencies, and monitoring can be conducted in cooperation with program developers. This technology is viable and available. To realize a comprehensive system, similar software for toddler, preschool, and after-school care must be completed and disseminated to middle-class communities.

A SYSTEM OF FAMILY ADVICE

The same demographic trends which indicate a growing need by the family for extra-family assistance in the supervision and care of children through day care also illustrate the need for child-rearing information to be readily available to parents.

In the past, parents looked to their extended family of grandparents, aunts, uncles, and lifelong friends for advice on how to handle particular child problems and how to organize family life to run smoothly. Often, the extended family assumed some of the child-care responsibilities and arranged activities which engaged all of the family members at once, thus enhancing family interactions. Perhaps most importantly, the extended family rendered valuable feedback and advice on standards of acceptability for children's social behavior.

The modern family finds itself separated from relatives and lifelong friends (Emlen et al., 1971; Low and Spindler, 1968) because of the high mobility of our society—18% of all families, or nearly 40 million U.S. citizens, change homes each year. Roughly 1 person in 15—a total of 13 million people—migrates across a county line annually. Nearly a third of all these people are in their 20's and have young children (U.S. Bureau of the Census, 1970; Commission on Population Growth and the American Future, 1972). These trends suggest that more families are living among neighbors with whom no adequate rapport has been established; consequently, unsolicited criticism or advice about child-rearing practices and the acceptability of children's behavior is neither wanted nor available. Furthermore, the increasing patterns of homogeneous age groupings within communities suggest that even if rapport is established, the majority of the neighbors of young parents are also inexperienced parents, and therefore are not qualified to give advice.

These inexperienced and isolated families will increasingly require, through other channels, the assistance traditionally provided by family and friends. Parent training programs, family counseling centers, and high-school family preparation courses are already well established in many communities and undoubtedly will be greatly expanded (Duncan, et al., 1973; LeShan, 1971). There will also be a growing demand for textbooks and paperbacks on child rearing, already sold in great volume to the public. Both these forms of assistance either advocate general approaches to child rearing or deal with the management of children displaying severe behavioral problems. Typically, they are aimed at giving parents a new attitude toward their children and the problems children face as they grow up. Alternatively, more specific child management guides attempt to give the parent a set of psychological principles which can be used to remediate a variety of child problems. Both kinds of advice require the parent to comprehend and embrace an entire theoretical approach, or learn a new set of skills. For this reason, participation and leadership are limited primarily to relatively well-educated parents or to desperate parents willing to undergo re-education in order to remediate severe child-rearing problems.

Society has not yet found a way to replace the most common child-rearing assistance once provided by the extended family: advice on solving chronic, everyday child-rearing problems. It appears from preliminary interview and observational data that a substantial portion of child-rearing problems can be accounted for in a relatively small number of specific times and places in a family's daily life. For example, sibling arguments and fights appear to be particularly common during the rush of morning preparation for school, and disruptive and argumentative behavior occurs frequently in public settings such as stores and restaurants.

Preliminary work at the Johnny Cake Child Study Center suggests that effective solutions to problems occurring at specific times and places can be communicated in an advice form amenable to presentation through public media systems, which represent the most economically feasible method of reaching the millions of parents faced with these problems (White House Conference on Children, 1970; *Merchandising Weekly*, 1972).

Unfortunately, little information is currently available from which to identify either problem times and places or the form of advice needed by parents. The information that is available concerning families consists mainly of survey-type conclusions which have typically been used to determine norms of developmental sequences, or major cultural and sociological variables which affect the family (e.g., Newson and Newson, 1968; Yarrow, Campbell, and Burton, 1968). While such studies are invaluable in providing norms concerning macro child-rearing practices of a large proportion of society, they lack the level of data necessary for formulating advice about specific family situations.

Direct observation of families has been used for studies of particular categories of behavior which were being experimentally remediated and for details of parent-child interactions (Hall et al., 1972; White and Watts, 1973; Herbert and Baer, 1972). But these studies have typically involved only one or two homes, and were not designed to sample a sufficiently large number of homes to determine any consistencies across families.

To collect detailed quantifiable information for identifying discrete situation-specific family problems and the form of advice required for their solutions would require the participation of a network of families. Particular times or places that tend to create problems can be identified through interviews, then direct observations can be made to identify advice needed to solve these problems. Once the general form of the advice is known, then the network of families could assist in the development and testing of the advice.

Use of such a network of families would allow the development of advice having several important characteristics. First, the problem conveyed would be immediately apparent on a common-sense basis and the solution readily acceptable to parents. If the problem can be recognized only from a particular theoretical framework, or the solution applied only after an introductory course in behavioral principles, very few parents would benefit. Parents must therefore be able to immediately recognize the problem as a problem. The solution should not involve the use of practices or materials which are unusual or may cause the parent to shy away from their use.

Our preliminary work in homes has identified several specific times and places that cause problems. Among these are mornings, before dinner, bedtime, shopping trips, dining out, and car travel. Rather than providing general advice, the system of family advice being developed at the Johnny Cake Child Study Center would solve specific problems by, for example, developing a schedule for morning responsibilities and fun, activity materials for pre-dinner time, or a management and enhancement program for family dining-out. Second, the advice could be developed to be easily communicable through the mass media, and therefore reach the largest proportion of parents economically and conveniently. For advice to be amenable to presentation through television, newspapers, radio, and magazines, it needs to be communicated in lay terms, to be applicable to specific concrete situations, and to be described briefly.

Finally, the advice would have two levels—it would provide for managing children's behavior and enhancing family interactions. We need to guard against developing advice which provides parents with quiet, docile kids, when what parents are looking for are ways in which the limited time the family has together can be more pleasant and significant for all members of the family. The enhancement in parent-child interactions may even prove to be of educational benefit to the child. Most parents may think that a trip to a shopping center isn't as educational as a day at school, but when you consider our public education systems, a shopping trip with Mom and Dad may have a lot to offer.

Now, let us consider how family advice of this sort is being developed to ensure that these features of the advice are incorporated and the advice is effective. There are three stages in this development—formulating advice, packaging advice, and disseminating advice. To formulate advice, first, recurring problems in daily family life must be identified. This is done by interviewing families to discover common problems, then observing in homes to determine what specific interactions, activities, and responsibilities make a particular time or place a problem. Second, the form of solution needed must be identified. This requires additional interviewing to find out what parents and children consider to be acceptable behaviors, procedures, and practices for the identified problem times and places. The third step is formulating a solution by combining all available information about an acceptable solution. Fourth, the proposed solution is tested by letting many cooperative families try out the solution and help in revising it. This testing, revising, and retesting continues until the solution appears to be effective and acceptable to most families. As the final step in this stage, the effectiveness of the solution is experimentally demonstrated using several naive families.

Once the advice has been formulated for a particular time or place, the emphasis moves to the second stage—packaging the advice. The first step of this stage requires identification of the particular consumer or audience for the advice. For example, advice might be custom-tailored to solve a problem particular to the single-parent family, or to a family of a given socioeconomic status, and this would have to be defined. The second step involves identifying how and when to reach the intended audience. For example, one might most effectively reach families faced with troubled mornings through morning radio and television spots or possibly the morning paper. Once the appropriate dissemination systems have been identified, the advice is packaged in the appropriate forms. Some types of advice could best be presented in magazine articles or stories in newspapers, whereas brief tips to parents might take the form of radio and television spots running 30 seconds, one minute, or three minutes. More complex advice could be made available through educational television, written materials available through mail requests, or as pamphlets available free in shopping centers. The next step, and probably the most important in formulating the advice, would involve testing the effectiveness of the advice package. First a number of cooperative families would be observed, then feedback from these families would be used in revising and retesting the advice package. When the package appears effective with these families, it would be tried with other families. This process of testing, revising, and retesting would be continued until a version of the advice package was found to be effective in remediating the problem in a large proportion of new families with whom it is used. As the final step, the effectiveness of the advice package would be experimentally demonstrated. The experimental documentation and subsequent publication of the results would help ensure that the advice packages were being adequately tested to meet the standards of scientific credibility.

Once the advice has been packaged, the emphasis moves to the third stage—disseminating the advice. This stage would again have feedback mechanisms to identify those advice packages which are having an impact and those which need further revision. During this stage the advice would be presented over the selected mass dissemination systems—television, magazines, audio-visual presentations for educational television, or hand-out pamphlets. The feedback mechanism of this stage would involve collecting and analyzing information obtained from circulation figures, listener polls, and interviews. It might also be possible to obtain objective measures of behavior change in some settings. All of these forms of information can be helpful in determining how the advice could be improved and revised to make it more effective.

Only through a three-stage system of this sort can effective, quality controlled advice be made available to millions of interested parents. To illustrate this system a little more clearly, let me present one of our programs which is currently in the first stage: formulating a solution.

Many parents have difficulty providing appropriate interaction with and supervision for their children at times when the parents' attention is elsewhere. Often, these parental activities could be both enjoyable and educational for children if a simple method of including the children could be specified to the parents. We are presently examining how one of these parental activities—shopping—can be transformed into an enjoyable family event (Macrae et al., in press).

During shopping trips, parents are usually absorbed in the activity of locating and purchasing certain products; therefore, children are merely tag-alongs, following the parents around, totally left out of the entire process and often forgotten completely. It is no surprise that merchants and parents in stores and shopping centers express very similar complaints about children's behavior in stores. Their views, expressed in interviews, support the fact that shopping trips are periods when minor but irritating problems occur. Through the interview process we also learned that most parents were interested in a better way of managing their children in stores and that they thought their children should have a chance to buy something if they were good. Thus the interviews provided us with specific information concerning the problem and the form of solution that might be appropriate; that is, the solution should manage the children's inappropriate and distracting behaviors and might include an opportunity for the children to buy something.

At the Johnny Cake Child Study Center we have access to a number of cooperative families with whom we worked to formulate a solution to the shopping problem. From general interview information collected previously, we drafted what we considered an acceptable and effective solution. Instructions describing a shopping program were developed and given to a couple of families. We informally observed the families in stores when they were using the program and when they were not. After several revisions in the procedures and instructions, we had the shopping program sufficiently refined so that use of the program resulted in many noticeable improvements.

We again revised the program using these families' suggestions and tested the program with a second set of families who further verified its effectiveness and acceptability. Also, while these families were using the program, we developed a measurement code for reliable observation of the children's behavior and parent-child interactions. This measurement code underwent revision until it accurately reflected the important changes which resulted from the shopping program—changes which were clearly evident to parents, store clerks, and observers.

The basic shopping program involved establishing rules of good shopping, then giving each child 50¢ of his allowance to spend at the end of the trip, provided the child did not distract the parent by breaking a rule. If the child did break a rule, a nickel of the allowance would be deferred to a future shopping trip when he or she displayed more responsible shopping behavior.

To demonstrate the effectiveness of the shopping program, we employed two families—the Smiths and the Joneses—each consisting of one parent and three elementary-school-age children. When they shopped, two observers followed the family through the store and recorded in 15-second intervals whether any child was distracting the parent with his or her behavior. In addition, the parent wore a tape recorder and recorded the sessions. After each session the observer listened to the tapes and scored whether each 15-second interval contained a distracting comment. When the parents began using the management package, distracting behavior and distracting comments both dramatically decreased.

The initial shopping program was found to have one problem: When the children stopped distracting the parents by roughhousing, handling merchandise, and making distracting comments, the children also stopped engaging in interesting conversation which had previously included social and educational comments about things in the store and shopping behavior. In order to enhance family interactions during shopping trips, an addition to the program was necessary. The fact became evident when the parents who assisted us began to see that they wanted more than just the management of their children's behavior. They suggested that shopping trips could also be made interesting and possibly educational for their children. An enhancement procedure was therefore added to the shopping program. This procedure consists simply of having the father, for example, talk to the children about shopping, telling the children what he is looking for, and asking them where it might be found. When they find what they are looking for, the father asks which brand would be the better buy. He asks them to compare quality, quantity, and price. He might explain how credit cards work and why they are useful to have. Or he might explain why a store has a catalogue department. In addition, the parent comments on interesting and unusual merchandise in the store and asks the children to describe how merchandise is used. This activity on the part of the parent gives the children many opportunities to comment appropriately on what is going on around them. And they were found to use these opportunities. In addition, the children can learn from these conversations. Instead of being simply tag-alongs, they can learn how the store is laid out. Instead of simply watching the parent pick a brand, they can learn about comparative shopping. Instead of thinking that using a credit card means you don't have to pay, they learn that the credit card stands for money. And while they learned these things, their distracting comments and behavior were maintained at a near zero level.

This example of the family shopping advice should help illustrate how Stage I is executed. After interviewing to find problems and acceptable solutions, a solution is formulated and tested, and its effectiveness is experimentally demonstrated. The shopping advice program will now go to Stage II, where the appropriate media system will be determined, the advice package will be formulated and tested, and then its effectiveness will be experimentally demonstrated. Finally, the shopping advice will reach Stage III where it will actually be disseminated while listener surveys, reader polls, and objective behavioral measures will be used for continuing evaluation.

It may be that family advice cannot be effectively communicated to parents through commercial and public media channels. Techniques to get parents to accept or "buy" the advice may not be available. Or parents may accept the advice but not follow it. It may well be that the "impersonal" commercial and public media are generally inappropriate for transmitting technology—even simple technology. It is anticipated that more of our research effort will be spent on dissemination strategies than on developing the advice itself. These efforts will contribute some technology on using mass media to disseminate behavioral advice. As an alternative, advice "packages," once developed and tested, could be disseminated to a more limited number of parents through public education channels, or *standards* for adequate child rearing and child care might be readily transmitted through the media and might be powerfully effective in prompting parents to seek out other child-rearing advice.

Hopefully, a system such as that described here can provide advice that is easily communicated, at a common-sense level, applicable to the recurring problem times and places of daily family life, and effective in managing child problems and enhancing family events for the educational benefit of the children.

SUMMARY

It is becoming increasingly obvious that American families are displaying an inability to socialize their children into healthy and productive citizens. It appears that the traditional sources of child-rearing advice and assistance have been lost. The modern family moves frequently to gain an economic, social, or geographic advantage. This mobility has taken its toll in isolating the family from the child-rearing support previously provided by relatives and close lifelong friends, who gave the inexperienced parent information on standards of appropriate child behavior, advice for solving common, everyday child-related problems, and assistance with child care. The modern family is typically located among neighbors who are also inexperienced parents and thus lack the repertoire necessary to assist each other in child rearing.

Some additional factors which may contribute to child-rearing difficulties experienced by the modern family are the stresses of divorce, working mothers, and single-parent families.

Hence, a societal problem is developing due to increased mobility, new economic and social stress, and lack of traditional extended family supports. Modern families have an increasing inability to socialize their children into healthy and normal citizens. If the trend continues at this exponential rate, the social and economic order of this country may be further impaired.

To address this societal problem, a *comprehensive system of child-rearing assistance for families* is needed. The primary focus of this assistance would be to supplement the family in those functions previously provided by the extended family. It appears that the child-rearing assistance once provided by the extended family might be characterized into two functions: (1) supplemental child care and supervision, and (2) parent education in child rearing. A comprehensive system of child-rearing assistance for families would provide quality community services that are economically feasible in supplementing the nuclear family in both of these functions.

Help for the family in child care and supervision can probably best be provided through day care centers for infants, toddlers, and pre-school-aged children. The needs of elementary-age children and adolescents would probably best be met by an after-school recreation program designed to actively engage them in games, sports, arts and crafts, and neighborhood citizenship. The Living Environments Group at the University of Kansas is developing day care and recreational programs to provide safe, enjoyable, educational care and supervision of children when parents cannot provide this attention due to work or other social requirements.

The need to provide the modern parent with the child-rearing information which was previously acquired from aunts, uncles, grandparents, and close friends must be addressed by behavioral researchers. The child-rearing advice developed should provide the family with solutions to the common recurring problems of daily family life.

Both of these family support functions should be scientifically verified to ensure that the technology is effective, and field tested to ensure that they are "packaged" appropriately for accurate and efficient dissemination.

Careful attention to demographic trends has allowed the professional staff of the Living Environments Group and the Johnny Cake Child Study Center to begin development of systems for comprehensive child-rearing assistance prior to the time when this becomes an urgent societal need. As the need for such intra- and extra-family assistance increases, these programs will be available in readily usable form for rapid dissemination and adoption.

REFERENCES

CATALDO, M. F., and RISLEY, T. R.: The organization of group care environments: The infant day care center. Paper presented at American Psychological Association, 1972.
CATALDO, M. F., and RISLEY, T. R.: Infant day care. In: R. Ulrich, T. Stachnik, and J. Mabry (Eds.), *Control of Human Behavior,* Vol. III. Glenview, Ill.: Scott Foresman, 1974.

Commission on Population Growth and the American Future: *Population and the American Future.* Washington, D. C.: U.S. Govt. Printing Office, 1972.

DOKE, L. A., and RISLEY, T. R.: The organization of day care environments: Required versus optional activities. *J. Appl. Behav. Anal.,* 5, 225-232, 1972.

DUNCAN, D., SCHUMAN, H., and DUNCAN, B.: *Social Change in a Metropolitan Community.* New York: Russell Sage Foundation, 1973.

EMLEN, A. C., DONOHUE, B. A., and LAFORGE, R.: *Child Care by Kith: A Study of the Family Day Care Relationships of Working Mothers and Neighborhood Caregivers.* Washington, D. C.: Office of Child Development, 1971.

GRAHAM, H. D., and GURR, T. R.: *Violence in America.* New York: New American Library, 1969.

HALL, R. V., AXELROD, S., TYLER, L., GRIEF, E., JONES, F. C., and ROBERTSON, R.: Modification of behavior problems in the home with a parent as observer and experimenter. *J. Appl. Behav. Anal.,* 5, 53-64, 1972.

HART, B. M., and RISLEY, T. R.: Using preschool materials to modify the language of disadvantaged children. *J. Appl. Behav. Anal.,* 7, 243-256, 1974.

HART, B. M., and RISLEY, T. R.: Incidental teaching of language in the preschool. *J. Appl. Behav. Anal.,* 4, 1975.

HERBERT, E. W., and BAER, D. M.: Training parents as behavior modifiers: Self-recording of contingent attention. *J. Appl. Behav. Anal.,* 5, 139-149, 1972.

HERBERT-JACKSON, E. W., O'BRIEN, M., PORTERFIELD, J., and RISLEY, T. R.: *Organization of the Infant Day Care Environment,* Lawrence, Kansas: Center for Applied Behavior Analysis, 1974.

KRANTZ, P. J., and RISLEY, T. R.: The organization of group care environments: Behavioral ecology in the classroom. *J. Appl. Behav. Anal.,* in press.

LELAURIN, K.: The organization of infant day care environments: An experimental analysis of some of the monitoring and management duties of the supervisor in a day care center for children under walking age. Ph.D. dissertation, Department of Human Development, U. of Kansas, 1973.

LELAURIN, K., CATALDO, M. F., and RISLEY, T. R.: Facilitating individualized care by public display of individual schedules. *J. Appl. Behav. Anal.,* in press.

LELAURIN, K., and RISLEY, T. R.: The organization of day care environments: "Zone" versus "man-to-man" staff assignments. *J. Appl. Behav. Anal.,* 5, 225-232, 1972.

LESHAN, E. J.: *The Conspiracy Against Childhood.* New York: Atheneum, 1971.

LINDEN, F.: Demographic forecasts. Paper presented to the Conference Board, Consumer Economics, November, 1973.

LOW, S., and SPINDLER, P. G.: *Child-Care Arrangements of Working Mothers in the United States.* Washington, D. C.: Children's Bureau Publication No. 461, 1968.

MACRAE, J. W., CLARK, H. B., McNEES, M. P., and RISLEY, T. R.: An experimental analysis of a management and enhancement program for family shopping trips. *J. Appl. Behav. Anal.,* in press.

Merchandising Weekly. New York: Billboard Publications, 1972.

MONTES, F.: Incidental teaching of beginning reading in a day care center. Ph.D. dissertation, Department of Human Development, U. of Kansas, 1973.

MONTES, F., and RISLEY, T. R.: Evaluating traditional day care practices: An empirical approach. *Child Care Quarterly,* in press.

MORRIS, B.: Finding someone responsible to care for the children. *The New York Times,* Jan. 7, 1974, p. 36.

National Center for Health Statistics: *Vital Statistics Report,* Washington, D. C.: U.S. Department of Health, Education and Welfare, 1974.

NEWSON, J., and NEWSON, E.: *Four Years Old in an Urban Community.* Chicago: Aldine, 1968.

PIERCE, C. H., and RISLEY, T. R.: Recreation as a reinforcer: Increasing membership and decreasing disruptions in an urban recreation center. *J. Appl. Behav. Anal.,* 7, 403-411, 1974a.

PIERCE, C. H., and RISLEY, T. R.: Improving job performance of neighborhood youth corps aides in an urban recreation program. *J. Appl. Behav. Anal.,* 7, 207-215, 1974b.

QUILITCH, H. R., and RISLEY, T. R.: The effects of play materials on social play. *J. Appl. Behav. Anal.,* 6, 573-578, 1973.

SHEPPARD, J., CATALDO, M. F., and RISLEY, T. R.: The generations design: An experimental design for evaluating the transmission of job skills across successive generations of workers. In preparation.

TWARDOSZ, S., CATALDO, M. F., and RISLEY, T. R.: Open environment design for infant and toddler day care. *J. Appl. Behav. Anal.,* 7, 529-546, 1974a.

TWARDOSZ, S., CATALDO, M. F., and RISLEY, T. R.: Infants' use of crib toys. *Young Children,* 29, 271-276, 1974b.

TWARDOSZ, S., CATALDO, M. F., and RISLEY, T. R.: Menus for toddler day care: Food preference and spoon use. *Young Children,* 30, 129-144, 1975.

TWARDOSZ, S., HASKINS, L., CATALDO, M. F., and RISLEY, T. R.: Staff-child ratios and staff-child interaction. In preparation.

United States Bureau of the Census: *Current Population Reports.* Series P. 20, No. 235. Washington, D. C., 1970.

VALDIVIESO-CEDENO, L.: The relative effects of seated vs. being held on the feeding behavior of infants in a day care setting. Master's thesis, Department of Human Development, U. of Kansas, 1972.

WHITE, B. L., and WATTS, J.: *Experience and Environment.* Englewood Cliffs, N. J.: Prentice-Hall, 1973.

White House Conference on Children: *Profiles of Children.* Washington, D. C.: U.S. Govt. Printing Office, 1970.

YARROW, M., CAMPBELL, J. D., and BURTON, R. V.: *Child-Rearing: An Inquiry into Research and Methods.* San Francisco: Jossey-Bass, 1968.

3

A Reward-Cost Analysis of the Single-Parent Family

ELAINE A. BLECHMAN

and

MARTHA MANNING

Single-parent families represent at least 11 percent of the U.S. population (U.S. Bureau of Census, 1973). They are as diverse in demographic characteristics and group behavior as are two-parent families. At the same time, the group composition of the single-parent family, a common denominator of all single-parent families, imposes selective access to reinforcers and selective changes in the behavior of single-parent family members.

Considerable research on the single-parent family has been reported in the U.S. since 1930 (cf. bibliographies by Herzog and Sudia, 1968, 1971; Schlesinger, 1969). Evidence will be presented in this paper to suggest that this body of research has largely disregarded normally functioning single-parent families and sought evidence of maladaptive behavior in members of single-parent families, particularly in the children. Several authors have drawn similar conclusions about single-parent family research (Herzog and Sudia, 1968, 1971; Kadushin, 1970; Selden, 1965; Sprey, 1967; Thomes, 1968). Although the detrimental effects of single-parent family membership have been emphasized by this body of research, the research results have not encouraged planners of primary prevention or secondary intervention to consider the unique treatment needs of single-parent families (exceptions are Stream, 1961; Stringer, 1967).

This paper proposes that behavioral differences and similarities among single-parent families vary reliably with their demographic characteristics. It suggests that rewards and costs commonly experienced by single-parent family members are a product of a few demographic and structural single-parent family characteristics. And it proposes that an awareness of the unique nature of the single-parent family should accompany planning for family member behavior change.

Transitions in the Single-Parent Family Population, 1900-1970

In 1900, 3.9 percent of the population of the United States were members of families with one adult head of household (U.S. Bureau of Census, 1973). In 1909, an article entitled "Alarming Changes in American Homes" (Benson, 1909) reflected the prevailing negative attitudes toward the single-parent family.

By 1970, 13.3 percent of the population of the United States were members of families with one adult head (Beck and Jones, 1970). According to Bohannon (1971), an even greater percentage of the population had probably lived in a single-parent family at one time in their lives. By 1970, divorce was a routine American social custom (Mead, 1971), unwed mothers of all social classes chose to raise their own children (Ferguson, 1965; Sauber and Corrigan, 1970), and men and women chose unwed and single adoptive or biological parenthood over married parenthood (Kadushin, 1970; Morgenstern, 1971).

The social science literature concerned with single-parent families in 1970 did not seem to have kept pace with changes in the population or in popular attitudes towards single parenthood. By 1970, volumes of social science studies about single-parent families had been produced (cf. Herzog and Sudia, 1968, 1971; and Schlesinger, 1969, for bibliographies). But only three articles discussed in detail how mental health services might be tailored to meet the needs of single-parent families (Herzog and Sudia, 1971; Stream, 1961; Stringer, 1967).

It is interesting to note that schizophrenics, who constituted a far smaller part of the population (1 percent), provoked disproportionately greater interest among social scientists. In the 1971-1973 *Psychological Abstracts,* 91 articles appeared about schizophrenics, while only 21 articles appeared about the single-parent family.

Neglect of the clinical treatment needs of single-parent families seems particularly unfortunate in light of information provided by Beck and

Jones (1970, p. 17) in a census report they compiled for the Family Service Association. Their results are displayed in Figure 1. They noted:

> Single-parent families are disproportionately heavy users of family service. Among sample families applying to agencies, 23 percent were headed by a woman as compared with only 11 percent of families in the general population. Applicants from single-parent families headed by a man were much less frequent—3 percent for both agency and U.S. families. Only 74 percent of agency families were intact as compared with 86 percent of U.S. families.
>
> During the 1960-1970 decade, single-parent families increased out of proportion to other groups as users of family service. For agencies reporting in both years, the proportion of agency families headed by a woman increased from 19.4 to 23.4 percent, while the corresponding increase for the general population was only from 9.3 to 10.8. During the same decade, broken families headed by a man increased from 2.1 to 3.5 percent of agency families, whereas this group in the general population changed little (from 2.9 to 2.8 percent).
>
> During this same period, there was a compensating downward shift in the proportion of intact families served by agencies (from 78.5 percent in 1960 to 73.0 percent in 1970), while for the general population, there was only a minor change (from 87.8 to 86.4 percent). Clearly, single-parent families are increasingly applying to family agencies for help with a wide range of family problems and crises.

Perhaps clinically oriented social scientists have ignored the single-parent family because their treatment models lead them to disparage this family type and provide them with few methods of changing single-parent family behavior without changing family composition. Freud's (1961) observations about family life seem to suggest that the single-parent family deprives children of role models and childhood experiences necessary for the acquisition of appropriate sex role behavior, for progress through successive developmental stages, and for satisfactory adult moral behavior. Others have suggested that a woman cannot manage social, economic, and psychological tasks outside of marriage (Decter, 1972; Graves, 1965; Rich, 1972; Staines et al., 1974; Vilar, 1972). Equipped with these attitudes towards the single-parent family, it is not surprising that many therapists have limited therapeutic strategies for the troubled single-parent family. They can either help the family accept a regrettable situation, prepare the parent for remarriage, or treat the family as if it were a two-parent family.

The experimental behavior analyst should be better prepared than

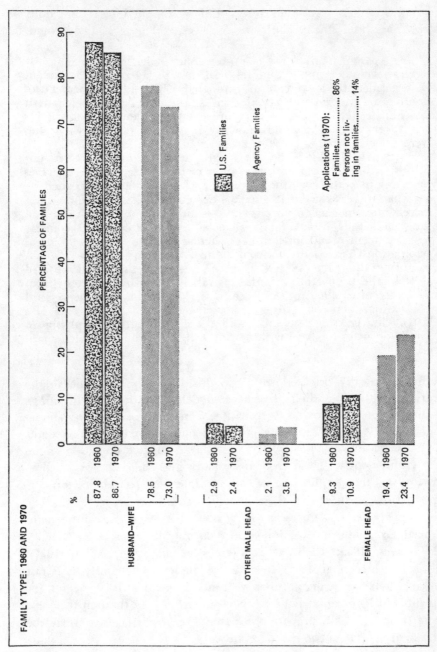

FIGURE 1: Percentage of U.S. families headed by single male parents, single female parents, and two parents, in 1960 and 1970. (Reprinted by permission from *Family Agency Clients: Who Are They? What Do They Want? What Do They Get?* by Dorothy Fahs Beck and Mary Ann Jones. New York: Family Service Association of America, 1972.)

the conventional therapist to ignore disparaging attitudes towards the single-parent family and to innovate prevention and intervention strategies for the single-parent family. The guiding philosophy of experimental behavior analysts seems to involve a readiness to view demographic and ecological characteristics as setting events (Bijou and Baer, 1966; Kantor, 1959) that selectively expose the individual to classes of reinforcers and selectively reinforce behavior. Demographic characteristics are not uniformly viewed as causes of irreversible structural change within the individual.

Social Science Research on the Single-Parent Family

The hypothesis that social scientists have shown abundant interest in the bad effects of the single-parent family was investigated by means of a literature search. *Psychological Abstracts* up to 1974 were searched, and the 75 articles found concerning single-parent families were classified by two raters. The earliest research on the single-parent family was three studies (Armstrong, 1932; Shaw and McKay, 1932; Weeks and Smith, 1939) that investigated the relationship between delinquency and membership in a single-parent family. These early studies prophesied the interest of researchers in the single-parent family for the next four decades. Studies fell into six categories:* effects of single-parent family membership on children—64 percent; theory and literature reviews—11 percent; effects of single-parent family membership on parents—8 percent; studies of small-group behavior—8 percent; demographic characteristics of single-parent families—5 percent; treatment of single-parent families—4 percent. (See Appendix I for these titles). One question summarizes the perspective of the bulk of this research: How much does single-parent family life interfere with the adjustment, appropriate sex role behavior, and educational achievement of children (particularly boys)? This literature is largely concerned with the causal relationship between single-parent family membership, delinquency, and pathology.

Many of these investigations of the single-parent family suffer from methodological flaws that jeopardize the internal and external validity of the research (for methodological discussion see Billingsley and Giovannoni, 1971; Herzog and Sudia, 1968, 1971; Sprey, 1967; Thomes, 1968). Many studies: (a) base causal inferences on correlational data, (b) draw conclusions about the true nature of the single-parent family from obser-

---

* Two readers grouped these articles in predetermined categories. In case of disagreement an article was considered unclassifiable.

vations of disturbed single-parent family members, and (c) conclude that the single-parent family induces pathology and deviancy at a higher rate than the two-parent family because single-parent family members are overrepresented in some penal and psychiatric facilities. This final approach ignores the possibility that the limited financial resources of single-parent families may restrict access to early private treatment and legal help, and thereby swell the proportion of single-parent family members found in public penal and psychiatric institutions (Billingsley and Giovannoni, 1971).

Unexpectedly, many empirical investigations of the single-parent family reveal fewer differences between children in single-parent and two-parent families than within each family type (cf., for examples, Herzog and Sudia, 1968, 1971; Kadushin, 1970; Selden, 1965; Sprey, 1967; Thomes, 1968); buttress a social learning perspective; and suggest that members of single-parent families are poorer and hence more likely than members of two-parent families to be found in public penal and psychiatric institutions.

The work of Aldous (1972) and Biller (1968, 1969, 1971, 1972) supported a social learning perspective on the behavior of single-parent family children. They reported that when single mothers reinforce their sons' masculine sex role behavior, their sons act appropriately masculine, regardless of father or male role model availability. In addition, they reported that peers and the mass media cue and reinforce masculine role performance among the sons of single parents.

Similarities and Differences Among Single-Parent Families

Awareness of behavioral diversity among families is muted by mass media presentations of ideal families and by social isolation of families with differing life-styles and compositions (Sussman, 1972; Turner, 1970). Rosenfeld and Rosenstein (1973) have suggested a family typology based on the degree and cause of parental absence as a first step in studying differences between families. Viewed through such a typology, some single-parent and two-parent families prove identical with respect to both the degree of total parent absence from the home and the relative social acceptability of cause of absence—business needs and physical illness versus psychiatric illness and alcoholism, for example. In support of such a typology, Biller (1972) has suggested that women and men in two-parent families, with partners who are frequently absent from home, function in many respects as if they were single parents.

In this paper, sources of behavioral diversity among real, not subjective, single-parent families will be examined. The single-parent family that includes only one adult parent (biological or adoptive) and one or more children will be considered. The two-parent family that functions as if it were a single-parent family derives financial and social benefits from its quasi two-parent status, and will not be considered here. The single-parent family that includes only adult self-sufficient children differs in resources from the single-parent family with dependent children, and will also not be considered here.

Demographic Characteristics of Single-Parent Families and Access to Rewards and Costs

Behavioral diversity among single-parent families might be related to a few salient demographic characteristics of families. Demographic characteristics, such as income level, mediate family member behavior in two ways: (a) they determine access to rewarding and punishing behavioral consequences, and (b) they affect members' output of certain classes of behavior.

Three characteristics of single-parent families—sex of the single parent, cause of parental absence, and role distribution in the family before parent loss—may introduce substantial diversity in the access of single-parent families to types and amounts of pleasurable and aversive consequences.

1. *The single-parent family's access to reward and costs may vary with the sex of the single parent.* The average income of female heads of household is significantly lower than that of male heads of household (Fuentes, 1970; U.S. Government Printing Office, 1963a). Hence the single-parent family, when headed by a female, has less access to financial, material, and social rewards (U.S. Government Printing Office, 1963b) than the two-parent family or the male-headed single-parent family. As a result, the female single parent is likely to command less material and social reinforcers to employ in contingent reinforcement of children's behavior, and the entire female-headed single-parent family is likely to be exposed to more of the noncontingent aversive outcomes associated with poverty.

There is reason to believe that community attitudes are more favorable towards single fathers than towards single mothers. Single fathers in 1970 headed 2.4 percent of all U.S. families, while single mothers headed 10.9 percent (see Figure 1). The portrayal of single parents in television situation comedies appears to support the assumption that single fathers are generally regarded more favorably than single mothers. Between 1970 and 1973, seven situation comedies featured single parents. In four of these shows, the single parent was male. Perhaps the single father is seen as a martyr who has volunteered for an exceptional task, while the single mother is seen as doing what she ought to do and deserving no special credit (de Charms, 1968). More favorable community attitudes directed towards the single father may mean that he is treated better by the children's schools, by social service agencies, by neighbors, and by work associates, than is the single mother. In turn, enhanced social prestige may provide the single father with abundant social reinforcement power in the home.

2. *The single-parent family's access to reward and costs may vary with the cause of parental absence.* The degree of social acceptability of the cause of single parenthood may function as a potent setting event, mediating the family's access to material and social rewards (Bohannon, 1971; Goffman, 1961; Waller, 1930). Widowed families and families with a physically ill member can expect more financial help through insurance payments, more prestige in the community, more favorable contact with welfare agencies, and more aid from both maternal and paternal extended families (Leichter and Mitchell, 1967) than can the family dismembered for socially unacceptable reasons.

Families dismembered due to socially unacceptable circumstances (divorce, psychiatric illness, desertion, unwed parenthood) are prone to numerous noncontingent material and social aversive consequences. Legislation directed at these families tends to be punitive and restrictive (e.g., proposals for sterilization of unwed mothers), while legislation directed at more socially acceptable family categories tends to be benign (e.g., bills to provide educational support to widows and orphans). Families dismembered by loss of a deviant parent are subject to negative attitudes within the community, and to self-castigation and lowered expectations within the family group.

The degree of social acceptability of the cause of single parenthood may also affect the family's subjective estimation of available rewards and costs. After a family has lost a parent for socially unacceptable reasons, members may compare their present to their past experiences and conclude that they are better off now than they were before (Thibaut and Kelley, 1959). Perhaps they no longer have bitter arguments within the family or unpleasant interactions with people and agencies outside the family.

After a family loses a parent for socially acceptable reasons, members may compare their present to their past experiences and conclude that they are worse off than they were before. An individual who provided significant material and social rewards and shared the family's labor is no longer present. When positive attitudes towards an absent family member are stronger than they were before the loss, the feeling of deprivation has been called idealization (Gebhard, 1971; Thibaut and Kelly, 1959). Idealization has been identified as a central ingredient in grief and mourning (Jensen and Wallace, 1956).

Thus the relative social acceptability of the cause of parental absence may result in a *real* change in a family's access to pleasant and aversive consequences. It may also result in a change in the family's *subjective evaluation* of such consequences.

3. *The single-parent family's access to reward and cost may vary with role distribution in the predismembered family.* Task and social-emotional functions can be distributed between two parents in accord with conventional sex role expectations, or they can be distributed with regard for each parent's available time and interests.

From World War II through the 1950's, mothers were found to be social-emotional leaders, and fathers were found to be task leaders in American and British middle-class families (Bott, 1955, 1956; Kenkel, 1957; Parsons et al., 1955). The leadership functions in small nonfamilial groups were also found to be distributed between a task and a social-emotional leader (Bales, 1953; Bales and Slater, 1955; Parker, 1958; Slater, 1955). In families and other small groups, the social-emotional leader was usually found to be the best-liked person in the group (Benne and Sheats, 1948; James, 1956). This research has been criticized for its neglect of a broad range of ethnic and social-class family types and for a tendency to idealize rather than describe families (Billingsley and Giovannoni, 1971). Nonetheless, in some two-parent families, task and social-emotional functions probably are distributed according to the sex of the parent.

Since 1950, research on distribution of leadership functions among parents has increasingly pointed to a liberalization of sex roles. Strodtbeck (1951), in a study of three American subcultures, reported that the marital partner who talked the most exercised the most power, regardless of the partner's sex. Blood and Hamblin (1958) described families in which labor distribution was determined by partner availability. Heiss (1962) reported that dating couples with a high degree of intimacy and familiarity rejected traditional sex-role allocations. O'Rourke (1963)

reported that traditional sex-role specialization around expressive behavior was observed much less in familiar home settings than in unfamiliar laboratory settings.

At the same time, small-group researchers described hierarchies which
served both task and social-emotional functions (Talland, 1957; Theodorson, 1957), and individuals who served both functions because of lack
of appropriate leaders to help them (Landsberger, 1955). Thus, distribution of social-emotional and task functions in a nontraditional manner
might be expected in increasing numbers of families.

Absence of a parent from a family decreases the possibilities for adult
leadership of the group and increases the responsibilities of the remaining adult. A decrease in the adult leadership of the family makes it likely
that some task and social-emotional functions will be neglected. This
may occur not only because one adult has less time and energy than two
adults, but also because one adult is less efficient than two at solving
certain problems (Goldman, 1966; Taylor and Faust, 1952).

The extent of detrimental effects caused by parent loss may depend
upon the distribution of social-emotional and task functions prior to
parent loss. Families in which functions were distributed according to
traditional sex-role expectations, or in any rigid fashion that precluded
the sharing of most tasks by both parents, are likely to experience
numerous aversive consequences as a result of parent loss. In these families, the remaining parent will be inexperienced at significant tasks,
and other family members may expect the single parent to fail at
these tasks.

The single parent who confronts tasks that formerly were inconsistent
with his or her role may experience role strain (Goode, 1960). The term
"role strain" encompasses several overt and covert verbal behaviors,
including (a) verbalization of pessimistic expectations about accomplishment of inconsistent tasks, and (b) verbalization of self-denigrating
evaluations while attempting to accomplish inconsistent tasks.

When the single parent is persistently inefficient at new tasks, one of
the children may take over some of the responsibility. An older child
may find a salaried job, help care for younger siblings, or aid in a variety
of household chores. In some families, children may take responsibility
in a maladaptive fashion for tasks neglected by the parent. A child may
imitate the behavior of the sick or deviant absent parent. If this behavior
helps the family explain their current unhappiness and if it helps the
family unite in an effort to improve the child's behavior, the family may
reward the child's maladaptive behavior (Koskoff and Weniger, 1949;

Parsons and Fox, 1952; Vogel and Bell, 1961). It is not clear how often children either directly assume responsibilities for inefficient parents or reduce the family's dissatisfaction with inefficient parents by means of deviant behavior.

No available evidence suggests short- and long-term effects of inefficient leadership by a new single-parent. However, it is possible to draw inferences from laboratory and field research on small groups. Member satisfaction may erode as children are forced to move out of their former roles into radically new ones. Such movement may increase social-emotional activity (i.e., talking about group problems) and reduce productivity (Bales and Slater, 1955, 1957; Heinecke and Bales, 1953; Shepherd and Weschler, 1955; Wheeler, 1957). All family members (parent and children) who made a successful adjustment to one type of family may lose some of their power when the leadership style changes (McCandless, 1942). Disagreement about the specific attributes of each family member's role may be associated with lowered family cohesiveness (Hall, 1955). Lowered consensus on family member status may be associated with lessened satisfaction with each family member's task performance (Heinecke and Bales, 1953). Family members who have acquired little experience at new tasks are likely to have little self-confidence (Kelman, 1950).

In contrast, the single-parent family that formerly distributed task functions on the basis of adult availability to perform these functions is less likely to suffer neglect of one set of functions, reallocation of these functions to a child member, role inconsistency, lowered productivity, reduced satisfaction, and impaired cohesiveness.

Both the sex of the single parent and the cause of parent absence affect the newly formed family's access to rewards and costs. However, neither of these conditions is readily changed. A third condition which affects access to rewards and costs—role distribution between parents before parent loss—can be altered. Families that anticipate the loss of a parent and families that have recently lost a parent could be trained to modify the distribution of family roles and relevant family attitudes. In particular, the new single parent could be trained in unfamiliar role behaviors and could be helped to change beliefs and feelings about the appropriateness of these behaviors for masculine and feminine sex roles. New single fathers may benefit from rehearsal of homemaking and empathizing behaviors; new single mothers may benefit from rehearsal of money management and assertive behaviors. As a part of parent retraining, parents might be trained to reinforce their own performance of newly acquired skills.

Behavioral uniformity among single-parent families might be related to the group composition of the family. The presence of only one adult parent with one or more children imposes common conditions upon single-parent families even though they differ in terms of sex of the single parent, cause of parent absence, and previous role distribution. These common conditions include leader strain, use of the two-parent family as a comparison group, and social isolation.

1. *Leader strain may uniformly reduce rewards and increase costs for the single-parent family.* We use the term "leader strain" to refer to the behavioral consequences of a situation in which one leader must carry out disparate tasks which overburden his or her available time and energy. Role strain, mentioned earlier, confronts leaders who must perform tasks which they feel they should not and cannot perform. Not all single parents confront role strain; that depends in part upon the pattern of role distribution prior to parent loss. But all single parents must endure some leader strain, since many of their obligations are incompatible for the same person at the same time (Gross et al., 1958; Simmel, 1955; Wispe, 1955).

The single parent faces behavioral objectives that include (1) gaining material reinforcement at work and in the community; (2) preparing family members to achieve at school; (3) reinforcing pleasant interactions among family members; and (4) training family members in effective social skills. Talcott Parsons (Parsons et al., 1955) proposed that the first two objectives (of group advancement in the outside world) belong to the group's task leader, while the other two objectives (of management of intragroup relations) belong to the group's social-emotional leader. He argued that the male and female parenting roles are consistently different because their behavioral objectives are so incompatible (Fiedler, 1958) that when one leader seeks both objectives he or she becomes confused, unhappy, and inefficient.

It may be that the behavioral components of task and social-emotional objectives are not in and of themselves mutually exclusive, but that adherents to traditional sex roles might construe one set of objectives to be impossible for them to achieve. In the absence of rigid beliefs about appropriate sex-role behaviors, simultaneous management of both task and social-emotional objectives merely demands greater efficiency and flexibility than does management of only one set of objectives.

The single parent must decide when to work towards task or social-emotional objectives. When a child studies inside on a sunny day while his friends play outside, the single parent must decide whether the child should be rewarded for achievement-oriented behavior or instructed to stop studying and go out to play. To bypass constant decision-making problems, the single parent must establish decision-making rules that indicate when to reinforce task and social-emotional objectives. For example, the parent may decide to reward play behavior during the day and study behavior after dark. Two-parent families also disagree about the appropriate method of encouraging task and social-emotional behavior. But two-parent families command more reinforcement power and more reinforcement opportunities. Therefore, the single parent must be quite efficient to achieve the same results as a moderately inefficient two-parent family.

The single parent must vigilantly organize time and resources to model and reinforce both task and social-emotional behavior. This means that the parent must often find time and money to work, pay for child care, attend to housekeeping chores, and spend time with the children. The same schedule might be accomplished more easily and at less cost by two parents; while one works the other cares for the children and the house.

Not all single parents are prepared to handle efficiently the broad range of time- and energy-consuming tasks confronting them. Nonetheless, some single parents attempt to accomplish both task and social-emotional parenting functions. The costs of this strategy for the unprepared parent may include endless indecision about appropriate behavior ("Should I leave work early when my child is sick?" "How can I play with my children and straighten up the house?"). The costs for the child may include uncertain expectations about the parent's behavior and dissatisfaction with the parent's leadership.

Other single parents, unprepared to juggle task and social-emotional demands, concentrate on one objective and abandon the other. The single parent who stays at home with young children and depends upon welfare payments, and the single parent who works and relies upon others to carry out a majority of child-care activities—both concentrate on one objective. The financial and social costs of the former strategy are obvious. The costs of the latter strategy, particularly when the single parent is female, include guilt about dereliction of traditional mothering responsibilities, and resentment of the children as an interference to professional advancement (Millett, 1972).

Prospective parents in Western society are not systematically taught to manage their time and resources in order to achieve their dual social-emotional and task objctives. They are expected to rear children who are emotionally and financially self-sufficient, and they are held responsible for their children's behavior when it falls short of this goal. They are expected to do this without close ties to an extended family and without adequate community-run child-care facilities. Single parents are likely to be least able to fulfill society's parenting expectations and, as a result, all members of the single-parent family are likely to experience reduced rewards and increased costs from family life.

Single parents would find it easier to discharge their parenting responsibilities if they were given explicit training in child behavior management. However, child behavior management training is insufficient unless the single parent is helped to establish priorities among parenting and other personal goals, and is trained to efficiently allocate time and money to accomplish these goals.

2. *Use of the two-parent family as a reference group may uniformly reduce the single-parent family's subjective rewards and increase the single-parent family's subjective costs.* Given the numerical predominance of two-parent families and cultural values that favor the two-parent family, it is likely that some members of single-parent families will regard their families as mutilated versions of the two-parent family. As a result, they may use the two-parent family as a reference group (Thibaut and Kelley, 1959), comparing their experiences with what they believe happens in two-parent families. If their acquaintance with two-parent families is limited, it is possible that single-parent family members will derive an idealized view of two-parent families from the mass media (Mayer, 1967). When they compare their outcomes with those they believe are achieved by members of the two-parent families, they will probably feel relatively deprived.

From the perspective of the child who compares the single-parent family with the idealized two-parent family, the following disadvantages to single-parent family membership emerge: in the single-parent family there is one less parent to approach with problems; there is no second parent to appeal to about unfair parental decisions; there is less time and attention available from the single parent; the single parent provides less diversity of viewpoints; the single parent can train the child in a more limited range of skills.

Single parents whose view of the two-parent family is idealized may conclude that they must carry out tasks that are equitably distributed between parents in the two-parent family.

Familiarity with a broad range of two-parent families and clear memories of prior experiences with an absent parent could dispel fantasies about the superiority of the two-parent family. Similarly, familiarity with a broad range of single-parent families could dispel the notion that single-parent family members are always disadvantaged. Realistic attitudes about single-parent and two-parent families might prevent single-parent family members from being subjectively dissatisfied with their experiences and might enable them to enjoy the unique opportunties afforded by single-parent family membership.

But realistic information about family life is not readily available in American society, particularly for young people. Television and schools provide inadequate information about family life (Mayer, 1967). The social isolation of the single-parent family, a topic to be discussed next, tends to prevent fruitful information exchange between single-parent and two-parent families. This serves to enhance ignorance about the variability of family experience.

3. *Social isolation of the single-parent family may uniformly reduce the single-parent family's rewards and increase the single-parent family's costs.* The single-parent family faces impediments to the formation and maintenance of pleasurable relationships with two-parent families. The single-parent family poses a threat to many two-parent families. It presents an example of a dissolved family to a family that may itself be in conflict, and it reduces sanctions against family dissolution (Miller, 1971). As a result, relationships between single-parent and two-parent families are often strained (Bohannon, 1971).

In addition, the single parent faces impediments to the formation and maintenance of satisfactory heterosexual relationships. Dating and parenting behaviors are regarded as mutually exclusive in American culture. No norms exist to guide the development of a socially sanctioned heterosexual relationship for the single parent (Gavai, 1967). Derogatory "merry widow" and "gay divorcée" stereotypes are likely to color perceptions of the single mother's behavior and to further impede her heterosexual adjustment.

When a single parent begins to form new sexual and affectional attachments, the children must share the parent's time and attention with the parent's friends. Memories of the loss of one parent together with diminished social reinforcement from the single parent may lead the children to fear abandonment. Children of remarried parents have been heard to express fears of abandonment long after remarriage has occurred (Bernard, 1956; Mead, 1971). The lack of kinship bond between the children and the stepparent may erode the taboo against incest (Mead, 1971) and abuse by the stepparent, and provide the realistic basis for children's fears about remarriage described in the folk tales of "Cinderella" and "Hansel and Gretel." At the same time, some children's fears about the stepparent may be highly unrealistic and yet may be strengthened by the attention of concerned natural and stepparents.

Barriers to familiarity between single-parent and two-parent families, a lack of norms regarding dating behavior by single parents, stereotypes concerning the sexual behavior of single parents, and conflict between the children and the parent's opposite-sex friends are all sources of single-parent family social isolation. Taken together, these conditions may be responsible for the loneliness and unsatisfactory social relationships described by many single parents (Freudenthal, 1959; Ilgenfritz, 1961).

Parents Without Partners, Inc. (Harris, 1966), and other single parents' social organizations successfully reduce social isolation and provide an appropriate reference group for some single parents. These groups seem to provide the least support to socially unassertive single parents, to lower-class and working-class single parents, and to single parents who maintain negative attitudes about single parenthood. The latter prefer not to be regarded as single parents and avoid the company of other single parents.

To reduce the social isolation of single parents who avoid social clubs, outreach and training procedures need to be developed. These single parents might benefit from realistic information about the dating behavior of other single parents and from preparation for children's reactions to parental dating. Some of these single parents might benefit from general social-skills training.

The three conditions related to the group composition of the single-parent family—leader strain, use of the two-parent family as a reference group, and social isolation—may diminish the family's real and subjective rewards and enhance its real and subjective costs. Widespread change in conditions responsible for unsatisfactory single-parent family life could be brought about by improvements in the family-life information provided by the mass media and by the schools. In addition, vulnerable single parents might be trained to use their time and resources to achieve their desired personal and parental goals; they and their children might be encouraged to compare their experiences with other single-parent families; and they might be trained to overcome impediments to satisfactory interpersonal relationships.

Demographic Characteristics of Single-Parent Families and Family Member Behavior

Demographic characteristics of single-parent families may act as setting events, directly affecting the probability of some classes of family member behavior. Two group characteristics distinguish single-parent families: (a) most single-parent families have, at one point in their history, lost an adult member; and (b) all single-parent families are composed of one adult and one or more child members. The relationship between these two group characteristics and family member behavior has not been documented. It is possible, however, to base tentative inferences upon laboratory and field small-group research.

1. *Decreased size of the single-parent family and temporary improvements in interpersonal behavior.* Decreased group size due to parent loss may give rise to positive, although not necessarily enduring, changes in the family's interactions. As the size of the group decreases, the frequency and intensity of statements of affection for other group members have been found to increase (Coyle, 1930). Decreased group size tends to increase individual interaction opportunities and may contribute to the improved social climate in smaller groups. Gibbs (1951) found that fewer people participated in group activities as the group increased in size. Dawe (1934) found in a kindergarten group that, as group size increased, the average number of remarks per child, percent of children participating, and total amount of discussion decreased. Positive effects of decreased family size caused by member death have been noted by Klein and Lindemann (1961), who reported heightened cohesiveness and increased intermember communication in mourning families. Not all categories of behavior increase as group size decreases (Bales and Borgatta, 1955), but the average rate of communication for all group members increases when a high interactor is removed from a group (Bovard, 1951; Stephan and Mishler, 1952; Strodtbeck and Hook, 1956).

This increase in statements of affection, together with a decrease in hostile statements, is particularly dramatic when a triad loses a member (Gamson, 1961; Mills, 1953; Simmel, 1902; Strodtbeck, 1954). Triads tend to break up into a two-person coalition aligned against the third. Loss of a member from a triad eliminates opportunities for competitive confrontations. Decomposition of a triad into a dyad changes not only communication rate but communication content. Wolff (1950) has found that messages in a dyad are more intimate. Decomposition of a mixed-sex group into a same-sex group also introduces favorable changes in communication content. South (1927) found less hostile content in messages sent in a same-sex group than in messages sent in a mixed-sex group.

Loss of a parent may temporarily increase the frequency of interaction and improve the content of communication between single parent and children. This is particularly likely if the absent parent was a high inter-actor, and if the single-parent family is a same-sex dyad. If favorable behavior change does briefly follow parent loss, primary prevention efforts should capitalize upon this change. Rather than attempting to change attitudes and teach new interaction skills, it would be simpler to teach family members to reinforce existing and favorable interaction patterns. In the absence of systematic reinforcement and in the presence of adverse environmental circumstances, favorable changes in inter-action are likely to vanish.

2. *Single-parent family group composition and nonreciprocal behavior control.* In every family the child's physical and social immaturity imposes a pattern of nonreciprocal behavior control upon the family. The parent controls a wealth of tangible and intangible behavior conse-quences. Positive reinforcers, negative reinforcers, time out, and punish-ment are all at the parent's disposal. Children control fewer behavior con-sequences; they primarily control behavior through the imposition and withdrawal of aversive consequences. They can impose time out by being sick in the middle of the night; punishment, by crying and misbehaving in the presence of company; negative reinforcement, by suddenly quiet-ing down. They have far less access to behavior management through positive material reinforcers, and they tend to be less skilled at the application of positive social reinforcers than their parents.

In the two-parent family, the partners are able to dilute the children's aversive control by cooperation. Parents of a newborn can alternate in waking up to feed the baby. Parents of a sick child can relieve one another from sickroom duty. But for the single parent there is no readily available help in the home to dilute the children's tendency to exert more aversive than positive control. The absence of adequate community child-care facilities (Guggenheimer, 1970; Lash, 1970) aggravates the child's aversive control.

It seems likely that in such an imbalanced relationship the single parent will eventually respond to the child's aversive control with even more aversive behavior, until the single-parent family is locked into the coercive spiral of aggression described by Patterson and Cobb (1971). Markedly imbalanced behavior control may produce a single mother who bitterly resents her children—because benefiting them costs her a high price (Millett, 1972). It may produce a martyred father, one who perpetually emphasizes how much good he gives and how much bad he receives. Finally, imbalanced behavior control may produce a parent who hesitates (despite professional advice) to exert positive control over the children. If the children punish him, a father may reason, why should he reward them?

As children mature, the positive material and social reinforcers that the parents command diminish in their effectiveness (Edwards, 1969). The adolescent, through working outside the home, can earn money as well as gain attention and praise from peers. Aversive consequences commanded by the parents also diminish in their effectiveness, since the adolescent can easily run away from parental punishment. At the same time, the adolescent's potential aversive control over the parent intensifies. Misbehavior is likely to be more costly, more embarrassing, and more worrisome than when he or she was younger.

The single parent has fewer avenues of escape and support in the face of conflict with adolescent children than do parents in the two-parent family. The single parent commands fewer material rewards and wields less aversive control than parents in the two-parent family. As a result, the single parent may be forced to relinquish control over the adolescent's behavior earlier than do parents in the two-parent family, and to have less impact on the socialization of the adolescent. For these reasons, the single parent must establish a relationship with the children based on positive social control. Only a parent-child relationship based on positive social control can possibly survive the changes in adolescent responsivity to parental reinforcement that characterize the parent-adolescent relationship.

More than parents in the two-parent family, the single parent needs to be informed about the likelihood that an imbalanced relationship will prevail during the childhood and adolescent years. Children in the single-parent family need to learn to use positive social reinforcement, and the single parent must learn to reward the children's use of positive social reinforcement.

Demographic Characteristics of the Single-Parent Family as
Mediators of Child Deviancy

At the beginning of this paper, a tendency was noted among social scientists to seek evidence that membership in the single-parent family brings with it heightened vulnerability to pathology. The quest for pathological effects of single-parent family membership was attributed in part to psychodynamic conceptions of child development, which postulate that normal child development demands the presence of two parents.

To some extent, the findings of greater deviancy among children of single parents are invalidated by poor research designs and by errors of reasoning. However, all evidence of greater deviancy among the children of single parents cannot be discounted. Demographic characteristics of single-parent families tend to diminish the rewards and enhance the costs of membership in the single-parent family. At times these characteristics promote conditions that overburden the already vulnerable family, mute the social reinforcement power of the parent, and increase the likelihood of conflict between parent and child.

The difficulties faced by the single-parent family are exacerbated by inadequate preparation for parenting, stereotyped information about families presented in the media and in schools, the inferior status of women, and the society's laissez-faire approach to the circumstances of child-rearing. These conditions, rather than an inherent flaw in the constitution of the single-parent family, may be largely responsible for any excess in child deviancy to be found among single-parent families.

Some of the impediments to enjoyable single-parent family life could be ameliorated by behavior and attitude change among single parents and their children.

In this paper some primary prevention and secondary intervention approaches to behavior and attitude change in the single-parent family have been proposed: (1) Train the new single parent to carry out tasks formerly accomplished by the absent parent and to self-reward performance of novel tasks. (2) Train the single parent to establish personal and parental priorities and to use limited time, energy, and material resources wisely. (3) Train the single-parent family to compare their outcomes to those of other single-parent families rather than to the outcomes of idealized two-parent families. (4) Prepare the single parents to overcome obstacles to satisfactory adult social relationships. (5) Capitalize on the brief period of increased positive interaction between parent and children that may follow one parent's departure; use this opportunity to reinforce the use of positive social control. (6) Educate the parent about the imbalanced relationship that often exists between single parents and children; provide the parent with cognitions that will interfere with an exploited, martyred self-concept. (7) Train the parent and children to avoid a spiral of aversive control and avoidance during adolescent socialization.

The Well-Functioning Single-Parent Family

Many well-functioning single-parent families have escaped the social scientists' attention. The characteristics that may be associated with superior functioning among new single-parent families were noted earlier. Families headed by a single male or a financially self-sufficient female, families dismembered due to socially acceptable causes, families in which the single parent has had prior experience with both social-emotional and task leadership functions, and families headed by a socially skilled parent are likely to be less vulnerable at the outset to the stressful conditions endured by all single-parent families.

There are probably many single parents who at first are at a disadvantage, but who gain in competence through exposure to fortuitous learning conditions. Among them are parents who learn to establish priorities among personal and parenting goals, and to work efficiently toward dominant goals; who acquire realistic attitudes about family life and compare outcomes with other single-parent families; who evolve a satisfactory balance of adult sexual and affectional needs with children's interests; and who rely predominantly upon positive social control during preadolescent and adolescent socialization.

Well-functioning single-parent and two-parent families probably rear children with equal success, but in a different manner and with different results. The single-parent family may lack the barriers of emotional intimacy that characterize the two-parent family. A certain degree of emotional detachment of children from parents may be necessary in the two-parent family to preserve the cohesiveness of the parental dyad. In contrast, the single-parent family may work best at high levels of self-disclosure and emotional coalition between parent and children.

The single-parent family appears to function best when the parent is self-sufficient. In contrast, many two-parent families appear to succeed precisely because of a complementary blend of emotional, social, and intellectual strengths and deficits. The two-parent family may even gain in cohesiveness at the expense of self-sufficiency in the two parents.

The single-parent family provides the self-sufficient adult parent with abundant freedom of choice in regard to the major decisions of the adult years. In contrast, adult members of successful two-parent families must take one another's preferences into account when deciding where to live, where to work, and with whom to associate.

The search for evidence of heightened pathology among members of single-parent families has obscured the unique contributions that may be made by adults socialized in well functioning single-parent families. These adults may be more self-sufficient and more tolerant of statistically deviant life-styles than adults reared in comparable two-parent families. They may be better equipped to successfully maintain nonconventional relationships, provide norms and role models for many family forms, and contribute to the dissemination and acceptance of alternatives to perpetual or serial monogamy.

APPENDIX I

ARTICLES LISTED IN *Psychological Abstracts* CONCERNING
SINGLE-PARENT FAMILIES, TO 1974

1. Effects of Single-Parent Family Membership on Children

a. Effects on children's adjustment

ALTHUS, W. D.: The broken home and factors of adjustment. *Psychol. Reports*, 4, 477, 1958.

BARTLETT, C. J., and HARROCKS, J.: A study of the needs status of adolescents from broken homes. *J. Genet. Psychol.*, 93, 153-159, 1958.

BILLER, H. B.: The mother-child relationship and the father-absent boy's personality relationship. *Merrill-Palmer Quarterly*, 227-241, 1971.

BURCHINAL, L.: Characteristics of adolescents from unbroken, broken, and reconstituted families. *J. Marriage and Family*, 44-51, 1964 .

DORPAT, T. L., JACKSON, J., and RIPLEY, H.: Broken homes and attempted and completed suicide. *Arch. Gen. Psychiat.*, 12, 213-216, 1965.

HAWORTH, M. R.: Parental loss in children as reflected in projective responses. *J. Proj. Tech.*, 28, 31-45, 1964.

HETHERINGTON, E. M.: Effects of father absence on personality development in adolescent daughters. *Devel. Psychol.*, 7, 313-326, 1972.

KELLY, J. M.: Self-concept development in parent-deprived children: A comparative study. *Grad. Res. in Ed. and Related Disc.*, 6, 30-48, 1970.

KOCH, M. B.: Anxiety in preschool children from broken homes. *Merrill-Palmer Quarterly*, 7, 225-232, 1961.

LANDIS, J.: A comparison of children from divorced and nondivorced unhappy marriages. *Family Life Coord.*, 11, 61-64, 1962.

LANGNER, T. S., and STANLEY, J. M.: *Life Stress and Mental Health*. New York: The Free Press, 1963.

MADOW, L., and HARDY, S. E.: Incidence and analysis of the broken family in the background of neurosis. *Amer. J. Orthopsych.*, 17, 521-528, 1947.

McCORD, J. W., McCORD, W., and THURBER, E.: Some effects of parental absence on male children. *J. Abnorm. and Soc. Psychol.*, 64, 361-369, 1962.

MISCHEL, W.: Father absence and delay of gratification. *J. Abnorm. and Soc. Psychol.*, 63, 116-124, 1961.

NYE, F. L.: Child adjustment in broken and unhappy unbroken homes. *Marriage and Family Living*, 19, 356-361, 1957.

PEDERSON, F. A.: Relationship between father absence and emotional disturbance in male military dependents. *Merrill-Palmer Quarterly*, 321-331, 1966.

ROSENBERG, M.: The broken family and the adolescent self image. In: G. Heiss (Ed.), *Family Roles and Interaction: An Anthology*. Chicago: Rand McNally, 1958. Pp. 516-532.

SCHOOLER, C.: Childhood family structure and adult characteristics. *Sociometry*, 35, 255-269, 1972.

SEARS, P.: Doll play aggression in normal young children: Influence of age, sex, sibling status, father's absence. *Psychol. Monographs*, 65 (6, Whole No. 323), 1951.

STOLZ, L. M.: Father Relations of Warborn Children. Palo Alto: Stanford U. Press, 1954.

SUGAR, M.: Divorce and children. *South. Med. J.*, 63, 1458-1461, 1970.

TILLER, P. O.: Father absence and personality development in children in sailor families: A preliminary research report. In: V. Anderson (Ed.), *Studies of the Family*, Vol. 2, Gottingen: Vandenhoek and Ruprecht, 1957. Pp. 115-137.

WYLIE, H. E., and DEGADO, H. A.: A pattern of mother-son relationship involving the absence of the father. *Amer. J. Orthopsych.*, 29, 644-649, 1959.

b. Effects on children's achievement

CARLSMITH, L.: Effect of early father absence on scholastic aptitude. *Harvard Ed. Rev.* 34, 3-21, 1964.

KRIESBERG, L.: Rearing children for educational achievement in fatherless families. *J. Marriage and Family*, 29, 228-301, 1967.

SANTROCK, J. W.: Relation of type and onset of father absence to cognitive development. *Child Devel.*, 43, 455-469, 1972.

WASSERMAN, H. L.: A comparative study of school performance among boys from broken and intact black families. *J. Negro Ed.*, 41, 137-141, 1972.

c. Effects on adolescent courtship

ANDREWS, R. O., and CHRISTENSEN, H. T.: Relationship of absence of a parent to courtship status: A repeat study. *Amer. Sociol. Rev.*, 16, 541-544, 1951.

d. Effects on children's delinquency

ARMSTRONG, C. P.: *660 Runaway Boys*. Boston: Badger, 1932.

GLUECK, S., and GLUECK, E.: *Delinquents in the Making*. New York: Harper, 1952.

MORAN, P. A.: The effect of father absence on delinquent males: Dependency and hypermasculinity. *Dissertation Abstr. Intl.*, 33, 1292-1293, 1972.

SHAW, C. R., and McKAY, H. D.: Are broken homes a causative factor in juvenile delinquency? *Social Forces*, 10, 514-525, 1932.

STERNE, R. S.: *Delinquent Conduct and Broken Homes: A Study of 1050 Boys*. New Haven: College and University Press, 1964.

WEEKS, H. A., and SMITH, M. G.: Juvenile delinquency and broken homes in Spokane, Washington. *Social Forces*, 18, 48-59, 1939.

e. Effects on children's father identification

ANCONA, L., BIANCHI, M. C., and BOCQUET, C.: Identification with the father in the absence of the paternal model: Research applied to children of naval officers. *Archivio di Psicologia, Neurologia and Psichiatria,* 24, 341-361, 1964.

BURNS, R. A.: The effect of father's absence on the development of a masculine identification of boys in residential treatments. *Dissertation Abstr. Int.,* 32, 4179-4180, 1972.

LAWTON, M. J., and SECHREST, L.: Figure drawings by young boys from father-present and father-absent homes. *J. Clin. Psychol.,* 18, 304-305, 1962.

LEICHTY, M. M.: The effect of father absence during early childhood upon the Oedipal situation as reflected in young adults. *Merrill-Palmer Quarterly,* 6, 212-217, 1960.

LYNN, D. B., and SAWREY, W. L.: The effects of father absence on Norwegian boys and girls. *J. Abnorm. Soc. Psychol.,* 59, 258-262, 1959.

NEUBAUER, P. B.: The one-parent child and his Oedipal development. In: A. Freud et al. (Eds.), *The Psychoanalytic Study of the Child.* Vol. 15. New York: International Universities Press, 1960. Pp. 286-310.

f. Effects on children's sex roles

ALDOUS, J.: Children's perceptions of adult role assignment: Father absence, class, race, and sex influences. *J. Marriage and Family,* 55-65, 1972.

BACH, G. R.: Father fantasies and father-typing in father-separated children. *Child Devel.,* 17, 63-80, 1946.

BARCLAY, A., and CUSUMANO, D. R.: Father absence, cross-sex identity, and field dependent behavior in male adolescents. *Child Devel.,* 38, 243-250, 1967.

BILLER, H.: A note on father absence and masculine development in lower class Negro and white boys. *Child Devel.,* 39, 1003-1006, 1968.

BILLER, H. B.: Father absence, maternal encouragement and sex role development in kindergarten age boys. *Child Devel.,* 40, 539-546, 1969.

HETHERINGTON, E. M.: Effects of parental absence on sex typed behaviors in Negro and white preadolescent males. *J. Pers. and Soc. Psychol.,* 4, 87-91, 1966.

MASINGALE, E. M.: Father absence as related to parental role play behavior. *Dissertation Abstr. Intl.,* 32, 7294, 1972.

RIBNER, S.: A test of the masculine protest theory of anti-social behavior. *Dissertation Abstr. Intl.,* 33, 400, 1972.

2. Theory and Literature Reviews on the Single-Parent Family

HERZOG, E., and SUDIA, C. E.: Fatherless homes: A review of research. *Children,* 15, 177-182, 1968.

HERZOG, E., and SUDIA, C. E.: *Boys in Fatherless Homes.* Washington, D. C.: U.S. Department of Health, Education and Welfare. Office of Child Development, DHEW Publication No. (OCD) 72-22, 1971.

KADUSHIN, A.: Single-parent adoptions: An overview and some relevant research. *Soc. Serv. Rev.,* 44, 263-274, 1970.

ROSENFELD, J., and ROSENSTEIN, E.: Towards a conceptual framework for the study of parent-absent families. *J. Marriage and Family,* 131-134, 1973.

SCHLESINGER, B.: *The One-Parent Family: Perspectives and Annotated Bibliography.* Toronto: U. of Toronto Press, 1969.

SELDEN, R. H.: Salutary effects of maternal separation. *Social Work,* 25-29, 1965.

SPREY, J.: The study of single parenthood: Some methodological considerations. *Family Life Coord.*, 16, 29-34, 1967.

THOMES, M. M.: Children with absent fathers. *J. Marriage and Family*, 30, 89-96, 1968.

3. Effects of Single-Parent Family Membership on Parents

BECKMAN, P. L.: Spouseless motherhood, psychological stress, and physical morbidity. *J. Health and Soc. Behav.*, 10, 323-334, 1969.

FREUDENTHAL, K.: Problems of the one-parent family. *Social Work*, 4, 44-48, 1959.

GAVAI, J. E.: Sex and the single parent. *Sexology*, 34, 148-150, 1967.

GEBHARD, P.: Postmarital coitus among widows and divorcées. In: P. Bohannon (Ed.), *Divorce and After*. New York: Anchor, 1971. Pp. 89-106.

HARRIS, E. T.: Parents Without Partners, Inc.: A resource for clients. *Social Work*, 92-98, 1966.

ILGENFRITZ, M.: Mothers on their own—widows and divorceés. *Marriage and Family Living*, 23, 38-41, 1961.

4. Studies on Small-Group Behavior

BEDELL, J. W.: Role reorganization in the one-parent family: Mother absent due to death. *Sociol. Focus*, 5, 84-100, 1971-72.

BURGESS, J. K.: The single-parent family: A social and sociological problem. *Family Coord.*, 19, 137-144, 1970.

GLASSER, P., and NAVARRE, E.: Structural problems of the one-parent family. *J. Soc. Issues*, 21, 98-109, 1965.

KOLIKOVA, A.: Emotional relationships of children toward their parents with a special view to family structure. *Psychologia a Patopsychologia Dietata*, 7, 13-28, 1972.

SCANZONI, J.: A social systems analysis of dissolved and existing marriages. *J. Marriage and Family*, 30, 452-461, 1968.

SCHLESINGER, B.: The widowed as a one-parent family unit. *Social Science*, 46, 26-32, 1971.

5. Demographic Characteristics of Single-Parent Families

BELL, R.: Lower class Negro mothers and their children. *Integrated Ed.*, Dec.-Jan., 2, 23-27, 1964-65.

BELL, R.: Lower class Negro mothers' aspirations for their children. *Social Forces*, 43, 493-500, 1965.

BESNER, A.: Economic deprivation and family patterns. *Welfare in Review*, 3, 20-28, 1965.

GLASSER, P., and NAVARRE, E.: The problems of families in the AFDC program. *Children*, 12, 151-156, 1965.

6. Treatment of Single-Parent Families

STREAM, H. S.: Treatment of mothers and sons in the absence of the father. *Social Work*, 6, 29-35, 1961.

STRINGER, E. A.: Homemaker service to the single-parent family. *Social Case Work*, 48, 75-79, 1967.

WOODRUFF, R. A., GRIZE, S. B., and CLAYTON, P. J., Divorce among psychiatric outpatients. *Brit. J. Psychiat.*, 121:562, 289-292, 1972.

REFERENCES

ALDOUS, J.: Children's perceptions of adult role assignment: Father absence, class, race, and sex influences. *J. Marriage and Family*, 9, 55-65, 1972.

ARMSTRONG, C. P.: *660 Runaway Boys*. Boston: Badger, 1932.

BALES, R. F.: The equilibrium problem in small groups. In: T. Parsons, R. F. Bales, and E. A. Shils, *Working Papers in the Theory of Action*. New York: Free Press, 1953.

BALES, R. F., and BORGATTA, E. F.: Size of group as a factor in the interaction profile. In: A. P. Hare, E. F. Borgatta, and R. F. Bales (Eds.), *Small Group Studies in Social Interaction*. New York: Knopf, 1955.

BALES, R. F., and SLATER, P. E.: Role differentiation in small decision-making groups. In: T. Parsons, R. F. Bales, et al., *The Family Socialization and Interaction Process*. New York: Free Press, 1955.

BALES, R. F., and SLATER, P. E.: Notes on "Role differentiation in small decision making groups": Reply to Dr. Wheeler. *Sociometry*, 20, 152-155, 1957.

BECK, D. F., and JONES, M. A.: Progress on family problems: A nationwide study of clients' and counselors' views on family agency services. *Family Service Association Census Report*, 1970.

BENNE, K. D., and SHEATS, P.: Functional roles of group members. *J. Soc. Issues*, 4, 41-49, 1948.

BENSON, A. L.: Alarming changes in American homes. *Pearson's Mag.*, 22, 711-718, 1909.

BERNARD, J.: *Remarriage*. New York: Dryden, 1956.

BIJOU, S. W., and BAER, D. M.: Operant methods in child behavior and development. In: W. K. Honig (Ed.), *Operant Behavior: Areas of Research and Application*. New York: Appleton, 1966. Pp. 718-789.

BILLER, H. B.: A note on father absence and masculine development in lower class Negro and white boys. *Child Devel.*, 39, 1003-1006, 1968.

BILLER, H. B.: Father absence, maternal encouragement and sex role development in kindergarten age boys. *Child Devel.*, 40, 539-546, 1969.

BILLER, H. B.: The mother-child relationship and the father-absent boy's personality development. *Merrill-Palmer Quarterly*, 1971, 227-241.

BILLER, H. B., and MEREDITH, D. L.: The invisible American father. *Sexual Behav.*, 2, 16-22, 1972.

BILLINGSLEY, A., and GIOVANNONI, J. M.: One-Parent family. *Encyclopedia of Social Work*. Vol. 1, 16th issue. New York: National Association of Social Workers, 1971.

BLOOD, R. O., and HAMBLIN, R. L.: The effect of wife's employment on the family power structure. *Social Forces*, 36, 347-352, 1958.

BOHANNON, P.: The six stations of divorce. In: P. Bohannon (Ed.), *Divorce and After*. New York: Anchor, 1971. Pp. 33-62.

BOTT, E.: Urban families: Conjugal roles and social networks. *Human Relations*, 8, 345-384, 1955.

BOTT, E.: Urban families: The norms of conjugal roles. *Human Relations*, 9, 325-341, 1956.

BOVARD, E. W., JR.: The experimental production of interpersonal affect. *J. Abnorm. and Soc. Psychol.*, 46, 521-528, 1951.

COYLE, G. L.: *Social Process in Organized Groups*. New York: R. R. Smith, 1930.

DAWE, H. C.: The influence of the size of the kindergarten group upon performance. *Child Devel.*, 5, 295-303, 1934.

DECHARMS, R.: *Personal Causation: The Internal Affective Determinants of Behavior*. New York: Academic Press, 1968.

DECTER, M.: *The New Chastity and Other Arguments Against Women's Liberation*. New York: Coward-McCann & Geoghegan, 1972.

EDWARDS, J. N.: *Familial behavior as social exchange. J. Marriage and Family,* 518, 526, 1969.

FERGUSON, E.: The social revolution in sexual behavior and standards. In: *Illegitimacy.* New York: National Council on Illigitimacy, 1965.

FIEDLER, F. E.: *Leader Attitudes and Group Effectiveness.* Urbana, Ill.: U. of Illinois Press, 1958.

FREUD, S.: A critique of Mill on women. In L. Marcus and S. Marcus (Eds.), Ernest Jones, *The Life and Work of Sigmund Freud.* New York: Basic Books, 1961. Pp. 117-118.

FREUDENTHAL, K.: Problems of the one-parent family. *Social Work,* 4, 44-48, 1959.

FUENTES, S. P.: Job discrimination and the Black woman. In *The Crisis,* 103-108, 1970.

GAMSON, W. A.: A theory of coalition formation. *Amer. Sociol. Rev.,* 26, 374, 1961.

GARDNER, R. N.: *The Boys' and Girls' Book About Divorce.* New York: Bantam, 1970.

GAVAI, J. E.: Sex and the single parent. *Sexology,* 34, 148-150, 1967.

GEBHARD, P.: Postmarital coitus among widows and divorcées. In: P. Bohannon (Ed.), *Divorce and After.* New York: Anchor, 1971. Pp. 89-106.

GIBBS, J. R.: The effects of group size and of threat reduction upon creativity in a problem solving group. *Amer. Psychol.,* 6, 324, 1951.

GOFFMAN, E.: *Stigma: Notes on Management of Spoiled Identity.* Englewood Cliffs, N. J.: Prentice-Hall, 1961.

GOLDMAN, M.: A comparison of group and individual performance when subjects have varying tendencies to solve problems. *J. Pers. and Soc. Psychol.,* 3, 604-607, 1966.

GOODE, W. J.: A theory of role strain. *Amer. Sociol. Review,* 25, 483-496, 1960.

GRAVES, R.: *Mannon and the Black Goddess.* New York: Doubleday, 1965.

GROSS, M., McEACHERN, A. W., and MASON, W. S.: Role conflict and its resolution. In: E. E. Maccoby, T. M. Newcomb, and E. L. Hartley (Eds.), *Readings in Social Psychology.* New York: Holt, 1958.

GUGGENHEIMER, E.: Child care and family services. In: *Women's Role in Contemporary Society: The Report of the New York City Commission on Human Rights,* September 21-25, 1970. Pp. 459-468.

HALL, R. L.: Social influences on the aircraft commander's role. *Amer. Sociol. Rev.,* 20, 292-299, 1955.

HARRIS, E. T.: Parents Without Partners, Inc.: A resource for clients. *Social Work,* 92-93, 1966.

HEINICKE, C., and BALES, R. F.: Developmental trends in the structure of small groups. *Sociometry,* 16, 7-38, 1953.

HEISS, J. S.: Degrees of intimacy and male-female interactions. *Sociometry,* 25, 197-208, 1962.

HERZOG, E., and SUDIA, C.: Fatherless homes: A review of research, *Children,* 15, 177-182, 1968.

HERZOG, E., and SUDIA, C. *Boys in Fatherless Homes.* Washington, D. C.: U.S. Department of Health, Education and Welfare. Office of Child Development, DHEW Publication No. (OCD) 72-133, 1971.

ILGENFRITZ, M.: Mothers on their own—widows and divorcées. *Marriage and Family Living,* 23, 38-41, 1961.

JAMES, J.: Verbal behavior in problem-solving small groups without formally designated leaders. *Research Studies, State College,* Washington, 24, 125-133, 1956.

JENSEN, G., and WALLACE, J.: Family mourning process. *Family Process,* October, 6, 56-66, 1956.

KADUSHIN, A.: Single parent adoptions: An overview and some relevant research. *Soc. Serv. Rev.*, 44, 263-274, 1970.

KANTOR, J. R.: *Interbehavioral Psychology*. Indiana: Principia, 1959.

KELMAN, H. C.: Effects of success and failure on "suggestibility" in the autokinetic situation. *J. Abnorm. and Soc. Psychol.*, 45, 267-285, 1950.

KENKEL, W. F.: Influence differentiation in family decision making. *Sociol. and Soc. Res.*, 42, 18-25, 1957.

KLEIN, D. C., and LINDEMANN, E.: Preventive intervention in individual family crisis situation. In: G. Kaplan (Ed.), *Prevention of Mental Disorders in Children: Initial Explorations*. New York: Basic Books, 1961.

KOSKOFF, Y. D., and WENIGER, F. L.: An adverse effect on the family resulting from radical change of personality in one member after prefrontal lobotomy. *Proceedings of the Association for Research in Nervous and Mental Diseases*, 29, 148-154, 1949.

LANDSBERGER, H. A.: Interaction process analysis of professional behavior: A study of labor mediators in twelve labor management disputes. *Amer. Sociol. Rev.*, 20, 566-575, 1955.

LASH, T.: Child care and family services. In: *Women's Role in Contemporary Society: The Report of the New York City Commission on Human Rights*. September 21-25, 1970. New York: Avon, 1972. Pp. 453-458.

LEICHTER, H. J., and MITCHELL, W. E.: *Kinship and Casework*. New York: Russell Sage Foundation, 1967. Pp. 22-24.

MAYER, J. E.: People's imagery of other families. *Family Process*, 6, 27-36, 1967.

McCANDLESS, B. R.: Changing relationships between dominance and social acceptability during group democratization. *Amer. J. Orthopsych.*, 12, 529-535, 1942.

MEAD, M.: Anomalies in American postdivorce relationships. In: P. Bohannon (Ed.), *Divorce and After*. New York: Anchor, 1971. Pp. 107-126.

MILLER, A. A.: Reactions of friends to divorce. In P. Bohannon (Ed.), *Divorce and After*. New York: Anchor, 1971. Pp. 63-86.

MILLETT, K.: The image of women in arts and letters. In: *Women's Role in Contemporary Society: The Report of the New York City Commission on Human Rights*. September 21-25, 1970. New York: Avon, 1972. Pp. 608-612.

MILLS, T. M.: Power relations in three-person groups. *Amer. Sociol. Rev.*, 18, 351-357, 1953.

MORGENSTERN, J.: A new face of adoption. *Newsweek*, September 13, 1971.

O'ROURKE, J. F.: Field and laboratory: The decision-making behavior of family groups in two experimental conditions. *Sociometry*, 26, 422-435, 1963.

PARKER, S.: Leadership patterns in a psychiatric ward. *Human Relations*, 11, 287-301, 1958.

PARKER, S., and KLEINER, R.: Characteristics of Negro mothers in single-headed households. *J. Marriage and Family*, 507-513, 1966.

PARSONS, T., and BALES, R. F., in collaboration with ZELDITCH, M. J., OLDS, J., and SLATER, P.: *Family Socialization and Interaction Process*. New York: Free Press, 1955.

PARSONS, T., and FOX, R. C.: Illness, therapy and the modern American family. *J. Soc. Issues*, 13, 31-44, 1952.

PATTERSON, G. R., and COBB, J. A.: A dyadic analysis of "aggressive" behaviors. In: J. P. Hill (Ed.), *Minnesota Symposium on Child Psychology*, Vol. 5. Minneapolis: U. of Minnesota Press, 1971.

RICH, A.: The Anti-Feminist Women. *New York Rev. of Books*, 19, 34-40, 1972.

ROSENFELD, J., and ROSENSTEIN, E.: Towards a conceptual framework for the study of parent-absent families. *J. Marriage and Family*, 131-134, 1973.

SAUBER, M., and CORRIGAN, E.: *The Six-Year Experience of Unwed Mothers as Parents.* New York: Community Council of Greater New York, 1970.

SCHLESINGER, B.: *The One-Parent Family: Perspectives and Annotated Bibliography.* Toronto: U. of Toronto Press, 1969.

SELDEN, R. H.: Salutary effects of maternal separation. *Social Work,* October, 25-29, 1965.

SHAW, C. R., and McKAY, H. D.: Are broken homes a causative factor in juvenile delinquency? *Social Forces,* 10, 514-525, 1932.

SHEPHERD, C., and WESCHLER, I. R.: The relation between three interpersonal variables and communication effectiveness: A pilot study. *Sociometry,* 18, 103-110, 1955.

SIMMEL, G.: The number of members as determining the sociological form of the group. *Amer. J. Sociol.,* 8, 1-46, 1902-03.

SIMMEL, G.: [Conflict.] (R. H. Wolff, trans.). In: R. Bendix (Ed. and trans.), *The Web of Group Affiliations.* New York: Free Press, 1955.

SLATER, P. E.: Role differentiation in small groups. *Amer. Sociol. Rev.,* 20, 300-310, 1955.

SOUTH, E. B.: Some psychological aspects of committee work. *J. Appl. Psychol.,* 11, 348-368, 1927.

SPREY, J.: The study of single parenthood: Some methodological considerations. *Family Life Coord.,* Jan.-April, 29-34, 1967.

STAINES, G., TAURIS, C., and JAYARATNE, T. E.: The queen bee syndrome. *Psychol. Today,* 7, 55-60, Jan. 1974.

STEPHAN, F. F., and MISHLER, E. G.: The distribution of participation in small groups: An exponential approximation. *Amer. Sociol. Rev.,* 17, 598-608, 1952.

STREAM, H. S.: Treatment of mothers and sons in the absence of the father. *Social Work,* 6, 29-35, July, 1961.

STRINGER, E. A.: Homemaker service to the single-parent family. *Social Casework,* 48, 75-79, February, 1967.

STRODTBECK, F. L.: Husband-wife interaction over revealed differences. *Amer. Sociol. Rev.,* 16, 468-473, 1951.

STRODTBECK, F. L., and HOOK, L. H.: *The social dimensions of a 12-Man Jury Table.* Unpublished manuscript, U. of Chicago Law School, 1956.

STRODTBECK, F. L., and HOOK, L. H.: A case for the study of small groups. *Amer. Sociol. Rev.,* 19, 651-657, 1954.

SUSSMAN, M. B. (Ed.): *Non-Traditional Family Forms in the 1970's.* Minneapolis: National Council on Family Relations, 1972.

TALLAND, G. A.: Role and status structure in therapy groups. *J. Clinical Psychol.,* 13, 27-33, 1957.

TAYLOR, D. W., and FAUST, W. L.: Twenty questions: Efficiency in problem solving as a function of size of group. *J. Exper. Psychol.,* 44, 360-368, 1952.

THEODORSON, G. A.: The relationship between leadership and popularity role in small groups. *Amer. Sociol. Rev.,* 22, 58-67, 1957.

THIBAUT, J. W., and KELLEY, H. H.: *The Social Psychology of Groups.* New York: Wiley, 1959.

THOMES, M. M.: Children with absent fathers. *J. Marriage and Family,* 30, 89-96, 1968.

TIGER, L.: *Men in Groups.* New York: Random House, 1969.

TURNER, R. H.: *Family Interaction.* New York: Wiley, 1970.

U.S. Bureau of the Census: *Current Population Reports,* Series P-20. Washington, D. C.: 1973.

U.S. Government Printing Office: *Report of the President's Commission on the Status of Women: American Women.* Washington, D. C.: 1963a.

U.S. Government Printing Office: *Report of the President's Commission on the Status of Women: Home and Community.* Washington, D. C.: 1963b.

VILAR, E.: *The Manipulated Man.* New York: Farrar Straus, 1972.

VOGEL, E. F., and BELL, N. W.: The emotionally disturbed child as the family scapegoat. In: N. W. Bell and E. F. Vogel (Eds.), *A Modern Introduction to the Family.* New York: Free Press, 1961.

WALLER, W.: *The Old Love and the New.* New York: Liveright, 1930.

WEEKS, H. A., and SMITH, M. G.: Juvenile delinquency and broken homes in Spokane, Washington. *Social Forces,* 18, 48-59, 1939.

WHEELER, D. K.: Notes on "Role differentiation in small decision groups." *Sociometry,* 20, 145-151, 1957.

WISPE, L. G.: A sociometric analysis of conflicting role-expectations. *Amer. J. Sociol.,* 61, 134-137, 1955.

WOLFF, K. H.: *The Sociology of George Simmel.* New York: Free Press, 1950.

4

The Positive Community: A Strategy for Applying Behavioral Engineering to the Redesign of Family and Community

L. KEITH MILLER, ALICE LIES, DAN L. PETERSEN,
and RICHARD FEALLOCK

B. F. Skinner foresaw in 1948 the possibility of using behavioral engineering to develop a more functional family and community structure (Skinner, 1948). His vision included the use of a token economy to organize the basic work of the community. It specifically included "housewifery" in the definition of this basic work as a step toward equalizing the sexes. It was designed to foster positive interactions between marital partners by eliminating the aversive control over the marital institution. It specified techniques for creating a more positive basis for parent-child interactions. These and many other proposed social innovations were labeled "The Good Life" by Skinner.

One does not have to agree with each of Swinner's proposals to be intrigued by the use of behavioral technology to design a more functional and reinforcing society. At the time that Skinner described his vision of The Good Life in *Walden Two,* the technology necessary for behavioral engineering did not exist. However, since then, a behavioral technology has developed with great rapidity. While this technology has been directed primarily at modifying abnormal behavior, it is clear that it is equally applicable to normal behavior. It may now be appropriate, as has been argued elsewhere (Miller and Lies, 1974), to begin using this well-established and successful technology to design and evaluate

91

more functional family and community structures.

Such a course of action is, of course, fraught with problems. Foremost among them is that society has not invited us to employ our skills in such a manner. In particular, no level of government is very likely to welcome, let alone invite, behavioral engineers to redesign their most sacred institutions. In the same vein, few people are likely to welcome the intrusions of well-meaning behavioral engineers into their families to redesign them; nor are they likely to sell their houses and invest in a risky Utopian venture in group living. Thus the application of behavioral technologies to the redesign of family and community structure is faced with what appear to be insurmountable difficulties in just getting started.

However, in spite of the poor outlook for such a use of behavioral technology, there is a strategy for getting started. That strategy might be likened to "shaping." Instead of starting by attempting the total ultimate redesign of the family and community, it may be possible to identify technologies that must be developed prior to that final step. In fact, it may be possible to identify a series of approximations that come closer and closer to the goal of a behaviorally engineered multi-family community.

The University of Kansas Experimental Living Project is one such initial approximation. The Experimental Living Project has been designed for unmarried university students. This has minimized the problem of having to persuade individuals living within established family patterns—individuals already presumably settled into relatively reinforcing routines—to undertake the risk of joining a project of uncertain outcome. While designing an effective group living arrangement for a student group is the starting point, it is only one of a series of proposed successive approximations to an experimental community involving a cross-section of the population.

THE UNIVERSITY OF KANSAS EXPERIMENTAL LIVING PROJECT

Thirty University of Kansas students live in the Experimental Living Project. About one-fifth are graduate students and the rest are undergraduates. They range in age from 18 to 28 years old, with about equal numbers of male and female members at any given time. The members' fields of study include business, psychology, behavior modification, social work, chemistry, and fine arts. Most of the members come from Kansas and Missouri, a few come from as far away as New York and California, and several come from other countries. Overall, the members seem to represent a random cross-section of the university population.

The Experimental Living Project is housed in a large three-story frame house. There are 29 private sleeping-study rooms, a lounge, an institutional kitchen, a snack kitchen, a dining-meeting room, a game room, storage rooms, and a shop. Each student has his or her own private room with a desk and bed in it. No contingencies apply to residents' private rooms while they live in them. Hence, students have their private areas as well as access to group areas. Students who do their share of the work pay an average rent of $43 per month.

The purpose of The Experimental Living Project has been to behaviorally engineer a positive, viable group living situation for single university students. The strategy of the Project has been to systematically accomplish three goals that lead up to this final stage. These three goals are based on an informal analysis of past group living situations. These goals were formulated to solve problems that had caused other groups to break up and to provide the Project with the positive advantage of group living.

The first goal has been to design an egalitarian, efficient worksharing system. This goal was formulated to solve two types of problems. First, an examination of why "communes" break up suggests that simply getting routine housework done is a major problem that frequently leads to interpersonal hassles sufficient to break up the group. Second, groups that do succeed in staying together frequently end up with one or more strong leaders or "managers" who see to it that the ordinary housework gets done. Yet avoidance of such an unequal sharing of authority is one of the major reasons that is given for the formation of experimental living groups. An egalitarian, efficient worksharing system would ensure that everyone does his or her fair share of the ordinary housework without any one member of the group having an unequal share of power.

The second goal has been to develop a "behavioral culture." Most individuals attracted to experimental groups seem interested in fully participating in running that group within a total democratic framework. On the other hand, Skinner foresaw a non-democratic system of "managers" to run such a system. Along with this, few behavioral programs have been open to complete democratic control by individuals living within them. Furthermore, one might guess that permitting individuals to vote on their own contingencies would lead to the gradual dilution of the contingency system. In a "behavioral culture," the relevant principles of behavior can be brought to bear on decisions involving the modification of the contingency system so that the system is retained and made more behavioral rather than eliminated and made less behavioral.

The third goal has been to develop a "positive verbal community." The ultimate goal of most individuals interested in experimental living is "togetherness." Such a state of affairs is rarely sustained after the initial euphoria usually involved in starting a new living group. Simply eliminating the hassles involved in worksharing and supervision will probably not automatically generate positive interpersonal interactions. Hence, the Project has set out to develop a systematic method for fostering a "positive verbal community."

At the time of this writing all three goals have not been totally accomplished. The following three parts of this paper describe the progress of the Project with respect to each of these three goals. *Part One: The Worksharing System* outlines the successful engineering of a worksharing system with an almost completed egalitarian coordinating system which manages the work. *Part Two: Behavioral Culture* gives the details of a rapidly developing behavioral culture in the Project. *Part Three: Positive Verbal Community* discusses the initial stages of the development of a systematic method for fostering positive interpersonal interactions. Finally, the last portion of the paper will discuss the prospects and problems involved in extending the Project further toward the creation of a viable experimental community.

PART ONE: THE WORKSHARING SYSTEM

The first goal of The Experimental Living Project was to design an egalitarian, efficient worksharing system. The initial efforts of the Project have been to accomplish this goal. Following is a detailed outline of: the components of the worksharing system; a set of worksharing programs in the worksharing system which manages the work through a coordinating system; and an overall evaluation of the worksharing system.

Components of the Worksharing System

There are three components to the Experimental Living Project's worksharing system: (1) behavioral specification of all the common chores in the project; (2) a mechanism for determining whether or not these chores have been done; and (3) a system for providing positive

TABLE 1

Lounge Inspection Checklist

LOUNGE

1. Pick up trash
2. Sweep up dirt
3. Vacuum or shake out rug
4. Empty and clean out ash trays
5. Empty trashbasket
6. Mop floor
7. Return items to proper place

consequences for people doing their share of the work. This system was behaviorally designed to prevent some people from not doing their share of the work and some from doing more than their share.

1. *Behavioral Specification.* The first component of the worksharing system is the behavioral specification of the common jobs in terms of an "inspection checklist"—a list of tasks which are essential to the completion of that job. Table 1 provides an example of an inspection checklist for cleaning the lounge. Each task has a definition that specifies what the outcome of that task must look like in order for it to be considered completed. Hence, when members sign up for a job they know exactly what that job entails.

2. *Accountability.* The second component of the worksharing system is "accountability." One positive result of the behavioral specification of jobs is that it makes possible a mechanism for determining whether or not these jobs have been done properly. Each night an inspector checks the routine jobs for that day according to standard inspection checklists and task definitions. Hence, members can be held accountable for the work they sign up for, and the Project is insured some quality control on how the common work gets done.

3. *Positive Consequences.* The third component of the worksharing system is a system providing positive consequences for the members who do their share of the work. Members are awarded "credits" for each job they do. When they move into the house, they agree to earn 100 credits per week in return for a rent reduction. Members can earn up to $40 rent reduction per month by doing their share of the work. This rent reduction is made possible because the Project is able to avoid hiring cooks, janitors, and handymen. The resulting saving permits the rent reduction. The remaining $43 per month in rent is used to cover unavoidable expenses such as mortgage, utilities, and the like. The fact that

members typically earn 98% of their possible rent reduction suggests the effectiveness of this contingency.

These three components together form the basis of the worksharing system. There are about 100 jobs that must be done each week. A list of these jobs and when they are to be done is posted once a week. Members then sign up for any combination of jobs they choose to do the next week. This sign-up system allows the members complete flexibility in choosing their jobs. They can sign up for only cleaning jobs. They can choose their jobs according to the time they have available the next week. Hence, members can freely choose their work.

Each house member signs up for a set of weekly jobs. Each weekly job has been timed and allotted 15 credits for each hour it takes to do that job. This credit allotment is adjusted according to the desirability of the particular job. Almost everyone likes to cook—so it gets 15 credits per hour. Not quite as many people like dishwashing—so it gets 25 credits per hour. Few people like to clean a greasy stove—so it gets 30 credits per hour. Adjustments upward or downward can be made by majority vote of the Project based on the difficulty or the ease of the job. Any adjustment to increase the credits for one job must be balanced by corresponding decrease in credits for another job in order to insure that all jobs in the Project get done. Since each member earns an average of 100 credits per week, the Project has a stable credit economy of about 3000 credits or about 200 man-hours worth of work a week.

The credit system is flexible. Earnings of over 100 credits a week can be saved for another week or given to a friend. Earnings of less than 100 credits a week can be made up by borrowing from past savings or from a friend. Otherwise, a small part of the rent reduction is lost. Past records of average credit weeks show that approximately 51% of the members earn all their 100 credits in one week; 37% have some credits saved; 7% have credits transferred to them; and 5% lose a small part of their rent reduction. Hence, the members need not do all their work each week; they can save up so that they can take off some time, or they can borrow from a friend during hard times.

There is one other important contingency in the worksharing system. Members who sign up for a job and fail to complete at least 50% of that job lose $2 of their rent reduction. This contingency insures that members with savings will not miss a job they signed up for simply because they don't need the credits. This contingency has virtually eliminated the problem of missed jobs.

Worksharing Programs

The work of the Experimental Living Project is administered within eight separate programs. These programs are: (1) cleaning; (2) food; (3) repair; (4) inspection; (5) financial; (6) rental; (7) educational; and (8) supervisory. All the work in these programs is part of the worksharing system.

Some jobs in each program referred to as "contract jobs" require special skills. These are the coordinating and supervisory jobs. However, each of these jobs is carefully specified so that members can be trained to do the job, and then be inspected, held accountable, and rewarded for doing their work just like any other job in the worksharing system. For each skilled job, there is a written manual and a three-month contract. Even the training procedures for these jobs are specified. Hence, no one person can corner the "expertise market" for any job.

Since these jobs involve training, the members sign contracts agreeing to do the job for three months. Hence the jobs are called "contract jobs" to distinguish them from weekly sign-up jobs. For example, a treasurer must know how to keep financial records, know how to handle house monies, and be responsible for the Project staying within its budget. These are not skills that most people have without training. Therefore, the treasurer is trained to follow standard financial procedures through a carefully programmed training manual. He or she is inspected according to that manual and held accountable for following it. The treasurer can be readily replaced and has no special power within the Project. Hence, there is no elite group of "managers" in The Experimental Living Project. The coordinators and supervisors are only a group of peers doing jobs for which they hold one another accountable.

Following is a description of each of the worksharing programs, the work done in each program, and the most important standard procedures of each program. All jobs, skilled or unskilled, are part of the worksharing system.

The Cleaning Program. The purpose of the cleaning program is to keep the public areas reasonably clean and neat so that members can live comfortably in the Project. All cleaning of bathrooms, mopping of halls, and picking up of common areas is done by Project members on a routine basis. One member in the Project holds the contract job of cleaning coordinator. This person is responsible for keeping a running inventory of the cleaning supplies and for putting these supplies in the various cleaning areas.

2. *The Food Program.* The purpose of the food program is to provide the members of the Project with one main meal a day at 6 p.m. The monthly food bill is $19 per month for approximately 27 meals. This averages about 75¢ per meal. The food program began in its present form when a semester menu for the house was put together. Each meal on this menu has a main dish, a vegetable, rice or potatoes, and a fruit or a dessert. Each week there are three or four hamburger main dishes, one chicken dish, one more expensive meat dish, and one or two meatless or fish meals. Hence, the semester menu provides the members with a variety of good food at a cheap price. In addition, the recipes are set up in such a way that most members can follow them. No cooking term is used without being defined, and what to do in emergencies is outlined. The food program has so simplified the job of cooking for 30 that even members with no prior cooking experience now cook. Also, men do about 50% of the cooking, shopping, and cleanup. Hence, sexual stereotyping has been virtually eliminated from this program.

Here is an explanation of how the food system works. Food is bought both wholesale and retail. In the cookbook there are already prepared wholesale shopping lists for each month as well as shopping lists for each week. The person who holds the contract job of food coordinator does the wholesale buying. Retail shopping is a sign-up job. Each week, the retail shopper first checks what is in the food storage pantry and then buys any additional items needed for the following week in a local grocery store. The food is cooked according to the recipes by two afternoon cooks who work from 4 to 6 p.m. After the meal, the kitchen and dining room are cleaned and the dishes are washed. Altogether the food program uses 630 credits or 42 man hours to feed 30 people each week, and 570 credits or 38 man hours to clean up after them. Past records show that these food jobs are done on the average about 95%.

3. *The Repair Program.* The repair program is now being developed. The purpose of this program is to have as many repairs done by members as possible. Members are taught some necessary repair skills. There are already some standard procedures for the repair program. One involves a set of detailed inspection sheets to locate repairs and needed maintenance in the Project. Another, which is partially developed, is a set of detailed job descriptions for the most commonly recurring jobs. These job descriptions are tested until the average house member can use them to make a satisfactory repair. In addition, a special program is being prepared that teaches a Repair Coordinator how to write and

test new job descriptions. The development of these procedures permits the Project to move gradually from reliance on an experienced handyman to the routine utilization of any member who wishes to sign up for a particular job. This has permitted increased participation by individuals not possessing extensive handyman skills, particularly women, thus reducing sexual stereotyping in the Program.

The Inspection System. As has been said before, the second component of the worksharing system is a mechanism for checking whether or not the jobs are completed in the Project. The basis of the mechanism is a group of members who hold the contract job of inspector. Each night at 8:00 an inspector goes around the Project, checks the routine common work according to the task definitions for each job, and passes or fails the job in the inspection checklist. There are two benefits of having regular daily inspections: first, the ratings provide the Project with consistent feedback on how the routine work of the Project is being completed; second, they are essential for keeping the worksharing system fair since they provide the membership with information for evaluating the work completed by each member of the Project.

So far, members have been trained to inspect through a verbal training procedure as the trainee accompanies a trained inspector on an inspection tour. The trained inspector explains how to inspect each task according to the task definitions. The trainee then does an independent inspection at the same time that the trained inspector is inspecting. Their inspection ratings are compared. The two inspection ratings must have a 90% total agreement. At this time, an inspection training manual is being developed and tested. After it is completed, this whole inspection training will be in written form. Such a manual will save training time and, hopefully, further standardize the inspection system. Once an inspector attains a 90% reliability, he or she signs a contract. After this, each inspector is checked once a week by a reliability inspector who is another trained inspector. Reliability with the inspector averaged 95%, with a range of 83% to 100% for 37 determinations during the first 60 weeks of the program.

5. *The Financial System.* The goal of the financial system is to have all Project monies handled by members of the Project in such a way that the house maintains a sound financial basis. The basis of the financial system is a Treasurer's Manual. This manual outlines the Project's budgeting system. It is set up so that any member with average arithmetical skills can keep financial books for the Project. The member who holds the contract job of treasurer is in charge of all incoming and

TABLE 2

1973-1974 Budget

Category	Monthly Allocation
Utilities	300
Small repairs	70
Major repairs	120
Cleaning supplies	50
Equipment	25
Pest control	15
Education	15
Insurance and taxes	120
Loan payment	250
Miscellaneous	25
Reserves	50
House improvements	250*
Food	570*
TOTALS	1860

* Based on an occupancy of 30.

outgoing monies. He is in charge of a budget of about $1800 a month. He allocates this money to various categories according to an established budget. Table 2 shows the allocation categories. As can be seen from this Table, this budget sets aside money for future expenses. For example $120 is set aside each month to pay insurance and taxes which is a once-a-year expense.

As a check on the treasurer there is a comptroller. The comptroller keeps all the permanent financial records for the Project. The comptroller keeps a parallel set of financial books for the Project. These books are compared with the treasurer's books once a month to ensure that no mistakes have been made in the accounting system. In addition, an auditor checks both sets of books once a month. This ensures that Project monies are not misused. It also protects the treasurer by ensuring that no one can accuse him of misusing Project monies. The job of the auditor will be explained in further detail under the Supervisory Program.

6. *The Rental Program.* The purpose of the rental program is to acquaint prospective members with the Project, to help incorporate new members into the worksharing system, and to collect rent from present members. Most of this work is done by a member who holds the contract job of Renter. The renter takes prospective members around the Project

and explains the worksharing system to them. Essentially this is a self-screening process. When prospective members decide to become members, they sign a contract specifying a rent payment schedule and agreeing to live by the rules of the Group Living Handbook. The Handbook will be described in detail later; briefly, it is an initial contract which one agrees to live by as a member of the Project. For instance, one agrees to earn 100 credits a week in return for a rent reduction. After agreeing to live by the Handbook, the new member makes an initial deposit that averages $127. This initial payment covers a $25 damage deposit; a $40 work deposit; a $43 rental payment, and a $19 food payment.

The $40 work deposit is a work bond for rent reduction. In other words, when members move into the Project they make this initial payment of $40. If they do all their work, they receive a rent reduction of $40. If they fail to do part of their work, they lose a proportional amount of rent reduction. Hence, if they have a $2 fine for missing a job, they receive only $38 rent reduction. This work deposit protects the Project from people who might move into the Project, not do any work for a month, and then move out. The work deposit is returned when a member moves out of the Project.

Once people make this initial payment, they are members of the Project. They are free to set up their private room as they wish until they check out, when the damage deposit and the work deposit are returned according to a standard checkout form. Hence, members who have done their work and not damaged their room receive $65 back when they leave.

7. *The Educational Program.* The purpose of the educational program is to develop an understanding of behavioral principles among the members of the Project. An innovative programmed test containing over 600 examples of behavioral principles in everyday settings is used (Miller, 1975). Residents sign up for the course and earn credits for each quiz they pass. About 300 credits per week are budgeted for this program. A more complete description of the program is presented in the section entitled "The Behavioral Culture."

8. *The Supervisory Program.* Jobs in this program involve overseeing all the work in the Project. The member who holds the contract job of "credit recorder" tallies up each member's credit balance at the end of the week according to credits saved or transferred, and amount of work completed that week. Credits are awarded for each job according to the inspection ratings on a percentage basis. If the job passes 90% of the inspection ratings, the full credits are awarded. However, if the job

passes between 80% and 89%, only 80% of the credits are awarded. If a job passes 70% to 79%, 70% of the credits are awarded; if it passes 60% to 69%, 60% of the credits are awarded; and if it passes 50% to 59%, 50% of the credits are awarded. If a job passes 49% or less, no credits are awarded and the member who signed up for the job loses a $2.00 rent reduction.

An "auditor" is responsible for inspecting according to an objective checklist all members holding contract jobs. At this time the auditor's job is not completely specified. It will be considered specified when any member can train for the job and take it over. At that time there will be reliability inspections to make sure that the auditor's job is done properly. Hence, the auditor will have no more power than any other member, but will only be one member who holds a contract job for which he or she is held accountable.

9. *Summary of the Worksharing Program.* The worksharing system consists of a set of weekly and contract jobs designed to totally define all work required in this particular group living situation. Members sign up once a week for weekly jobs. They are trained for and sign a longer-term contract for "contract" jobs. All jobs are objectively defined, thereby permitting members agreeing to those jobs to be held accountable through a system of objective inspections. Members are consequated for doing their jobs by means of a rent reduction that on the average reduces the monthly rent from $83 to $43.

Evaluation of the Worksharing System

The prior sections of this paper have outlined a behavioral approach to group living. This approach has specified in behavioral term the major components of a system of group living. However, a critical feature of applied behavior analysis is the empirical analysis of such behavioral systems. Such an analysis may take a number of forms. The most common form is a single-subject experimental analysis of reliably observed behavior. A brief summary of the results of three such experiments will be presented in this section; for a more detailed account see Feallock and Miller (in press).

A second form of evaluation has been termed "social validation" by the Achievement Place Research Group (Fixsen et al., in press). Social validation is an important evaluative procedure when the social significance of target behaviors is not obvious. Thus, social validation may not be relevant when self-destructive behavior is being modified, but it may be relevant when specific target behaviors, such as those relating to cooks, for example, are being modified. One would like to know whether the individuals eating the food consider it to be "good." Social validation involves obtaining a quantifiable sample of the verbal behavior of relevant judges (such as the people eating the food) with respect to their description of it. If they describe it as being "good," then this would be evidence supporting the significance of the specified target behaviors; if it is rated as being "poor," then this would be evidence opposing the significance of the specified target behaviors. A simple rating methodology using Likert scales is used in this evaluative procedure. The results of a "social validation" evaluation are presented in this section.

A third form of evaluation might be termed "cost effectiveness." This involves determining the costs of the program compared to other programs with similar goals. A complete cost-effectiveness analysis would involve the direct measurement of the effectiveness of the comparable programs and their relative costs. The goal of most applied programs will probably be to provide either the same effectiveness at a cheaper cost or greater effectiveness at no more cost. The results of a partial cost-effectiveness analysis are presented in this section. These results compare the relative costs of various living situations; however, a detailed comparative analysis of relative effectiveness has not yet been completed.

1. *Experimental Analysis of The Worksharing System.* Three major experiments were done to determine the functionality of different aspects of the worksharing system. The inspection system, the credit system, and the rent reduction consequence were all analyzed in single-subject designs. In all three of these experiments, percent of cleaning done was the dependent variable. The full procedure and day-by-day data will be published at a later time.

The first experiment analyzed the importance of inspection in the worksharing system. Is it possible that people would do their cleaning jobs without being held accountable for doing them? It was found that when credits were given without regard to the inspection ratings, the mean percentage of cleaning done was 57%, with a range of 50% to 61%. When credits for cleaning jobs were contingent upon the inspection ratings, the mean percentage of cleaning done rose to 98%, with a range of 96% to 100%.

The second experiment in the Project was done to determine the importance of the credit system in getting the cleaning done. Is it possible that members would clean the common areas in a group living situation just because they wanted a clean house? It was found that when no credits were given for cleaning, the average percent of cleaning done was only 49%, with a range of 34% to 67%. However, when credits were given for cleaning, the average percentage for cleaning done rose to 94%, with a range of 88% to 100%.

The third experiment analyzed the importance of the contingent rent reduction consequence to the worksharing system. Is it possible that a credit system in and of itself would maintain cleaning behaviors? Is it also possible that there are enough social consequences in a group living situation to maintain members' cleaning behaviors, particularly since the work of each member is reported publicly through the credit system? When members received the maximum monthly rent reduction regardless of the number of credits they earned or the inspection ratings, an average of only 77% of the cleaning was done, with a range of 65% to 84%. When the maximum monthly rent reductions were awarded only to those members who earned 100 credits per week, an average of 92% of the cleaning was done, with a range of 83% to 98%.

It can be concluded from the results of these three experiments that high percentages of cleaning done in the worksharing system are maintained only when the members are held accountable for their work and consequated for doing it. All three components (inspection system, contingent credits, and rent reduction consequences) were found to be functional for the worksharing system. These three experiments illustrate the point that the worksharing system was not only behaviorally designed but also empirically tested for its functionality.

2. *Social Validation.* All of the worksharing system would be of no value if the members did not enjoy living in The Experimental Living Project. Hence, we asked the members: "Over all, how much do you enjoy living here, compared to a dorm?" Members were asked to rate this question on a 7-point scale. A rating of 1 meant that members enjoyed living in the Project very little in comparison to a dorm, and a rating of 7 meant they enjoyed living in the Project much more than living in a dorm. A dorm was chosen as the comparison because almost all of the members had lived in a dorm at one time. The average rating for this question was 5.7. Thus, the members indicated that they enjoyed living in the Experimental Living Project much more than in a dorm.

Several other questions were asked of the members. The purpose of these questions was to assess what components they liked the least. Again a seven-point scale was used, and the dormitory was the comparison. The next question asked was: "How clean is the house kept, compared to a dormitory?" The average rating was 4.1. This means that members said the Project was at least as clean as a dorm.

The next question asked of the members was: "How good is the food, considering the price, compared to a dormitory?" The average rating was 6.3. This was the highest rating of any program. Members said they enjoyed the food much more than food in the dormitory.

Members were asked: "How rapidly are repairs made here, compared to a dormitory?" The average rating was 4.0. Members said that repairs were made as fast in the Project as in the dorm.

Finally, members were asked: "To what extent is the rent money that you pay spent in ways that benefit you, compared to a dormitory?" The average rating was 5.9. Members said that their rent money was spent in ways that benefited them more often than in a dormitory.

These data indicate that members describe the effectiveness of the program at producing a clean and well-repaired living environment as comparable with dormitories. They also indicate that members describe the effectiveness of the program in producing cheap food and utilizing their rent money to their benefit as exceeding the dormitory. Data indicate that the members describe the overall program as producing a living environment that they enjoy living in considerably more than they enjoy living in a dormitory. Thus, if the residents of the program are relevant judges, one may conclude that the behavioral program has produced a valid specification of target behaviors for the creation and maintenance of a satisfactory group living environment.

3. *Cost Effectiveness of the Work Sharing System.* One of the primary advantages of living in The Experimental Living Project is economic. The average rental payment in the Experimental Living Project is $43 per month. According to the University of Kansas Housing Association, the monthly rental payment for private rooms in a University of Kansas dormitory is $78. A three-bedroom apartment with three occupants rents on the average for $69 per month, while a studio apartment rents for $110 a month, and a one-bedroom apartment rents for $127. All of the apartment figures are for the city of Lawrence, Kansas, and are based on an article in *University Daily Kansas* (Spring, 1973). The Experimental Living Project is a cheaper place to live than any other comparable living arrangement. This is especially true when one considers the fact that the rental for the Project includes utilities and most apartments do not include utilities in their rental payments.

Another economic consideration is the cost of food. In the Experimental Living Project it costs $19 per month for one main meal a day, 6 days a week. This is approximately 27 meals at a cost of 75¢ per meal. In a dormitory, the cost for the same number of evening meals per month is $47.69, or $1.76 per meal. The dormitory costs include the expense of hiring people to do preparation and cleanup.

These data indicate that The Experimental Living Project is relatively cheaper for both space and food than other comparable living arrangements. One additional datum that would be of considerable interest here would involve a comparison of time costs—that is, whether it takes members more hours of housework to live in The Experimental Living Project than elsewhere. The apparent time involved in living in the Project is about six to seven hours per week. Casual discussions with individuals living elsewhere suggest that the amount of time involved in housekeeping and cooking in non-dormitory settings is about the same. Dormitory living, however, probably involves less time since meals and most janitorial work are provided.

4. *Summary of Evaluations.* Three different types of evaluations have been undertaken to date. The first involves the experimental analysis of important components of the program. This evaluation indicates that inspections, credit assignments, and rent reductions are all crucial to maintenance of a high level of cleaning behavior. By implication, one may guess that these same components are important for other target behaviors. However, systematic data have not yet been gathered on this question. Other components of the worksharing system, such as the contract and the training programs, have not yet been evaluated.

The second type of evaluation suggests that the outcomes produced by the target behaviors selected for the major programs in the worksharing system are compared favorably with the outcomes obtained in dormitories. This provides some evidence that the target behaviors are of practical significance and not simply arbitrary behaviors.

The third type of evaluation indicates that The Experimental Living Project is cheaper than any comparable alternative.

Overall, then, these evaluations suggest that The Experimental Living Project has defined a worksharing system that is functional in maintaining common work, that the outcomes of the resulting work are rated favorably by residents of the Project, and that the environment is cheaper than comparable alternatives. One might argue from these results that the Project produces a more effective group living environment at a cheaper cost than comparable alternatives. However, a firm conclusion with respect to this question must await a more comprehensive program of evaluation.

PART TWO: BEHAVIORAL CULTURE

A major goal of the Project is to permit members to have complete democratic control over the system. Implementation of this goal means that all aspects of the program must be capable of being modified by the members, including the target behaviors, the behavioral specifications, and the contingencies. With such control, it is possible for members of the Project to gradually eliminate all aspects of the behavioral system. This creates a problem, since such decisions as increasing credit payments for a job or reducing the stringency of criteria for completing a job can lead to relatively immediate reinforcement. Thus one might expect that members would come under the control of such immediate consequences and be relatively less influenced by the long-term consequences of making these changes (such as a dirtier house and poorer food).

Several strategies have been developed to cope with these problems. First, an orderly system of self-government has been set up with specified rules for changing any component of the Project. Second, a lengthy handbook has been prepared, spelling out and explaining the rules of the Project. Third, a course in which members are taught behavioral concepts has been organized. All three of these strategies have been developed with the goal of influencing how members discuss issues involved in changing the behavioral system and how they vote on them. The three strategies will be outlined next.

1. *Self-Government.* The rules for self-government provide the mechanism by which the members can change the existing rules of the Project. One important provision is that any change of the behavioral system requires a majority vote of 75%. This ensures that a solid majority of members are in favor of making the proposed changes. Any proposed changes must be brought up at the weekly meeting of the membership. It is at the meeting that any decisions for the Experimental Living Project are made. Not only do all members have access to the decision-making apparatus but they are paid 15 credits for attending the weekly meeting. Hence, the operation of the system is completely turned over to the members in a democratic form of self-government.

2. *Handbook.* The Handbook states the rules that all members agree to live by when they move into the Experimental Living Project. In it, the worksharing system and programs are described and a set of social rules stated. An example of a social rule is: "Any stealing in the Project from the Project or from another member is grounds for immediate

eviction." Hence, people who sign their contract are agreeing to work within the system and live by its rules. Another important component of the Handbook is the set of rules outlined above for self-government in the Project.

3. *Educational Program.* Potentially the members could vote out major components of the worksharing system. The likelihood of this happening is diminished by the educational program. The purpose of the educational program is to develop a behavioral culture in the Project that will encourage the use of behavioral approaches to group problems. In a broad sense, the educational system includes the reading of the Handbook and the training for any specialized contract jobs in the Project. However, it more specifically means an introductory course on behavioral analysis.

The text used for this introductory course is *Principles of Everyday Behavior Analysis* (Miller, 1975). This text consists of 26 lessons. Members are paid 15 points every time they pass a quiz on one lesson with a score of 90% or better. From the text, they learn behavioral principles in such a way that they generalize to everyday settings involving normal adults. The teaching procedure used in this text is called "generalized programming" (Miller and Weaver, 1975). Research has shown that students who master this program can correctly answer novel questions on a "generalization post-test" with a mean of 75% or better in comparison to pre-test scores of 15% (Miller and Weaver, 1975). At the time of this writing, 21 out of 30 residents have taken the course. These members seem to be able to verbalize the principles of behavioral analysis and apply them to decisions relating to the behavioral system in the Project.

4. *Social Validation.* Again the question may be asked about the members' satisfaction with these procedures. While this is a difficult question to answer, there are some data that partially answer this question. The members were asked to rate their answers to several questions on a 7-point scale. For the question: "How many undesirable rules are there compared to a dormitory?" the average rating was 5.9. Members said there were fewer undesirable rules in the Project than in a dormitory. In response to the question: "How much influence do you have in determining important aspects of the Project compared to a dormitory?" the average rating was also 5.9. Members said that they had more influence in determining important aspects of the Project than they had in a dormitory. It should be noted that members have never voted out any of the important components of the worksharing system or programs.

Hence, from this data one could conclude that members are satisfied with the system and are willing to work to continue it.

PART THREE: POSITIVE VERBAL COMMUNITY

A methodology for creating a positive pattern of interactions between group members is now being developed. It is hoped that this will lead to a happier, more functional "culture." In this context, culture refers to the verbal behavior of the group and the rules by which members of the group socially reinforce and punish each other. The goal is to teach members how to use social reinforcement to increase the rate of positive statements that others make in their presence while at the same time decreasing the rate of "downers" that others make in their presence. Don Whaley has designed such a culture, which he calls the "positive verbal community" (Whaley, 1973).

At the present time an extensive program is being developed for training members in specific behaviors and stimulus situations that are important for the core of a positive community (Fawcett and Miller, 1974). This program teaches members how to sincerely praise other people, using positive praise statements and a description of what is being praised. It teaches them how to enhance this reinforcement with follow-up questions. It also teaches members how to "graciously accept compliments" by reinforcing people for complimenting them. Thus, a pattern of positive interactions would be built. Also, people are taught to deal with negative statements through the prompting and reinforcement of incompatible positive statements (and extinction if that fails). The training program involves programmed instructions—so that trainees can verbally describe the rules of such a culture—as well as a programmed role-playing component that teaches them to actually engage in the behavior in the appropriate stimulus situation.

The positive verbal community may be viewed in two ways. First, it may be viewed as an end in its own right. It specifies a pattern of positive social interactions between members that are designed to be reinforcing and that may lead to a greater feeling of "togetherness." Thus, such a community would be intrinsically desirable.

However, the positive verbal community may well have a second, potentially even more important result. If members can be taught to use positive verbal statements to contingently reinforce behavior that is desirable within the Project, it can be a powerful tool for social change. Patterns of behavior that are disruptive, nonproductive, and annoying can be eliminated through reinforcement of alternative behaviors. Behaviors that the individuals would like to increase may be capable of being influenced and possibly even maintained by such contingent social reinforcement. It is conceivable that such contingent social praise could replace the rent reduction contingency for all or some members. Or it could be used to produce new and more functional cultural patterns within the membership of the group. That is, it may provide a systematic procedure for redesigning cultures (Skinner, 1961, 1971).

While the feasibility of a positive verbal community is not yet known, some small-scale testing of the training procedures has indicated that they are feasible. And the informal reactions of the trained individuals has been favorable. A full development and evaluation of this promising technique is now beginning. Further conclusions will have to await the outcome of that program of research.

FUTURE DIRECTIONS

In the introduction it was noted that there are three major goals of the Experimental Living Project. The goal of effectively sharing the work and creating an egalitarian system of management has been largely accomplished at this time. The Project is kept clean, well-fed, repaired, and properly financed through the basic programs within the worksharing system.

The goal of developing a behavioral culture has been fairly well-established at this point. The Handbook has provided an initial set of rules as well as rules for changing the rules. The behavioral course has modified most members' discussion of behavioral issues in such a way as to ensure against the gradual elimination of the behavioral system. The remaining step at this point is to extend the course so that the actual skills of creating innovative behavioral specifications and contingency systems can be taught. In this way the membership will be completely self-sufficient without the need of outside behavioral consultants. This step is just now being worked on and will undoubtedly require a major effort.

The goal of developing a positive verbal community is in the development stage. A specification of many of the relevant target behaviors has been undertaken and a training procedure is now being tested.

With reasonable approximations of each of the three basic goals in existence, it is realistic to start looking ahead. If the goal is a multi-family community, then there are at least two major behavioral engineering tasks ahead of us. The first is the development of an approach to marital stability within such a group setting. The various behavioral approaches to remediating troubled marriages might be adapted to making average marriages sound enough to withstand the problems of group living (Azrin, Naster, and Jones, 1973). Jealousy, both sexual and social, is likely to be a major problem in a group of married individuals. We therefore see the development of strategies for dealing with that problem to be of utmost importance. Toward this end, we are now in the planning stage to create a group living situation for married students without children. Such a project will involve a direct replication of the procedure in use in the Experimental Living Project, plus the development and evaluation of programs to promote marriages sound enough to survive within a group living situation.

The second major task is to develop a reasonable method for including children in such a community. This will require some systematic set of rules that all adults will enforce for all the children. Such rules will probaby have to be set up in the form of a handbook to which all new families subscribe. The rules in such a handbook would be subject to change within the self-government program.

With these problems solved, it is possible to foresee an initially small group of families coming together, working out the remaining technologies of multi-family living, and starting to extend their membership with the goal of creating an independent, behaviorally engineered community. Such a community could consider creating their own school—a major, if somewhat far-off, reinforcer for most of us. Such a community could begin exploring the extension of the worksharing system to several economic ventures within their own community. A small farming component could be examined with the goal of making the community more self-sufficient. Community governmental and legal systems could be designed with a behavioral engineering base. In short, behavioral engineering could be applied to a range of community problems in a systematic way.

While these extensions are obviously far in the future, it is possible to foresee a conservative and sound approach to developing such an experimental community. This approach probably involves engineering the basic technologies needed in group living first for unmarried students, then for married students with no children, and finally, for families of any description. The establishment of such a multi-family living group will signal the first step toward a behaviorally engineered community. When such a step is taken, it will represent an actualization of

Skinner's proposal to apply behavioral engineering to designing a better community and society capable of creating for all of its members The Good Life.

REFERENCES

AZRIN, N. H., NASTER, D. J., and JONES, R.: Reciprocity counseling: A rapid-learning-based procedure for marital counseling. *Behav. Res. and Ther.*, 11, 365-382, 1973.

FAWCETT, S. B., and MILLER, L. K.: *Positive Conversation Training Manual.* Lawrence, Kans.: mimeo, 1974.

FEALLOCK, R., and MILLER, L. K.: The design and evaluation of a worksharing system for experimental living. *J. Appl. Behav. Anal.* (in press).

FIXSEN, D. L., PHILLIPS, E. L., PHILLIPS, E. A., and WOLF, M. M.: Training teaching ing parents to operate home treatment programs. In: M. E. Bernal (Ed.), *Training in Behavior Modification.* Monterey, Cal.: Brooks/Cole (in press).

MILLER, L. K.: *Principles of Everyday Behavior Analysis.* Monterey, Cal.: Brooks/Cole, 1975.

MILLER, L. K., and LIES, A.: Everyday behavior analysis: A new direction for applied behavior analysis. *Behav. Voice*, 2, 1-10, 1974.

MILLER, L. K., and WEAVER, F. H.: The use of "concept programming" to teach behavioral concepts to university students. In: J. Johnson (Ed.), *Behavior Research and Technology in Higher Education.* Springfield, Ill.: Charles C Thomas, 1975.

SKINNER, B. F.: *Beyond Freedom and Dignity.* New York: Knopf, 1971.

SKINNER, B. F.: The design of cultures. *Daedalus,* Summer, 523-546, 1961.

SKINNER, B. F.: *Walden Two.* New York: Macmillan, 1948.

University Daily Kansas: Spring, 1971.

University of Kansas Housing Association: Spring, 1974.

WHALEY, D.: *Hope.* Kalamazoo: Behaviordelia, 1975.

Section II

GENERALIZATION AND
MAINTENANCE

Commentary

A persistent problem for behavioral approaches to the family, as well as for behavioral approaches generally, has been the question of the degree to which the effects of treatment generalize over situations, behaviors and persons, and the extent to which they maintain themselves over time. Much of the behavioral literature, including the various social learning formulations of personality (Mischel, 1968), has been explicit with respect to the notion that generalization is something that doesn't just happen, but rather is a function of the degree to which it is programmed. This notion reflects the strong emphasis placed on situational determinants of behavior, and the idea that behavior is situation specific. If the intervention takes place in one environment, then transfer of behavior change to other situations cannot be assumed unless there is "comparability" across situations (Mash & Terdal, 1976). The definition of what constitutes comparability is itself a complex problem.

The first paper in this section, by Conway and Bucher, provides an extensive review of the evidence for transfer and maintenance of treatment effects in behavior change programs with children. In addition to a review of the empirical basis for transfer, the paper serves to provide a conceptual base for asking questions about generalization. For example, a major difficulty in assessing the generality of effects relates to what other situations or behaviors are to be observed. The extremely large number of possible areas which may be potentially affected by family intervention efforts creates a complex measurement problem, in that it is difficult to identify and assess all of these areas. The scope and extensiveness of this problem are apparent in a paper by Willems (1973).

Behavior modification programs have attempted to deal with the question of generalization in at least two ways. The first, which has been by far the most prevalent, is the focus of intervention in the natural environment, employing as mediators people who are indigenous to the situation. Bucher and Conway review studies which have involved, for example, parents, teachers, and peers as mediators of change. It is believed that if intervention occurs in the situation of interest, then the question of transfer across situations is superfluous. Although this approach would seem to have face validity, it does assume that there is an identifiable, discrete, and unitary situation designated as "the natural environment." In actuality, given what we know about the importance of setting events in the regulation of behavior, it would seem more appropriate to talk about "natural environments." When intervention occurs in the home or the classroom, it is likely that each of these situations in turn reflects a composite involving a multiplicity of more restricted stimulus conditions having differential controlling properties for behavior. Consequently, intervention involving parents, which takes place in the home, is not likely entirely to circumvent the question of transfer of effects across situations.

Where intervention has taken place in environments extrinsic to the individual's life situation, questions of generalization have been dealt with in a similar fashion to that described above. Frequently, an attempt is made to simulate the conditions which exist, or are likely to exist, in the natural environment both in terms of antecedent and consequent stimulus events. Such programs often involve a proportionately greater number of artificial controls in the initial stages, with attempts to make the program more "lifelike" as it progresses. Included here are token programs (O'Leary & Drabman, 1971) which are gradually faded out, and programs which attempt to modify the schedules of reinforcement in a way that will be congruent with the schedules in the environment which the person is functioning in, entering, or reentering. While this approach is different from naturalistic intervention in some ways, it is essentially the same in the way that it attempts to deal with the generalization question—creating as much similarity as possible between the "treatment" environment and the "natural" environment.

A less prevalent, but increasingly more frequent, approach to the generalization questions associated with behavior change effort is represented in those programs which attempt to provide the individual with a self-controlling strategy that may be employed across a number of situations. Implicit in such cognitive mediational approaches is the notion that the family members can be taught a general coping strategy which will permit them to deal with a wide range of situations. In a sense, this approach attempts to change the person directly, and the situation indirectly by altering the way in which the person will react to it. Rather than being taught to respond to all situations, the individual is given a general response style which presumably will be applicable across a wide range of conditions. There is some evidence to suggest that such types of programs may promote a greater degree of generalization. Approaches to generalization involving reprogramming the natural environment, as well as approaches which attempt to utilize cognitions in the mediation of transfer, are extensively discussed in the paper by Conway and Bucher.

The questions raised in the paper by Conway and Bucher relating to the generalization of treatment effects across situations suggest the need for careful and systematic cross-situational assessment. The specification and identification of characteristic features of different situations, in terms of both the cues being presented and the behaviors occasioned by these cues prior to any intervention, would seem to be an important consideration. In other words, would treatment in one context more readily generalize to another context than would be the case if the situations were reversed? These issues are dealt with extensively in the next paper, by Johnson, Bolstad and Lobitz, within the context of intervention programs for the family and school environments.

Johnson et al. consider initially the pre-intervention consistency across home and classroom environments. It is clear from their discussion that the level of consistency will depend upon the specific measures which are used for its determination. For example, while there may be little consistency between the absolute rates of different responses across situations, there may be a high degree of consistency in terms of viewing the child as being deviant in both settings. In this regard, it is important to recognize that very different rates of responses in different situations may lead to similar outcomes (e.g., referral to treatment) because of the specific and differential performance expectations and criteria characteristic of each situation. A major point, then, is that any assessment of cross-situational consistency or treatment generalization is inextricably bound to the unit of analysis and measuring instrument being used to make the assessment.

The paper by Johnson et al. also sensitizes individuals involved with family intervention to the *possibility* that intervention in a particular situation may produce adverse effects in other nonintervention situations. This failure to generalize, or "contrast effects," is suggested by the data presented by Johnson et al., in which improvements in the home are accompanied by decrements in the classroom, and vice versa. Several explanations for this finding are discussed.

The assessment and modification of family behavior in the natural environment has been shown to have a number of strengths. In the context of the present discussion, promoting generalization is especially important. However, it has also been shown that naturalistic assessment and intervention strategies are procedures that may be costly compared to efforts that may occur in more artificial environments. Having people "come to the office" is likely to be less costly than "home visits" and observations. Consequently, if assessments which occur in less naturalistic contexts can be shown to be correlated with the occurrence of significant behaviors in significant environments, such procedures would have some advantages.

The next paper, by Martin, Johnson, Johanson, and Wahl, examines the degree to which analogue measures of family behavior correlate with more naturalistic measures. Martin et al. consider the empirical literature and report the results of a research study examining this question. Although the data reported by Martin et al. suggest that there may be little correlation between behavior in analogue and home environments, it is important to recognize that these conclusions may only be drawn in relation to the specific types of analogue measures being employed. The predictive power of analogue assessment may be directly related to the nature of the analogue situation being used and the characteristics of the measuring instrument being employed. The issue here is similar to that raised in relation to making comparisons across different naturalistic environments. Additional discussion of the issues involved in the use of analogue assessment are presented in the paper by Terdal, Jackson, and Garner. The next paper, by Bernal, Delfini, North, and Kreutzer, compares the behavior of deviant and normal populations of kindergarten and first-grade boys across the home and school situation. As was the case in the paper by Johnson et al., multiple measures are used to examine the degree of cross-situational consistency. In addition to examining this question, the study also serves to provide a base of normative data for studying this population of children and their social environment. It is believed that such normative data are evident in the paper by Patterson in the next section of this volume. Additional normative information of this sort is also presented for deviant and normal boys in the paper by Delfini, Bernal, and Rosen, and for normal and developmentally delayed groups in the paper by Terdal, Jackson, and Garner. In summary, the papers presented in this section provide an extensive conceptual and empirical base for the consideration of problems relating to the generalization and maintenance of intervention efforts with families.

REFERENCES

MASH, E. J., and TERDAL, L. G.: *Behavior-Therapy Assessment: Diagnosis, Design and Evaluation.* New York: Springer, 1976.

MISCHEL, W.: *Personality Assessment.* New York: Wiley, 1968.

O'LEARY, K. D., and DRABMAN, R.: Token reinforcement programs in the classroom: A review. *Psychol. Bull.,* 75, 379-398, 1971.

WILLEMS, E. P.: Behavioral technology and behavioral ecology. *J. Appl. Behav. Anal.,* 7, 151-165, 1974.

5

Transfer and Maintenance of Behavior Change in Children: A Review and Suggestions

JOHN B. CONWAY

and

BRADLEY D. BUCHER

Questions of transfer (across settings and behaviors) and maintenance (across time) of behavior change are important ones for any change agent. Our focus in this paper is to review and suggest applied behavioral strategies for promoting transfer and maintenance of changes in children.

In assessing any behavior change effort, there appear to be at least three important questions: What behavior(s) was changed? Under what stimulus conditions was the behavior changed? For how long a time was the changed behavior maintained?

Applied behavior analysis has been primarily concerned with specifying the functional relationship between targeted behaviors and their immediate and consequent stimulus conditions. As Baer et al. (1968), among others, have suggested, "A behavioral change may be said to have generality if it proves durable over time, if it appears in a wide variety of possible environments, or if it spreads to a wide variety of related behaviors" (p. 96). Thus, questions of transfer include the co-variations among target and other, nontarget behaviors, and the generality of behavior changes across settings or environments or, perhaps more precisely, beyond the stimulus conditions that induced the change; in addition, maintenance or durability of changes across time is seen as an important practical concern. For the purpose of providing a rather

119

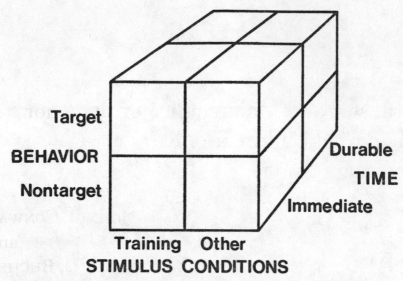

FIGURE 1. Some outcome questions: What *behavior* was changed, under what *stimulus conditions,* and for how long a *time?*

complete picture of the possible outcomes of any change effort, these three dimensions (i.e., changes across *behaviors, stimulus conditions* and over *times*) may be combined as in Figure 1.

Although Patterson (1969) suggested that applied behavior analysis must move beyond the "whoopee-we-did-it" stage, involving the redis-covery of the Law of Effect, clearly the majority of our "analytic" work has been concerned with investigating a rather narrow range of behav-ioral changes—i.e., specifying the *training* stimulus conditions that in-duce *immediate* change in *targeted* behavior. As Figure 1 suggests, at least seven additional outcomes are possible and probably desirable if a change effort is to have a practical, therapeutic impact.

Let us look only at targeted behavior change for the moment. Three questions may be posed beyond the concern with immediate change under a specific set of training stimulus conditions. First: Are the train-ing stimulus conditions able to maintain the changed behavior across time? While we may suspect that the behavior will be maintained as long as the stimulus conditions that induced the change are intact, the evidence for such durable, long-term change is sparse. Might not some components of the stimulus conditions require modification over time? Second: Do changes transfer beyond a limited set of training conditions?

Stimulus topographies may be seen as comprised of at least two sets of stimuli—the controlling antecedent and consequent conditions and all other coincidental and, perhaps, irrelevant stimulus conditions in the training environment. If the stimulus consequences that induced a change in behavior are transferred across other, nontraining environments, then the behavior change may be seen as having some stimulus generalizability. For example, a therapist may successfully engineer a family environment so that changes in the child's behavior initially induced by therapist consequences are maintained by similar parent consequences, thus leading to a transfer of the changed behavior across some stimulus conditions. On the other hand, do behavior changes endure in the absence of those stimulus conditions (usually consequent) responsible for inducing the initial change? In other words, if the reinforcing or punishing consequences are withdrawn or absent in another environment, will the changed behavior be resistant to extinction? What are effective strategies for programming resistance to extinction beyond training and in nonsupportive environments? The third question about the generalizability of targeted behavior change combines the previous two: Is the behavior change maintained over time and under nontraining stimulus conditions? For example, a particularly important question concerns the parents' ability as change agents to maintain changes in a child's behavior over time and after therapist support is removed. How might we program such a durable supportive family environment?

The outcome questions we have posed thus far have included only changes in targeted behaviors; Figure 1 raises a similar set of four possible outcome effects for nontargeted behaviors. The basic question here concerns relationships or covariations among behaviors. Are there functional relationships between target and nontarget behaviors? Are there groups of behaviors (or response classes) which change together, even though the environment may be acting directly on only some of them? Are there hierarchical arrangements among responses and can superordinate responses be identified and targeted for change? Immediate changes in nontargeted behaviors may be observed under a particular set of training stimulus conditions. If so, then further questions about the generalizability of these nontargeted behavior changes become important. Are the changes in nontarget behaviors transferred across stimulus conditions and durable over time?

Some applied behavior analysts (e.g., Lovaas et al., 1973) have seen the time dimension or questions about the durability of behavior changes as relatively meaningless. If a child's behavior is largely a function of immediate stimulus consequences, then behaviors will be maintained as long as stimulus consequences are supportive. The durability of behavior changes has some obvious practical importance, however, and becomes an especially crucial question in evaluating the social relevance of a change effort. Certainly, practical questions of how to *maintain* supportive stimulus conditions are important strategic ones for social engineers.

The multiple questions raised by considering maintenance over time and transfer across behaviors and stimulus conditions clearly merit careful outcome research if answers and strategies are to emerge. That transfer and maintenance are not automatic but rather must be strategically planned has been echoed frequently (e.g., Bandura, 1969; Kanfer and Phillips, 1970; Kazdin and Bootzin, 1972; Krasner, 1971). It has become axiomatic that behavior changes in children are reversible (e.g., Kazdin, 1973; O'Leary and Kent, 1973) and situation specific (e.g., Birnbrauer, 1968; Herman and Tramontana, 1971; O'Leary et al., 1969; Wahler, 1969b).

In some isolated cases reporting unprogrammed generalization, questions of why or how behavior change was generalized remain unanswered. Blanchard and Johnson (1973) reported some generalized, albeit inconsistent, behavior changes across classrooms resulting from the contingent application of tangible rewards and punishments, while they found no generalized changes due to differential teacher attention. To what can this generalization be attributed? As another recent example, Lovaas et al. (1973) suggest some fairly impressive generalization of behavior changes in autistic children. They reported transfer of targeted as well as nontargeted behavior changes to very dissimilar settings (with no supportive consequation for desired behaviors) while the children were in their hospital training program. Suggestions are certainly available to account for these generalized changes, but controlled analyses are lacking. They were also apparently successful in retraining some parents so that desired behavior changes were maintained over several years, but again the effective components of their social engineering strategies remain unspecified. These studies represent important examples of measurement of changes across stimulus conditions, other behaviors, and time. It is only through similar efforts that effective strategies will emerge for programming transfer and maintenance.

A variety of strategies for promoting transfer and maintenance of behavior change have been suggested. Strategies for the transfer and maintenance of targeted behavior change across stimulus conditions will be reviewed first. Reprogramming natural environments so that they initiate and maintain behavior changes in children has increasingly become the strategy of choice for applied behavior analysts. In addition, there are a number of strategies for planning or promoting transfer which do not involve reprogramming. Since practical planning for transfer often includes reprogramming, as well as other strategies, this distinction is somewhat arbitrary but, for convenience, each of these two sets of strategies will be reviewed separately. Finally, evidence for transfer across other, nontargeted behavior will briefly be considered.

REPROGRAMMING NATURAL ENVIRONMENTS

The design, implementation, and evaluation of strategies for reprogramming social environments are probably the top priority goals for the present generation of behavior modifiers and, indeed, many of the papers in this volume are focused around such strategies within family environments. It is not our intention to extensively review the rapidly increasing amount of research dealing with the *initiation* of changes in social environments, but rather to focus some critical attention on strategies for *maintaining* such changes once initiated.

The intervention model adopted by social engineers may simply be elaborated following Tharp and Wetzel (1969). In order to initiate changes in a target child's behavior as it occurs in his or her social environment (traditionally, home or school), it is often necessary to modify the stimulus conditions (usually the consequences) that support an undesired behavior and/or that do not support a desired behavior. Other people in the child's social environment (parents, teachers or peers) are the dispensers of consequences, and hence their behavior will initiate and maintain any change in the target child's behavior. Social engineers thus become a step removed from the target child, and their efforts are directed toward modifying the behavior of dispensers (or mediators), which in turn controls the child's behavior. Tharp and Wetzel have labeled this intervention model a triadic one (consultant-mediator-target) in contrast to the traditional dyadic therapeutic model and have reemphasized the role of the mediator as the primary change agent.

Adoption of the triadic intervention model has afforded behavior modifiers with answers to some of the questions about transfer and maintenance of behavior change in children. "Transfer across settings must be engineered, stimulus conditions must be rearranged to support any change." "Changes will be durable as long as the stimulus conditions are supportive." The real social engineering questions, however, are concerned with initiating and maintaining those rearranged stimulus conditions: how to initiate change in parents, teachers, and peers, and especially how to maintain these changes across time; or how changed mediator behaviors are transferred across situations, other problem behaviors, or other children. Questions of transfer and maintenance remain largely unanswered; the focus of these questions has simply been shifted from children's to mediators' behavior. Strategies for the initiation of changes in parent, teacher, and peer behavior will briefly be reviewed, followed by suggestions for maintaining supportive mediator behavior.

Parents as Mediators

Patterson (1971) and Berkowitz and Graziano (1972) have reviewed behaviorally-based parent training programs, and the status of such programs does not appear to have substantially altered in the last three years. The bulk of behavioral parent training programs have been able to demonstrate short-term changes in targeted child behaviors. Before proceeding to the question of how well these reprogrammed parenting behaviors are maintained, it is worth noting that only recently have studies evaluated the comparative effectiveness of parent training programs. Baer's (1971) criticisms of Tharp and Wetzel's (1969) evaluation procedures are applicable to all those reviewed. Evaluations have rarely gone beyond an AB design and, as such, are incapable of demonstrating that changes were not coincidental or, indeed, specifically to what any changed child behavior may be attributed. The Patterson and Reid (1973) evaluation of 11 consecutive referrals to their Institute, while employing systematic data collection and multiple outcome criteria, suffers from the same shortcoming. Reversals, multiple baseline designs, or the use of comparison groups (Kazdin, 1973; O'Leary and Kent, 1973) are necessary at this stage.

Recently, three published studies have provided controlled comparison data. Wiltz and Patterson (1974) reported some initial evidence that the Oregon Research Institute's parent intervention package for conduct-disordered boys (e.g., Patterson et al., 1973) produced favorable changes compared to an untreated, waiting-list control over a five-week period. Walter and Gilmore (1973) compared the same intervention package with a placebo treatment. Attention and expectations were similar in both treatment and placebo groups. The outcome results indicated an overall significant decrease in targeted deviant child behaviors only under the treatment condition, while boys of the placebo families showed a nonsignificant increase in targeted deviant behavior. The treatment period lasted only four weeks and, unfortunately, no follow-up was done.

Alexander and Parsons (1973), working with delinquent families, compared a short-term behaviorally oriented family intervention program with a client-centered family groups program, a psychodynamic family program, and a no-treatment control. Their behavioral intervention program produced significant changes in three family process interaction measures, but also led to a reduced recidivism rate (26%) over a 6-18 month follow-up. This reduced recidivism rate compared favorably with a county-wide rate of 51% and rates ranging from 47%-73% across the other comparison groups. While not as well controlled or as specific in its outcome measures as that of Walter and Gilmore (1973), this study affords an excellent and much needed field study with follow-up measures on a socially relevant criterion.

The question of maintaining supportive parent behaviors is one of reinforcement control, i.e., of what controls or maintains the parents' behavior. Indeed, difficulties are not infrequently encountered even in initiating changes in parents' behaviors. Some parents have little invested in training programs and may only be involved through coercion by courts or schools. In some instances (e.g., Patterson and Reid, 1970) attempts have been made to arrange arbitrary reinforcers, such as money, contingent upon the parents' appropriate behavior; or, at times, therapists have had to rely largely on negative reinforcement to maintain parent participation (e.g., Reid and Hendriks, 1973, report a case in which the father finally implemented a program to keep the therapist from "bugging" him). Once a program is initiated by parents and a change in child behavior is demonstrated, these changes are often reinforcing for the parents. Not only may the desired change in the child be reinforcing by itself, but the parents may legitimately attribute such a change to their own efforts. Following current notions of attribution theory (Winett, 1970), the incidence of further similar parent behavior should be maintained over time. However, immediate changes in child behavior do not seem to be reinforcing for all parents. Supportive parent behavior is often initiated and maintained largely by external therapist control. When therapist control is primarily through negative reinforcement and the parents' participation is primarily avoidance behavior, there is very little reason to suspect that the parents' changed behavior will continue after therapist control is withdrawn. Similarly, if the parents' participation is a function of therapist-delivered arbitrary reinforcers, one cannot expect those behaviors to be maintained in the absence of continued reinforcement. To a greater or lesser extent, therapist control in terms of explicit demands is necessary in any change effort. If possible, fulfillment of such demands should be reinforced by positive social consequences from the therapist. Any necessary use of arbitrary, nonsocial reinforcers must be faded out for maximal maintenance.

Although follow-up data are sparse, there are certainly many instances of durable changes in parents' behavior following behavioral intervention programs. There appears, however, to be no systematic study of the variables maintaining durable changes in parenting. Two suggestions were offered above: fading out the use of arbitrary reinforcers and increasing use of positive social therapist control. Patterson and Reid (1970) suggest that children may be trained to be more reinforcing to the parents, thus increasing their "sending" status and providing the necessary reciprocity in reinforcement patterns to maintain the parents' behavior. Reengineering efforts should strive to effect initial and immediate changes in the child's behavior, even if the initial targeted change is in a simple, nonthreatening behavior. Therapist-parent program contracts might include increasing levels of parent participation contingent upon demonstrated changes in the child's behavior. Training parents in groups may have some advantages in providing peer support and pressure for maintained supportive parenting. Clearly, booster sessions, perhaps best organized with groups of parents, should facilitate maintenance.

Finally, a recent study by Lavigueur et al. (1973) is noteworthy. Following a program of differential attention and time-out implemented by the mother, the authors document a generalized change in a nontarget sibling's behavior. The mother's behavior toward the nontarget sibling paralleled her behavior toward the target child. It was not possible, however, to directly attribute the change in the nontarget child's behavior to differential mother behavior, as the change could also have been due to a change in the target child's status as a facilitating stimulus (Patterson, 1973). In either case, this study demonstrates a transfer in the mother's behavior across stimulus conditions (from targeted to nontargeted child) and, with respect to the change in the nontargeted child's behavior, adds another dimension to our initial conceptualization of transfer and maintenance. The effects of intervention on nontarget children is an important concern that warrants future investigation.

Teachers as Mediators

Teacher reprogramming efforts have been extensively employed by social behavioral engineers in the past decade. Teacher training and direct intervention strategies have been reviewed at Banff 3 (Hall and Copeland, 1972; Patterson et al., 1972), and the use of token economies in the classroom has also been well reviewed recently (Kazdin and Bootzin, 1972; O'Leary and Drabman, 1971). Our emphasis, however, as with parent reprogramming, is on the transfer and maintenance of reprogrammed teacher behavior. There is certainly some overlap among strategies but teacher training, direct intervention, and token systems will be considered separately for convenience.

Early efforts at teacher training relied heavily on teaching principles of differential attention, with time out procedures for disruptive classroom behavior and occasionally aversive consequences (e.g., Haughton, 1968). Reprogramming strategies included some didactic training, often in seminars. At least a dozen references are available (e.g., Buckley and Walker, 1970; Homme et al., 1970; O'Leary and O'Leary, 1972) and now widely used in such formal training efforts. In addition, Hall and Copeland (1972), among others, include presentations by fellow teachers of behavioral programs in school settings, and supervised classroom practice with continued feedback. With few exceptions, most studies (reviewed by Patterson, 1971) have reported that teachers were able to successfully alter classroom behavior after such training. What maintains the teacher's behavior as a change agent? Brown et al. (1969) provided a striking demonstration of external consultant control of teacher behavior. Using an ABAB design, these authors altered social reinforcement (via the consultant in the classroom with the teacher) contingent upon appropriate teacher attention. The data suggested that appropriate teacher behavior was clearly under the control of the consultant's social consequation, and appropriate teacher behavior, of course, controlled the target child's behavior. Hall and Copeland's (1972) Responsive Teaching Model attempts to make provisions for initiating teacher participation through professional and/or academic credits. It also attempts to maintain teacher support from other workshop participants and other more experienced teachers, principals, and professionals. As such, the Responsive Teaching Model represents a well planned social engineering enterprise. Whether in fact this model, or other similar ones, actually does maintain changes in teachers' classroom behaviors across time remains to be demonstrated.

The Oregon Research Institute's direct intervention strategy (e.g., Patterson et al., 1972; Hops and Cobb, 1973) may be distinguished from others in several respects: it focuses on a targeted child (or children); initial child behavior changes are engineered directly by the behavioral consultant; and attempts are made to maintain changed child behavior through teacher and/or peer control. Direct classroom intervention by the behavioral consultant has some advantages, especially in reducing the high initial teacher-response cost (expenditure of time) involved in altering high rates of deviant behavior. Direct intervention usually has involved the use of a "work box" or signaling apparatus placed near the target child. The "work box" provides immediate feedback to the child for appropriate as well as inappropriate behaviors. Backup reinforcers for points registered on the "work box" may be individual ones, but more frequently have been group rewards (delivered to the entire class). Transfer of desired target child behavior changes has been reported over times when the "work box" is not in operation. Once changes have been initiated, control of the "work box" may be transferred to the teacher, with continued back-up reinforcers supplied for appropriate child behavior. In subsequent stages the "work box" has been faded out, with reliance on programmed peer-teacher and/or parent support. At this stage, parent and teacher training techniques may be instituted as reviewed above. Patterson et al. (1972) report excellent results in increasing appropriate behaviors in deviant target children. Further, four- to six-month follow-ups have clearly demonstrated that these behavior changes were maintained. These results are among the most favorable in the literature and, as Patterson and Reid (1973) point out elsewhere, they deserve independent replication.

Token economy systems have afforded the most expedient intervention strategy for altering the deviant behaviors of whole classrooms. The often noted shortcoming has been the lack of evidence regarding transfer and maintenance of behavior changes beyond the token-culture classroom. Kazdin and Bootzin (1972) recently reviewed the evidence suggesting that changes are not transferred to nontoken classroom situations, nor are they maintained once token systems are withdrawn. Since this review we are aware of only one marginally favorable report of maintained behavior change after the abrupt termination of a special class token system (Dalton et al., 1973). This study reports that gains in achievement test scores (arithmetic and language) for a group of retarded children were maintained over one year. Kazdin and Bootzin (1972) offered several suggestions for programming maintained behavior changes following token systems, including: the gradual removal of token reinforcement; stepwise token systems; intermittent, delayed, and varied schedules; varied stimulus conditions for appropriate behavior; self-reinforcement; increased reliance on social and natural consequences; and a reprogramming of the natural environment.

Walker and Buckley (1972) reported the first systematic evaluation of reprogramming strategies following the termination of a token economy classroom. Primary-school-age children with academic and behavioral problems spent two months in a special experimental classroom employing a token economy system. Upon completion of the experimental classroom intervention, children were randomly assigned to one of three maintenance strategies or to one control group and returned to their original classrooms. The maintenance strategies were as follows: teacher training in behavior engineering techniques; equating stimulus conditions which involved maintaining experimental classroom techniques (including social and token reinforcement and aversive control administered by the regular teacher) in the regular classroom; and a peer reprogramming procedure which involved group reinforcement contingent upon appropriate target child behavior. Control group children were returned to their regular classrooms with no follow-up support or reprogramming efforts. Across all children, the experimental classroom token procedures increased the mean percent appropriate behavior from 45% during a baseline period to 90% at the end of treatment. During the two-month follow-up, mean percent appropriate behaviors were 70%, 68%, 64%, and 59% for peer reprogramming, equating stimulus conditions, teacher training, and control groups respectively. Post-hoc analyses indicated that peer reprogramming and equating stimulus conditions group means were significantly different from the mean of the control group, while the teacher training group and the control group means did not significantly differ. As Cone (1973) has pointed out, these data may be analyzed in other ways (using change scores or analysis of covariance) with different results, but even with Walker and Buckley's (1972) analysis the results do not suggest reliable differences across maintenance strategies. Further, the practical significance of differences between the control and three maintenance strategies may be limited. The importance of this study, however, should not be underestimated. Systematic evaluation of maintenance strategies is crucial at this point, not only in the development of token systems, but in all efforts aimed at reprogramming natural environments.

Peers as Mediators

The cooperation of peers as mediators of behavior change in other target children, while not as extensively enlisted as that of parents and teachers, has been given increasing attention in recent efforts to re-engineer social environments. We will first briefly summarize the literature on initiating supportive peer stimulus conditions, as it has not been systematically reviewed. Our focus, once again, is on the maintenance of supportive peer environments once they have been successfully initiated, and the evidence here is practically nonexistent.

An important role for peers has been recognized both in serving as facilitating stimuli (Patterson, 1973) and providing supportive consequences for deviant child behavior (Buehler et al., 1966; Solomon and Wahler, 1973). Assuming, then, that peers function as important agents of behavior control in natural environments, especially in classrooms, several strategies for enlisting peers as agents of behavior change have been implemented. First, individual peers have served as contingency managers for one or more target children. Second, reinforcement contingencies have been implemented on a group-wide basis, where the group shares in the consequences for the behavior of any group member. Finally, both of the above strategies may be combined with a peer group member managing contingencies that are shared by the entire group.

Peers have been trained to monitor the behavior of a target child and dispense nonsocial and social reinforcers contingent upon appropriate behavior (e.g., Nelson et al., 1973; Patterson et al., 1969; Solomon and Wahler, 1973; Surratt et al., 1969). For example, Nelson et al. (1973) paired target children with a peer manager at a summer camp for the behaviorally disordered and neurologically impaired. Intervention plans were drawn up for each target child specifying one target behavior, behavioral goal, responsibilities for the peer manager and adult counselor, and the reinforcers (activities and consumables) for both the target and peer manager. From the brief report given, it appears that peer managers served as mediators between the target child and the counselor, reminding the target of inappropriate and appropriate behavior and checking with the counselor for reinforcers. In this case, as well as in others, varying degrees of adult control entered into the intervention, and indeed it is impossible to separate the multiple controlling conditions (adult external control, nonsocial reinforcers, peer social reinforcers).

Solomon and Wahler (1973) demonstrated that peers may support the deviant behavior of others in the group and that peer social reinforcement may be manipulated to change that deviant behavior. Five disruptive children in a sixth-grade class of 30 were chosen as targets. Another five children who ranked high on "popularity" and "willingness to cooperate with adults" were selected as "therapists." The classroom seating was arranged so that each target child was seated adjacent to one "therapist" child. Peers in training attended a group meeting in which differential reinforcement and extinction were discussed, and problem, and desirable target children behaviors were observed on videotape. In addition, they had daily meetings with the teacher to discuss their records of attention to problem or desired behaviors. An ABAB design assessed the role of peer ("therapist" child) social attention on the target children's problem behavior. The results very nicely demonstrated the controlling function of peer social attention on problem behavior.

In recent developments of the teaching-family model at Achievement Place, Phillips and his colleagues (Fixsen, Phillips, & Wolf, 1973; Fixsen, Wolf, & Phillips, 1973; Phillips et al., 1973) have explored semi self-government and elected peer manager systems. Predelinquent youths at Achievement Place have been trained in the skills involved in a democratic decision-making process, including developing group-wide rules, reporting rule violations, deciding guilt, and assigning consequences. In an important series of experiments Phillips et al. (1973) concluded that an elected peer manager system of administering tasks and assigning consequences was just as effective as, and preferred over, a teaching-parent administered point system. Under the elected peer manager system peer managers were elected democratically each week, and their duties included assigning and supervising a variety of daily tasks and activities in each of which the managers had the authority to give or take away points for their peers' behavior. Phillips et al. (1973) speculate that perhaps the elected peer manager system was most attractive because it allowed the peers to have contingencies for one another— "The manager had immediate contingencies for his workers and the workers had the remote contingency of not reelecting that particular manager" (p. 558). A variety of manipulations with the peer manager system demonstrated the crucial importance of the managers' point giving and taking authority without which they were practically ineffective. Point consequences based on the performance of their peers were usually in effect for the managers, i.e., the peer managers gained or lost points depending upon the satisfactory completion of tasks by their peers. The effectiveness of the manager system was only slightly reduced, however, under a condition where the peer managers could neither make nor lose points themselves, but where they could still give and take away points for their peers' performance. This suggests that the managers' behavior was maintained by variables other than nonsocial rewards, and probably by the opportunity to exercise authority over their peers. Although these findings need replication and extension to tasks other than bathroom cleaning (the only dependent task variable in this study), they clearly have important implications for the utility of peer mediation in small group living situations. Of course, as Fixsen et al. (1973) point out, the evaluation of Achievement Place has been on a "procedural" level to date, and whether behavioral changes initiated at Achievement Place transfer to other settings or are maintained over time remains unanswered.

Instituting group contingencies for the behavior of a single target child within the group has been quite effectively used in very rapidly eliminating problem behavior and increasing appropriate behavior. Wolf and Risley (1967) reported that a group-wide point system was more effective in decreasing the disruptive classroom behavior of a target child than an individual-based point reinforcement system. Apparently a group-wide contingency initiates supportive (and often coercive) peer behavior. The Oregon group (e.g., Patterson and Reid, 1970; Patterson et al., 1969) has used group-wide contingencies to alter the deviant classroom behavior of a target child, but usually in combination with teacher, parent, or other individual peer supoprt.

Walker and Buckley (1972), in the peer reprogramming condition of their previously mentioned study on generalization strategies, enlisted the active support and cooperation of peer groups in a unique manner. When he returned to his regular classroom, the target child was given opportunities twice a week to earn points for appropriate social and academic behavior. Points were exchanged for a group reinforcement for the entire class. During the two weekly opportunities to earn points, the child's behavior was monitored and rewarded via a "work box." In addition, these opportunities to earn points were contingent upon acceptable behavior during intervals between these "work box" periods. If, at the teacher's discretion, the target child's behavior was unacceptable between the two weekly sessions, the next scheduled opportunity to earn points was cancelled. This peer reprogramming strategy was at least as effective as other strategies in maintaining behavioral changes gained during the special experimental classroom token systems.

Another interesting example of peer-mediated support was provided by Walker and Hops (1973). In attempting to increase social interactions in a withdrawn target child in one experiment, the authors trained the classroom peers in social interaction skills (via a symbolic modeling procedure) and then implemented a group-wide contingency in which points were earned by the peer group for every social interaction initiated *by the target child.* In another experiment, following training in social interaction skills for both the target child and the peer group, contingencies were implemented for both the child and the peer group. The target child earned points contingent upon any social interaction initiated by any peer and, conversely, the peer group earned points contingent upon interactions initiated by the target child. In addition, *both* the target and the peers had to achieve a predetermined number of points before *either* could exchange their points. The target's backup reward was a preselected individual reinforcement, while her peers' was a preselected group reinforcement. Both of these two exeprimental conditions were effective, though the latter reciprocal reinforcement strategy produced the most dramatic change in social interactions. Interestingly, in the first experiment, peers greatly increased their rate of initiating interactions with the target even though they were never reinforced for doing so. Both these experiments employed ABAB designs, and in reversal (second baseline) conditions the rates of social interactions were maintained initially, but quickly decreased. Hence, the point systems were clearly the effective controlling variables for social interactions in this study and, as the authors suggest, the extent to which behaviors are maintained following withdrawal of tokens is unanswered by this study.

Group consequences have also been applied contingent upon the behavior of *any* and *all* group members, with the group sharing the consequences of any individual member's behavior (e.g., Packard, 1970; Schmidt and Ulrich, 1969; Barrish et al., 1969). The "good behavior game" has withstood replication (Harris and Sherman, 1973; Medland and Stachnick, 1972) and appears to be effective in reducing disruptive classroom behavior. With some procedural variations, the good behavior game involves dividing the class into two teams and arranging competitions between teams in which the reinforcing consequences are delivered to the entire team for appropriate behavior. Medland and Stachnick (1972) and Harris and Sherman (1973) have examined some of the components in the good behavior game, and particularly relevant to this discussion is the finding in both studies that some appropriate behavior was maintained in the absence of winning consequences. Comparisons of the good behavior game with other classroom control techniques (e.g., individual token systems) have yet to be published. Herman and Tramontana (1971) found group and individually administered reinforcement equally effective in reducing disruptive behavior during procedures in a contrived experimental situation and in the classroom. On the other hand, under quite different circumstances, Phillips et al. (1973) found a group consequence (individually assigned tasks but group consequences) somewhat less effective than individual consequences (individually assigned tasks with individual consequences).

Finally, it is worth noting the extensive use of group competitions and contingencies and of peer managers in the Soviet Union (as reported by Bronfenbrenner, 1962, 1967). In pursuing the goal of developing a strong collectivistic morality, the Soviets have relied heavily upon peer group control established as early as possible. Team or unit competitions with group-wide rewards and punishments are established across a variety of social units. As early as the first grade many of the monitoring and consequating functions are given over to children in the units and, by the third grade, according to Bronfenbrenner's descriptions, the degree of peer group control is indeed extensive. Based on these reports, there is very little doubt that a carefully programmed strategy of ever increasing peer control can maintain the behavioral objectives of parents and teachers. The similarity between some of the peer reengineering strategies just reviewed and the Soviet efforts is striking and only infrequently noted.

Transfer to Nonprogrammed Environments

In this section we discuss the problems faced by therapists planning treatment for an extreme case: an extra-treatment environment over which they have little or no control. Treatment itself may occur outside the environment or in a special tetmporary modification of that environment. We assume, however, that treatment is restricted to temporary programming and that treatment does not change the client's environment or the behavior patterns of significant persons therein.

We must begin by recognizing the artificiality of this case for treatment of behavior problems of children in the home and school. In such settings, behavior modifiers will typically prefer to work with natural controlling agents. In some cases, however, reprogramming the environment cannot be carried far or must be omitted. In behavior therapy for problems of outpatient adults one must typically accept this disadvantage. One must look for training methods that release the client from the control of those contingencies that formerly maintained maladaptive behavior—e.g., removing the effects of harmful contingencies or putting the client in touch with reinforcing potentialities in the environment that were not previously being used—so that an environment that formerly did not support adaptive behavior will come to do so.

Let us begin by stating a basic assumption involved in this treatment approach. Behavior modifiers suppose that the functional relations between events and behavior that are observed in the laboratory also regulate behavior in the natural environment. Laboratory research thus gives us basic principles to work from. Contingent events that exert such powerful control in the laboratory also control the pattern of behavior outside. Thus, understanding behavior in the natural environment requires understanding the potential contingencies for behavior that exist there. It also requires, of course, an understanding of the discriminative abilities of the subject and the reinforcing or punishing potential of various behavioral consequences. This set of assumptions gives us a method of attack on the problem of transferring behavior change to the natural environment. We must inquire what contingencies maintain the undesirable behaviors, what contingencies exist to control more adaptive behaviors, and what behaviors or training programs are necessary to potentiate them.

Strategies for obtaining transfer of treatment depend on our answers to these questions. These answers should ideally be obtained by careful examination of the environment to which transfer is desired. Given the deficiencies in our current knowledge, however, we must rely to a degree on conceptual models of those environments. In some cases, these environments appear suitable to support changed behavior with little effort on the part of the therapist; in other cases, the environment appears quite challenging.

We look first at some problems that exist in environments that appear to support changes toward more adaptive functioning, then at environments that do not—recognizing the rather speculative nature of this division of environments. In addition, we look at recent conceptual models using cognitive constructs as mediators of behavior and at models for obtaining transfer through self-control strategies.

Supporting Environments

One can evaluate the success of transfer of treatment to the natural environment through follow-up studies. A follow-up is a routine recommendation for studies of conventional psychotherapy. However, behavior modification studies often ignore follow-up, and there has been some justification for this lack of concern. Many behavior modification studies have aimed only to demonstrate time-and-situation-limited behavior control. Follow-up observations taken in an environment for which the contingencies are unknown would add little to our knowledge of the variables that control behavior. But if a procedure is to be advanced as practically useful, follow-up is crucial, and most crucial if the procedure does not involve reprogramming the environment.

In two treatment areas, follow-up in the natural environment has been frequent, and good results have been found. These are in treatment of fears by desensitization and in treatment of enuresis by variations of the bell-and-pad conditioning device. Treatment of fears, or specific aversion reactions, by desensitization shows low relapse rates (Paul, 1969). It is not difficult to post-dict this finding from a behavioral model of the environmental contingencies that maintain the aversion. Aversion reactions are assumed to be acquired behaviors; the aversive stimuli typically have no genuinely harmful qualities. On the other hand, aversion behaviors frequently create serious social or other problems, which are relieved by successful treatment. Treatment thus leaves the client with a new set of behaviors for which the environmental consequences are more reinforcing than otherwise, and so nonphobic behavior is maintained.

Enuresis research, too, shows good follow-up results in most studies (Lovibond and Coote, 1970). Post-diction of this finding is also not difficult. The behaviorist typically views enuresis as a learning deficit rather than as an acquired behavior. Bed-wetting has an immediate consequence that is likely to be aversive, and delayed consequences, such as social disapproval and withdrawal of reinforcers, may be so as well. Training in appropriate behavior gives the child a means of avoiding these aversive stimuli without substituting others. This model thus leads to the deduction that training in these skills gives access to reinforcing events which, in many cases, will be adequate to maintain them.

There are other behavior problems for which the environmental factors that maintain the behavior may fit one or the other of these two paradigms. Inappropriate or low-rate social behavior in children (and adults) may be viewed either as resulting from learning deficits or from acquired aversive reactions to social interactions, or perhaps both. School phobias have also been seen as fitting either paradigm. For either model, an appropriate modification of the behavior may be expected to persist in the post-treatment environment. Of course, the treatments appropriate for these two paradigms may be quite different, as Ayllon et al. (1970) illustrate in their analysis of a school phobia.

Another example of behavior that often persists after it is once produced is peer interaction among children. Studies of this behavior, involving use and withdrawal of contingent adult attention, have frequently found that it persists after attention is finally withdrawn. Using some of these adults, Baer and Wolf (1970) developed the concept of a behavior trap—a behavior pattern which, once begun, produces environmental consequences that maintain the behavior. Leading children into such traps appears to be highly desirable if behavior change is to persist in the environment. Baer and Wolf illustrate this concept with a study showing how adult social reinforcement for peer group interaction could lead the child to enter the peer group reinforcement system so that social interaction would persist when the adult contingency was withdrawn.

Several other studies show similar results (Allen et al., 1964; Hopkins, 1968; Hall and Broden, 1967). The studies all used variations of reversal designs. In this design, if persistence of behavior is to be tested, the experimental contingency (e.g., adult social reinforcement for peer interaction) is occasionally withdrawn to check if interaction persists. Adult reinforcement may also be made gradually more and more intermittent. When the reversal to baseline, or the probe sessions, shows continued interaction without the maintaining experimental contingency, control of behavior is assumed to be transferred to other contingencies (e.g., peer interaction). This assumption should be tested more carefully, however, since failure of behavior to return to baseline may also be due to lack of experimental control. An alternative test method is shown by Hopkins (1968), who studied maintenance of smiling in a retarded child. Smiling was first reinforced with candy, but Hopkins aimed to transfer smiling to the environment, using answering smiles or social interaction as the reinforcer. When he found that withdrawal of candy reinforcement was not followed by decrease in smiling, Hopkins added a check to test what aspect of the environment had assumed control of the response. He placed a sign on the subject requesting that he be ignored if he smiled but attended to if he did not. Smiling decreased, and returned when the request on the sign was reversed.

Another design possibility is to use multiple baselines to observe behavior change both in a treatment environment and in the natural environment. This design has been used in several studies, but most have found little generalization across environments. In an exception to this rule, Johnston and Johnston (1972) treated a pair of speech deficient children in a classroom, using a multiple baseline combined with an ABA procedure. They attempted to establish each child as a cue for articulate speech in the other. Good articulation showed generalization to the nontreated play environment shared by the two children. Maintenance of more articulate speech here may be presumed to lie in its potentially greater effectiveness for obtaining a variety of reinforcing events; however, maintenance of behavior change after treatment ended was not shown. Kazdin and Polster (1973) used a multiple baseline, with behavior of two adult retardates providing the two response lines. Performance of the two subjects in a sheltered workshop was compared in order to study effects of gradual versus abrupt withdrawal of token reinforcement on social behavior. Gradual withdrawal produced more lasting effects.

Nonsupportive Environments

In some other areas, transfer of behavior changes from controlled environments is less reliably observed. Results of token systems and attention control procedures in school settings commonly show that reinforcement systems can increase attention or output in school tasks, but deterioration is common when baseline conditions are reintroduced (Kazdin and Bootzin, 1972). Post-diction can, of course, supply a variety of models to explain the difficulty. One may suppose that the desired behavior is not adequately reinforced under natural conditions, or that other reinforcers compete, and the behavior change program does not alter the strength of these contingencies.

If we do not permanently reprogram the classroom, we must look for contingencies already in effect there. After all, even in classes with misbehaving students, the behavior of other students is more appropriate. How this result is achieved is not clearly known. One contingency we know something about—peer attention—seems almost exclusively directed toward undesirable behavior (Solomon and Wahler, 1973). Such data support the conjecture that some environments may be quite hostile to effective behavior change. These include some hospital wards, classrooms, and homes (Rosenhan, 1973; Ullmann and Krasner, 1969). Not only are adaptive behaviors often not effectively reinforced, but available reinforcement may maintain or even shape maladaptive responses.

In general, however, we are relatively ignorant about the typical contingencies in natural environments. Contingencies may well be available for appropriate behavior, either in the classroom or in the home, but the children may not be sampling them, or may not have learned the association between these events and their behavior. Even under the best circumstances there are likely to be major differences between contingencies in treatment settings and those in the natural environment. Quick behavior change is desirable in treatment, but the contingencies that produce it will likely bear little resemblance to those in natural settings, where rewards for appropriate behavior are often delayed, intermittent, or based on large packages of behavior. In such cases, an environment that has many favorable features may still fail to support the treatment change.

One common tactic to bridge the gap between environments is to use training procedures that increase resistance to extinction. Perhaps then the changed behavior can be maintained long enough for the natural environmental contingencies to take control. One such tactic is to thin out reinforcement schedules gradually, as illustrated by some previously cited studies (Kazdin and Polster, 1973). Another is use of aversive control, as in the use of punishment for enuresis using the bell-and-pad technique. Punishment can have long-lasting effects if complete suppression of the punished response is obtained (Azrin and Holz, 1966), particularly if alternative responses for reinforcement are available. A variant is avoidance training, which is sometimes difficult to separate conceptually for punishment. Avoidance and punishment training, in various combinations with classical conditioning procedures, have been used with adults for treatment of homosexuality and other sexual problems, overeating, smoking, and alcoholism (Bucher and Lovaas, 1968). The problems of transferring treatment effects from the clinic to the environment to the post-treatment setting have been noted infrequently, and some data have accumulated concerning the complexities that surround relapse (Hore, 1971).

It seems unlikely that techniques designed to delay extinction or relapse can have permanent success unless the changes are supported by the environment. Some treatments of adults have recently been devised to take account of the therapeutic changes the environment will most readily support. These include: attempts to train social drinkers rather than complete abstainers (Mills et al., 1971); use of interpersonal facilitation as an aid to control of smoking (Janis and Hoffman, 1971); and analysis of discriminative control over smoking, with treatment aimed at extinguishing acquired environmental controls over the behavior (Upper and Meredith, 1970; Bernard and Efran, 1972).

Let us look now at some of the factors that affect transfer to the natural environment. An analysis of available contingencies in these environments can be helpful in devising treatment programs in settings where natural contingencies seem to make transfer difficult. We look at the two categories of controlling events that are primarily involved in the analysis of environmental control of behavior—consequences and antecedents.

Consequent events. In their summary of their work on token economies, Ayllon and Azrin (1968) state that transfer of gains made in these economies can best succeed if behaviors are trained that will continue to be reinforced after training. Behavior modification procedures often employ strong and easily delivered reinforcers. Many classes of behavior may be shaped and maintained with food reinforcement in a controlled environment, but most of those behaviors will not be directly or even indirectly maintained by food outside. Token systems involve a much greater variety of reinforcers, but again the association between behavior and its immediate and ultimate payoff is likely to be quite different from that in the natural environment. Thus, at the least, shifting from token control to natural controls will typically involve a shift in the consequences that maintain behavior (Ferster, 1967).

In planning a program for a given client, we need specific information about the contingencies that are available for behavior in the several environmental settings where the client lives; but we know rather little about what reinforcers control behavior in natural environments. One helpful technique, often used in token economies, is to observe the rates of the client's typical activities in various settings. Access to activities is then used as a reinforcer. This work reveals something of the variety of events that clients will work to sample. When such observations are carried out in natural settings, it is noteworthy how many activities involve complex skilled interaction with the environment. In children, reinforcing activities include cooperative and competitive games and sports, and others, such as those connected with reading, motor skills, and speech, that require considerable skill. Thus, these reinforcing activities are not available to everyone, and they may not be available to our clients. Training clients in these skills is thus one of the major ways to achieve behavior change that will persist when the artificial contingencies that created the change are removed.

It is unclear whether or when activities should be considered as having the status of primary reinforcers, or as being links in chains with other reinforcers at their terminus. In the sense that activities often require considerable prior learning to make them accessible, they do not fit the usual definition of primary reinforcers (Millenson, 1967). However, many activities seem also not to be acquired reinforcers, in that their reinforcing effectiveness seems not to be maintained by reinforcers extrinsic to the typical consequences of the activity. Apart from this issue, however, it seems clear that access to activities often has highly persistent reinforcing effects, and many activities require a considerable background of experience to make them effective. It follows that introducing such activities into children's repertoires can permanently change the reinforcing capacities of their environments and promote enduring behavior change. A successful treatment program to increase reading skill, for example, can result in new reinforcers for a child that are more potent than teacher attention and praise. Reading ability gives access to innumerable behavior options in the natural environment, and some of these options will inevitably lead to reinforcers. Reading can also result in intrinsic payoff; that is, it may not require external reinforcers to maintain its rate. The method used to train such skills may be important in potentiating them as intrinsic reinforcing activities. At present we know far too little about the characteristics of activities that make them reinforcing, or about how we can best train skilled behaviors so that once they are acquired they will have these reinforcing characteristics (Premack, 1965).

A second approach to the problem of an inadequately reinforcing environment is to establish secondary reinforcing stimuli. The most common of such stimuli for children are attention and praise from adults. Thus it is important to understand how adult praise, smiles, greetings, etc., acquire and maintain their function as secondary reinforcers in natural environments. There is a great deal of laboratory research in social reinforcement effects. Even for the most intractable subjects, autistic children, Lovaas and his colleagues have studied methods of creating social interaction as reinforcers (Lovaas, Freitag et al., 1966; Lovaas, Schaeffer, and Simmons, 1965). Success in this training gave the therapists greater control over the children's behavior when primary reinforcement was not consistently given. However, laboratory training procedures may not resemble the contingency conditions that occur naturally to produce and maintain social consequences as reinforcers in the natural environment.

Insofar as social reinforcers have a secondary, acquired character, they must be maintained by association with primary reinforcers, and their power depends on the continuation of this association. In this respect, social reinforcement resembles a less controlled version of a token reinforcement procedure, and successful transfer of social reinforcement to the natural environment would depend on whether, and how, the effectiveness of social consequences in the environment are maintained by association with other reinforcers. Wahler (1969a) noted this problem in his study of techniques for obtaining parental social control of oppositional behavior. However, studies of the effects of teacher praise and attention have not provided much data about how social contingencies are related to other characteristics of teacher behavior in the classroom. Such work seems necessary if the teacher attention is to be evaluated with respect to its potential effectiveness for maintaining a treatment result after the child has returned to his unprogrammed class.

Antecedent events. Stimuli associated with reinforcing events can acquire both reinforcing and cueing properties. The secondary discriminative properties of such stimuli have generally been easier to demonstrate. They serve an important discriminative function in coherent sequences of behavior by helping to sustain behavior when primary reinforcers are not immediately or consistently delivered. Thus, transfer of behavior from training to natural environmental conditions may depend on the similarity or adequacy of the cueing conditions in the two settings. A frequently encountered problem in treatment is that the child appears to make inadequate use of the discriminative cues for reinforcement that exist in the environment. If training is to transfer outside the treatment setting, it seems important to discover and train those cues that are reliably available.

Adequate use of environmental cues frequently requires signals that mediate later rewards, or rewards that are contingent on sizeable chunks of behavior. Training in the use of acquired stimulus features is involved in recent studies of the programming of self-care behaviors (O'Brien et al., 1972) and of complex sequences of academic behaviors such as arithmetic (Grimm et al., 1973). These activities are examples of behavior chains that operate to obtain rewards in the natural environment. Their acquisition reprograms the environment in the sense that they change its cueing and reinforcing capacity for the child.

There is much research on variables controlling transfer across settings. Training in even simple discriminative skills may not transfer. In some recent studies, Campione and Beaton (1972) and Campione (1973) have investigated variables controlling whether discriminative cues used for solving certain kinds of problems will continue to be used under certain changes in problem formats. These and other studies show that transfer is not automatic. Training of skills, then, should be done so that the cues that are available in training to guide the skilled behavior are very similar to those in the environment in which the skills are to be exercised.

Training techniques in discrimination learning tasks may also contribute to transfer and to the stability of performance under changes of reinforcement contingencies. Terrace (1969) found differences in behavior during extinction in comparing discrimination training with and without errors, and with and without continuous reinforcement. Similarly, Battig (1966) noted effects of training on transfer in paired associate learning tasks. He concluded that interference between items in a list has a facilitating effect on learning between tasks; intra-task interferences may facilitate precise discrimination of reliable cues.

In discussing problems of providing treatment for nonsupportive environments, we have found very few studies of methods to produce transfer to such environments. In fact, perhaps the major conclusion of this discussion is to point out the need for analysis of the environments in which behavior change is to be maintained; to discover not only the reinforcers that are available for the client, but what schedules apply, what behaviors will be necessary to produce them, and what cueing functions the environment can provide for these behaviors. If treatment conditions do not take account of these features of the client's natural environment, treatment transfer may fail.

In an important paper, Bijou et al. (1968) discussed techniques for discovering contingent relationships in the natural environment. These techniques have been too little used, so that problems of transfer are most often discussed on the basis of inadequate knowledge. A major effort in this direction is represented by Patterson's (1973) extensive analysis of the stimulus control exerted by family members over the noxious behaviors of an aggressive child in the home. Both antecedent and consequent events were observed. Another rating system, for use in the home, to determine antecedents and consequences of problem behavior has been offeered by Mash et al. (1973).

A similar approach is through the systematic analysis of typical environments to determine how behavior is influenced by variations in their organization and composition. Risley and his colleagues have been carrying out such analyses for day care environments (Risley and Cataldo, 1974). This work is valuable as an aid both in programming environments and in evaluating the potential of existing environments to maintain particular behaviors. Such data are crucial for examining the prospects for transferring training to outside environments.

Cognitions as Mediators of Transfer

The past generation of behavior theorists, following Skinner (1953), have maintained that the inclusion of cognitive mediating variables in a science of human behavior is premature and counterproductive until a functional analysis of environmental, observable conditions proves inadequate. This position, of course, has been an important strategic and pragmatic one for the development of behavior theory. Certainly, present-day behavioral models, and especially behavioral change efforts, have expanded the "narrow-band" S-R formulation of human behavior to include private events as mediators of behavior and change (e.g., Bandura, 1969, 1971; Kanfer and Phillips, 1970; Jacobs and Sachs, 1971). Some recent attention has been focused on the role of cognitions as important mediators of the transfer and maintenance of behavior change in the absence of immediate external environmental support.

Self-control (or self-regulation, self-management) has emerged as one of the most widely discussed cognitive events within behavior therapies. The so-called techniques of behavioral self-control may be presented in a fairly straightforward fashion, and their efficacy in promoting and maintaining behavior change may likewise be evaluated. There appears to be a good deal of confusion, however, about some fundamental issues of self-control. What precisely is mean by "self"-control? How is it acquired and maintained?

The utility of some formulations of self-control is severely restricted by their vagueness (e.g., Goldfried and Merbaum, 1973; Marston and Feldman, 1972). Most behavior theorists (including Cautela, 1969; Goldiamond, 1965; Kanfer and Karoly, 1972; Mahoney, 1972) define self-control following Skinner (1953), and very little confusion arises around the observation that just as man may control the behavior of others by arranging the relevant environmental conditions, so too may he control his own behavior by arranging the same kinds of conditions. Kanfer (1971) has simply labeled as self-control responses any response made by an organism to modify the probability of any other response. Again, there is very little doubt that certain responses (called self-controlling responses) affect the probability of certain other responses (called controlled responses). Indeed, it is difficult to think of any response emitted that does not affect the probability of some other response in the organism's repertoire. Most behavioral formulations of self-control have been restricted to instances in which a self-controlling response decreases the probability of some other response being controlled. For example, the control of behaviors which lead to immediate positive but delayed aversive consequences (such as overeating, alcoholism, cigarette smoking) is often conceptualized as a problem in self-control, and any response which inhibits, that is, which facilitates avoidance or escape of, such behaviors, is seen as a self-control response.

Instances of self-control, as defined simply following Skinner (1953), clearly exist; but why are self-controlling responses initiated or how are they acquired and maintained? Most behavioral formulations agree that the ultimate origin of self-control behavior lies in the individual's social learning history, but very few adequate descriptions of the development of self-control are available. (Premack and Anglin's, 1973, discussion is a notable exception.) It appears to be with respect to how self-control behaviors are *maintained* in the absence of immediate external support that some disagreement arises.

There are, in general, two somewhat divergent paradigms offered to explain the maintenance of self-control behaviors. On the one hand, self-control behaviors may be seen as maintained predominantly by external stimulus events. Ferster (1970) simply suggested that self-control responses are negatively reinforcing in that they reduce the probability of the delayed aversive consequences resulting from the behavior to be controlled. Stuart (1972) has argued the case for the *situational* determination of so-called self-control behaviors and, adhering to the logic of a Skinnerian science of human behavior, concludes that "there is as yet no reason to ascribe the controlling conditions for self-control responses to any agency other than the external environment" (p. 135). Likewise, Gewirtz (1971) dismissed self-control as an "intra-psychic cognitive-act euphemism" that may readily be explained in an operational learning analysis with the conception of functional response classes (and S-R chains) maintained by intermittent environmental reinforcement. On the other hand, others have emphasized the role of mediating cognitive events in maintaining self-control behaviors. The theoretical models of self-control proposed by Bandura (1969, pp. 32-38 and 615-622; 1971) and Kanfer (1971; Kanfer and Karoly, 1972) suggest mediating roles for self-evaluation and self-reinforcement in maintaining self-control behaviors.

These models warrant a bit of elaboration, since they appear to have generated most of the research into the techniques of self-control with children. The starting point is the assumption that there are times when the contiguous environmental conditions do not control behavior (e.g., Kanfer and Karoly, 1972, p. 406). Kanfer and Karoly suggest that self-initiated performance promises or contracts regulate behavior in the absence of external supports. "The antecedents of . . . self-control," they conclude, "lie in the discrepancy between self-observation and the performance promise, followed by self-reinforcement aimed at reducing the discrepancy" (Kanfer and Karoly, 1972, p. 408).

Bandura (1969, 1971) likewise has postulated the utility of self-evaluation and self-reinforcement as mediators in maintaining self-control processes. In questioning why individuals may deny themselves available immediate rewards or why they may punish themselves, Bandura suggested that self-evaluative responses acquire secondary reinforcing properties through repeated association with primary or social reinforcement. Bandura (1971) further suggested that:

> Once the evaluative properties of differential accomplishments are well established, favorable or adequate matches with adopted standards are likely to elicit self-reactions that, in turn, give rise to self-rewarding or self-punishing behavior. At this stage the whole process becomes relatively independent of external reinforcement, but remains dependent upon cognitive evaluations based on the match between self-prescribed standards, performance, and the attainments of reference models (p. 263).

These working models of self-control, then, include three principal components: self-monitoring, self-evaluation, and self-reinforcement. Most of the recent literature in this area with children has attempted to demonstrate that some or all of these components of self-control may be trained and that, once trained, behavior may be maintained by "self-control." Again, the paradigm for training in self-control has generally followed procedures outlined by Bandura (1969, p. 620). After behavior change has been induced via external reinforcement, direct training in self-reinforcement may be initiated. This may be achieved by gradually transferring evaluative and reinforcing activities from change agents to the children themselves. Thus rewards are now made contingent not only upon the desired behavior, but also upon accurate evaluation by the children of their own behaviors, as judged by an external change agent. Reinforcing activities may likewise be transferred so that the children both evaluate their own behavior and reinforce themselves accordingly. With the gradual thinning of arbitrary nonsocial rewards, the ultimate aim of such training is to produce a level of functioning at which the children can maintain their own behavior with minimum external supports.

The self-reinforcement component has been most heavily researched. Studies of self-reinforcement with children in the laboratory have followed Bandura and Perloff's (1967) demonstration that children can impose their own achievement standards and reinforce themselves appropriately. Felixbrod and O'Leary (1973) found that contingent reinforcement of self-imposed academic performance standards was as effective as externally imposed standards in maintaining the arithmetic problem solving behavior of second graders. In extending their procedures over six sessions, however, they also found that the children imposed consistently more lenient standards upon themselves over time.

A variety of attempts to program self-control behaviors have been reported in classroom settings, usually within a token economy system. Broden et al. (1971) successfully employed self-recording to increase study behavior and decrease disruptive behavior in two eighth grade children. As in other studies with adults (e.g., McFall, 1970), it is probable that self-monitoring alone may lead to initially consistent, but small and short-lived, behavior changes. It is encouraging to note, however, that Knapczyk and Livingston (1973) reported highly accurate self-recording of academic behavior in a group of junior high school special education (EMR) students.

Lovitt and Curtiss (1969) found that higher academic work rates were achieved when their 12-year-old subject arranged his own contingency requirements compared to teacher-imposed, but identical, contingencies. This finding has not been replicated to our knowledge, but several subsequent studies have demonstrated that self-determined reinforcement standards are able to maintain classroom behavior as well as do externally determined contingencies.

Glynn (1970) compared self-determined, experimenter-determined, and chance-determined reinforcement contingencies for academic performance of ninth graders. Children in the self-determined group were allowed to determine their own amount of token reinforcement, up to an externally imposed limit; identical amounts of reinforcement were given to yoked children in the chance-determined group; and arbitrary performance standards were imposed on the experimenter-determined group. Both self-determined and experimenter-determined reinforcement produced higher rates of academic performance than chance-reinforcement or a no-reinforcement control. In subsequent phases, all experimental groups were allowed to self-determine their amounts of reinforcement, and their differential past token reinforcements influenced subsequent rates of self-determined reinforcement. Of particular interest was that the previously chance-reinforced group never appeared to recover from their experience with unpredictable amounts of reinforcement, i.e., they did not increase their academic performance even when allowed to determine their own amounts of reinforcement. Glynn et al. (1973) extended some of these self-control procedures to a token system with second graders. After fairly extensive training in on-task classroom behavior supported by a group-wide contingency, individual contingencies were introduced, with each child responsible for assessing his or her own behavior as "on-task" or "not on-task" (the teacher defined on-task behavior). Reinforcement was then available as before, but contingent upon the child's own assessment. Results indicated that these self-control procedures maintained the on-task classroom behavior (that had been initiated by the externally arranged and monitored group contingency).

Kaufman and O'Leary (1972) likewise found that self-evaluation maintained (over six and seven days) low rates of disruptive behavior in a classroom of adolescent psychiatric patients. After three months under a token system, the responsibility for the evaluation of pupil behavior was transferred from the teacher to the individual pupil. Under this self-evaluation phase, the pupils rated themselves on disruptive behavior, and their own token ratings were then exchanged for back-up reinforcers. Disruptive behavior was maintained at its previously established low rates, but the pupils gradually gave themselves the highest possible ratings, and their own ratings were not significantly related to teacher ratings made independently during this phase.

Santagrossi et al. (1973) have recently reported a failure to replicate these short-lived effects with self-evaluation. Again using an adolescent psychiatric patient population, they found self-evaluation without any contingency to be ineffective in altering disruptive classroom behavior. A token economy system produced dramatic reductions, but subsequent attempts to introduce self-evaluation with back-up reinforcers (as in Kaufman and O'Leary, 1972) led to increases in disruptive behavior as well as nonveridical self-ratings (pupil self-ratings did not match teacher ratings nor independent observer ratings). An attempt to promote accurate self-ratings by reinforcing accurate matches between pupil and teacher ratings and punishing (points subtracted) discrepancies was abruptly terminated after one day during which pupil disruptive behavior increased sharply in opposition to the matching procedure. This group of adolescents was no doubt a difficult one to work with, and the self-evaluation procedures here were probably introduced too abruptly with little or no shaping.

Drabman et al. (1973) included appropriate shaping in self-evaluation behavior with good results. A standard, teacher-administered token program reduced disruptive behavior and increased academic work in an after-school remedial reading class for third-grade boys. Matching procedures were then initiated as in Santagrossi et al. (1973) and followed by four phases during which reinforcement for accurate matches were gradually faded out. In the final phase (lasting 12 days), token reinforcement was entirely contingent upon the children's self-evaluations. Decreased disruptive behaviors and increased work behaviors were maintained throughout the matching, fading, and self-evaluation phases. Self-evaluations were generally consistent with teacher evaluations during all phases (Median $r = .70$).

One final series of studies by Johnson and his colleagues (Bolstad and Johnson, 1972; Johnson, 1970; Johnson and Martin, 1973) has explored one of Bandura's testable hypotheses—that behaviors maintained by self-delivered reinforcement are more resistant to extinction than those maintained by reinforcement from an external agent. These studies report a small but consistent superiority of self-reinforcement in the initial stages of extinction. That is, when all external rewards for a particular behavior were withdrawn, those children who had been delivering the rewards to themselves maintained their behavior longer in the absence of any external rewards than did those who had been rewarded by an external agent. Johnson suggested, as has Bandura, that these results may be due to the conditioning of self-evaluative responses as secondary reinforcers and that, once established through self-reinforcement procedures, the secondary reinforcing properties of positive self-evaluation may serve to maintain behavior in the absence of external rewards. The experimental evidence is weak at best, however, and even this short-lived effect may be explained in other ways or may be simply a chance effect.

In each of the preceding examples of self-control, varying degrees of control by experimenters or change agents have, of course, been present. Instances of self-monitoring, self-evaluation, and self-reinforcement have been of relatively short duration and have always been initiated under external direction and probably supported by external control. Indeed, if one defines self-reinforcement as Morgan and Bass (1973) have, then no adequate demonstration of the phenomenon yet exists and, further, such demonstration may be impossible under controlled conditions. They consider self-mediated reinforcement to exist only in the absence of any external control (including experimenter/change agent demand characteristics) and in situations where the individuals are free to reward themselves at any time regardless of their behavior. These criteria are clearly also implicit in Bandura's and Kanfer's formulations as outlined above, and neither have been met in any of the research cited here. This is not to deny the existence of self-reinforcement or self-control, but it is worth noting that such phenomena (as described by Bandura and Kanfer) may be unobservable under laboratory or controlled conditions.

Children may be explicitly trained in any of the components of self-control, but are these self-control behaviors transferred and maintained beyond the controls of the training agent? How are "performance promises" or "contracts" or "self-prescribed standards" initiated, developed, and maintained in children? How can such standards be explicitly trained, and do they transfer beyond training conditions? Certainly further refinements in explicitly training some of these self-control components are required, but it must further be demonstrated that such instances of self-control transfer beyond the externally supporting stimulus conditions of the training environment and maintain behavior in environments with little or no external support. A few recent behavioral explorations of self-control (e.g., Logan, 1973; Premack and Anglin, 1973) have been especially well formulated and have speculated in some detail about the social learning development of self-control behaviors. Premack and Anglin (1973), within an operant framework, define self-control much as Bandura and Kanfer have, including performance standards and self-denial as the crucial motivational (moral) system acquired through socialization and built largely upon avoidance. Although their discussion of socialization and conscience formation is not novel, their specification of the learning parameters involved is important, especially if they can be demonstrated in animal analogue experimentation. The gap from these speculations to behavioral interventions with problem children is large, indeed, and it has yet to be demonstrated that self-control mechanisms can be trained in children.

A few additional research areas focusing on cognitive events as mediators of behavior change and facilitators of transfer warrant brief consideration. Meichenbaum (1973) has pioneered the development of cognitive self-guidance programs which train individuals to use their private speech for orienting, organizing, regulating, and self-praising functions toward the end of greater self-control. For example, Meichenbaum and Goodman (1971) trained impulsive children to talk to themselves and effectively modified their impulsivity on a variety of psychometric tests. As might be expected, however, they failed to find any transfer to the classroom, and to our knowledge no evidence for the transfer of self-instructions beyond the demand characteristics of the training environment is available. Proponents of attribution theory (cf., Winett, 1970, for a review of its relevance to behavior therapy) have speculated that attitude and behavior change will be more durable across situations and time when individuals attribute changes in their behavior to themselves rather than to external manipulations. A couple of studies with adults may be viewed as supporting this hypothesis (Davison et al., 1973; Davison and Valins, 1969). These data are limited to placebo drug effects, and there is presently no clear demonstration of the utility of attribution theory beyond drug- versus "self"-induced effects.

RESPONSE TRANSFER

In this closing section we will briefly consider the sparse experimental evidence for transfer of behavior changes across other, nontargeted, responses. As they were posed earlier, questions here are focused around covariations among responses. The existence of functionally related groups of behavior or response classes is often noted, yet beyond this basic assumption very little has been done toward identifying response classes in individual children (or adults) or across groups of subjects. These questions are surely of great importance in planning and evaluating change efforts. If we were able to specify covariations among behaviors, then intervention strategies might be much more carefully planned. But this is several steps ahead of our present knowledge about response classes. First, careful identification is required of any collateral changes in other behaviors following changes in targeted behaviors.

Research in generalized imitation in children (after Baer et al., 1967) has led to the reinterpretation of imitative behaviors as functionally related members of a generalized response class. Gewirtz and Stingle (1968) have outlined the development of imitation in children as a class of diverse but functionally equivalent behaviors that are acquired and maintained via intermittent external reinforcements. Once an imitative behavioral unit is trained in a child the discriminative occasion (usually cues from adults) indicating that an imitative response is *likely* to be reinforced comes to control imitative behavior in the child, even in the absence of immediate reinforcement (e.g., Burgess et al., 1970; Garcia et al., 1971; Peterson and Whitehurst, 1971). The establishment of a generalized imitative class of behaviors has been especially useful in training specific skills such as speech (e.g., Lovaas et al., 1966; Wheeler and Sulzer, 1970).

A number of studies have reported desirable collateral changes in nontargeted behaviors in autistic or retarded children following intervention (e.g., Lovaas et al., 1973; Lovaas and Simmons, 1969; Risley, 1968). After self-stimulatory behavior patterns have been eliminated in these children, training procedures usually involve building appropriate social behaviors, and the emergence of a variety of other, nontrained, social behaviors has sometimes been noted. It may be assumed that adults rather quickly become discriminative stimuli for a functionally related class of appropriate social behaviors in these children, as they also appear to become for very young normal children. As discussed above, social behaviors are often supported by naturally occurring communities of reinforcers, and they may also be another example of behaviors which readily acquire functional equivalence. Several training programs with socially withdrawn children have found that once a few social behaviors have been initiated, others, not specifically trained, sometimes emerge (e.g., Buell et al., 1968; Whitman et al., 1970).

Wahler et al. (1970) observed some difficult-to-interpret covariations between stuttering and other secondary problem behaviors. Differential parental attention for oppositional behaviors in one child and for distraction and frequent activity shifts in another child were accompanied by changes in stuttering. An ABAB design demonstrated that stuttering covaried directly with changes brought about in these secondary problem behaviors. Wahler further examined the temporal relationships between the two behaviors and found no evidence for common stimulus conditions controlling both, nor was there any evidence of coincident differential attention to fluent and stuttered speech. These functional relationships were puzzling, and all that can presently be said is that these secondary problem behaviors and/or their environmental contingencies were apparently in some unknown way related to stuttering.

More attention to collateral changes in nontargeted behaviors is needed before we can begin to piece together evidence for functionally related response classes. The precision and careful recording of multiple responses by Lovaas et al. (1973) serves as an outstanding example. In one of the few other examples of multiple behavior recording, Sajwaj et al. (1972) explored some of the effects of extinction on a variety of other nontargeted behaviors. Some of the undesirable "side effects" they found in using extinction procedures in isolation might be post-dicted (cf., Bandura, 1969, pp. 50-51), but theirs appears to be the first well documented demonstration that extinction procedures in isolation may reinitiate or increase other (sometimes undesirable) behaviors in a child's repertoire. It is important to observe that response classes may be comprised of inversely as well as directly covarying behaviors, and further attention to identifying members of functional response classes is long overdue.

REFERENCES

ALEXANDER, J. F., and PARSONS, B. V.: Short-term behavioral intervention with delinquent families: Impact on family process and recidivism. *J. Abnorm. Psychol.*, 81, 219-225, 1973.

ALLEN, K. E., HART, B. M., BUELL, J. S., HARRIS, F. R., and WOLF, M. M.: Effects of social reinforcement on isolate behavior of a nursery school child. *Child Devel.*, 35, 511-518, 1964.

AYLLON, T., and AZRIN, N. H.: *The Token Economy: A Motivational System for Therapy and Rehabilitation.* New York: Appleton-Century-Crofts, 1968.

AYLLON, T., SMITH, D., and ROGERS, M.: Behavioral management of a school phobia. *J. Behav. Ther. and Exper. Psychiat.*, 1, 125-138, 1970.

AZRIN, N. H., and HOLZ, W. C.: Punishment. In: W. K. Honig (Ed.), *Operant Behavior: Areas of Research and Application.* New York: Appleton-Century-Crofts, 1966. Pp. 380-447.

BAER, D. M.: Review of R. G. Tharp and R. J. Wetzel, *Behavior Modification in the Natural Environment. Contemp. Psychol.*, 16, 396-398, 1971.

BAER, D. M., PETERSON, R. F., and SHERMAN, J. A.: The development of imitation by reinforcing similarity to a model. *J. Exper. Anal. Behav.*, 10, 405-416, 1967.

BAER, D. M., and WOLF, M. M.: The entry into natural communities of reinforcement. In R. Ulrich, T. Stachnik, and J. Mabry (Eds.), *Control of Human Behavior*, Vol. I. New York: Scott, Foresman, 1970. Pp. 319-324.

BAER, D. M., WOLF, M. M., and RISLEY, T. R.: Some current dimensions of applied behavior analysis. *J. Appl. Behav. Anal.*, 1, 91-97, 1968.

BANDURA, A.: *Principles of Behavior Modification.* New York: Holt, Rinehart and Winston, 1969.

BANDURA, A.: Vicarious and self-reinforcement processes. In R. Glaser (Ed.), *The Nature of Reinforcement.* New York: Academic Press, 1971. Pp. 228-278.

BANDURA, A., and PERLOFF, B.: Relative efficacy of self-monitored and externally imposed reinforcement systems. *J. Pers. and Soc. Psychol.*, 7:111-116, 1967.

BARRISH, H. H., SAUNDERS, M., and WOLF, M. M.: Good behavior game: Effects of individual contingencies for group consequences on disruptive behavior in a classroom. *J. Appl. Behav. Anal.*, 2, 119-124, 1969.

BATTIG, W. F.: Facilitation and interference. In: E. A. Bilodeau (Ed.), *Acquisition of Skill*. New York: Academic Press, 1966.

BERKOWITZ, B. P., and GRAZIANO, A. M.: Training parents as behavior therapists: A review. *Behav. Res. and Ther.*, 10, 297-317, 1972.

BERNARD, H. S., and EFRAN, J. S.: Eliminating versus reducing smoking using pocket timers. *Behav. Res. and Ther.*, 10, 399-401, 1972.

BIJOU, S. W., PETERSON, R. F., and AULT, M. H.: A method to integrate descriptive and experimental field studies at the level of data and empirical concepts. *J. Appl. Behav. Anal.*, 1, 175-191, 1968.

BIRNBRAUER, J. S.: Generalization of punishment effects—A case study. *J. Appl. Behav. Anal.*, 1, 201-211, 1968.

BLANCHARD, E. B., and JOHNSON, R. A.: Generalization of operant classroom control procedures. *Behav. Ther.*, 4, 219-229, 1973.

BOLSTAD, O. D., and JOHNSON, S. M.: Self-regulation in the modification of disruptive classroom behavior. *J. Appl. Behav. Anal.*, 5, 443-454, 1972.

BRODEN, M., HALL, R. V., and MITTS, B.: The effect of self-recording on the classroom behavior of two eighth-grade students. *J. Appl. Behav. Anal.*, 4, 191-199, 1971.

BRONFENBRENNER, U. Soviet methods of character education: Some implications for research. *Amer. Psychol.*, 17, 550-564, 1962.

BRONFENBRENNER, U.: Response to pressure from peers versus adults among Soviet and American school children. *Int. J. Psychol.*, 2, 199-207, 1967.

BROWN, J., MONTGOMERY, R., and BARCLAY, J.: An example of psychologist management of teacher reinforcement procedures in the elementary classroom. *Psychol. in the Schools*, 6, 336-340, 1969.

BUCHER, B., and LOVAAS, O. I.: Use of aversive stimulation in behavior modification. In: M. R. Jones (Ed.), *Miami Symposium on the Prediction of Behavior, 1967: Aversive Stimulation*. Coral Gables, Fla.: U. of Miami Press, 1968. Pp. 77-145.

BUEHLER, R. E., PATTERSON, G. R., and FURNISS, J. M.: The reinforcement of behavior in institutional setting. *Behav. Res. and Ther.*, 4, 157-167, 1966.

BUELL, J., STODDARD, P., HARRIS, F. R., and BAER, D. M.: Collateral social development accompanying reinforcement of outdoor play in a preschool child. *J. Appl. Behav. Anal.*, 1, 167-173, 1968.

BUCKLEY, N. K., and WALKER, H. M.: *Modifying Classroom Behavior*. Champaign, Ill.: Research Press, 1970.

BURGESS, R. L., BURGESS, J. M., and ESVELDT, K. C.: An analysis of generalized imitation. *J. Appl. Behav. Anal.*, 3, 39-46, 1970.

CAMPIONE, J. C.: The generality of transfer: Effects of age and similarity of training and transfer tasks. *J. Exper. Child Psychol.*, 15, 407-418, 1973.

CAMPIONE, J. C., and BEATON, V. L.: Transfer of training: Some boundary conditions and initial theory. *J. Exper. Child Psychol.*, 13, 94-114, 1972.

CAUTELA, J. R.: Behavior therapy and self-control: Techniques and implications. In: C. M. Franks (Ed.), *Behavior Therapy: Appraisal and Status*. New York: McGraw-Hill, 1969. Pp. 323-340.

CONE, J. D.: Assessing the effectiveness of programmed generalization. *J. Appl. Behav. Anal.*, 6, 713-716, 1973.

DALTON, A. J., RUBINO, C. A., and HISLOP, M. W.: Some effects of token rewards on school achievement of children with Down's syndrome. *J. Appl. Behav. Anal.*, 6, 251-260, 1973.

DAVISON, G. C., TSUJIMOTO, R. N., and GLAROS, A. G.: Attribution and the maintenance of behavior change in falling asleep. *J. Abnorm. Psychol.*, 82, 124-133, 1973.

DAVISON, G. C., and VALINS, S.: Maintenance of self-attributed and drug attributed behavior change. *J. Pers. and Soc. Psychol.*, 11, 25-33, 1969.

DRABMAN, R. S., SPITALNIK, R. and O'LEARY, K. D.: Teaching self-control to disruptive children. *J. Abnorm. Psychol.*, 82, 10-16, 1973.

FELIXBROD, J. J., and O'LEARY, K. D.: Effects of reinforcement on children's academic behavior as a function of self-determined and externally imposed contingencies. *J. Appl. Behav. Anal.*, 6, 241-250, 1973.

FERSTER, C. B.: Arbitrary and natural reinforcement. *Psychol. Record, 17,* 341-347, 1967.

FERSTER, C. B.: Comments on paper by Hunt and Matarazzo. In: W. A. Hunt (Ed.), *Learning Mechanisms in Smoking.* Chicago: Aldine, 1970. Pp. 91-102.

FIXSEN, D. L., PHILLIPS, E. L., and WOLF, M. M.: Achievement Place: Experiments in self-government with predelinquents. *J. Appl. Behav. Anal.*, 6, 31-47, 1973.

FIXSEN, D. L., WOLF, M. M., and PHILLIPS, E. L.: Achievement Place: A teaching-family model of community-based group homes for youth in trouble. In: L. A. Hamerlynck, L. C. Handy, and E. J. Mash (Eds.), *Behavior Change: Methodology, Concepts and Practice.* Champaign, Ill.: Research Press, 1973. Pp. 241-268.

GARCIA, E., BAER, D. M., and FIRESTONE, I.: The development of generalized imitation within topographically determined boundaries. *J. Appl. Behav. Anal.*, 4, 101-112, 1971.

GEWIRTZ, J. L.: The roles of overt responding and extrinsic reinforcement in "self-" and "vicarious-reinforcement" phenomena and in "observational learning" and imitation. In: R. Glaser (Ed.), *The Nature of Reinforcement.* New York: Academic Press, 1971. Pp. 279-309.

GEWIRTZ, J. L., and STINGLE, K. C.: The learning of generalized imitation as the basis for identification. *Psychol. Rev.*, 75, 374-397, 1968.

GLYNN, E. L.: Classroom application of self-determined reinforcement. *Appl. Behav. Anal. 3,* 123-132, 1970.

GLYNN, E. L., THOMAS, J. D., and SHEE, S. M.: Behavioral self-control of on-task behavior in an elementary classroom. *J. Appl. Behav. Anal.*, 6, 105-113, 1973.

GOLDFRIED, M. R., and MERBAUM, M.: A perspective on self-control. In: M. R. Goldfried and M. Merbaum (Eds.), *Behavior Change Through Self-Control.* New York: Holt, Rinehart and Winston, 1973. Pp. 3-34.

GOLDIAMOND, I.: Self-control procedures in personal behavior problems. *Psychol. Reports,* 17, 851-868, 1965.

GRIMM, J. A., BIJOU, S. W., and PARSONS, J. A.: A problem-solving model for teaching remedial arithmetic to handicapped young children. *J. Abnorm. Child Psychol.*, 1, 26-39, 1973.

HALL, R. V., and BRODEN, M.: Behavior changes in brain-injured children through social reinforcement. *J. Exper. Child Psychol.*, 5, 463-479, 1967.

HALL, R. V., and COPELAND, R. E.: The responsive teaching model: A first step in shaping school personnel as behavior modification specialists. In: F. W. Clark, D. R. Evans and L. A. Hamerlynck (Eds.), *Implementing Behavioral Programs for School and Clinics.* Champaign, Ill.: Research Press, 1972. Pp. 125-150.

HARRIS, V. W., and SHERMAN, J. A.: Use and analysis of the "good behavior game" to reduce disruptive classroom behavior. *J. Appl. Behav. Anal.*, 6, 405-418, 1973.

HAUGHTON, E.: Training counselors and advisers of precision teaching. Paper presented at the meeting of the CEC Convention, New York, April 1968.

HERMAN, S. H., and TRAMONTANA, J.: Instructions and group versus individual reinforcement in modifying disruptive group behavior. *J. Appl. Behav. Anal.*, 4, 113-120, 1971.

HOMME, L., CSANYI, A. P., GONZALES, M. A., and RECHS, J. R.: *How to Use Contingency Contracting in the Classroom.* Champaign, Ill.: Research Press, 1970.

HOPKINS, B. L.: Effects of candy and social reinforcement, instructions, and reinforcement schedule leaning on the modification and maintenance of smiling. *J. Appl. Behav. Anal.,* 1, 121-130, 1968.

HOPS, H., and COBB, J. A.: Survival behaviors in the educational setting: Their implications for research and intervention. In: L. A. Hamerlynck, L. D. Handy, and E. J. Mash (Eds.), *Behavior Change.* Champaign, Ill.: Research Press, 1973. Pp. 193-208.

HORE, B. D.: Life events and alcoholic relapse. *Brit. J. Addiction,* 66, 83-88, 1971.

JACOBS, A., and SACHS, L. B.: *The Psychology of Private Events: Perspectives on Covert Response Systems.* New York: Academic Press, 1971.

JANIS, I. L., and HOFFMAN, D.: Facilitating effects of daily contact between partners who make a decision to cut down on smoking. *J. Pers. and Soc. Psychol.,* 17, 25-35, 1971.

JOHNSON, S. M.: Self-reinforcement *vs.* extrenal reinforcement in behavior modification with children. *Devel. Psychol.,* 3, 148-149, 1970.

JOHNSON, S. M., and MARTIN, S.: Developing self-evaluation as a conditioned reinforcer. In: B. Ashem and E. G. Poser (Eds.), *Behavior Modification with Children.* New York: Pergamon, 1973. Pp. 69-78.

JOHNSTON, J. M., and JOHNSTON, G. T.: Modification of consonant speech-sound articulation in young children. *J. Appl. Behav. Anal.,* 5, 233-246, 1972.

KANFER, F. H.: The maintenance of behavior by self-generated stimuli and reinforcements. In A. Jacobs and L. B. Sachs (Eds.), *The Psychology of Private Events: Perspectives on Covert Response Systems.* New York: Academic Press, 1971. Pp. 39-59.

KANFER, F. H., and KAROLY, P.: Self-control: A behavioristic excursion into the lion's den. *Behav. Ther.,* 3, 398-416, 1972.

KANFER, F. H., and PHILLIPS, J. S.: *Learning Foundations of Behavior Therapy.* New York: Wiley, 1970.

KAUFMAN, K. F., and O'LEARY, K. D.: Reward, cost, and self-evaluation procedures for disruptive adolescents in a psychiatric hospital school. *J. Appl. Behav. Anal.,* 5, 293-309, 1972.

KAZDIN, A. E.: Methodological and assessment considerations in evaluating reinforcement programs in applied settings. *J. Appl. Behav. Anal.,* 6, 517-531, 1973.

KAZDIN, A. E., and BOOTZIN, R. R.: The token economy: An evaluative review. *J. Appl. Behav. Anal.,* 5, 343-372, 1972.

KAZDIN, A. E., and POLSTER, R.: Intermittent token reinforcement and response maintenance in extinction. *Behav. Ther.,* 4, 3861391, 1973.

KNAPCZYK, D. R., and LIVINGSTON, G.: Self-recording and student teacher supervision: Variables within a token economy structure. *J. Appl. Behav. Anal.,* 6, 481-486, 1973.

KRASNER, L.: The operant approach in behavior therapy. In: A. E. Bergin and S. L. Garfield (Eds.), *Handbook of Psychotherapy and Behavior Change.* New York: Wiley, 1971. Pp. 612-652.

LAVIGUEUR, H., PETERSON, R. F., SHEESE, J. G., and PETERSON, L.: Behavioral treatment in the home: Effects on an untreated sibling and long-term follow-up. *Behav. Ther.,* 4, 431-441, 1973.

LOGAN, F. A.: Self-control as a habit, drive, and incentive. *J. Abnorm. Psychol.,* 81, 127-136, 1973.

LOVAAS, O. I., BERBERICH, J. P., PERLOFF, B. F., and SCHAEFER, B.: Acquisition of imitative speech by schizophrenic children. *Science,* 151, 705-707, 1966.

LOVAAS, O. I., FREITAG, G., KINDER, M. I., RUBENSTEIN, B. D., SCHAEFER, B., and SIMMONS, J. Q.: Establishment of social reinforcers in two schizophrenic children on the basis of food. *J. Exper. Child Psychol.,* 4, 109-125, 1966.

LOVAAS, O. I., KOEGEL, R., SIMMONS, J. Q., and LONG, J. S.: Some generalization and follow-up measures on autistic children in behavior therapy. *J. Appl. Behav. Anal.*, 6, 131-166, 1973.

LOVAAS, O. I., SCHAEFER, B. M., and SIMMONS, J. Q.: Building social behavior in autistic children by use of electric shock. *J. Exper. Res. in Pers.*, 1, 99-109, 1965.

LOVAAS, O. I., and SIMMONS, J. Q.: Manipulation of self-destruction in three retarded children. *J. Appl. Behav. Anal.*, 2, 142-158, 1969.

LOVIBOND, S. H., and COOTE, M. A.: Enuresis. In: C. G. Costello (Ed.), *Symptoms of Psychopathology: A Handbook.* New York: Wiley, 1970. Pp. 373-396.

LOVITT, T. C., and CURTISS, K. A.: Academic response rate as a function of teacher and self-imposed contingencies. *J. Appl. Behav. Anal.*, 2, 49-53, 1969.

MAHONEY, M. J.: Research issues in self-management. *Behav. Ther.*, 3, 45-63, 1972.

MARSTON, A. R., and FELDMAN, S. E.: Toward the use of self-control in behavior modification. *J. Consult. and Clin. Psychol.*, 39, 429-433, 1972.

MASH, E. J., TERDAL, L., and ANDERSON, L. The response-class matrix: A procedure for recording parent-child interactions. *J. Consult. and Clin. Psychol.*, 40, 163-164, 1973.

McFALL, R. M.: Effects of self-monitoring on normal smoking behavior. *J. Consult. and Clin. Psychol.*, 35, 135-142, 1970.

MEDLAND, M. B., and STACHNIK, T. J.: Good-behavior game: A replication and systematic analysis. *J. Appl. Behav. Anal.*, 5, 45-52, 1972.

MEICHENBAUM, D. H.: Cognitive factors in behavior modification: Modifying what clients say to themselves. In: R. D. Rubin, J. P. Brady, and J. D. Henderson (Eds.), *Advances in Behavior Therapy*, Vol. 4. New York: Academic Press, 1973. Pp. 21-36.

MEICHENBAUM, D. H., and GOODMAN, J.: Training impulsive children to talk to themselves: A means of developing self-control. *J. Abnorm. Psychol.*, 77, 115-126, 1971.

MILLENSON, J. R.: *Principles of Behavior Analysis.* New York :Macmillan, 1967.

MILLS, K. C., SOBELL, M. B., and SCHAEFER, H. H.: Training social drinking as an alternative to abstinence for alcoholics. *Behav. Ther.*, 2, 18-27, 1971.

MORGAN, W. G., and BASS, B. A.: Self-control through self-mediated rewards. In: R. D. Rubin, J. P. Brady, and J. D. Henderson (Eds.), *Advances in Behavior Therapy*, Vol. 4. New York: Academic Press, 1973. Pp. 117-126.

NELSON, C. M., WORELL, J., and POLSGROVE, L.: Behaviorally disordered peers as contingency managers. *Behav. Ther.*, 4, 270-276, 1973.

O'BRIEN, F., BUGLE, C., and AZRIN, N. H.: Training and maintaining a retarded child's proper eating. *J. Appl. Behav. Anal.*, 5, 67-72, 1972.

O'LEARY, K. D., BECKER, W. C., EVANS, M. B., and SAUDARGAS, R. A.: A token reinforcement program in a public school: A replication and systematic analysis. *J. Appl. Behav. Anal.*, 2, 3-13, 1969.

O'LEARY, K. D., and DRABMAN, R. S.: Token reinforcement programs in the classroom: A review. *Psychol. Bull.*, 75, 379-398, 1971.

O'LEARY, K. D., and KENT, R.: Behavior modification for social action: Research tactics and problems. In: L. A. Hamerlynck, L. C. Handy, and E. J. Mash (Eds.), *Behavior Change.* Champaign, Ill.: Research Press, 1973. Pp. 69-96.

O'LEARY, K. D., and O'LEARY, S. G.: *Classroom Management: The Successful Use of Behavior Modification.* New York: Pergamon Press, 1972.

PACKARD, R. G.: The control of "classroom attention"; A group contingency for complex behavior. *J. Appl. Behav. Anal.*, 3, 13-28, 1970.

PATTERSON, G. R.: Paper presented at the First Banff International Conference on Behavior Modification, Banff, Alberta, 1969.

PATTERSON, G. R.: Behavioral intervention procedures in the classroom and in the home. In: A. E. Bergin and S. L. Garfield (Eds.), *Handbook of Psychotherapy and Behavior Change.* New York: Wiley, 1971. Pp. 751-775.

PATTERSON, G R.: Changes in status of family members as controlling stimuli: A basis for describing treatment process. In: L. A. Hamerlynck, L. C. Handy, and E. J. Mash (Eds.), *Behavior Change*. Champaign, Ill.: Research Press, 1973. Pp. 169-192.

PATTERSON, G. R., COBB, J. A., and RAY, R. S.: Direct intervention in the classroom: A set of procedures for the aggressive child. In F. W. Clark, D. R. Evans, and L. A. Hamerlynck (Eds.), *Implementing Behavioral Programs for Schools and Clinics*. Champaign, Ill.: Research Press, 1972. Pp. 151-201.

PATTERSON, G. R., COBB, J. A., and RAY, R. S.: A social engineering technology for training aggressive boys. In: H. E. Adams, and I. P. Unikel (Eds.), *Issues and Trends in Behavior Therapy*. Springfield, Ill.: Charles C Thomas, 1973. Pp. 139-224.

PATTERSON, G. R., and REID, J. B.: Reciprocity and coercion: Two facets of social systems. In: C. Neuringer and J. Michael (Eds.), *Behavior Modification in Clinical Psychology*. New York: Appleton-Century-Crofts, 1970. Pp. 133-177.

PATTERSON, G. R., and REID, J. B.: Intervention for small families of aggressive boys: A replication study. *Behav. Res. and Ther.* 11, 383-394, 1973.

PATTERSON, G. R., SHAW, D. A., and EBNER, M. J.: Teachers, peers and parents as agents of change in the classroom. In: F. A. M. Benson (Ed.), *Modifying Deviant School Behaviors in Various Classroom Settings*. Eugene, Ore.: Department of Special Education, College of Education, U. of Oregon, 1969, Monograph No. 1. Pp. 13-48.

PAUL, G. L.: Outcome of systematic desensitization, II. In: C. R. Franks (Ed.), *Behavior Therapy: Appraisal and Status*. New York: McGraw-Hill, 1969. Pp. 105-159.

PETERSON, R. F., and WHITEHURST, G. J.: A variable influencing the performance of generalized imitative behaviors. *J. Appl. Behav. Anal.*, 4, 1-10, 1971.

PHILLIPS, E. L., PHILLIPS, E. A., WOLF, M. M., and FIXSEN, D. L.: Achievement Place: Development of the elected manager system. *J. Appl. Behav. Anal.*, 6, 541-561, 1973.

PREMACK, D.: Reinforcement theory. In: D. Levince (Ed.), *Nebraska Symposium on Motivation, 1965*. Lincoln, Neb.: U. Nebraska Press, 1965. Pp. 123-180.

PREMACK, D., and ANGLIN, B.: On the possibilities of self-control in man and animals. *J. Abnorm. Psychol.*, 81, 137-151, 1973.

REID, J. B., and HENDRIKS, A. F. C. J.: Preliminary analysis of the effectiveness of direct home intervention for the treatment of predelinquent boys who steal. In: L. A. Hamerlynck, L. C. Handy, and E. J. Mash (Eds.), *Behavior Change*. Champaign, Ill.: Research Press, 1973. Pp. 209-220.

RISLEY, T. R.: The effects and side effects of punishing and autistic behaviors of a deviant child. *J. Appl. Behav. Anal.*, 1, 21-34, 1968.

RISLEY, T. R., and CATALDO, M. F.: Evaluation of planned activities: The pla-check measure of classroom participation. In: P. O. Davison, F. W. Clark, and L. A. Hamerlynck (Eds.), *Evaluation of Social Programs in Community, Residential and School Settings*. Champaign, Ill.: Research Press, 1974.

ROSENHAN, D.: On being sane in insane places. *Science*, 179, 250-257, 1973.

SAJWAJ, T., TWARDOSZ, S., and BURKE, M.: Side effects of extinction procedures in a remedial preschool. *J. Appl. Behav. Anal.*, 5, 163-175, 1972.

SCHMIDT, G., and ULRICH, R.: Effects of group contingent events upon classroom noise. *J. Appl. Behav. Anal.*, 2, 171-179, 1969.

SANTAGROSSI, D. A., O'LEARY, K. D., ROMANCZYK, R. G., and KAUFMAN, K. F.: Self-evaluation by adolescents in a psychiatric hospital school token program. *J. Appl. Behav. Anal.*, 6, 277-288, 1973.

SKINNER, B. F.: *Science and Human Behavior*. New York: Macmillan, 1953.

SOLOMON, R. W., and WAHLER, R. G.: Peer reinforcement control of classroom problem behavior. *J. Appl. Behav. Anal.*, 6, 49-56, 1973.

STUART, R. B.: Situational versus self-control. In: R. D. Rubin, A. A. Lazarus, M. Fensterheim, and C. M. Franks (Eds.), *Advances in Behavior Therapy*, Vol. 3. New York: Academic Press, 1972. Pp. 129-146.

SURRATT, P. R., ULRICH, R., and HAWKINS, R. P.: An elementary student as a behavioral engineer. *J. Appl. Behav. Anal.*, 2, 85-92, 1969

TERRACE, H. S.: Extinction of a discriminative operant following discrimination learning with and without errors. *J. Exper. Anal. Behav.*, 12, 571-582, 1969.

THARP, R. G., and WETZEL, R. J.: *Behavior Modification in the Natural Environment.* New York: Academic Press, 1969.

ULLMANN, L. P., and KRASNER, L.: *A Psychological Approach to Abnormal Behavior.* Englewood Cliffs, N. J.: Prentice-Hall, 1969.

UPPER, D., and MEREDITH, L.: A stimulus control approach to the modification of smoking behavior. *Proceedings of the Annual Convention of the American Psychological Association*, 5 (pt. 2), 739-740, 1970.

WAHLER, R. G.: Oppositional children: A quest for parental reinforcement control. *J. Appl. Behav. Anal.*, 2, 159-170 (a), 1969.

WAHLER, R. G.: Setting generality: Some specific and general effects of child behavior therapy. *J. Appl. Behav. Anal.*, 2, 239-246 (b), 1969.

WAHLER, R. G., SPERLING, K. A., THOMAS, M. R., and TEETER, N. C.: The modification of childhood stuttering: Some response-response relationships. *J. Exper. Child Psychol.*, 9, 411-428, 1970.

WALKER, H. M., and BUCKLEY, N. K.: Programming generalization and maintenance of treatment effects across time and across settings. *J. Appl. Behav. Anal.*, 5, 209-224, 1972.

WALKER, H. M., and HOPS, H.: The use of group and individual reinforcement contingencies in the modification of social withdrawal. In: L. A. Hamerlynck, L. C. Handy, and E. J. Mash (Eds.), *Behavior Change.* Champaign, Ill.: Research Press, 1973. Pp. 269-308.

WALTER, H. I., and GILMORE, S. K.: Placebo versus social learning effects in parent training procedures designed to alter the behavior of aggressive boys. *Behav. Ther.*, 4, 361-377, 1973.

WHEELER, A. J., and SULZER, B.: Operant training and generalization of a verbal response form in a speech deficient child. *J. Appl. Behav. Anal.*, 3, 139-148, 1970.

WHITMAN, T. L., MERCURIO, J. R., and CAPONIGRI, V.: Development of social responses in two severely retarded children. *J. Appl. Behav. Anal.*, 3, 133-138, 1970.

WILTZ, N. A., and PATTERSON, G. R.: An evaluation of parent training procedures designed to alter inappropriate aggressive behavior boys. *Behav. Ther.*, 5, 215-221, 1974.

WINETT, R. A.: Attribution of attitude and behavior change and its relevance to behavior therapy. *Psychol. Record*, 20, 17-32, 1970.

WOLF, M. M., and RISLEY, T. R.: Analysis and modification of deviant child behavior. Paper read at the American Psychological Association meeting, Washington, September 1967.

6

Generalization and Contrast Phenomena in Behavior Modification with Children

STEPHEN M. JOHNSON, ORIN D. BOLSTAD,
and GRETCHEN K. LOBITZ

Requests for special treatment of a child usually come from the adult authorities in either the school or the home. In most cases, the adults in one setting perceive the child to be more of a problem than do those in the other, and referral for treatment is usually *initiated* by this "primary" source. Not infrequently, however, the adults in the primary problem setting attribute the difficulties they have with the child to the adults in the other setting. Although this accusatory attribution occurs in both directions, our experience would suggest that it most frequently leads to referral when teachers blame the "home environment" for a child's behavior problems in school. Teachers may recommend or demand that parents seek counseling for their child and/or themselves to remedy the problems which the teacher experiences. Although it is probably less frequent, the converse situation also occurs— parents seek out alternative school placement or special educational programs because of their difficulties with the child at home.

This research was supported by National Institute of Mental Health Grant MH 19633. The authors wish to thank Andrew Christensen for his work in helping complete various aspects of this study. The authors relied heavily in this research on the assistance and cooperation of the staff of the Center at Oregon for Research in the Behavioral Education of the Handicapped (CORBEH). All of the school behavior modification programs described here were conducted through this Center and the present research could not have been done without the generous cooperation of this group. In particular, the authors would like to express their appreciation for the help of Hill Walker, Hy Hops, Charles Greenwood, and the late Joseph Cobb.

Even when the issues are not so clear, the responsible clinician must always wonder to what extent a referred child has difficulties in each of these two important settings. To what extent are the problems exhibited in one setting demonstrated in the other? Which setting would provide either the initial or primary focus of treatment? To what extent can successful treatment in one setting be expected to generalize to the other? When parents or teachers attribute their own difficulties to the environment created by the other, should the clinician accept their formulation or attempt to redefine the problem? Because clinical decisions involve individuals, the answers to these questions cannot be simple or unitary. However, it is hoped that the data reported here on cross-situational assessment of children treated in either the school or home will provide guidelines for formulating answers in individual cases.

The present research was designed to answer two basic questions: (1) Do children who are referred for treatment of behavior problems in one setting also exhibit such behavioral problems in the other? and (2) Does behavior modification treatment in the primary setting have any systematic effect on children's behavior in the other (secondary) setting?

There have been a number of studies on the generalization of treatment effects from the treated to similar but untreated settings in educational and institutional environments (e.g., Kuypers et al., 1968; Meichenbaum et al., 1968; O'Leary et al., 1968; Walker et al., 1975; Walker et al., 1971). With the exception of the Walker et al. (1971) report, these studies yielded no evidence of positive generalization, and the Meichenbaum et al. (1968) study yielded trends suggesting behavioral contrast.*

When the present research project was begun, only two studies involving very small samples had been reported on the generalization of behavior change from the home to the school (Martin, 1967; Wahler, 1969). Since then, a few additional reports have emerged on the issue of generalization of children's behavior and behavior change across these settings.

Martin's (1967) investigation differs from most others to be reviewed

---

* As employed here, contrast effect simply refers to the situation in which a treatment program appears to effect a desired change in the treated setting (e.g., a decrease in aggressive behavior) but the opposite in another, untreated setting (e.g., an increase in aggressive behavior). This is a less technical and more general definition than is typically employed in research on this phenomenon. The more commonly used technical definition will be detailed in the discussion section together with a presentation of the implications of controlled laboratory research on behavioral contrast for work in applied settings.

in this context because it does not involve behavioral observation assessment in *both* settings and involves an intervention which is somewhat different from the usual behavior modification employed in the other investigations. In this study, four children exhibiting behavior problems and underachievement were selected for study. All children and their parents were assessed in a structured laboratory setting on dimensions of dyadic communications. In addition, the children's teachers were asked to describe the children's behavior on the Peterson Problem Checklist (Peterson, 1961). Two of these children and their parents were then exposed to six intervention sessions over a two-week period in the clinic. These sessions were directed at modifying problematic interaction patterns through instruction and reinforcement. The two other families served as no-treatment controls. Results indicated that reductions in negative parent-child interaction for the treated families were accompanied by marked improvement in the teachers' ratings of the children. Changes on the interaction measures were less dramatic for control children. Teacher ratings showed a less favorable rating at post-assessment for one control subject but a somewhat more favorable rating for the other. Teachers were uninformed as to which children were treated and which were not. This early pilot investigation, then, showed some weak evidence for generalization on the basis of teacher ratings.

Wahler (1969) selected two children who exhibited similar behavior problems in the home and school. The children received behavior modification treatment in the home setting through parent training. Although the children's behavior changed appropriately in the homes, their problem behaviors in school remained at baseline level. Skindrud (1972) examined behavioral results with four boys who exhibited behavior problems in both settings, but received initial treatment only for the home problems. The results of this study substantiated Wahler's (1969) findings in showing significant change in the home but no change in the school. The question of pre-intervention generalization was not addressed in either the Wahler (1969) study or the Skindrud (1972) study since the subjects were selected because they exhibited behavior problems in both settings. In a report of early results from the present project, Walker, Hops, and Johnson (1975) examined the home behavior of five children referred for special classroom treatment for conduct behavior problems. Results showed that only one of the five children exhibited a rate of deviant behavior at home which would be considered problematic by normative standards. Unfortunately, the only child who was deviant at home dropped out of the program. The other four all showed a modest but nonsignificant increase ($p < .06$, two-tailed) in their deviant behavior rate at home after behavior modification treatment in a special classroom. This trend suggests a behavioral contrast effect.

Wahler (1973) reported on six children observed both in home and school after referral for treatment. Of the five children who showed behavioral disturbance in at least one setting, only one demonstrated any cross-situational consistency in behavior problems. Wahler (1974) has also given a very detailed report on three other children observed and serially treated over a two-year period in both settings. Although two of these children were perceived to have problems in both settings, the specific behavioral clusters which were problematic differed. In two cases, treatment in one setting seemed to have unpredicted effects on behavior in the other. In one case, desired increases in studying at school were accompanied by an undesired increase in self-stimulation and a decrease in social interaction at home. In the second case, desired decreases in oppositional behavior at home seemed to be accompanied by unexpected increases in oppositional behavior and peer interactions at school. While the second case could in a general way be characterized as an example of behavioral contrast, the phenomena illustrated in the first are obviously more complex.

In a recently completed study, discussed in Chapter 8 of this volume, Bernal et al. report on the preintervention generality of children's behavior in school and home settings. Twenty-one children were observed in both settings employing the same coding system. Four behavioral summary scores reflecting Desirable, Annoying, and Deviant Behavior, and the Child's Ratio of Compliance were used. Cross-situational correlations on these variables were all negligible and nonsignificant. In another recently completed report, Patterson (1974) noted that 17 of the 27 conduct-problem children treated in his project displayed problems at school as well as in the home.

Several investigators, coming out of another research tradition, have correlated parents' ratings of children's behavior or traits with similar ratings obtained by teachers (e.g., Becker, 1960; Rutter & Graham, 1966; Wolff, 1967). In general, these investigators found low and nonsignificant correlations between such ratings. Wolff (1967) did find, however, that as a group, children referred for outpatient or hospital treatment received higher behavior disturbance scores from teachers than did the control group children.

Thus, the more global findings as reported by Wolff (1967) and Patterson (1974) give evidence for some cross-situation generality while the other research reviewed generally suggests little or no generality. With the exception of Martin's (1967) early results, no study has provided evidence for either generalization or contrast in behavior change across these settings. The interpretation of all of these earlier reports is complicated, however, by the generally small size of the samples involved and the lack of control group comparisons. The present research attempted to remedy these difficulties. In addition, this research examined both the relationship of preintervention behavior across settings and the generalization effects of intervention in one setting on behavior in the other. Finally, in this research, both observational data and parent or teacher reports were examined to answer the generalization questions.

METHOD

Subjects

Thirty-five children, selected because they were perceived to have behavior problems in either the home or school, were employed in this study. Fifteen of these children were referred for outpatient treatment for "active" behavior problems in the home setting. Families remaining in the program received family intervention treatment as described in Eyberg and Johnson (1974) and will hereafter be referred to as the "home-problem" sample. The mean age of the children in this sample was 8.5 years (range, 5.3 to 12.8). Twelve children, hereafter referred to as the "school-problem" sample, were referred for treatment of behavior problems in the school setting. Four of these children received behaviorally oriented treatment in a special classroom designed for "acting-out" children as described elsewhere (Walker, Hops, and Fiegenbaum, 1971; Walker, Hops, and Johnson, 1975). One child dropped out of this program. Three others received behaviorally oriented treatment in a similar special classroom designed to deal with children who displayed excessive social withdrawal as described by Walker, Hops, and Greenwood (1974). The four remaining children were treated in their regular classrooms for excessive acting-out behavior under behavioral programs directed by J. Cobb and H. Hops (Hops and Hutton, 1974). The mean age of children in the entire school-problem sample was 7.9 years (range, 6.4 to 9.1).

Eight children were recruited for research purposes and selected because their teachers perceived them to have behavior problems at school sufficiently severe to *warrant* referral for special treatment. This group, which was recruited in the same manner as the school-problem sample, will hereafter be referred to as the "school-problem control" sample. The mean age of children in this sample was 7.5 (range, 7.2 to 8.3). In the school-problem sample, children were accepted for treatment only if behavioral data confirmed the presence of teacher-perceived behavior problems. In the school-problem sample, teacher perception of the child's serious behavior problems was sufficient for inclusion but, as the results will indicate, the two school-problem samples were essentially equivalent. Similarly, in the home-problem sample, the parents' perception of serious behavior problems was sufficient to warrant initial assessment.

Measurement Instruments

Walker Problem Behavior Identification Checklist. The Walker Problem Behavior Identification Checklist (Walker, 1970) was administered to the children's teachers. This 50-item, weighted checklist of behaviors yields a total behavior problem score and five separate factor scores. The total score has been shown to have a split-half reliability of .98. Further, the total score has been shown to reliably discriminate between normal and behaviorally disturbed children as defined by other criteria. Normative data have been collected on a 21-teacher sample involving ratings of 534 children in grades four, five, and six (Walker, 1970). In the present study, Walker's (1970) guidelines were followed in defining a child as behaviorally disturbed if his score was one standard deviation above the normative mean.

Bi-Polar Adjective Checklist. The Bi-Polar Adjective Checklist was administered to the parents of all the children before and after their respective treatments. This 47-item checklist originated by Becker (1960) calls for parental description of the child and yields five factor scores for parents as derived by Patterson and Fagot (1967). In previous research (Lobitz, G., and Johnson, 1975), this measure has been found to discriminate well between referred and nonreferred children on all five factors. Normative data has been collected in this laboratory on a sample of 146 parents of 73 children between the ages of 4.0 and 8.0 years of age. Analyses of these data indicated that the Aggressiveness, Activity, and Conduct Problem factors correlate highly, and their sum has been found to discriminate very well between referred and nonreferred children (Lobitz, G., and Johnson, 1975). For the purposes of the present investigation, children whose score fell one standard deviation above the normative mean for children aged 6.0-8.0 were considered to be perceived as behavior problems by their parents.

Home Observations

Home observations were conducted under the same conditions and with the same coding system as employed in earlier normative research on child behavior and family interaction (e.g., Johnson et al., 1973). The observations were conducted for 45 minutes each day during the hour prior to the family's regular dinner time when all family members were usually present. Five families in the school-problem sample were observed for three days; all other observation statistics are based on five days of observation. All family members were required to be present and remain in a specified two-room area during the observations. Further, home observation rules prohibited interaction with the observer, operation of the television set, and the presence of visitors in the home. The parents were instructed to try to behave as they would if no observers were present and to present as representative a picture of their family as possible.

A revision of the observational system developed by Patterson et al. (1969) was employed. This revised system utilizes 35 distinct behavior categories to record all the behaviors of target children and family members who interact with them.

On the basis of previous research, 15 behaviors were designated as "deviant" for children, and the sum of the rates of these behaviors was designated as the child's deviant behavior score. The deviant behaviors are demand attention, violation of standing command, destructiveness, high rate behavior, humiliation, noncompliance, physical negativeness, smart talk, teasing, tantrums, whining, yelling, threatening command, ignoring, and negativism. These behaviors were most consistently described by a sample of 146 parents of young children to be deviant. Previous research has indicated that these behaviors tend to receive a relatively high proportion of negative consequences from the social environment (Wahl et al., 1974) and that there is a strong relationship between the average parent rating of the behavior as deviant and the average family's tendency to respond to it in a negative manner (Adkins and Johnson, 1972). The validity of the child deviant behavior score is also enhanced by the finding that it discriminates significantly between a group of children referred for outpatient treatment of behavior problems and a matched nonreferred group (Lobitz, G., and Johnson, 1975).

Other research has demonstrated that when parents are instructed in home observations to make their children appear deviant the child deviant behavior score is reliably and dramatically higher than when they are instructed to make them appear nondeviant (Johnson and Lobitz, 1974). W. Lobitz and Johnson (1974) have replicated this finding in families with both deviant and nondeviant children and demonstrated that this discrepancy is primarily due to parents' ability to make their children appear deviant. Previous research has also indicated that the child deviant behavior score has high stability over time (Johnson and Bolstad, 1973). The child's deviant behavior score was used as the central dependent variable from the home observation in this study. Normative data are available on this home observation statistic for a sample of 73 children between the ages of 4.0 and 8.0. For the purposes of this study, a child was considered deviant on this measure if he or she fell one standard deviation above the mean for children between the ages of 6.0 and 8.0 ($N = 40$).

Observations were made by a group of young female research assistants. The observers were trained continuously on a weekly basis throughout the period involved in this study. Except for a few information leaks, the observers were unaware of the status of the children, the treatment stage, and the purpose of hypothesis of this study. A different observer was always employed for the baseline and termination assessments on any given child.

A calibrating observer accompanied the regular observer for one day of observation on 49 occasions covering all 32 families. The observer agreement was computed by a correlation between the two data sets on the deviant behavior score, as recommended by Johnson and Bolstad (1973) and Hartmann (1975). The correlation between the sets of observers on the overall deviant behavior proportion was .94.

School Observations

In general, children were observed in their classrooms on five consecutive days for 30 minutes per day. These periods were chosen on a random basis. Due to the usual fluctuation in school scheduling, observers obtained an average of 142.78 minutes of behavioral data per child. The children's classroom behavior was coded by the system developed by Cobb and Hops (1972). This system contains 37 code categories and was used to record the behavior of the target children as well as all of their interactions with their teachers and peers. This system was used on all the children except the first five school-problem children observed. These children were observed on a system devised by Walker (1971).

For the school observation system used on all other children, 11 codes of the total 37 were selected on an a priori basis to represent child deviant behavior in the classroom situation. This deviant behavior code comprised the dependent variable from this data source. Deviant behavior codes were call out, look at another, talk about other material, play, disruptive behavior, physical negative, noisiness, inappropriate locale, noncompliance to management commands, noncompliance to academic commands, and noncompliance to disciplinary commands.

The observers were trained continuously on this coding system, and the same procedures as outlined above were employed to keep the observers unaware of the children's status and treatment stage in the research.

Observer agreement was checked in 26 separate sessions, using the percent agreement calculation system for all codes employed. To count as an agreement, both observers were required to see the same behavior in the same 10-second block. Agreements were calculated for target children, and teacher and peer behaviors. The average percent agreement in this sample was 87.88%.

Unfortunately, there are no adequate normative data on this coding system. However, on the basis of previous experience with this system in classrooms, the authors designated a cutoff score for considering children to be deviant by this measure. Thus, on each of the two measures used in the home and school, a deviant cutoff score was operationalized to help answer the questions posed.

RESULTS

The question of preintervention generalization will be considered first. At the most general level, it may be asked: What proportion of those children referred for treatment of behavioral difficulties in one setting exhibited similar difficulties in the other? This question may be answered both in terms of the observed rates of relevant behaviors in the secondary setting and by the report of significant adults in that setting. For this initial analysis, the school-problem sample and the school-problem control sample were combined. This was done because the recruitment procedures were nearly identical for both samples, and the

TABLE 1

Percentage of Children in Each Sample Demonstrating
"Deviance" on Each of Four Measures

	Walker	*School Observation*	*Becker* *M*	*F*	*Home Observation*
School Problem Sample	82%	100%	67%	78%	45%
Home Problem Sample	67%	50%	100%	100%	47%

teacher ratings and observed deviancy levels of both groups were quite
similar. The mean Walker score for the school-problem sample was 27;
for the control sample, it was 31. This difference was not significant
($t < 1$). The deviant behavior scores in school were also similar and
not significantly different (school-problem sample deviant behavior percent mean $= 25.66\%$, control sample deviant behavior percent mean $=$
28.41%).

It will be recalled that, except for observed deviance in the school,
children were characterized as "deviant" on each measure on which they
scored beyond one standard deviation as defined by the appropriate
normative sample. Since such a normative sample was not available for
the school observation data, an arbitrary cutoff point was established
based on previous research with similar observation systems. Any child
whose deviant behavior exceeded 20% of his total behavior was characterized as deviant in the school. The proportion of children considered
deviant by each measure in each of the two samples is presented in
Table 1. Considering the combined school-problem sample first, it can
be seen that for the 11 children for whom Walker Problem Behavior
Identification Checklist scores were available, 82% of them would be
considered deviant in the primary (school) setting. For the same children, 100% had deviant behavior scores in the classroom. It will be
recalled that the first five school-problem children in this project were
observed under a different coding system than that used for the other
children, and their teachers were not administered the Walker Problem
Behavior Identification Checklist. The behavioral data on these children
as reported in Walker, Hops, and Johnson (1975) clearly indicate, however, that they were deviant in the classroom as determined by systematic
observation, and their teachers referred them because of active behavior
problems. Thus, it was considered appropriate to include these children
in the overall analysis of behavioral generalization in the secondary
(home) setting.

For the combined school-problem sample $(N = 19)$, 42% would be considered deviant at home by the home observation criteria. This observed percentage significantly exceeded the expected percentage based on available normative data $(\chi^2 = 9.76, p < .01)$. Using the parent rating scale, 67% of the mothers and 78% of the fathers gave ratings to their children which would place them in the deviant category. The Chi-Square for both proportions was significant beyond the .01 level of confidence. Thus, by all criteria, a greater than chance proportion of the school-problem children were documented to have behavior problems in the home setting.

Considering the home-problem sample, it can be seen by reference to Table 1 that 100% of both mothers and fathers described their children as deviant via the verbal report measure. Only 47% of these children, however, had deviant behavior scores which were one standard deviation above the normative mean. Possible reasons for this discrepancy have been discussed at length elsewhere (Eyberg and Johnson, 1974; Lobitz, G., and Johnson, 1975). Similar results have been reported by Hendriks (1972) on children seen in G. R. Patterson's laboratory.

Sixty-seven percent of these children referred for home problems were perceived to exhibit significant behavioral difficulties in the classroom by teachers as measured by the Walker Problem Behavior Identification Checklist $(\chi^2 = 21.87, p < .01)$. By the behavioral observation criterion, 50% of these children were classified as showing problematic behaviors at a rate designated deviant $(> 20\%)$.

At a more precise level, it may be asked to what extent the behavioral rates and behavior ratings correlated across the two settings. This question must, however, be answered in the context of considering the validity of the measures used. In other words, before considering the correlation between the teachers' rating of a child in school and his or her deviant behavior rate at home, the correlation between the parents' rating of home behavior and the actual behavior in that setting must be considered. All such correlations should be examined with a full recognition of the considerable error variance that can be introduced by the use of different raters responding to the rating scale forms. It is known that the trained observers operate under highly similar response sets in examining children's behavior, but it is to be expected that different parents and teachers approach rating scales with different response sets. This factor introduces considerable error variance in the scores obtained and would at least partially account for the low correlations obtained in other research where different raters were used

TABLE 2

Rank Order Correlations Between Four Measures
on All Children

	T Walker	School Deviant Behavior	Becker M	Becker F	Deviant Behavior Percent
Walker Checklist	—	—	—	—
School Deviant Behavior %	.01	—	—	—
M	—.04	.20	—	—
Becker F	.28	.21	—	—
Home Deviant Behavior %	.35*	.03	—.07	.10	—

* p < .05.

(Becker, 1960; Rutter and Graham, 1966; Wolff, 1967). Nevertheless, since ratings by parents and teachers are used to label children as deviant, it is of considerable interest to know to what extent these ratings may be used to estimate a child's observed deviancy. The rank order correlations relating all measures on all children in this sample are presented in Table 2. Examination of Table 2 will reveal that all correlations were negligible, and all but one were not significant. Very little relationship was documented between parents' and teachers' ratings of children and their behavior in either the primary or secondary settings. The one exception to this involved the correlation between the Walker Problem Behavior Identification Checklist and the observed deviant behavior percent in the home. Since only one of the nine correlations was significant, however, this rather weak relationship should be cautiously interpreted. These correlations should also be examined in light of the fact that the sample examined here is an extreme one in terms of the deviancy levels in both settings and that the full range of the population is not represented. This factor would also tend to lower the magnitude of correlations.

Behavior Change

In examining the question of generalization of behavior change, it is first necessary to document change in the primary setting. In each analysis which follows, changes will be examined in both the primary and secondary settings, and these changes will be compared with those observed in the school-problem control group. In each case, the within-group changes were tested by the use of paired-observation t-tests. Comparisons with the school-problem control group were accomplished using 2 x 2 analyses of variance with repeated measures on one factor (time). The group x time interaction in these analyses was the critical test of differential group change over time. All deviant behavior proportions were subjected to arc-sin transformations before statistical analyses.

The school-problem control group should be considered a quasi-control group (as in Campbell and Stanley, 1966), especially with regard to the home-treated sample. In spite of some differences in recruitment procedures and pre-post time lag, the school-problem control sample bears considerable similarity to the home-treated sample in terms of pre-intervention scores on both parent report and home observation data. In addition, these control-group data represent one of very few examples of research where such behavioral data have been collected on an untreated sample.

School-problem samples. The three school-problem samples will be considered separately, since the treatment procedures and results differed somewhat for each. The first four cases to be considered were children referred for active behavior problems in the school setting and treated in a special classroom under the direction of H. Walker. The behavioral data on the children treated in this classroom have been analyzed in detail in Walker, Hops, and Johnson (1975). This analysis clearly demonstrated that the children's behavior consistently improved in the classroom from baseline to termination as a consequence of treatment in this special classroom ($p < .01$).

An examination of the changes in the secondary setting for this sample, however, revealed that the children's deviant behavior at home increased in every case, from a pre-intervention average of 1.35% to a termination average of 2.85%. A t-test for paired observations revealed that this reliable change approached statistical significance ($t = 3.04$, $df = 3$, $p < .06$). A contrast of this group with the school-problem control group is of questionable meaning because the pre-test deviant behavior mean of the control group of 9.71% was considerably higher than that of the treated group ($t = 2.73$, $df = 10$, $p < .05$). In addition, the pre-post time lag of home observation differed appreciably between these two groups. The lag was 3.55 months for the treated group, but only 2.05 for the control group. Although the deviant behavior decreased slightly to 8.35% in the control group while it increased for the treated group, the 2 x 2 analysis of variance on these data did not yield a significant group x time interaction.

The second school-treated sample involved three children referred to another structured classroom, under the direction of H. Walker, which was designed to deal with children exhibiting excessive social withdrawal. The behavioral data again clearly showed that the deviant behavior of these children was dramatically reduced at school. Unfortunately, the baseline data for one of these subjects were lost; but data on the other two subjects indicate that inappropriate behavior was reliably reduced from a baseline level of 63% to a post-intervention level of 33%. In addition, the post-intervention data on the other child indicate that his deviant behavior percent was 7.14 after intervention— clearly well within normal limits. In addition, H. Walker's data on this child further support the fact that a clear reduction in inappropriate behavior was observed from baseline to follow-up in the regular classroom (59% reduction). Although statistical analyses of these data are somewhat questionable because of the very small sample size, it is interesting to note that the changes in the two cases for which data are complete were sufficiently dramatic to be statistically significant both by the paired observation t-test ($p < .025$) and by contrast to the school-problem control group ($p < .01$).

In this same sample, however, the rates of deviant behavior in the home increased for two of the three children. Unlike the previous sample, the two children who evidenced increases in deviant behavior at home were initially in the deviant range on this measure. One child increased from a baseline level of 14.3% deviant behavior at home to a post-intervention level of 22.2%; the other child, from 6.3% to 9.0%. In the third case, deviant behavior decreased from a baseline average of 2.0% to a post-intervention average of .1%. The average pre-post time lag of home observation was quite comparable for this group and the control group—2.19 months for the treated group versus 2.05 for the control group. The average increase for these three cases was not statistically significant, however, either by paired observation t-tests or by contrast with the school-problem control group in a 2 x 2 analysis of variance. And, in contrast, parents consistently rated their children as improved at termination on the Becker Bi-Polar Adjective Checklist ($p < .10$ for both mothers and fathers).

It is interesting to note that six of the seven children who were treated with these very effective special classroom programs showed a concurrent increase in deviant behavior as measured in the home. The average deviant behavior percent at home increased in the treated group from 4.0% at baseline to 6.1% at termination ($t = 1.82$, $df = 6$, $p < .06$) while the control group mean decreased from 9.7% to 8.4%. Although the deviant behavior percents were higher for the control group at both points, these differences were not significant. A contrast was performed between the seven children treated in the special classroom with the eight control children. The 2 x 2 analysis of variance revealed that the group x time interaction was not statistically significant, but the trend is sufficiently obvious to be of interest ($F = 2.08$, $df = 1,13$, $p < .20$).

The third school-problem sample involved four children treated in their regular classrooms in a program under the direction of J. Cobb and H. Hops. The changes in the overall percent of inappropriate classroom behavior did not, in and of themselves, support the efficacy of that program, but other data sources do provide evidence of desired changes. The inappropriate behavior percent showed a nonsignificant increase from a preintervention level of 26% to a post-intervention level of 33%. A closer examination of the data revealed, however, that these four children had relatively high rates of high intensity, acting-out behavior. The high intensity deviant behaviors coded in this system were preselected—disruptive behavior, physical negative, noisiness, inappropriate locale, noncompliance to management commands, noncompliance to academic commands, and noncompliance to disciplinary commands. The average high intensity deviant behavior percent decreased from 8.19% to 5.93%. The decrease which was realized in three of these four cases approached significance by a paired observation t-test ($t = 1.78$, $df = 3$, $p < .10$, one-tailed). In addition, all four children were given improved scores by their teachers on the Walker Problem Behavior Identification Checklist. A paired observation t-test indicated that this reduction also approached significance ($t = 2.18$, $df = 3$, $p < .07$). The average pre-post time lag of home observation was 2.44 months for this group as compared to 2.05 months for the control. The positive changes observed both on the Walker Problem Behavior Identification Checklist and on the high intensity deviant behavior scores were not significant when contrasted with the school-problem control group in a 2 x 2 analysis of variance. In general, then, the evidence of positive change in the primary setting is less persuasive for this sample than for those cases treated in the special classroom.

For these four children, there was no evidence of either positive generalization or contrast effects in the secondary setting as measured either by the parents' responses on the Becker Bi-polar Adjective Checklist or by the observational data. For the group as a whole, the changes in these measures were negligible and nonsignificant.

Home-treated sample. Complete data at baseline and termination in both settings are available on only 8 of the 15 children originally referred for home treatment. This attrition is due to children being referred elsewhere for treatment after the initial assessment ($N = 5$), families dropping out of treatment ($N = 1$), or the fact that treatment was completed in the summer months when school was not in session ($N = 1$). All the parents in this sample described their children more favorably at termination than at baseline on the parent rating form. These changes were significant for both mothers ($t = 6.38$, $df = 6$, $p < .005$) and fathers ($t = 3.65$, $df = 6$, $p < .005$). As indicated earlier, no change in parent ratings was observed in the control group. Two separate analyses of variance on mother and father ratings comparing these two groups reveal significant groups x sessions interaction at the .05 level of confidence.

Consistent with previous research (Eyberg and Johnson, 1974), the deviant behavior score derived from observation did not document the efficacy of treatment in the primary (home) setting (paired observation $t > 1$). Other behavioral data, however, did document such beneficial changes. For example, when those behaviors which were directly related to treatment programs were isolated, there was an overall 46% reduction in targeted deviant behaviors. This difference approached statistical significance ($t = 1.54$, $df = 7$, $p < .10$). Parent-collected data on treated behavior problems indicated an average reduction of 64% from baseline to termination. Thus, there was evidence of change in the primary setting on the basis of observed targeted behaviors, parent attitude, and parent-collected data, but the changes in overall observed deviant behavior were disappointing. As indicated earlier, there was no appreciable change in the deviant behavior rate of the control group, and the 2 x 2 analysis of variance yielded a nonsignificant group x time interaction on total deviant behavior.

Examination of data in the secondary (school) setting for this sample indicates that the average teacher rating on the Walker Problem Behavior Identification Checklist was virtually identical at both testing periods (27.16 at baseline versus 27.33 at termination). Thus, there was not a significant pre-post change on this measure, and a comparison with the control group revealed no significant main effects or interactions.

The observational data from the classroom are presented in Figure 1

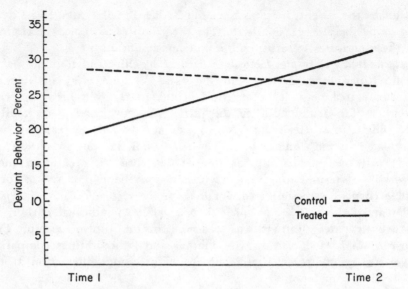

FIGURE 1. Observed deviant behavior in school for the home-treated and school-problem control samples at two time points.

for the home-treated and school problem control samples. As can be seen, the control group mean is higher than the home-treated mean at baseline, but the difference was not significant $(t < 1)$. On the average, the behavior of the treated children increased somewhat from baseline to termination, and this increase occurred for four of the five children on whom such data were collected.* This increase was not significant by a paired observation (within group) t-test $(t = 2.04, df = 4, p < .12,$ two-tailed). The behavior of the school-problem control group improved slightly but not significantly $(t < 1)$. The 2 x 2 analysis of variance contrasting the home-treated and school-problem control groups yielded a significant group x sessions interaction $(F = 5.46, df = 1,11, p < .05)$. This interaction is obviously a function both of the slight improvement in the control group and the noticeable deterioration in the home-treated group. Thus, by this observational measure, there is some evidence of a contrast effect in the classroom as a function of treatment

---

* School observation could not be obtained on three of the eight children due to unavoidable delays in training coders. Thus, there were eight children with Walker Problem Behavior Identification Checklists at baseline and termination, but only five children with a similar set of school observations.

in the home. The quasi-control nature of the comparison group should not be lost sight of. In particular, it should be clarified that the time lag between school assessments was considerably longer for the home-treated sample than for the school-problem control sample (3.48 months versus 1.79 months).

DISCUSSION

The results of this study seem to provide persuasive evidence for pre-intervention generality of children's behavior problems across settings. Children who were perceived to have behavioral difficulties in one setting had a good chance of demonstrating deviance in the other. This was true both in terms of the behavior ratings by significant adults in the alternate setting and in terms of objective behavioral observation by trained observers. These results lend some support to the commonly held belief that high levels of behavioral deviance in children have some cross-situational consistency. By the same token, it should be emphasized that these same results indicate that children who have problems in one setting do not necessarily have them in the other.

It is interesting to note in examining Table 1 that the verbal report measures always designated a higher proportion of children as deviant than did the observational measures. This was true for both the primary setting and the secondary setting. Such results for the primary setting may simply reflect the referral process. When parents or teachers refer their wards for special treatment, they are likely to indicate on verbal report inventories that the children are in fact deviant. Of more interest is the fact that this same trend holds for the secondary setting. For example, 67% of the mothers and 78% of the fathers of children who experienced school problems rated their children in the deviant range on the Becker Bi-Polar Adjective Checklist. The home observation data indicated that only 45% of these children would be rated as deviant by this criterion. The same trend may be observed in comparing the proportion of children in the home-problem sample who were characterized as deviant by their teacher and by the school observation (63% versus 50%). These discrepancies may be partially due to communication between the parents and teachers, and reflect more of a social labeling process than an accurate perception of the children's behavior in the secondary setting.

Although these results as presented in Table 1 are analyzed in a very global fashion, this presentation seems to be most relevant, particularly for applied purposes. To the present authors, it does not seem necessary to document that the same clusters of behavior problems are represented in both settings to demonstrate the generality of behavior problems. The school and home settings are very different, and behaviors which are inappropriate in one may be quite appropriate in the other. The school setting is generally a much more restrictive and prescriptive one, in which a far greater number of behaviors are inappropriate. This probably accounts for the fact that a deviant behavior percent of 6% is in the deviant range in the home while such a percent at school would generally be viewed as very low indeed.

Neither does it seem necessary to demonstrate high correlations between the deviant behavior rates in both settings. While in the present study the rank order correlations between school deviance and home deviance as measured by any criterion were very low, children who were deviant in one setting had a far higher probability than would be expected by chance of being deviant in the alternate setting. The various methodological problems outlined earlier could be expected to contribute to lowering these correlations. These problems include the variability in response sets that individuals use when completing verbal report questionnaires, and the fact that there is a rather restricted range of scores in this generally deviant sample. The observational data in the classroom are particularly restricted in range, thereby contributing to low correlations.

In Chapter 8 of this volume Bernal et al. report similar analyses on a sample of 21 kindergarten and first grade boys involved in a home-treatment program. These investigators also found low correlations between behavioral scores across school and home settings. Thirty percent of these boys scored beyond one standard deviation of the normative mean established in their laboratory on various disruptive school behaviors. This represents nearly twice the expected proportion and, although it reflects slightly less generality than that catalogued here, the finding seems consistent with the present results. On low rate, high amplitude deviant behaviors, however, the home-treated and normative samples were found to be quite similar. Parent and teacher report data were collected but not reported in a similar form. In attempting to integrate the results of these two investigations, it is well to consider that the children in the Bernal et al. study were considerably younger than those observed in the present research. In addition, the families involved in that study were recruited for the home treatment program rather than being selected on the basis of community or self referral.

These differences could well be related to any differences in cross-situational consistency as catalogued by observation or verbal report measures.

In considering the issue of behavior change generalization, the fairly consistent trends in the direction of behavioral contrast are of interest and potentially of considerable importance. Such trends were clearly present in the changes in school behavior of those subjects treated in the home context and in the home-recorded behavior of those children treated in the special structured classrooms. No such effects were apparent, however, for those school-problem children treated in their regular classrooms. These trends should be interpreted with caution because of the small sample sizes involved, the relatively small magnitude of the effects, and the marginal statistical significance of many of the results. Nevertheless, the consistency of these trends across samples seems to warrant the most serious attention. While the present authors are not at all confident that these results will reliably replicate, the present findings together with the results of several other investigations lead to the conclusion that such contrast effects *can* occur. Thus, a review of the available literature on such effects and the various explanations accounting for them seems warranted.

A review of behavior modification studies indicates that such contrast effects are not without precedent. Meichenbaum et al. (1968) treated institutionalized behavior-problem adolescent girls by initially reinforcing appropriate classroom behavior during the afternoon but not during the morning. The proportion of appropriate behavior in the afternoon class increased from a baseline average of 46% to 65% during the first week of intervention and 83% during the second week. At the same time, however, appropriate behavior in the morning class declined from a baseline average of 54% to 52% during the first week and 36% during the second week. Skindrud (1972) subjected this data to statistical analysis and found that the reduction from baseline observed in the second week was significant at the .10 (two-tailed) level of confidence. Nine of the ten subjects in this experiment showed a reduction of appropriate behavior in this nonreinforced period. In addition, the authors report anecdotally that one subject clearly stated that she and her classmates would not "shape up" without reinforcement. Although less persuasive, both Skindrud (1972) and Wahler (1974) have discussed individual cases in which children's improvement in the treated setting was accompanied by undesirable behavioral changes in another setting. Such changes in individual cases may merely reflect chance fluctuation, but it seems noteworthy that these investigators considered the effects of sufficient substance to discuss them at length.

Two separate areas of more basic research yield data which may bear on the present concerns. The first is the body of research on the behavioral contrast effect. The second is that research in the attribution theory literature which involves the concept of "overjustification."

Contrast effects have been demonstrated with animal subjects placed on multiple reinforcement schedules. A multiple schedule is one in which at least two schedules of reinforcement are alternately applied with different discriminative stimuli associated with each schedule. Contrast effects are said to occur when (a) the reinforcement schedule associated with one discriminative stimulus (S_1) is altered, (b) the response rate associated with that stimulus (S_1) is altered, and (c) the response rate to the alternate discriminative stimulus (S_2) changes in the opposite direction from that observed for S_1.

The description of one experiment which demonstrates the contrast effect may clarify the usual procedure. Reynolds (1961) trained pigeons to respond to both a green and red light as discriminative stimuli. Both stimuli were associated with the same variable interval (VI3′) schedule of reinforcement. After five sessions of such training, the animals were subjected to discrimination training through a cessation of reinforcement in the presence of the green light. The results indicated that as the animals decreased their rate of responding to the green light, they increased their rate of responding to the red light. Such an increase in response to the unaltered stimulus is termed a positive transfer. The term "negative transfer" is applied to the phenomenon in which the response rate to the altered component increases while the response rate to the unaltered component decreases.

Research on contrast effects is quite extensive, and several reviews of these studies are available in the literature (e.g., Dunham, 1968; Freeman, 1971; Terrace, 1966). Two basic explanatory hypotheses have been proposed with reference to the contrast effect. Terrace (1966) and Amsel (1958) have argued that positive contrast effects may be due to some kind of emotional arousal elicited by extinction or time-out. Others have argued that while this emotionality hypothesis may be a viable one for explaining positive contrast, it appears less persuasive in the explanation of negative contrast. Reynolds and Limpo (1968) have argued that contrast is a more or less lawful phenomenon affected by changes in the *relative* amount of reinforcement associated with the discriminative stimuli. Thus, in the earlier experiment by Reynolds (1961), there is *relatively* more reinforcement in the presence of the red light when the green light is associated with extinction procedures. For a more extensive discussion of these theoretical controversies, the reader is referred to Freeman (1971) and Dunham (1968). Although the contrast effects observed in the animal literature are somewhat more precisely defined than the more global contrast changes observed in the present study, the explanatory concepts used may shed light on the contrast effect phenomena observed in treatment studies such as the present one.

Attribution theorists have frequently demonstrated that extrinsic reward can differentially influence one's attitudes or behaviors. According to attribution theory, such effects are due to changes in the individuals' perception of the causes of their behavior (cf. Bem, 1967, 1972; Nisbett and Valins, 1971). Theories of self-perception emphasize the importance of individuals' accounting for their own behavior and postulate that individuals will perceive their behavior as externally directed if externally controlled contingencies are sufficiently salient and unambiguous. When external contingencies are not apparent or appear insufficient to maintain behavior, the individuals will tend to attribute their behavior to more intrinsic motivations. This theorizing is most germane to the present concerns for the derivation of the "overjustification" hypothesis. Lepper et al. (1973) define this hypothesis as ". . . the proposition that a person's intrinsic interest in an activity may be undermined by inducing him to engage in that activity as an explicit means to some extrinsic goal" (p. 130). These authors and others (e.g., Deci, 1971; Nisbett and Valins, 1971) have reasoned that if external reinforcement or justification for behavior is "psychologically oversufficient," individuals may tend to perceive their engaging in that behavior as externally determined and of less intrinsic value. This proposition would predict that such "overjustification" would result in a subsequent decrease in the relevant behavior in situations in which the external reinforcement or justification was absent. Although Nisbett and Valins (1971) reviewed a few reinterpreted experiments which gave some evidence for this hypothesis, there has been rather little direct experimental testing of it.

An experiment by Lepper et al. (1973), however, using a subject population and setting which make it highly relevant to the present concerns, provides persuasive support for the "overjustification" hypothesis. In this experiment, nursery school children were provided the opportunity of engaging in a drawing activity in a relatively unstructured classroom situation. Those subjects who demonstrated some sustained participation in drawing were selected as subjects for the experiment. Children were brought to a separate experimental room and asked to engage in drawing for a six-minute period. One-third of the children contracted to engage in the activity in order to obtain an extrinsic reward—a decorated certificate which had been found to be reinforcing for nursery school children in previous research. One-third were simply asked to engage in the drawing task and were given the same reward without any prior expectation. The third group received no reward. After all selected subjects in one classroom had completed the procedures, the drawing materials were reintroduced into the classroom. In line with the expectations, the children in the expected reward condition engaged in drawing only about half as much as children in the other two groups ($p < .025$). The amount of drawing behavior did not differ significantly between the two control groups. The overjustification hypothesis was supported in this experiment because the reduction in target behavior was observed only in the group where the reward had been contracted for or expected.

The results reported by Lepper et al. (1973) and by Meichenbaum et al. (1968), taken together with the present findings, should at least alert one to the possible adverse behavioral effects that may be involved with the use of extrinsic reinforcers. While a good deal of research is available to suggest that these effects do not always occur (e.g., Kuypers et al., 1968; O'Leary et al. 1968; Walker, Mattson, and Buckley, 1971), the authors are convinced that such negative "side effects" *can* occur. The reasons for the occurrence of such effects are far from clear, but the theoretical propositions put forward to explain both behavioral contrast and "overjustification" provide some useful suggestions.

Both the school and home behavior modification programs to which children in the present sample were exposed were quite complex, involving the use of many procedures, including token reinforcement, social reinforcement, response-cost contingencies, time-out, and extinction. These procedures were employed both for the purpose of increasing the rates of desired behavior and decreasing the rates of undesired behavior. It is possible to envisage the operation in these cases of any of the explanatory processes already introduced. For example, it is conceivable that the use of response-cost, extinction, and time-out procedures could have produced sufficient frustration in one setting to affect an increase in the rate of undesired behaviors in the other. This explanation is, however, the least plausible to the present authors since such effects would probably be most apparent in the initial phases of treatment and of rather little consequence by the time programs were terminated. While such effects could be responsible for some initial behavioral contrast, it appears less likely that they would be responsible for contrast measured at termination. Second, it is quite possible that the subjects perceived the change in *relative* reinforcement provided in the unaltered setting, and responded accordingly. That is, the reinforcement for appropriate behavior in the unaltered setting would presumably have been relatively less, and the reinforcement for inappropriate behavior would have been relatively greater. This shift could lead to an associated decrease in appropriate behavior and/or an increase in inappropriate behavior in the unaltered setting.* Finally, it is conceivable that such changes occurred *because* of changes in the children's intrinsic motivation associated with the relevant behaviors.

In considering the overjustification explanation, it is relevant to consider that observational studies of children in both the classroom and home indicate that the proportion of appropriate child behavior is generally quite high even for the most deviant children (e.g., see Johnson et al., 1973; Lobitz, G. and Johnson, 1975; Patterson, Chapter 11, this volume; Walker, Mattson, and Buckley, 1971). Thus, it is possible that in some cases the reinforcement of appropriate behavior in one setting will cause it to be perceived as less intrinsically valuable and will effect its decrease in a nonreinforced setting. In this connection, it is of interest to note that all four children in the present sample who were treated for "acting-out" behavior in the structured classroom showed deviant behavior rates below the normative mean in the home before intervention and reliably increased in rate after intervention. Three of the four children who increased in deviant behavior in school after treatment in the home showed initial baseline levels of deviance in school below the 20% cutoff. It should be pointed out, in contrast, that there were also cases in the school-treated and home-treated samples where baseline levels were initially above the cutoff score and in which an increase in deviant behavior was also observed. In addition, it should be pointed out that simple regression to the mean effects could account for such changes in extreme scores. That is, the regression to the mean phenomenon would predict that extreme scores would tend to approach the mean on a second testing.

Irrespective of these considerations, it is also quite possible and con-

---

* It should be pointed out here that the level of control achieved in laboratory studies of behavioral contrast cannot be achieved in the natural setting. Thus, while no change in contingencies was *programmed* in the secondary, untreated settings, there is no guarantee that some changes did not occur. It is possible, for example, that teachers changed the way they responded to the children they knew to be in treatment elsewhere and that such changes contributed to the observed effects.

gruent with some clinical experience that children *can* perceive "bad" behavior as the antecedent condition for the introduction of a reinforcement system and, further, that they will use this realization to manipulate the adults in the environment (as in Meichenbaum et al., 1968). We have had the experience, for example, that children reinforced for certain classes of compliance to commands may refuse to obey other commands unless reinforcement is instituted for them. It appears unlikely that such maneuvers would occur cross-situationally with different adult authorities, but such a phenomenon is not inconceivable. It is likely in dealing with human subjects, using complex behavior modification programs, that multiple processes may be active to account for contrast phenomena, depending on the modification system employed and the individuals involved.

Although the evidence is at this point scanty, there are data to suggest that negative "side effects" in the form of contrast phenomena *can* occur. As a consequence, it would seem incumbent on those who employ such programs to recognize this possibility and to make some attempt to check for contrast. In addition, it would seem advisable to consider procedures which would minimize the possibility of such side effects. To the present authors, it would seem likely that this could be accomplished by greater use of natural and social consequences and, when this is not possible, employment of the most rapid fading from tangible to natural and social consequences. The "overjustification" hypothesis would seem to argue for the use of the most minimal extrinsic contingencies possible, of whatever kind. In discussing the implications of self-perception theory and research for behavior modification, Kopel and Arkowitz (1975) made the same recommendations and reviewed additional research consistent with it. Self-perception theory would predict that if a reward were very minimal yet associated with response emission, it would lead one to perceive the emitted behavior as intrinsically valuable, thereby effecting an increase in its future probability under nonrewarded circumstances. This theoretical viewpoint leads one to consider the possibility of fading from an initially sufficient or oversufficient reward to an "insufficient" reward (i.e., a reward which would not initially maintain behavior). If this could be accomplished with adequate behavioral maintenance, both positive generalization across settings and resistance to extinction might be enhanced.

Another possible approach, consistent with self-attribution notions, would involve enhancing the individuals' perception of self-determination in spite of the existence of powerful external contingencies. In other words, it can be emphasized to the individuals that their behavior is completely under their own control; the environment may respond to their behavior in a contingent fashion, but it is completely up to them how they will respond to those contingencies. For a dramatic example of this approach, the reader is referred to a case study by Milton Erickson reviewed by Haley (1973, pp. 213-221).

In some situations, it may be productive to frankly label the use of extrinsic contingencies as prosthetic and actively encourage the individuals to work toward the ultimate goal of their removal. This would seem particularly salient in situations where high status individuals are not subjected to such prosthetic treatment (e.g., peers, older siblings, parents, etc.). Some token economy programs in institutions appear to have been designed with this concept in mind (e.g., Atthowe and Krasner, 1968).

Alternatively, the perception of self-determination would seem clearly enhanced by the use of self-management procedures. Among other things, such procedures would include the subject's involvement in establishing and administering the contingencies applied to him. Although the effects have often been found to be weak, there is evidence to suggest that self-administered contingencies produce behavior which is more resistant to extinction (Bolstad and Johnson, 1972; Johnson, 1970; Johnson and Martin, 1973; Kanfer and Duerfeldt, 1967). In addition, the available evidence argues for the clinical utility of training in self-instruction for behavior change (e.g., Meichenbaum, 1971; Monohan and O'Leary, 1971).

In any case, the present results do suggest that serious consideration should be given to the possible adverse effects of extrinsic contingencies. These results lend support to the admonitions of O'Leary and Drabman (1971) and O'Leary et al. (1972) that behavior modifiers should seriously face these questions and use powerful extrinsic contingency programs only after other less intrusive procedures have failed, and then with discretion.

The results of the present study are fully consistent with most other work on the generalization question in showing that unprogrammed positive generalization rarely, if ever, occurs. It seems clear from the accumulation of research data that children should be treated in the setting where they are having difficulty. There is little reason to expect positive generalization from one setting to the other, and children who have difficulty in school and home settings should probably receive simultaneous treatment in both settings. If positive generalization across settings is desired, active programming of such generalization appears to be required.

REFERENCES

ADKINS, D. A., and JOHNSON, S. M.: What behaviors may be called deviant for children? A comparison of two approaches to behavior classification. Paper presented at the meeting of the Western Psychological Association, Portland, Ore., April 1972.

AMSEL, A.: The role of frustrative non-reward in non-continuous reward situations. *Psychol. Bull.*, 55, 102-119, 1958.

ATTHOWE, J. M., and KRASNER, L.: A preliminary report on the application of contingent reinforcement procedures (token economy) on a "chronic" psychiatric ward. *J. Abnorm. Psychol.*, 73, 37-43, 1968.

BECKER, W. C.: The relationship of factors in parental ratings of self and each other to the behavior of kindergarten children as rated by mothers, fathers, and teachers. *J. Consult. Psychol.*, 24, 507-527, 1960.

BEM, D. J.: Self-perception: An alternative interpretation of cognitive dissonance phenomena. *Psychol. Rev.*, 74, 183-200, 1967.

BEM, D. J.: Self-perception theory. In: L. Berkowitz (Ed.), *Advances in Experimental Social Psychology*, Vol. 6. New York: Academic Press, 1972.

BOLSTAD, O. D., and JOHNSON, S. M.: Self-regulation in the modification of disruptive classroom behavior. *J. Appl. Behav. Anal.*, 5, 443-454, 1972.

CAMPBELL, D. T., and STANLEY, J. C.: *Experimental and Quasi-Experimental Designs for Research*. Chicago: Rand McNally, 1966.

COBB, J. A., and HOPS, H.: Coding manual for continuous observation of interactions by single subjects in an academic setting. Report Number 9, Center at Oregon for Research in the Behavioral Education of the Handicapped, U. of Oregon, Eugene, 1972.

DECI, E. L.: Effects of externally mediated rewards on intrinsic motivation. *J. Pers. and Soc. Psychol.*, 18, 105-115, 1971.

DUNHAM, P. J.: Contrasted conditions of reinforcement: A selective critique. *Psychol. Bull.*, 69, 295-315, 1968.

EYBERG, S. M., and JOHNSON, S. M.: Multiple assessment of behavior modification with families. Effects of contingency contracting and order of treated problems. *J. Consult. and Clin. Psychol.*, 42 (4), 594-606, 1974.

FREEMAN, B. J.: Behavioral contrast: Reinforcement frequency or response suppression? *Psychol. Bull.*, 75, 347-356, 1971 .

HALEY, J.: *Uncommon Therapy: The Psychiatric Techniques of Milton H. Erickson, M.D.* New York: Norton, 1973.

HARTMANN, D. P.: Notes on methodology: 1. On choosing an interobserver reliability estimate. *J. Appl. Behav. Anal.*, 1975, in press.

HENDRIKS, A. F. C. J.: Observed deviancy and age differences in deviant and normal boys. Unpublished manuscript, Oregon Research Institute, Eugene, 1972.

HOPS, H., and HUTTON, S. B.: CLASS: A standardized in-class program for acting-out children. I. Preliminary investigations. Report Number 13, Center at Oregon for Research in the Behavioral Education of the Handicapped, U. of Oregon, Eugene, 1974.

JOHNSON, S. M.: Self-reinforcement vs. external reinforcement in behavior modification with children. *Devel. Psychol.*, 3, 148, 1970.

JOHNSON, S. M., and BOLSTAD, O. D.: Methodological issues in naturalistic observation: Some problems and solutions for field research. In: L. A. Hamerlynck, L. C.

Handy, and E. J. Mash (Eds.), *Behavior Change: Methodology, Concepts and Practice.* Champaign, Ill.: Research Press, 1973. Pp. 7-67.

JOHNSON, S. M., and LOBITZ, G. K.: Parental manipulation of child behavior in home observations. *J. Appl. Behav. Anal.,* 7, 23-31, 1974.

JOHNSON, S. M., and MARTIN, S.: Developing self-evaluation as a conditioned reinforcer. In: B. A. Ashem and E. G. Poser (Eds.), *Adaptive Learning: Behavior Modification with Children.* New York: Pergamon, 1973. Pp. 69-78.

JOHNSON, S. M., WAHL, G., MARTIN, S., and JOHANSSON, S.: How deviant is the normal child? A behavioral analysis of the preschool child and his family. In: R. D. Rubin, J. P. Brady, and J. D. Henderson (Eds.), *Advances in Behavior Therapy,* Vol. 4. New York: Academic Press, 1973. Pp. 37-54.

KANFER, F. H., and DUERFELDT, P. H.: The effects of pre-training on self-evaluation and self-reinforcement. *Perceptual and Motor Skills,* 25, 237-246, 1967.

KOPEL, S. A., and ARKOWITZ, H.: The role of attribution and self-perception in behavior change: Implications for behavior therapy. *Genet. Psychol. Monographs,* 1975, in press.

KUYPERS, D. S., BECKER, W. C., and O'LEARY, K. D.: How to make a token system fail. *Exceptional Children,* 35, 101-109, 1968.

LEPPER, M. R., GREEN, D., and NISBETT, R. E.: Undermining children's intrinsic interest with extrinsic reward: A test of the "overjustification" hypothesis. *J. Pers. and Soc. Psychol.,* 28, 129-137, 1973.

LOBITZ, G. K., and JOHNSON, S. M.: Normal vs. deviant children: A multi-method comparison. *J. Abn. Ch. Psychol.,* 1975, in press.

LOBITZ, W. C., and JOHNSON, S. M.: Parental manipulation of the behavior of normal and deviant children. *Child Dev.,* 1975, in press.

MARTIN, B.: Family interaction associated with child disturbance: Assessment and modification. *Psychotherapy: Theory, Research and Practice,* 4, 30-35, 1967.

MEICHENBAUM, D.: Cognitive factors in behavior modification: Modifying what clients say to themselves. Paper presented at the Fifth Annual Meeting of the Association for the Advancement of Behavior Therapy, Washington, D. C., September 1971.

MEICHENBAUM, D. H., BOWERS, K. S., and ROSS, R. R.: Modification of classroom behavior of institutionalized female adolescent offenders. *Behav. Res. and Ther.,* 6, 343-353, 1968.

MONOHAN, J., and O'LEARY, K. D.: The effects of self-instruction on rule-breaking behavior. *Psychol. Reports,* 28, 1059-1066, 1971.

NISBETT, R. E., and VALINS, S.: *Perceiving the Causes of One's Own Behavior.* New York: General Learning Press, 1971.

O'LEARY, K. D., BECKER, W. C., EVANS, M., and SAUDARGAS, R. A.: A token reinforcement program in a public school: A replication and systematic analysis. *J. Appl. Behav. Anal.,* 2, 3-13, 1968.

O'LEARY, K. D., and DRABMAN, R. S.: Token reinforcement program in the classroom: A review. *Psychol. Bull.,* 75, 379-398, 1971.

O'LEARY, K. D., PAULOS, R. W., and DEVINE, V. T.: Tangible reinforcers: Bonuses or bribes? *J. Consult. and Clin. Psych.,* 38, 1-8, 1972.

PATTERSON, G. R., and FAGOT, B. I.: Selective responsiveness to social reinforcers and deviant behavior in children. *Psychol. Rec.,* 17, 369-378, 1967.

PATTERSON, G. R., RAY, R. S., SHAW, D. A., and COBB, J. A.: Manual for coding of family interactions, 1969 revision. Document #01234. Available from ASIS/NAPS, c/o Microfiche Publications, 305 E. 46 St., New York, N. Y. 10017.

PETERSON, D. R.: Behavior problems of middle childhood. *J. Consult. Psychol.,* 25, 205-209, 1961.

REYNOLDS, G. S.: Behavioral contrast. *J. Exper. Anal. Behav.,* 4, 57-71, 1961.

REYNOLDS, G. S., and LIMPO, A. J.: On some causes of behavioral contrast. *J. Exper. Anal. Behav.*, 11, 543-548, 1968.

RUTTER, M., and GRAHAM, P.: Psychiatric disorder in 10- and 11-year-old children. *Proc. Royal Soc. Med.*, 59, 382-387, 1966.

SKINDRUD, K.: Generalization of treatment effects from home to school settings. Unpublished manuscript, Oregon Research Institute, Eugene, 1972.

TERRACE, H. S.: Stimulus control. In: W. K. Honig (Ed.), *Operant Behavior: Areas of Research and Application.* New York: Appleton-Century-Crofts, 1966. Pp. 271-344.

WAHL, G., JOHNSON, S. M., JOHANSSON, S., and MARTIN, S.: An operant analysis of child-family interaction. *Behav. Ther.*, 5, 64-78, 1974.

WAHLER, R. G.: Setting generality: Some specific and general effects of child behavior therapy. *J. Appl. Behav. Anal.*, 2, 239-246, 1969,

WAHLER, R. G.: Deviant child behavior in home and school settings: Some categories for comprehensive description. Part 1 of progress report on NIMH Research Grant MH18516-01A1, U. of Tennessee, 1973.

WAHLER, R. G.: Some structural aspects of deviant child behavior. Unpublished manuscript, U. of Tennessee, 1974.

WALKER, H. M.: The Walker Program Behavior Identification Checklist, 1970. Available from Western Psychological Services, 12031 Wilshire Boulevard, Los Angeles, Cal.

WALKER, H. M.: Early identification and assessment of behaviorally handicapped children in the primary grades. Report Number 2, Center at Oregon for Research in the Behavioral Education of the Handicapped, U. of Oregon, Eugene, 1971.

WALKER, H. M., HOPS, H., and FIEGENBAUM, W. E.: Deviant classroom behavior as a function of change in setting, social and token reinforcement, and cost contingency. Report Number 3, Center at Oregon for Research in the Behavioral Education of the Handicapped, U. of Oregon, Eugene, 1971.

WALKER, H. M., HOPS, H., and GREENWOOD, C. R.: Modification of social withdrawal within an experimental class setting. Paper presented at the 52nd Annual Convention of the Council for Exceptional Children, New York, April 1974.

WALKER, H. M., HOPS, H., and JOHNSON, S. M.: Generalizations and maintenance of classroom treatment effects. *Behav. Ther.*, 6, 188-200, 1975.

WALKER, H. M., MATTSON, R. H., and BUCKLEY, N. K.: The functional analysis of behavior within an experimental classroom setting. In: W. C. Becker (Ed.), *An Empirical Basis for Change in Education.* Chicago: Science Research Associates, 1971. Pp. 236-263.

WOLFF, S.: Behavioral characteristics of primary school children referred to a psychiatric department. *Brit. J. Psychiat*, 113, 885-893, 1967.

7

The Comparability of Behavioral Data in Laboratory and Natural Settings

SANDER MARTIN, STEPHEN M. JOHNSON,
SANDRA JOHANSSON, and GAIL WAHL

Behavioral assessment of parent-child interaction has taken many forms. Traditionally, psychology has relied on both the controlled laboratory experiment and the observation of behavior in the natural environment to gather data about human behavior. Although research is carried out in both these settings, few psychologists have investigated the comparability of behavioral data from one setting to the other. Wiggens (1973) suggests that such investigations are especially important if one wishes to make generalizations from behavioral data recorded in the laboratory to behavior in the "real" world. He states that prediction of behavior in real-life situations is usually assumed to be the goal of most psychological measurement procedures. He further notes that investigators have not been concerned with the problem of the comparability of laboratory and naturalistic data, or with the generalizability of behavioral data from one natural setting to another.

The object of the present study was to assess the relationship of behavioral data taken in analog situations and similar data based on naturalistic observation.

Laboratory Measures of Behavior

Experimental laboratory procedures have remained the most popular methods of research in psychology. Among the reasons for this popularity are the control and economy allowed by these methods. Control of the experimental situation enables the investigator to hold certain variables constant and to manipulate others. Thus, the experimenter can make statements about the behavior of the subject and attribute them to the prearranged conditions of the experiment. Control of the experimental situation also allows the investigator to decide on the unit of measurement to be emphasized. Laboratory equipment can be designed to record complex chains or simple molecular units of behavior. Furthermore, control of the experimental environment allows the investigator to standardize procedures, minimizing factors which decrease comparability across subjects.

A second factor weighing heavily in favor of the laboratory method of investigation is the efficiency of its data yield in terms of both time and money. The investigator does not have to go out "into the field" for subjects; they come to him, or her. Furthermore, the equipment need not be transported from place to place. The investigator can also prearrange conditions so that particular behaviors of interest, which may occur at low base rates in the natural environment, are readily elicited during the experimental session. Thus, the experimental method in psychology provides very efficient and economical ways of gathering data.

Behavioral analog measures of parent-child interaction. A number of investigators have constructed laboratory analog measures of parent-child interaction in order to take advantage of the economy and control offered by this method. The behavioral analogs, as defined here, all involve procedures in which one part of an adult-child dyad is both programmed and simulated, while the other is the object of investigation.

Parent-child analogs were developed in part because data from more naturalistic measures of parent-child interaction were extremely unreliable and difficult to interpret because of ineffective systems of analysis. Furthermore, analogs were able to overcome the problems of earlier parent-child interaction studies which suffered from the drawbacks of exclusive use of correlational analyses. The behavioral analog allowed an investigator to make statements specifying direction of influence. One recent example is provided by Berberich (1971), who investigated children's control over adults' behavior. The analog method allowed him to test a number of theoretically derived hypotheses through procedures in which preprogrammed child behaviors were held constant across all subjects while adults' reactions provided the dependent variable. As a result, Berberich was able to make statements concerning the direction of causation in these adult-child interactions. Rothbart and Maccoby (1966) used analog procedures to control for certain variables which might influence an adult's reaction to a real child. The authors presented subjects with a standardized tape recording of a child's voice and observed the parents' responses to the standardized stimuli it contained.

In the studies noted above, the part of the child was held constant and the behavior of the parent was the object of investigation. It is equally plausible to create behavioral analogs where the parent's behavior is held constant and the behavior of the child is the object of investigation (e.g., Haley, 1968).

Although these investigators have assumed that the subjects' behavior in the analog is representative of their behavior in the "real" world, no research has been done to test this assumption.

The problem of generalization. A number of authors have cited the dangers of relying on behavioral data from laboratory experiments as the basis for generalization about behavior in natural environments. Scott and Wortheimer (1962) suggest that both the behavior and the functional relationships observed in the laboratory may be peculiar only to the artificial conditions of the psychological experiment. Willems (1969) states that it is seductively easy to be content with results obtained in manipulated laboratory experiments and to assume that caution is the only requirement for generalization (p. 64). He also criticizes the laboratory experiment in terms of the time factor, noting that the brevity of most experimental studies causes the subjects to perceive that the consequences of their behavior will be terminated when the study is completed. This is rarely the case in real-life situations. Brunswik (1955) used the terms "artificial tying and untying" of variables to criticize the artificiality of the laboratory experiment. Artificial tying refers to the situation in which experimental variables are made to co-vary in ways that may never be duplicated in real life. Artificial untying refers to the situation in which variables which naturally co-vary are separated for experimental investigation. Breland and Breland (1966), referring to the artificial use of punishment (pp. 62-70), provide numerous examples of such artificial tying and untying.

Pugh (1966) suggests that the social situation in which the experimental task is performed limits its generalizability to everyday or natural phenomena, and Milgram (1963) has effectively demonstrated the "unnatural" control over subjects which experimenters are able to exert.

Unfortunately, few studies have actually been done to confirm or disconfirm any assumptions about the relationship between behavior in the experimental setting and behavior in the natural setting. Many of the investigations which do exist in this area have involved the study of animal behavior. For example, Kortlandt (1962) observed the behavior of chimps in controlled (zoo) settings and in naturalistic (wilderness) settings. Kortlandt found that chimps tended to be listless and essentially arboreal in the zoo setting, whereas they were observed to be more lively and alert, and essentially terrestrial, in wilderness settings.

There has been a paucity of literature in this area of research on humans, especially children. Barker et al. (1943) induced experimental frustration in a number of two- to five-year-old children at play. The authors found that these children reverted to modes of play typical of much younger children. Fawl (1963) challenged the relevance of these findings. His study involved analysis of 16 days of observation taken from a study done by Barker and Wright (1955) describing the daily activities of 18 children. Fawl analyzed the data for goal blockage, frustration, and the accompanying effects of frustration. He found that blocked goals, when they did occur, did not induce the kind of regression described in Barker et al.'s (1943) earlier study. These few studies suggest that much more definitive research must be done to investigate the relationship between behavioral data obtained in experimental and naturalistic settings.

Naturalistic Measures of Behavior

Naturalistic measures impose relatively few restrictions or artificial conditions on the persons being observed, and thus capitalize on the realism of *in situ* behavior. Advocates of naturalistic observation claim that these measurement procedures catalogue more of the total impact of the relationship between individuals and their environment. Unfortunately, naturalistic measures achieve realism at the cost of experimental control, since the experimenter is able to obtain data only on those behaviors which happen to occur during the observation period. Naturalistic investigations have also been plagued with the problem of creating sufficiently valid and reliable measurement units. Naturalistic researchers have accumulated much data, but as Caldwell (1968) states, ". . . there has been the dilemma of what to do with such records after they have been obtained." (p. 76)

Recently a number of behavioral coding systems have been developed which allow an observer to behave systematically in the face of an unpredictable environment and, fortunately, these systems have also proven useful to observations in the laboratory (Merrill, 1946; Rothbart and Maccoby, 1966; Patterson et al., 1969). A number of investigators have used these new coding systems to study parent-child interaction. The obvious face validity of such naturalistic methods has seemingly contributed to the lack of research on the generalizability of behavioral estimates based on such samples. Other than the studies investigating those behavioral effects of being observed (e.g., Bales, 1950; Bechtel, 1967; Lindsley, 1966; Patterson and Harris, 1968; Purcell and Brady, 1966), little research exists providing evidence of the validity of naturalistic data. Yet, if one can assume that the naturalistic home setting is the closest approximation to everyday parent-child interaction, one could use behavior observed in this naturalistic setting as a criterion measure for checking experimental measures of parent-child interaction.

In summary, there has been a serious lack of research into the representativeness and the generalizability of behavioral data on parent-child interaction obtained in laboratory and naturalistic settings. Most researchers have made generalizations from behavioral data obtained in the laboratory to the same behavior in the "real" world, with no evidence that such generalizations are valid. This deficit leaves in serious doubt the legitimacy of statements about behavior beyond the confines of any particular experimental situation.

The object of the present study was to examine the comparability of laboratory and naturalistic measures of parent-child behavior. The concern of the present study was with the cross-situational consistency of behavior; the aim was to establish the extent to which various measures designed to investigate the same behaviors yield comparable results.

METHOD AND PROCEDURE

Subjects

Thirty-three families were recruited through radio, television, and newspaper advertising and were paid $20 for their participation. Eligible families were required to have: (a) both parents living in the home; (b) four children or fewer; (c) no member of the family currently under psychiatric care; and (d) a target child (a four- to six-year-old) with no history of psychiatric treatment.

Measurement Instruments

All subject families were required to take part in the following procedures: (a) five 45-minute sessions of home observations; and (b) two 30-minute sessions of parent-child interaction analogs.

Home Observation. Each family was observed five consecutive week-days for 45 minutes on each occasion. A trained observer coded the target child in his or her interaction with the rest of the family. Observations were held when all members of the family were at home. Typically, this was one hour before the supper hour. Families were required to comply with the following rules: (a) all family members be present; (b) all family members remain in a specified two-room area; (c) the observer not be interrupted; (d) the television set not be turned on during observations; (e) no telephone calls or visitors be accepted.

In order to investigate the reliability of the observational data, a calibrating observer joined the original observer during one of the five nights of observation for 17 of the sample families.

Analog measures of parent-child interaction. The two analog measures used in the present study resemble those analogs reported in the literature for studying aspects of parent-child interaction (Berberich, 1971; Rothbart and Maccoby, 1966). The analogs consisted of a series of simulated parent-child interaction situations. The procedures involved only the parents and did not require the target child. In both analogs, the behavior of the analog child was programmed, while the parents' behavior was the object of study. Parents' immediate reactions to specific child behaviors were recorded in the analog situations. Parents were told to respond to the analog child as if it were their own four- or five-year-old.

Analog I. The first analog followed the general format outlined by Berberich (1971). In this procedure, the parent was asked to teach the analog child a marble drop task. The parent was seated in one room and the "programmed analog child" (experimenter) was seated in the adjoining room. Both individuals faced a display board containing five heavy plastic tubes which passed through the panel and extended into both the adult's and the analog child's rooms. The tubes were approximately one-half inch in diameter, allowing a small marble to pass through them. The five tubes were slanted toward the parent's room and emptied into five separate clear plastic cups situated in front of the parent. The parent was instructed to require the child to deliver marbles in particular sequences. The parent was free to communicate with the child in any way and was provided with a penny-dispensing apparatus for the purpose of reinforcing the child for desired behavior. The parent was told that the analog child's behavior was programmed to respond to the instructions and consequences which the parent provided. Actually, the behavior of the analog child was invariate across all parents.

The following is a description of apparatus and procedures for Analog I:

A parent was brought into the experimental room and seated before the display board. On the board directly above each of the plastic tubes and facing both rooms was a series of colored symbols. The tubes were also numbered from one to five.

The analog child's room contained a tray filled with colored marbles which the experimenter could deliver to the parent on command. The parent was instructed to read a set of directions asking the analog child to deposit particular colored marbles down specified tubes. The panel also contained a slot for dispensing pennies and a slot for returning pennies. This allowed the parent to present or take away pennies. Parents were given a container of 200 pennies to use as they saw fit. Parents could retrieve pennies from the child by signaling the experimenter that they would like pennies returned. The parent indicated the number of pennies to be returned by depressing a lever which sounded a tone. The number of tones determined the number of pennies to be returned.

A light was mounted directly in the center of the panel and labeled "out of seat." The parent was informed that this light would activate whenever the child left to play with some toys available at the other end of the room. The parent was further informed that when the child returned the light would go off.

After going over the instructions with the parent, the experimenter entered the analog child's room and signaled the parent to begin.

The analog child (experimenter) responded to parental instructions from a prearranged program which included the following range of behaviors: (a) correct; (b) incorrect; (c) partially correct; (d) leave; (e) high rate. The latter two were defined as deviant child behaviors. Under the leave condition, the experimenter switched on the small "out of seat" light visible to the parent. The light remained on until 15 seconds after the parent's first command directing the child to return to the seat. Under the high-rate condition, the examiner chose five marbles, all of one color, and dropped them down one of the tubes as rapidly as possible.

The parent variables of interest in this analog were the amounts of parental social and nonsocial reward and punishment as a function of correct, incorrect, partially correct, and noncooperative responses by the child.

Each session was recorded and, at a latter time, the parents' responses were coded, using a limited number of the codes suggested by Patterson et al. (1969).

Analog II. The second analog measure resembled that used by Roth-bart and Maccoby (1966). In this procedure, the parents were asked to respond to a standard audio tape recording on which a series of parent-child interaction situations had been enacted. The role of the child was programmed on the tape and the parents were asked to respond to this tape as they would to their own child under the same circumstances. In any given sequence the parents listened to a short taped interaction; the tape then stopped and the parents were asked to do three things: (a) indicate their intention to respond positively, nega-tively, or neutrally to the child's behavior; (b) say what they would say; (c) say what they would do.

The following is a description of apparatus and procedures for Analog II:

> A parent was seated at a table containing a small microphone, a tape recorder holding the stimulus material (analog child's voice), and a small panel with three buttons labeled positive, negative, and neutral.
>
> The parent was asked to imagine that he was at home with his child (the target child); that he was attempting to do his income tax, and the child was in the same room with him. The parent was also asked to imagine a second scene in which he and his child were playing together.
>
> The parent was told that the analog child would be engaging in a number of activities. Whenever a bell sounded on the tape, the parent was to stop the recorder and to respond to the preceding segment of the tape in the following three ways: First, the parent was to signal his intentions in responding by depressing one of three buttons on a panel directly in front of him (labeled positive, nega-tive, and neutral). The parent was told to press the positive button whenever it was his intention to reward or encourage the previous child behavior. The negative button was to be pressed if the parent intended to punish, discourage or ignore the child's behavior. The neutral button was to be pressed if neither reward nor punishment was intended. Second, the parent was to respond verbally to the child in the same manner he would to his own child engaged in similar behavior. Third, the parent was to state what physical action he would take, if any, if his child were engaged in similar behavior.
>
> When the three tasks were completed for the first taped segment, the parent was instructed to start the recorder, listen to the next analog sequence, and repeat the same three tasks.

The analog child was chosen by recording a number of young chil-dren between the ages of six and seven reciting a prepared script. The voice selected for the present study was one which three judges were unable to distinguish as either male or female. The analog child engaged in a number of activities classed deviant and non deviant by the Patterson et al. (1969) coding system.

Observation Coding System

The observation coding system used for all measurement settings in the present study was a revision of one developed by Patterson et al. (1969). This system utilizes 35 behavior categories which are distinct from one another and which are directly observable. The categories are designated by code letters and are hand written by an observer as they occur. The code is based on pinpointing a target individual and recording all behaviors directed toward this individual and all behaviors that this individual directs toward those around him or her. In the present study, the code centered on four- to six-year-old "target" children. For convenience, all interactions in the home and structured laboratory settings were coded in a framework of 30-second intervals and each observer was equipped with a 30-second stopwatch and signaling apparatus. In general, observers recorded three interactions per 30-second period. Interactions were defined as patterns of behavior consisting of an action and a response. The behavioral code allowed a minimum of one action and one response and a maximum of two actions and two responses per interaction. On the basis of data collected from responses to a question given to parents of sample children, behavioral codes were designated as either deviant or nondeviant. Furthermore, by agreement among experimenters, behavior codes were designated as either positive, negative, or neutral consequences.

Observers

Observers were undergraduate and graduate students in psychology who were trained to use the coding system and received course credit for their participation. All observers were trained to a criterion of 70% reliability and were continually checked throughout the study by a calibrating observer.

Observer agreement was tested by very stringent criteria; to count as an agreement, both observers had to agree at the same time on the agent, the code, and the interaction sequence. Observer agreement percent equalled the number of agreements divided by the sum of the number of agreements and disagreements.

Observer agreement was calculated for 17 of the sample families by a calibrating observer who joined the regular observer for one of the five home observations. The mean agreement score for all observers was 65%. It should be noted that the level of agreement expected by chance is less than 5%.

An alternative index of agreement was computed by correlating observer and calibrator on total number of deviant behaviors reported. The correlation based on one day of observation was .78. The same strategy was applied to each individual behavior code, resulting in a median correlation of .88 for the 19 codes which occurred for five or more children.

RESULTS

All parent responses to the analog "children" were placed in either positive, negative, or neutral categories. Parent responses to their own children in the home setting were coded in the same maner.

In Analog I both Verbal and Material responses were possible, and in Analog II parents' Intentions, Verbalizations, and Actions were scored.

The analog data were inspected with the purpose of attending to three questions: (1) What was the relationship between parent's verbal and nonverbal responses within the same setting? (2) What were the correlations between parents' responses to Analog I and their responses to similar events in Analog II? and (3) How did parental consequations to deviant and nondeviant child behavior under analog conditions compare with parental consequations to the deviant and nondeviant behavior of their own children at home.

Analog II presented the opportunity to study the relationship between parents' Intentions and Verbal responses. More specifically, the question posed was: If parents noted an intention to reward or punish, was this followed by a verbal statement congruent with that intention? If congruence occurred, an agreement score was recorded. Agreement scores for each parent were computed by summing agreements and dividing by agreements plus disagreements. The Analog II Action category was dropped due to its lack of use by most parents. The mean agreement scores for Analog II are presented in Table 1.

Correlations between parents' Intentions and Verbal responses in Analog II, according to deviant and nondeviant child behavior, proved to be both significant and positive, but only for positive consequences to deviant and nondeviant behavior categories. These data are presented in Table 2.

TABLE 1

Parents, Positive, Negative, and Neutral Mean
Percent Agreement Scores for Analog II

Parent Behavior	Mean	Standard Deviation
Positive	.73	.14
Negative	.80	.09
Neutral	.45	.20

TABLE 2

Product-Moment Correlations Between Intention
and Verbal Categories of Analog II

Parents' Response		Deviant	Child Behavior		Non-Deviant	
	Both Parents	Fathers	Mothers	Both Parents	Fathers	Mothers
Positive	.50**	.45**	.55**	.44**	.47**	.42*
Negative	.09	.07	—.01	.10	.08	.02
Neutral	—.05	—.27	.11	.06	—.24	—.18

* $p < .05$ ** $p < .01$.

The data from Analog I also presented an opportunity to assess
parent consistency between Verbal and Material categories. Correlations
between these two Analog I categories for parents' positive, negative,
and neutral responses to deviant and nondeviant child behavior failed
to reach significant levels.

The second focus of attention was the relationship between Analogs
I and II. Since the Verbal response category was common to both
Analogs, an estimate of relationship could be achieved by correlating
parents' positive, negative, and neutral verbal responses to deviant and
nondeviant child behavior under each analog condition. Correlations
proved to be nonsignificant across all categories.

Consistency between parents' responses to children in the Analogs
and their responses to similar behavior in the home was the third area
of investigation. Correlations for parents' responses in Analog I and
their responses to similar child behavior in the home are presented in
Table 3.*

---

* The reader will notice the addition of a Compliance/Noncompliance category
for home data. The similarity between compliance and nondeviant behavior and
noncompliance and deviant behavior provided the experimenter the opportunity to
investigate the possibility that there might be some relationship between compliant
and noncompliant child behavior in the home and nondeviant and deviant behavior
in the analogs.

TABLE 3

Product-Moment Correlations Between Parents' Responses to
Child Behavior in Analog I and at Home

Parent Response	Child Behavior	Verbal			Material		
		Both Parents	Fathers	Mothers	Both Parents	Fathers	Mothers
Positive	Nondeviant	−.19	−.30	−.02	−.11	−.29	−.07
	Deviant	.03	.09	−.03	−.13	−.20	.04
	Compliance	−.20	−.35**	−.01	−.30**	−.29	−.30
	Noncompliance	−.01	.10	−.13	−.21	−.27	−.07
Negative	Nondeviant	.05	.11	.01	.03	.10	−.04
	Deviant	−.14	−.07	−.24	−.07	−.16	−.01
	Compliance	.10	.08	−.06	.19	.24	−.04
	Noncompliance	−.19	−.14	−.09	−.16	−.43**	.12
Neutral	Nondeviant	−.09	−.17	.10	−.26**	−.36**	−.17
	Deviant	−.15	−.15	−.17	−.22	−.35**	−.03
	Compliance	−.11	−.13	−.09	−.20	−.28	−.15
	Noncompliance	−.15	−.32	−.10	−.12	−.36**	.36**

** $p < .05$.

TABLE 4

Mean Percent Positive and Negative Consequences Provided by Mother
and Father to Deviant and Nondeviant Child Behavior in
the Home Setting, Analog I and Analog I

Consequence	Agent	Behavior	Home	Setting Verbal Analog I	Verbal Analog II
Positive	Mother	Nondeviant	.67	.79	.72
		Deviant	.49	.29	.19
	Father	Nondeviant	.70	.71	.69
		Deviant	.43	.31	.27
Negative	Mother	Nondeviant	.02	.18	.12
		Deviant	.13	.68	.64
	Father	Nondeviant	.02	.18	.10
		Deviant	.15	.67	.52

It is interesting to note an inverse relation between fathers' responses
in the home and in Analog I. Though interpretation of results should
be attenuated by the possibility that three significant correlations could
have occurred by chance, it is important to point out that the "material-
Father" column contains four correlations above chance levels.

The correlations between parents' responses to the Analog II child
and their responses to similar behavior in the home were also computed. Though four correlations reached levels of significance greater
than .05, approximately three would have been expected by chance.
Closer inspection of the data revealed no particular constellation of
significant correlations as found in the Analog I data.

A second part in the investigation of parents' responses to children
in the Analogs and their responses to their own children at home was
to pursue the possibility that while there might not be a strong relationship between individual parents' responses from one setting to the
other, group data might reflect the same general results for parents in
both settings. The question of interest was whether parents responded
to deviant and nondeviant child behavior with generally the same
pattern of responses in the Analogs as in the home.

Table 4 contains means for fathers' and mothers' positive and negative responses to deviant and nondeviant child behavior in both home
and analog settings. Inspection of the data comparing mean parent
responses in analog and home settings revealed that: (a) mothers and
fathers did not differ significantly in the manner with which they con-

sequated deviant and nondeviant child behavior; (b) both parents consequated deviant child behavior significantly more negatively $(p < .001)$* and nondeviant child behavior more positively $(p < .001)$ regardless of setting; (c) the magnitude of this effect was found to be far greater in the Analogs than in the home setting.

Discussion

The present data suggest several conclusions. First, the lack of significant correlations between parents' behavior in Analogs I and II suggests that these represent entirely independent measures of parent behavior. Second, there is little or no relationship between parents' responses toward the analog children in the laboratory setting and their responses to similar sets of antecedent events involving their own children in the home setting. It is important to point out that many of the significant correlations found for fathers in Analog I were in a negative direction, indicating that an entirely opposing set of responses would be expected from analog to home. One would be committing a serious error in generalizing from a father's behavior in one setting to his responses in the other. Finally, grouped comparison of parents' responses to child behaviors in both home and analog settings revealed that similar response patterns were used in consequating deviant and nondeviant child behaviors. Parents tended to respond to nondeviant child behaviors more positively and to deviant behaviors more negatively regardless of setting. This effect was, however, more pronounced in the analog than in the home. Also, no differences were found between fathers' and mothers' consequence patterns in either setting. These results suggest that the analog may be of some use in predicting simple relationships for a group, but it is clear that the analog had no value in predicting behavior to the home setting for the single case.

Present results are consistent with the few research studies which have compared the behavior of children across situations (Bernal, Chapter 8, this volume; Dysart, 1973). These studies reinforce Mischel's (1968) conclusions that behaviors which are often construed as stable traits actually are highly specific and dependent on the details of the evoking situations and the response mode employed to measure them.

---

* Results for both home and Analog measures were analyzed by two-by-two Analyses of Variance for Repeated measures. Separate analyses were done for positive and negative consequences.

REFERENCES

BALES, R.: *Interaction Process Analysis.* Cambridge: Addison-Wesley, 1950.

BARKER, R., DEMBOW, T., and LEWIN, K.: Frustration and regression. In: R. Barker, J. Kounin, and H. Wright (Eds.), *Child Behavior and Development.* New York: McGraw-Hill, 1943. Pp. 441-458.

BARKER, R., and WRIGHT, H.: *Midwest and Its Children: The Psychological Ecology of an American Town.* New York: Row, Peterson, 1955.

BECHTEL, R.: The study of man: Human movement and architecture. *Transaction,* May, 53-56, 1967.

BERBERICH, J.: Adult child interactions: I. Correctness of a "child" as a positive reinforcer for the behavior of adults. Unpublished manuscript, U. of Washington, 1971.

BRELAND, R., and BRELAND, M.: *Animal Behavior.* New York: Macmillan, 1966.

BRUNSWIK, E.: Representative design and probabilistic theory in a functional psychology. *Psychol. Rev.,* 62, 193-217, 1955.

CALDWELL, B.: A new approach to behavioral ecology. In: J. P. Hill (Ed.), *Minnesota Symposium on Child Psychology,* Vol. 2. Minneapolis: U. of Minnesota Press, 1968.

DYSART, R.: A behavioral description of family interactions in the home and in the clinic. Unpublished doctoral dissertation, University of Houston, 1973.

FAWL, C.: Disturbances experienced by children in their natural habitats. In: R. G. Barker (Ed.), *The Stream of Behavior.* New York: Appleton-Century-Crofts, 1963. Pp. 99-126.

HALEY, J.: Testing parental instructions to schizophrenic and normal children. *J. Abnorm. Psychol.,* 73, 559-565, 1968.

KORTLANDT, A.: Chimpanzees in the wild. *Scientific Amer.,* 206, 128-138, 1962.

LINDSLEY, O.: An experiment with parents handling behavior at home. *Johnstone Bull.,* 27-36, 1966.

MERRILL, B.: A measurement of parent-child interaction. *J. Abnorm. and Soc. Psychol.,* 41, 37-39, 1946.

MILGRAM, S.: Behavioral study of obedience. *J. Abnorm. and Soc. Psychol.,* 67, 371-378, 1963.

MISCHEL, W.: *Personality and Assessment.* New York: Wiley, 1968.

PATTERSON, G., and HARRIS, A.: Some methodological considerations for observation procedures. Paper read at the Annual Convention of the A.P.A., San Francisco, 1968.

PUGH, D.: Modern organizational theory: A psychological and sociological study. *Psychol. Bull.,* 66, 235-251, 1966.

PURCELL, K., and BRADY, K.: Adaptation to the invasion of privacy: Monitoring behavior with a miniature radio transmitter. *Merrill-Palmer Quarterly,* 12, 242-254, 1966.

ROTHBART, M., and MACCOBY, E.: Parents' differential reaction to sons and daughters. *J. Pers. and Soc. Psychol.,* 4, 237-243, 1966.

SCOTT, W., and WORTHEIMER, M.: *Introduction to Psychological Research.* New York: Wiley, 1962.

WIGGENS, J.: *Personality and Prediction: Principles of Personality Assessment.* Read-

WIGGENS, J.: *Personality and Prediction: Principles of Personality Assessment.* Reading, Mass.: Addison Wesley, 1973.

WILLEMS, E.: Planning a rationale for naturalistic research. In: E. Willems and H. Raush (Eds.), *Naturalistic Viewpoints in Psychological Research.* New York: Holt, Rinehart, and Winston, 1969. Pp. 44-71.

8

Comparison of Boys' Behaviors in Homes and Classrooms

MARTHA E. BERNAL, LEO. F. DELFINI,
JUEL ANN NORTH, and SUSAN L. KREUTZER

The behaviors of boys referred as deviant in the home were examined to evaluate the degree of consistency of their behavior from home to classroom. Data were collected during the conduct of a research project designed to identify and treat boys whose parents referred them because they presented behavior problems which consisted of frequent non-compliance and disruptive behaviors. The 21 boys who were so identified were the subjects of this study; prior to treatment, a series of home and school observations were done by trained observers using naturalistic observation methods.

Attention recently has been paid to the generation of data regarding the natural, unprogrammed behavior of children and their social environment (e.g., Wahl et al., 1972; Johnson et al., 1973; Patterson et al., 1972; Werry and Quay, 1969). As Johnson et al. (1973) have argued, these data can provide a basis from which to infer the degree of deviance of a child from his peer group. A second type of information that can be generated by such data is the extent to which the same child's behaviors vary from one setting to another, e.g., in home and school. Predictions about a child's conduct in unsampled settings made on the

This research was supported by NIMH grant No. 20922 awarded to the senior author. We are deeply grateful to Leola Schultz, who helped collect, process, and analyze the data; to Sandra Tamayo, who typed this manuscript; and to Orin D. Bolstad, who reviewed it prior to presentation at the Banff Conference. The cooperation and assistance of the Denver Public Schools, and in particular of Dr. Gerald Elledge and Mr. Orville Turner, are gratefully acknowledged.

basis of known behavior in a given setting are based upon the assumption of cross-situational behavioral consistency. This assumption has not been seriously challenged and investigations of the consistency of behavior across different naturalistic settings using behavioral observation are few.

One study by Wahler (1969) reported on the degree of generalization from home to school of the effects of behavior modification in two young boys. The deviant boys presented similar problems in the two settings, but successful modification of child behaviors in the home did not generalize to the classroom setting. However, subsequent contingency changes in the classroom for both boys produced increases in desirable, and decreases in undesirable, behaviors.

In Chapter 7 of this volume, Martin et al. report on their investigation of parental responses toward children and find no relationship between parent behaviors in home and laboratory settings. However, they were comparing parents' responses toward their own children in the home with responses to laboratory children who were not their own. Due to this confounding of the setting and stimulus variables, conclusions about the consistency of parental reactions were restricted. They also review studies dealing with the cross-situational consistency assumption, and conclude that, while it is unsupported by most animal and human research, some factors do increase this consistency. The degree of structure of a task, the similarity of behaviors sampled, and the similarity of situations may increase the correlation between behaviors in different settings.

In Chapter 6 of this volume reporting a study of consistency across home and school settings of baseline or pretreatment behaviors, as well as generalization of behavior change after treatment, Johnson et al. find no evidence of cross-situational consistency or positive generalization in a group of 35 behavior problem children. These findings corroborate Wahler's (1973) earlier report that only one of five children showing behavior problems in one setting also presented problems in the second setting. In contrast to previous studies, Johnson et al.'s data were based on a larger sample, and an added refinement was that the children's behaviors in the home were compared with normative data for other children of the same age. Normative data for the school setting were unavailable, and a cutoff score for deviance in the classroom was arbitrarily designated. Nevertheless, such use of a single score for each setting permitted statements about the proportion of subjects found to be average or deviant in comparison to a sample of children in similar

TABLE 1

Characteristics of Deviant Group and
Their Families

| Age in yrs. & mos. | Grade | | Socioeconomic | | No. Children | | No. Parents | |
	K	1st	Level*		in Family		Single	Two-Parents
Range 5-6 to 7-7	13	8	Range	1-6	Range	1-4	8	13
Mean 6-5			Mean	3.2	Mean	2.3		
Median 6-3			Median	3.0	Median	2.0		

* Scores were based on Edwards' Occupational Grouping Scale. Lowest occupational levels are coded 6 and the highest are coded 1.

settings. A normative standard for definition of children's deviance has been used rarely in the behavior modification literature. In Johnson et al.'s comparison, the Patterson et al. (1969) scoring system was used in the home, and the Cobb and Hops (1972) system in the school.

In the present report, the same multivariate scoring system (Bernal and North, 1972) was used in both home and school settings, and in addition normative data for both home and classroom were available. The use of the same scoring system permitted an analysis of similarly coded behaviors across settings as well as comparison of various types of children's behaviors in each setting.

METHOD

Subjects and subject selection. The subjects were 21 kindergarten and first grade boys who were enrolled in regular classrooms in the Denver Public Schools. One boy was repeating the first grade. These subjects were recruited into a Family Intervention Project being conducted for the purpose of locating and treating boys who were identified as discipline problems in the home by their parents. Evaluation of the behavior modification parent training treatment was based primarily on naturalistic observation data of child behaviors collected in the child's home and classroom. Characteristics of the boys and their families are presented in Table 1.

Identification of the boys was carried out with the assistance of the schools. Letters were sent to the parents of boys in the kindergarten and first grades from 22 schools whose principals agreed to cooperate. The letters listed the following behaviors: fails to obey, fights, talks back, interrupts, teases, damages things, cries and fusses. Parents were told that if their boy displayed two or more of these behaviors to an excessive degree at home, and they wished to obtain help, they could return an enclosed family information form. An introductory letter from the school district office was also enclosed.

A total of 1,857 letters were mailed, 154 sets of parents returned the information forms and 81 met the following preliminary selection criteria: the designated problem boys lived with their immediate families only, i.e., there were no relatives or friends in the home; there were no mentally or physically handicapped children; there were no more than four children in the family; and they were permanent residents with no plans to move out of the area. Both intact and single-parent families were allowed to participate.

The next step in the selection process was to call the parents of the deviant boys to further screen them to assure that both parents were concerned about the boy, were willing to set two appointments per week, and agreed to come to the laboratory for a group meeting to obtain further information about the offered service. In addition, parents who were experiencing severe marital difficulties manifested by previous separation or threats of divorce were asked to select themselves out. Boys who had previously been referred to mental health or school facilities for help were accepted provided they were not currently in treatment.

Of the 79 parents who were reached by telephone, 50 met the above criteria and 33 kept the appointment for the group meeting. At the meeting, the contract into which they were asked to enter was explained to them: they were provided with a free-of-charge teaching service carried out mostly in their homes and designed to help them manage their child more effectively in exchange for their cooperation in allowing the collection of observation data in the home and in their boy's classroom, and continued participation in a twice-per-year set of observations over two years of time.

Following screening by telephone and the group meeting, there was a further dropout of families; these dropout data and the use of excuses given at different contact points as predictors of dropout have been reported elsewhere (Bernal, Kreutzer, North and Pelc, 1973). Dropouts were self-selected and not eliminated by the research staff except as they failed to meet the designated criteria.

Observations were scheduled with those parents who agreed. They were told that when each set of observations was completed they would be paid $10. The next step was to collect home and school observation data.

Procedure

Dependent variables. A multivariate behavioral coding system (Bernal and North, 1972) developed for the purpose of recording both home and classroom behaviors of primary grade discipline problem boys was used. Four major categories were scored for the target child: Compliance-Noncompliance, Desirable, Annoying, and Deviant. These categories represented very broad classifications with arbitrarily designated labels under which were subsumed various types or classes of behavior which were more narrow and specific. In addition, two major behavior categories were scored for the parents or teacher. These categories were Commands and type of Attention. Attention from peers was scored in the classroom only. The Attention category also contained a number of classes of attention which were fairly specific and well defined. Whenever a given behavior could not be scored by the observer, use was made of an Unscorable category. Absence of the target child was scored in an Out column, and the child was scored for being in time-out.

The term "behavior class" was used to designate those types of child, parent, and teacher behaviors itemized under each of the major behavior categories. These categories, and the behavior classes subsumed under each category, are listed below with brief definitions and abbreviations used to denote them. A more complete description of the codes can be found in the Appendix.

BEHAVIOR CODES

Child Behaviors

Compliance-Noncompliance

Desirable

> On Task
> Physical Positive
> Appropriate Verbal Interaction
> Appropriate Nonverbal Interaction
> Altruism

Annoying

> Verbal Abuse
> Whining
> Noisemaking

Nonverbal Abuse
Motor Behavior (scored at home only if child must be seated
   to complete a task)
Inappropriate Task (scored only at school)

Deviant

Namecalling
Destructive
Physical Negative

Adult Behaviors

Commands

Original Command
Repetition of the Command
Negative Command
Delayed Command (Compliance cannot be scored)

Adult or Peer Attention

Verbal and Physical Positive
Negative
Physical Negative and Punishment
Spanking
Time Out
No Attention

Coding sheets had a standard format which permitted scoring by pen-
ciling in the correct spaces, and each side was divided into four sections
each of which corresponded to a 15-second time sample (TS). A modified time-sampling system was used such that only the first occurrence
within 15 seconds of a behavior class under each category could be
scored. That is, the system allowed for scoring of Desirable, Annoying,
and Deviant categories of child behavior within each TS, but no more
than one behavior class within each of these child categories could be
scored. For a given category, the maximum rate per minute (RPM)
that could be scored was 4, or 240 per hour. Data were punched onto
IBM cards for processing.

Observer training and interobserver agreement. Four observers, all
women, collected the data for this study. One observer was highly experienced and knowledgeable about the research goals and acted as the
calibrating observer; the other observers were naive. After each observation, the naive observers were asked to write their hypotheses about the
goals of the research. This monitoring of observer hypotheses was used

to check for experimenter bias, but in no case did any observer indicate she knew we were comparing discipline-problem and normal boys. The most common hypothesis was that the study concerned the care and treatment of speech problems, probably because many of the boys had varying articulation difficulties.

Observers were trained prior to the beginning of data collection for the present study; details of that training have been presented elsewhere (Bernal, Kreutzer, North, and Pelc, 1973). Briefly, they were required to reach a 75% level of overall agreement on three out of five consecutive observations, and then an overt check (i.e., the observer knew she was being checked) was done once a week for each observer. Calibrating sessions to review scoring procedures and codes were held once weekly.

Three kinds of agreement calculations yielded *overall* agreement scores, *category* agreement scores for the Desirable, Annoying, and Deviant behavior categories, and *chain* agreement scores for Percent Compliance.. The overall agreement determination, which required that two observers agree on 82 possible cells within each 15-second TS, was computed by counting the number of perfectly matching TS's and dividing by the total number of TS's scored on a given observation, or:

$$\frac{\text{Agreement on occurrences} + \text{nonoccurrences}}{\text{Number of TS's scored}}$$

Category agreement was computed similarly, except that agreement on occurrence of any class within a category was required; i.e., so long as two observers agreed that some behavior (or none at all) listed under any of the class codes within a category occurred, an agreement was scored. Agreement for Percent Compliance was computed differently due to the complexity of the measure. Agreement on the behavioral chain consisting of a command (original, repeated, or negative) followed by compliance or noncompliance within 30 seconds was required. Overall agreement and category agreement were computed for all agreement checks during the study. However, for chain agreement, ten subjects for whom agreement was checked in the home and ten subjects in the school were selected at random, and agreement on the chain was computed for each observation by the formula:

$$\frac{\text{Total number of chain agreements on occurrences}}{\text{Total number of commands}}$$

For the deviant subjects at home, the mean overall agreement was .73. Category agreement scores were very high, averaging .94 for Desirable, .95 for Annoying, and .99 for Deviant. Percent Compliance chain agreement averaged .62. At school, mean overall agreement was .82, category agreement scores were as high as in the home, and chain agreement for Percent Compliance averaged .77.

Observation procedures and normative data collection. Standard observation procedures included the use of a battery-operated pacer which provided a single audio signal every 15 seconds into an earphone; when observers checked agreement, a second earphone was used. Four observations were conducted in each setting within a period of two weeks.

In the home, observations were conducted when all family members were in view of the observer, the television set was turned off, the radio was turned off or at low volume, no telephone calls were made, and no visitors were present. Once a time of day was selected as a convenient time by the family (but no observations were done during mealtimes) for the first observation, all subsequent observations were conducted at the same time on weekdays. The observers scored continuously for 30 minutes on the child identified as the subject, yielding 120 minutes of data over the four observations. Parent Commands and parent Attention also were scored.

Normative home data were obtained from a group of 21 boys identified by their parents as being no more disruptive or showing no more behavior problems than average boys. Selection and data-collection procedures for this sample are described in Chapter 9 of this volume, which compares the deviant and normal groups' home behavior. Observation procedures for these boys were the same as for the deviant group.

In the classroom, teachers were asked to select a fairly structured period during the day; observations typically were conducted during reading or arithmetic periods. In order to reduce the subject's reactivity to being observed, the observer who collected classroom data was not the same one who collected home data. Only one deviant subject per classroom was observed. In the classroom, observation of each deviant subject was alternated with observation of a peer every minute so as to obtain classroom normative peer data with which to compare the subjects. Instructions for the scoring of these peers were that observers should score the behaviors of as many boys as possible, but no less than four different boys. This sampling procedure yielded 15 minutes of data per observation for each subject and each peer, or a total of 60 minutes for each real and each peer subject over the four observations.

Scores for classroom peers were combined to form a single composite score per variable for each "peer." Teacher Commands and teacher and peer Attention were also scored.

Home and school data for all samples were collected between December and the following May. Collection of data in the two settings was scheduled concurrently so that all observations were completed within the same two weeks of time. The only exception was one deviant subject who, due to absence from school and scheduling changes associated with the annual administration of school achievement tests, was observed in the home one month before he was observed in the classroom.

Walker Problem Behavior Identification Checklist (WPBIC). Mothers of the deviant boys and their teachers were asked to fill out the WPBIC immediately following the end of the observations. WPBIC data were not obtained for the home and school normative samples. At the request of the public school administration, items 8, 22, 31, 37, and 44 were deleted for both home and school use.

RESULTS

Measures. This paper reports only child behavior data; parent, peer, and teacher attention will be reported in a separate paper. Data for Desirable, Annoying, and Deviant behavior categories were expressed as a rate per minute (RPM) measure modified by the restriction on RPM of the time-sampling technique used. The measure of child compliance was Percent Compliance—the number of compliances that occurred whenever a parent or teacher issued a command divided by the number of commands given. For each of these four dependent variables describing child behavior, total RPM or Percent was obtained for each of four observations, and the average overall scores per child were computed over the four observations.

Consistency of behavior across settings. Table 2 presents the means and standard deviations for the Desirable, Annoying, Deviant, and Percent Compliance categories, as well as for the behavior classes subsumed under the Desirable and Annoying categories. Pearson product moment correlations are presented for examination of the degree of relationship between behaviors coded in the home and school. To the extent that behavior is consistent across settings, these correlations should reflect that consistency.

Correlations were not computed when 7 or more of the 21 boys were

TABLE 2

Means, Standard Deviations, and Product Moment
Correlations for Home and School Deviant Group

Behavior Code	Home Mean	SD	School Mean	SD	r*
Desirable	3.38	.56	3.35	.63	—.06
On Task	1.37	.45	3.20	.61	.13
Physical Positive	.06	.11	....**	....	
Verbal Interaction	1.76	.48	.11	.09	—.13
Nonverbal Interaction	.22	.25	.09	.08	
Altruism	....	....	....	....	
Annoying	.91	.54	1.00	.78	.03†
Verbal Abuse	.69	.41	.41	.42	—.12
Whining	.06	.07	....	....	
Noisemaking	.07	.07	.02	.02	
Nonverbal Abuse	.09	.09	.08	.11	
Motor	....	....	.24	.34	
Inappropriate Task	not scored		.21	.27	
Deviant	.11	.23	....	....	
Namecalling	.04	.05	....	....	
Destructive	....	....	....	....	
Physical Negative	.07	.19	....	....	
% Compliance	69.54	17.99	85.55	17.24	—.23

* No correlation between settings was computed for a code when 7 or more *S*'s were at zero rate.
** Dashes indicate that mean and SD were not reported because 14 or more *S*'s were at zero rate for this code.
† This correlation does not include data for the Inappropriate Task class which was scored only in school.

at zero RPM in either setting. In the classroom, a number of boys complied 100% of the time, producing a restricted score range, and thereby accounting in part for the low correlation between settings for Percent Compliance. For the other variables, the correlations were low and nonsignificant.

Internal consistency of measurement. Odd-even reliabilities were calculated by correlating scores for observations 1 and 3 with 2 and 4 for subjects in each setting. In the home, these product moment correlations were .78 for Desirable, .73 for Annoying, and .60 for Percent Compliance. In the school, the correlations for these same categories were .71, .83, and .81, respectively. Correlations were not computed for the Deviant category because of the large number of zero scores.

Normative comparisons. An alternative to correlational analysis was

TABLE 3

Normative Data for Normal Home Sample and
Composite Classroom Peers

| Category | Home | | | School | | |
Variable	Mean	SD	1 SD Cutoff	Mean	SD	1 SD Cutoff
% Compliance	84.71	10.50	74.20	90.40	10.89	79.51
Desirable	3.66	.21	3.45	3.36	.54	2.82
Annoying	.58	.30	.88	.87	.48	1.35
Deviant	.03	.06	.09	.01	.02	.03

to determine which children showed extreme behaviors in each of the two settings, i.e., whether the more deviant boys at home were also the more deviant in the classroom. Johnson et al. (1974) characterized a child as deviant on a given variable when the child scored beyond one standard deviation of the normative group's mean. A similar strategy was used here; in the home, each deviant child's scores were compared with the scores for the normal home sample, and in the school the deviant child's scores were compared with those of the composite peer group. The deviant children in each setting—those who scored either above or below one standard deviation of the Normal group mean (the cutoff) in the direction of unacceptability or more acceptable behavior —were identified. Table 3 presents the means, standard deviations, and cutoff scores for the major behavior categories for the normal home sample and the composite classroom peer group. The frequencies of deviant boys above and below the cutoffs for each setting were cast in a 2 x 2 table and the Fisher test (Siegel, 1956) was computed for each behavior category. None of the tests were significant; boys who were above the normative mean in degree of unacceptable behaviors at home did not tend to be above the mean at school, and vice versa.

Setting comparisons. The distributions of the children, identified by subject number, are provided in Figures 1-4. Each figure presents data for a given behavior category in the home and in the school. The deviant sample's mean and one standard deviation above the mean in the direction of unacceptable behavior were marked for each variable. These figures permitted the location of a given deviant subject's score in relation to his own group in both settings. For example, subject 80, who was above one standard deviation for his group in an unacceptable direction in terms of his Percent Compliance at home, had a compliance score

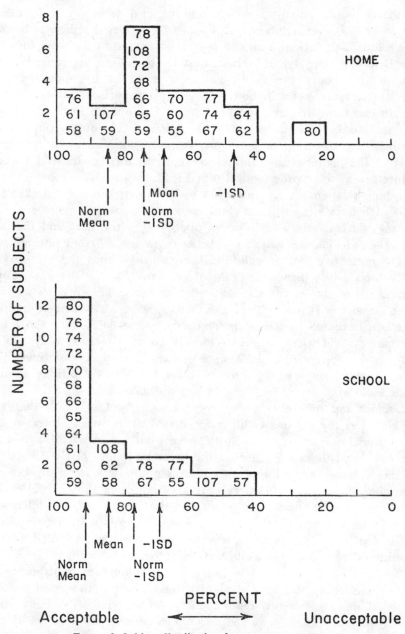

FIGURE 1. Subject distribution for percent compliance.

in the classroom which was within one standard deviation of the mean. Location of subject number 80 in Figures 2-4 reveals that he was beyond one standard deviation in an unacceptable direction in the home only for the Desirable category, in both settings for the Annoying category, and considerably above the group mean in terms of his more extreme Deviant category scores in both settings. In comparison, subject 70 was within one standard deviation for Percent Compliance in both settings, but he was beyond one standard deviation of his own group in an unacceptable direction in Desirable, Annoying, and Deviant behaviors only in the home setting. Similar comparisons can be drawn for other subjects so as to provide more detailed information about complex relationships between setting and types of behaviors. It appeared that the type of behavior in which a child engaged that was extreme even for his own deviant group varied from one child to the next and that the boys showed differing patterns of behavior in the different settings.

The normative group means and standard deviations also are marked on Figures 1-4 to provide a point of reference for the deviant group's scores. For example, for the Annoying category, Figure 3 shows that nine deviant boys, or 43% of the sample, were above one normative standard deviation in the home, and six boys, or 30%, were above one normative standard deviation in the classroom. However, only two of these boys, subjects 70 and 80, were this extreme in both settings. The lack of correlation between group scores in the two settings became clear by looking at the relative standing of individual subjects.

Deviant and normative group comparisons. Another result that was striking was the apparent difference between the mean scores of the deviant and normative groups in the home, but not in school. Statistical comparison of these differences in the home by Delfini et al. (Chapter 9 of this volume) showed that the deviant group was lower in Percent Compliance, had fewer Desirable, more Annoying, and more Deviant behaviors than the normative group. On the other hand, no differences were found between the deviant and normative groups in the classroom for any of the category or class variables using the two-tailed Mann-Whitney U test (Bernal, Kreutzer, Garlington, and North, 1973).

Behavioral differences in the two settings. Differences between means of main category scores of deviant subjects in the two settings were analyzed using two-factor, repeated-measures analyses of variance computed for the Desirable and Annoying variables, with settings as one factor and observations as the second factor. No significant differences between settings in rates of Desirable and Annoying behaviors were

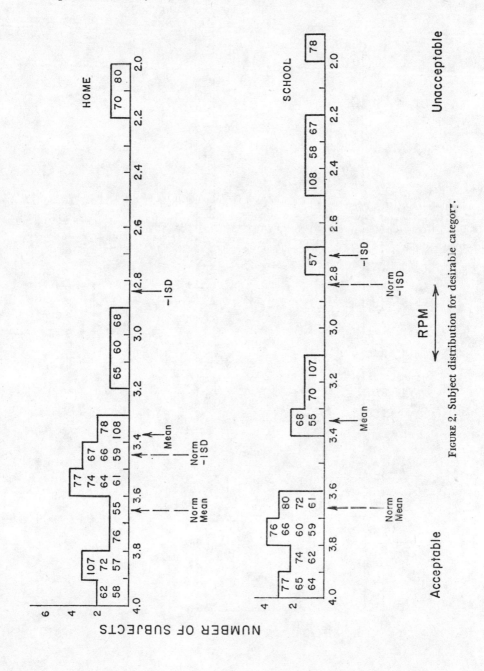

FIGURE 2. Subject distribution for desirable categor.

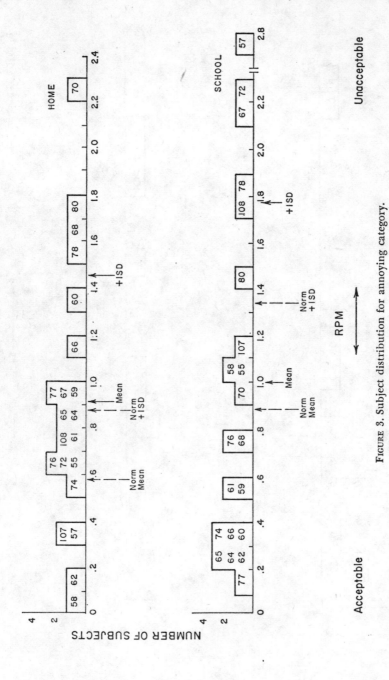

FIGURE 3. Subject distribution for annoying category.

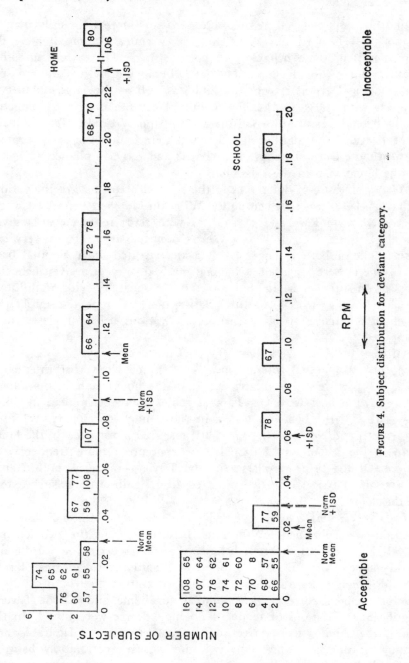

FIGURE 4. Subject distribution for deviant category.

found; the boys engaged in Desirable behaviors more frequently than in Annoying behaviors, but as a group they emitted approximately the same levels of these behaviors in both settings. There were no other main or interactional effects. The large number of zero scores for subjects on the Deviant category variable, as well as the large number of subjects with 100% Compliance, required the use of a nonparametric analysis for these variables. On the basis of the Wilcoxin Matched Pairs Test (Siegel, 1956), significant differences were found; the deviant group showed more Deviant behavior ($p < .01$) and less Compliance ($p < .01$) in the home than in the classroom.

The significance of differences in the rates of occurrence of the various behavior classes was tested using the Wilcoxin Matched Pairs Test whenever there were few cases of subjects with zero frequency of a given variable. When a given behavior class occurred at a zero or very low rate in one or both settings, the data were treated on a nominal basis and subjects were regarded as having any frequency of a given behavior class or zero frequency. In this case, the McNemar Test for Significance of Changes (Siegel, 1956) was used. Using these two tests, the significance levels of differences in occurrence of the various behavior classes were computed.

Of the behavior classes in the Desirable category, Physical Positive ($p < .01$), Verbal Interaction ($p < .01$), and Nonverbal Interaction ($p < .05$) occurred to a greater extent in the home than in the school. However, the boys were On Task at school more often than at home ($p < .01$). Of the behavior classes in the Annoying category, Whining ($p < .001$) and Noisemaking ($p < .01$) occurred more often in the home than in the school and Motor Behavior occurred more frequently in school. Of the behavior classes in the Deviant category, both Namecalling and Physical Negative occurred to a significantly greater extent in the home ($p < .01$).

Intercorrelations among behaviors and settings. Although low correlations were obtained for the same behaviors across the two settings, correlations between different behavior categories occurring within and between the two settings were useful in identifying the degree of relationship among the variables. Table 5 presents a matrix of Pearson product-moment correlations computed for home and school. Several significant correlations of moderate to high degree were found. In the home, the significant negative correlation between the Desirable and Annoying categories and the significant positive correlation between Desirable behavior and Percent Compliance attested to the inverse rela-

TABLE 4

Correlation Matrix for Home and School
Behavior Categories

	2	3	4	5	6
(1) Desirable—Home	—.90†	.45*	—.06	.09	—.47*
(2) Annoying—Home		—.38	.00	.00	.39
(3) % Compliance—Home			—.32	.21	—.23
(4) Desirable—School				—.70†	.48*
(5) Annoying—School					—.45*
(6) % Compliance—School					

* $p < .05$.
† $p < .01$.

tionship between acceptable and unacceptable behavior and the direct relationship between acceptable behaviors. Similar directional relationships were found in the classroom. Curiously, occurrence of Desirable behavior in the home was inversely related to Percent Compliance in the school.

WPBIC Ratings and Observed Child Behavior

Pearson product-moment correlations were computed between the WPBIC teacher ratings and child behavior in the classroom, and between WPBIC mother ratings and child behavior at home. Table 5 presents these correlations between Percent Compliance, Desirable, and Annoying categories and WPBIC Scales 1, 3, and the total WPBIC scores. Scale 1 represents a factor called Acting-out which includes disruptive, aggressive, defiant behaviors, while Scale 3 represents a Distractability factor, characterized by short attention span and inadequate study skills. The two scales are correlated ($r = .67$); acting-out children frequently manifest high rates of inattention and distractibility (Walker, 1970).

In the home, correlations for the behavioral variables and the WPBIC were about zero, except for the low negative correlations between Percent Compliance and the total WPBIC score. In the classroom, correlations between the Desirable and Percent Compliance categories and the mothers' WPBIC ratings were negligible, but moderate and positive relationships were found between Scales 1 and 3 and the Annoying category. The total WPBIC score correlated significantly ($r = .51$, $p < .05$) with Annoying behaviors.

TABLE 5

Pearson Product-Moment Correlations between WPBIC and
Observation Data† for 17 Deviant Subjects

Raters		% Compliance	Behavior Category Desirable	Annoying
Mothers				
	Scale 1	—.33	.05	—.09
	Scale 3	—.34	.01	.12
	Total	—.35	.08	.08
Teachers				
	Scale 1	.18	.01	.39
	Scale 3	.13	—.06	.44
	Total	.07	—.04	.51*

* $p < .05$.
† Data for the home were correlated with mother ratings; data for the school were correlated with teacher ratings.

Teacher-parent WPBIC correlations. Correlations also were computed between teacher and mother ratings; these correlations were .47 for Scale 3 and .34 for the total WPBIC score. Correlations for Scales 1, 2, 4, and 5 were near zero, and none of these correlations were statistically significant.

DISCUSSION

The major task of this report has been to investigate the comparability of behavioral data from one setting to another, using naturalistic observation data obtained on a group of deviant boys. These boys were referred by their parents because they presented certain behavior problems at home. In another report (Chapter 9, this volume), this same group of boys was found to be behaviorally different from boys identified by their parents as normal at home. While these results established that the two groups were different at home, the present report sought to determine the extent to which the deviant group's behavior was stable across settings, i.e., in home and classroom. Correlations and comparisons of the levels of various behaviors in the two settings provided empirical evidence that the children behaved differently in their homes and classrooms. The boys did not tend to maintain similar levels of behaviors or their relative order in their own group from one setting to the other. In comparison to their normative group, boys who behaved in a deviant manner in one setting did not necessarily behave similarly in the other setting. Apparently, the settings contained functional properties which elicited different behavior patterns.

As a group, the boys tended to be less compliant, and to display higher frequencies of namecalling, hitting, whining, and noisemaking in the home than in the classroom. They also engaged to a greater extent in such acceptable behaviors as positive physical contact and verbal and nonverbal interaction in the home, while in the classroom most of their acceptable behavior consisted of being on task—studying, reading, listening, writing, and generally attending to schoolwork. In the classroom the children's range of both unacceptable and acceptable behaviors tended to be restricted as compared to the home.

Results presented here are consistent with Wahler's (1969) report, based on data collected on two boys, that children's deviant and desirable behaviors conformed to contingencies present within the settings, i.e., behavior tended to be setting-specific. Comparison of the results of the present report with the more elaborate ones of Johnson et al. (Chapter 6, this volume) was somewhat difficult, since these investigators used a single overall "deviance" score as their observation measure and a different scoring system was used here. These investigators used two groups of children, one labeled deviant at home and the other labeled deviant at school. The relationship between behavior in the home and school was examined for each group, yielding a two-way look at children's behaviors in settings unlike the referral setting, as contrasted with the home-to-school examination provided by the present study. Using an index of deviance computed by comparison of deviant subjects' data with normative data, they found that 45% of the school-problem sample were deviant according to home observation, and 50% of the home-problem sample were deviant according to school observation. In the present study, 30% of the home-problem boys were beyond one standard deviation of the normative group mean in various disruptive behaviors according to school observation. However, only 14% of the home-problem boys were beyond one standard deviation in higher amplitude aggressive behaviors such as hitting and namecalling in the classroom. Both the Johnson et al. and the present results agreed about the fact that *some* proportion of boys identified as behavior problems in one setting tended also to show them in the other.

The low and generally nonsignificant correlations between the WPBIC and observation data were consistent with Johnson et al.'s report for both home and school settings and with Bolstad's (1974) comparison of teacher ratings and observed classroom behaviors in a "least well behaved" group. In the Johnson et al. study, as well as in the present one, the use of different raters introduced error variance which could account for the low correlations. Thus, adult report bore little relationship to child behavior, particularly in the home, where such relationships were expected between the referring parents' ratings and observation data. Since various items were deleted from the WPBIC prior to adult ratings, no comparisons could be made between children's WPBIC scores and normative data available from other investigators using the WPBIC.

One implication of the major results of this study is that, for primary-grade school children, statements or findings about their behaviors should not be readily generalized from one setting to another. In particular, rates of behaviors observed in a clinic, school, playground, or laboratory setting are not necessarily representative of the children's behavior at home, and behavior rates observed in the home cannot be regarded as criterion measures for assessing the validity of observations made in other settings. Most likely, the most valid assessment of a child's behavior rate is one which is conducted in the setting in which the problem behavior occurs.

APPENDIX

Scoring System Codes

1. *Commands*

Original command: A direct, reasonable request to do or stop doing something.

Negative command: An original command given in a threatening, humiliating, angry, or nagging manner.

Repetitions: An original command or negative command is repeated.

Delayed command: A command that doesn't require compliance or initiation of compliance immediately.

2. *Compliance-Noncompliance*

Compliance: When a child complies within 30 seconds of a command, he is scored as having complied.

Noncompliance: When a child fails to obey a command within a maximum of 30 seconds, he is scored as noncompliant. This is an arbitrary definition of compliance, and only those commands which can be obeyed within the short period of time are scored.

3. Annoying Behavior

Annoying behavior includes child behavior which is bothersome or disruptive, but which is not physically aggressive or destructive and does not pose any threat of damage to anyone. The following are the classes of Annoying behavior which are scored.

Verbal Abuse: Yelling, talking back, arguing, bossing, making nonsounds, interrupting, insisting or threatening verbally to do something that has been forbidden, talking without permission, and criticizing others.

Whining: Whining, crying, whimpering, and sulking.

Noisemaking: Kicking at objects noisily but not destructively, running, hopping, stomping, tapping, banging, dragging furniture noisily, or using objects to make noise.

Nonverbal Abuse: Disrespectful hand gestures, sticking out tongue, grabbing, doing or threatening nonverbally to do something previously forbidden, other forms of nonverbal teasing, obvious cheating.

Motor Behavior: The child is in his seat and engaged in some motor behavior such as bending over while seated, rocking in his chair, sitting straddled backwards in his chair, kneeling with both legs on the chair, looking over at someone else's work or table. Scored at home only when a child must be seated to complete a task.

Inappropriate Task: Working on the wrong material when told to do something else, or there is some clear indication that there is something else the child should be doing. Scored only at school.

4. Deviant Behavior

Deviant behavior is more extreme than Annoying, and usually cannot be tolerated or ignored. The following classes of deviant behavior are scored.

Namecalling: Use of profanity, derogatory terms, and foul language whether directed to specific person or not.

Destructiveness: Destroying or threatening to destroy physical objects.

Physical Negative: Physical attacks or attempts to attack another person. The attack must be of sufficient intensity to potentially inflict pain.

5. Desirable Behavior

This category includes acceptable behavior other than compliance.

On Task: Working on assignment or engaging in any task prescribed by the teacher; raising hand in order to be recognized by the teacher.

Physical Positive: Physical reactions of affection, warmth, and approval.

Verbal Interaction: Speaking in a manner appropriate to the situation; for example, engaging in conversation, asking and answering questions, making statements relative to the situation.

Nonverbal Interaction: Appropriate play and work with other persons with no verbal exchanges occurring.

Altruism: Doing or offering to do some common kindness for someone else.

6. *Parent, Teacher and Peer Attention*

Reactions to the child's scored behaviors are Attention. The following classes of Attention are scored:

Verbal and Physical Positive: Statements of verbal expressions, even though they are affectively neutral, and praise, compliments, approval, physical reactions of warmth, affection and approval.

Negative: Verbal statements of criticism, correction, derogation, name-calling, half compliments, threats of punishment, negative facial expressions and gestures indicating disapproval, and denials of requests.

Physical Negative: Physical restraints, coercion, pulling, yanking or other forms of physical aggression, removing child from the group, depriving him of privileges or objects, making him stay after school.

Spanking: Hitting the child on the buttocks with the hand.

Time-out: Sending the child to a specified room or other enclosed area for the purpose of isolating him as punishment. Child may be isolated visually from the company of others in the classroom.

No Attention: Neither verbal nor physical response to the child.

REFERENCES

BERNAL, M. E., KREUTZER, S. L., GARLINGTON, G., and NORTH, J. A.: Comparison of real and composite subjects in the classroom. Unpublished manuscript, 1973. May be obtained from the senior author at the Department of Psychology, U. of Denver, Denver, Colo. 80210.

BERNAL, M. E., KREUTZER, S. L., NORTH, J. A., and PELC, R. E.: Scoring system for home and school: Rationale, use, reliability, and validity. Paper presented at the meetings of the American Psychological Association, Montreal, 1973. May be obtained from the senior author at the Department of Psychology, U. of Denver, Denver, Colo. 80210.

BERNAL, M. E., and NORTH, J. A.: Scoring system for home and school. Revision X. Unpublished manuscript, 1972. May be obtained from the senior author at the Department of Psychology, U. of Denver, Denver, Colo. 80210.

BOLSTAD, O. D.: The relationship between teacher ratings and observed behavior of children in the classroom. Unpublished doctoral dissertation, U. of Oregon, Eugene, 1974.

COBB, J. A., and HOPS, H.: Coding manual for continuous observation of interactions by single subjects in an academic setting. Report No. 9, July, 1972, U. of Oregon, Contract No. NPECE—70—005, OEC—70—4152 (607), Bureau of Educationally Handicapped, U.S. Office of Education.

JOHNSON, S. M., WAHL, G., MARTIN, S., and JOHANSSON, S.: How deviant is the normal child and his family. In: E. D. Rubin, J. P. Brady, and J. D. Henderson (Eds.), *Advances in Behavior Therapy*, Vol. 4. New York: Academic Press, 1973. Pp. 37-54.

PATTERSON, G. R., RAY, R. S., SHAW, D. A., and COBB, J. A.: Manual for coding of family interactions, 1969 revision. Document #01234. Available from ASIS/NAPS, c/o Microfiche Publications, 305 E. 46 St., New York, N. Y. 10017.

PATTERSON, G. R., COBB, J., and RAY, R. S.: Direct intervention in the classroom: A set of procedures for the aggressive child. In: F. W. Clark, D. R. Evans, and L. A. Hamerlynck (Eds.), *Implementing Behavioral Programs in Educational and Clinic Settings*. Champaign, Ill.: Research Press, 1972.

SIEGEL, S.: *Nonparametric Statistics for the Behavioral Sciences*. New York: McGraw-Hill, 1956.

WAHL, G., JOHNSON, S. M., JOHANSSON, S., and MARTIN, S.: An operant analysis of child-family interactions. *Behav. Ther.*, 5, 64-78, 1974.

WAHLER, R. G.: Setting generality: Some specific and general effects of child behavior therapy. *J. Appl. Behav. Anal.*, 2, 239-246, 1969.

WAHLER, R. G.: Deviant child behavior in home and school settings: Some categories for comprehensive description. Part 1 of progress report on NIMH Research Grant MH18516-01A1, U. of Tennessee, 1973.

WALKER, H. M.: *Walker Problem Behavior Identification Checklist Manual*. Los: Angeles: Western Psychological Services, 1970.

WERRY, J. W., and QUAY, H. C.: Observing the classroom behavior of elementary school children. *Exceptional Children*, 35, 461-470, 1969.

9

Comparison of Deviant and Normal Boys in Home Settings

Leo F. Delfini, Martha E. Bernal,
and Paul M. Rosen

The purpose of this paper is to compare the behavior of primary grade boys who were identified by their parents as presenting behavior problems at home (deviant group) with boys identified by their parents as being no more disruptive than the average boy (normal group). Comparisons were made in the boys' homes by trained observers using naturalistic observation methods.

Current literature in child psychopathology includes a number of comparisons of conduct-problem clinic-referred children, and nonproblem nonreferred children. These comparisons have been done using symptom rating checklists completed by parents or by experimenters during parent interviews (e.g., Connors, 1970; Speer, 1971; Wolf, 1967), and behavioral observations in natural environments such as classrooms (e.g., Werry and Quay, 1969; Nelson, 1971), recreation centers (Wodarski and Pedi, 1972), and homes (Patterson, Chapter 11, this volume). Some have used combinations of behavioral observation and parent report inventories (e.g., Lobitz and Johnson, 1974).

The majority of symptom checklist studies have shown that clinic-referred and nonreferred children differed in frequency and intensity of

This research was supported by NIMH grant No. 20922 awarded to the second author. We are deeply grateful to Leola Schultz, who helped collect, process, and analyze the data, to Sandra Tamayo, who typed this manuscript, and to Orin D. Bolstad, who reviewed it prior to presentation at the Banff Conference. The cooperation and assistance of the Denver Public Schools, and of Dr. Gerald Elledge and Mr. Orville Turner, in particular, is gratefully acknowledged.

conduct disorder characteristics such as acting out and antisocial behaviors, and personality disorder symptoms such as shy, inhibited, anxious behaviors (see Connors, 1970; Speer, 1971; Wolf, 1967).

One problem with parent report methods is that such reports may be contaminated by differences in the parents' subjective estimates or threshold of tolerance for certain symptoms, when in reality the deviant children's behaviors might not differ from those of the average child (Connors, 1970). This possibility was investigated by Shepherd et al. (1966), who reported that a nonreferred normal child population included many children with behavior disturbances comparable to those of referred deviant children. These investigators also reported that mothers of the referred children were more likely to experience various emotional problems, less tolerance for stress, and less ability to cope with their children than mothers of nonreferred children. Thus, information regarding child behavior based solely upon parents' ratings remains ambiguous.

Unfortunately, observation data which could shed some light on this problem have tended to provide conflicting results; children variously classified as deviant sometimes, but not always, show more deviant and less desirable behavior than their normal counterparts. Successful differentiation of these two groups seems to depend upon a number of factors. For example, Wodarski and Pedi (1972) found only minimal differences in behavior between antisocial and normal boys in a recreation center. They concluded that this finding might have been due to a lack of correspondence between the behaviors they observed and the behaviors (e.g., truancy, theft) that referring agents used to classify the children as deviant. They also noted that the settings (home, school, neighborhood) within which classification or labeling and observations took place were quite different. In the recreation center the structured group activities and interaction with adults probably served to decrease the likelihood of occurrence of the antisocial behaviors that the deviant children might emit in their usual environments.

Similar failures to find consistency of behavior across settings have been reported elsewhere. In Chapter 8 of this volume, for example, Bernal et al. find that in a group of children who presented conduct problems at home, the most deviant children at home were not necessarily the most deviant in school.

Several recent studies have found differences between deviant and normal children when they were observed in the setting where they were labeled. Both Werry and Quay (1969) and Nelson (1971) reported that children who were labeled deviant in the classroom exhibited significantly higher rates of deviant behavior and significantly lower rates of task-oriented, desirable behaviors in their classrooms than matched normal children. In another study, Lobitz and Johnson (1974) found that children who were referred to a clinic by their parents for "active behavior problems" (e.g., aggressiveness, disobedience, hyperactivity) emitted a significantly greater proportion of deviant, and a significantly smaller proportion of positive, behaviors during home observations than matched normal subjects. No differences were found between the two groups when they were observed during a structured clinic situation. This finding tended to agree with results of other studies reviewed by Lobitz and Johnson (1974) in which failure to find differences between clinic-referred and nonreferred children in a laboratory or in a clinic waiting room might have been due to the failure of deviant behavior to transfer from the usual environment to a different setting.

One implication of these results is that when comparing deviant and normal children by observational methods, differences are more likely to be found when the children are observed in the setting in which they were labeled. These differences also may be accentuated when the behaviors measured are similar to those used to classify the groups, as Wodarski and Pedi (1972) have pointed out. In the present study the behaviors observed and measured in the boys' homes where they were labeled corresponded closely to the behavioral criteria that parents used to differentiate the groups. Thus, it was expected that deviant boys would show lower rates of acceptable, and higher rates of unacceptable, behavior compared to a normative group of nondisruptive boys.

METHOD

Subjects and subject selection. The subjects were 21 deviant and 21 normal boys in the kindergarten and first grades of the Denver Public School system. All were enrolled in regular classrooms, and only one boy who was in the deviant group was repeating a grade. Characteristics of the two groups shown in Table 1 indicate that the groups were not perfectly matched on several variables such as socioeconomic level, number of intact or two-parent families, and number of children per family. However, these differences between groups reached significance only for number of intact families. Matching of the groups was not possible because the families of normal boys who volunteered to participate were intact families who tended to be of higher socioeconomic level.

TABLE 1

Characteristics of Deviant and Normal
Boys and Their Families

Age in yrs. & mos.	Grade K	1st	Socioeconomic Level*		No. of Children in Family		Single	No. Parents Two-Parents
			DEVIANT GROUP					
Range 5-6 to 7-7	13	8	Range	1-6	Range	1-4	8	13
Mean 6-5			Mean	3.2	Mean	2.3		
Median 6-3			Median	3.0	Median	3.0		
			NORMAL GROUP					
Range 5-5 to 7-1	15	6	Range	1-6	Range	1-4	0	21
Mean 6-3			Mean	2.4	Mean	3.0		
Median 6-3			Median	1.0	Median	3.0		

* Scores were based on Edwards' Occupational Grouping Scale. Lowest occupational levels are coded 6 and the highest are coded 1.

The deviant subjects were recruited into a family intervention project being conducted for the purpose of locating and treating boys who were identified by their parents as showing behavior problems in the home. Letters sent to parents through the schools for recruitment of deviant boys listed the following behaviors: fails to obey, fights, talks back, interrupts, teases, damages things, cries, and fusses. Parents were told that if their boy displayed two or more of these behaviors to an excessive degree at home, and they wished to obtain help, they could return an enclosed information form. The letter designed to recruit normal boys was sent three months later. It stated that the same research project that had been trying to locate behavior problem boys was now interested in obtaining volunteer families whose kindergarten or first grade boy was regarded as being no more disruptive than the average boy. The stated purpose for studying these children was to determine to what extent average boys of this age behaved disruptively. Additional details regarding deviant subject recruitment and subject screening criteria which applied to both normal and deviant subjects are reported in Bernal et al. (Chapter 8, this volume).

For recruitment of normal boys, 600 letters were mailed from 10 of the 22 Denver schools cooperating in this research; the principals of only these 10 schools consented to this additional mailing. The number of sets of normal children's parents who responded to the letter was 62. Twenty-six of these families met the initial selection criteria presented in Chapter 8 and were subsequently contacted by telephone. The most critical criteria were, briefly, that the boys lived with their immediate families, were physically and mentally normal, and had no previous referral for psychological or psychiatric problems, and that their parents were free of serious marital difficulties as manifested by previous separation or threats of divorce. The deviant and normal boys for whom observation data are reported here are those boys whose parents cooperated for four observation periods.

All families were offered $10 for taking part in the study, which required them to return an enclosed information form and complete a set of four home observations. The major differences in recruitment of deviant and normal boys, aside from the difference in selection criteria, were that (1) the normals were recruited later in time than the deviant boys and came from schools whose principals were highly cooperative, and (2) the normals' parents were given full information about the project (including that they would be paid for taking part) when they were called by telephone the first time, whereas the deviant boys' parents were first invited to a group meeting following the initial telephone contact. At this group meeting they obtained full details of the project and learned they would be paid for observations.

Scheduling of observations. The order of data collection for deviant and normal subjects was not random; data were collected on 15 of the 21 deviant subjects between December and the following February 21. The rest of the deviant subjects were observed between February 21 and May 30, during which time all normal group data collection occurred.

Dependent variables. A multivariate behavioral coding system (Bernal and North, 1972), developed for the purpose of recording both home and classroom behaviors of primary grade discipline problem boys, was used. Four major categories were scored for the target child: Compliance, Desirable, Annoying, and Deviant behaviors. In addition, two major behavior categories, Commands and type of Attention, were scored for the parents.

Under each of the behavior categories were subsumed various behavior classes. These categories, and the behavior classes subsumed under each category are shown below. Detailed descriptions of the coding system, observers and their training, agreement checks, and other details of data collection are presented in Chapter 8.

Agreement calculations. Four different types of agreement were calculated. *Overall* agreement was idiosyncratic to the scoring format used, was easiest to compute, and was the most stringent. Agreement on all

82 cells within a 15-second time sample was required. *Category* agreement required that two observers agree that any behavior class within a category occurred or did not occur, and was scored for Desirable, Annoying, and Deviant categories. Due to the complexity of the Percent Compliance measure, *chain* agreement was computed; it required that observers agree on the command-compliance chain that was scored within 30 seconds of time. Finally, *class* agreement was computed for the Command category, i.e., observers were required to agree on the type of command given, but only for Commands, Repetitions of Commands, and Negative Commands. Delayed Commands were not scored for agreement because by definition a child could not comply with a Delayed Command within 30 seconds.

Overall and category agreement were calculated for all 42 agreement checks done during data collection. However, chain agreement and class agreement were computed for ten subjects for each group chosen at random.

For the deviant subjects, overall agreement averaged .82, and category agreement scores were high, averaging .94 for Desirable, .93 for Annoying, and .99 for Deviant. Chain and class agreements were lower, averaging .62 for Percent Compliance and .58 for Commands. For the normal group, overall agreement averaged .82 and category agreement scores were as high as for the deviant group. Chain agreement for Percent Compliance averaged .57 and class agreement for Commands averaged .58.

Observation procedures. Observations in the home were conducted when all family members were in view of the observer, the television set was turned off, the radio was turned off or at low volume, no telephone calls were made, and no visitors were present. Once a family selected a convenient time of day (but no observations were done during mealtimes) for the first observation, all subsequent observations were conducted at that time on weekdays. The observers scored continuously for 30 minutes on the child identified as the subject, yielding 120 minutes of data over the four observations. Parent commands and parent attention were also scored but data for attention are not reported here.

RESULTS

Data reduction. Scores for child Desirable, Annoying, and Deviant behaviors were expressed in rates per minute (RPM) modified by the restriction on rate of the time sampling technique used. Parent Commands and child Compliance were expressed in frequency per observation. Another measure of child compliance, Percent Compliance, was computed by dividing the number of child compliances during an observation by the number of parents' commands in that observation. A score for each of these variables was obtained for each observation and these scores were individually averaged over the 21 subjects in each group to yield 8 means per behavior category (4 observations x 2 groups).

Parent Command data were further analyzed according to whether the commands were original, repeated, or negative commands. Scores for each of these classes of commands were expressed in percentages of the total commands given, and were computed by dividing the frequency of a command class by the frequency of total commands per observation.

To compare groups in terms of the types of commands given, it was necessary to omit mother-only families because of the differences in number of commands that could occur in single versus two-parent families. When mother-only families were omitted, there remained 16 sets of parents in the deviant group. Since the normal group was composed solely of two-parent families, five families were selected out of the analysis at random. In each group the individual subjects' percentages within each command class were averaged over fathers and mothers separately. Mean percentage scores for a command class during each observation were then averaged over the four observations to yield six mean command class scores per group; i.e., for each group, there were data for the three command classes for fathers and for the three command classes for mothers.

Main behavior category differences between groups and observations. Two-factor analyses of variance (AOV) of Percent Compliance, Compliance, Desirable, and Annoying categories, and parent Commands were conducted, with one factor consisting of groups (deviant vs. normal) and the other observations (four repeated measures). The analyses of Desirable and Annoying behaviors showed that deviant boys exhibited significantly ($F = 4.24$, $df = 1/40$; $p < 0.05$) lower rates of Desirable category behaviors, and significantly ($F = 5.88$, $df = 1/40$; $p < 0.05$) higher rates of Annoying category behaviors than the normal boys. There were no changes in Annoying or Desirable behavior rates over observations for either group. Means and standard deviations of Desirable, Annoying, and Deviant behaviors expressed in RPM are presented in Table 2.

Because many of the normal boys emitted zero rates of the more ex-

TABLE 2

Means and Standard Deviations of Main Child Behavior Categories

Behavior Category	Subjects	Index	Observations				Mean 1-4
			1	2	3	4	
Annoying	Normal	Mean	.54	.73	.48	.57	.58
RPM		SD	.24	.64	.24	.46	.30
	Deviant	Mean	.75	1.04	.87	.97	.91
		SD	.58	.75	.85	.63	.55
Deviant	Normal	Mean	.01	.07	.01	.02	.03
RPM		SD	.01	.19	.02	.05	.06
	Deviant	Mean	.06	.16	.13	.10	.11
		SD	.09	.45	.29	.21	.22
Desirable	Normal	Mean	3.71	3.49	3.78	3.65	3.66
RPM		SD	.22	.49	.20	.33	.21
	Deviant	Mean	3.51	3.36	3.33	3.43	3.41
		SD	.37	.78	.79	.56	.50

TABLE 3

Means and Standard Deviations of Compliance and Related Parent Behaviors

Behavior Category	Subjects	Index	Observations				Mean
			1	2	3	4	
Percent	Normal	Mean	72.5	83.9	83.0	79.1	79.6
Compliance		SD	23.4	16.6	16.0	19.3	10.5
	Deviant	Mean	71.2	64.5	69.3	64.8	67.4
		SD	21.4	25.3	23.7	22.8	17.6
Compliance	Normal	Mean	6.14	7.47	6.52	5.19	6.33
Frequency/		SD	5.08	6.40	5.67	3.80	
Observation	Deviant	Mean	14.29	6.71	7.47	7.71	9.04
		SD	6.23	3.90	4.84	6.70	
Command	Normal	Mean	8.23	8.47	7.47	6.23	7.48
Frequency/		SD	6.36	7.36	6.19	3.67	
Observation	Deviant	Mean	21.85	10.90	10.80	11.14	13.65
		SD	8.87	6.28	7.13	8.41	

treme Deviant category behaviors, a nonparametric test comparing the groups in terms of number of subjects who emitted any Deviant Category behavior seemed more appropriate than AOV comparing mean differences in behavior rate. For this purpose a chi-square analysis was performed using a 2 x 2 table which compared deviant versus normal subjects with respect to occurrence and nonoccurrence of Deviant behavior. The results of this analysis showed that compared to normal boys a significantly greater number of deviant boys emitted Deviant behaviors ($\chi^2 = 4.20$, $df = 1$, $p < .05$).

Compliance behaviors were subdivided into three dependent variables: parent Commands, children's Compliance, and Percent Compliance. Group x observations analysis of each of the three variables showed significantly ($F = 4.69$, $df = 1/40$; $p < 0.05$) lower Percent Compliance in the deviant group, a greater frequency of Commands that almost reached significance at p .05 for deviant children's parents, and no difference between groups in frequency of Compliance ($p > 0.05$). There were no changes in behavior for either group over observations. Means and standard deviations of Percent Compliance, Compliance, and Commands are presented in Table 3.

In summary, the main category analyses suggest that deviant children showed a lower percentage of Compliance, a higher rate of Annoying behaviors, and a lower rate of Desirable behaviors than normal children. It also appeared that a significantly larger proportion of the deviant children emitted the more extreme Deviant behaviors which occurred at low rates in both groups, and that deviant children's parents tended to give more commands, although this difference did not quite reach significance.

Differences in types of commands. To obtain a more detailed picture of parents' command behavior, each of the three Command classes (i.e., First Commands, Repeat Commands, and Negative Commands) was subjected to a two-factor analysis of variance, with one factor consisting of parents (mother versus father) and the other groups (deviant versus normal). The three analyses showed that the parents of deviant children tended to give a significantly ($F = 9.02$, $df = 1/60$, $p < .01$) greater percentage of Negative Commands than the normal children's parents. There were no differences ($p > 0.05$) in percentage of First Commands or Repeat Commands between the groups; however, mothers gave a significantly ($F = 4.84$, $df = 1/60$; $p < 0.05$) greater percentage of First Commands compared to fathers. This difference between parents in First Commands occurred not because fathers emitted more Repeat or Nega-

TABLE 4

Pearson Product-Moment Correlations* between Main Behavior Categories

Group	*Behavior Categories*				
Normal	Com-pliance	Commands	Annoy-ing	Deviant	Desirable
% Compliance	.15	.02	−.31	−.16	.27
Compliance		.99†	−.18	.03	.19
Commands			−.11	.13	.13
Annoying				.30	−.65†
Deviant					−.16
Deviant					
% Compliance	.24	−.23	−.38	−.62†	.50**
Compliance		.87†	.43**	−.17	−.25
Commands			.63†	.18	−.54**
Annoying				.54**	−.89†
Deviant					−.70†

* Note diagonal entries have been omitted.
** $p < .05$.
† $p < .01$.

tive Commands, but because in several families they gave no commands at all during any of the observation periods. Despite the greater percentage of Negative Commands given by deviant children's parents, it should be noted that the percentages of both Negative Commands and Repeat Commands were relatively small compared to percentages of First Commands for both groups, as shown in Figure 1.

Relationship among main behavior categories. Pearson product-moment correlations between all combinations of the six variables were computed for deviant and normal subjects separately and are presented in Table 4. In general, behaviors considered acceptable (e.g., Desirable, Percent Compliance) tended to be inversely related to those considered unacceptable (Annoying, Deviant). There also were a greater number of significant correlations in the deviant group and a tendency for correlation coefficients to be of greater magnitude than in the normal group.

Another set of relationships that appeared to distinguish deviant and normal groups was the association between parents' Commands and child's Desirable and Annoying behaviors. In the deviant group there was a high positive correlation ($r = .63$, $p < .01$) between parents' Commands and the child's Annoying behavior rate, and a high negative

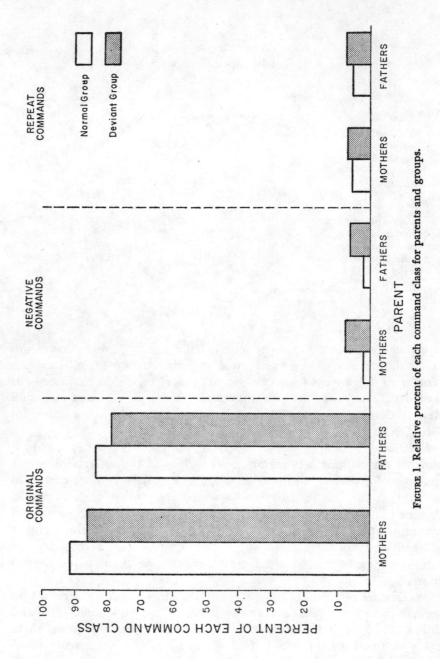

FIGURE 1. Relative percent of each command class for parents and groups.

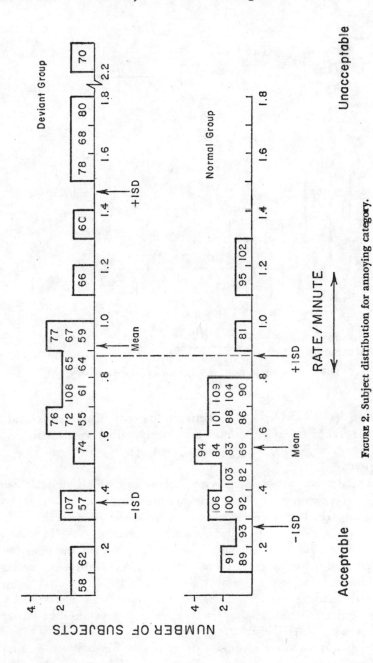

FIGURE 2. Subject distribution for annoying category.

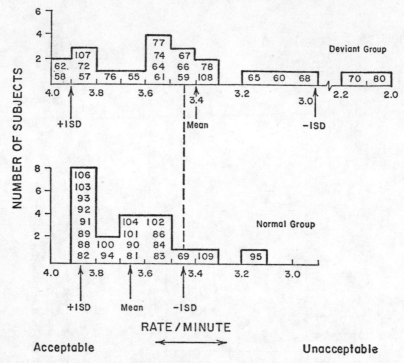

FIGURE 3. Subject distribution for desirable category.

correlation $(r = -.54, p < .05)$ between parents' Commands and the child's Desirable behavior rate. The corresponding coefficients in the normal group were low, nonsignificant, and opposite in sign $(r = -.11, .13,$ respectively).

Normative comparisons and distribution of individual subjects' scores. Although comparisons of main category behaviors showed that group differences reached statistical significance, there was considerable overlap in the range of scores of the deviant and normal subjects. This overlap is illustrated in Figures 2 through 5. Each figure shows the distribution within a given behavior category of normal and deviant boys' scores by subject numbers which are shown in the boxes. Individual subjects' scores were examined to determine whether boys who overlapped with or were similar to normal boys on one variable would be similar to normal boys on other variables.

The criterion for determining whether a deviant boy was similar to the normal boys was based on an index used by Johnson et al. (Chapter

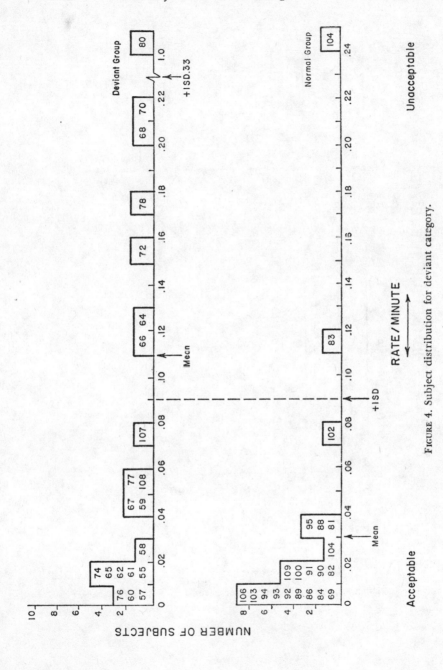

FIGURE 4. Subject distribution for deviant category.

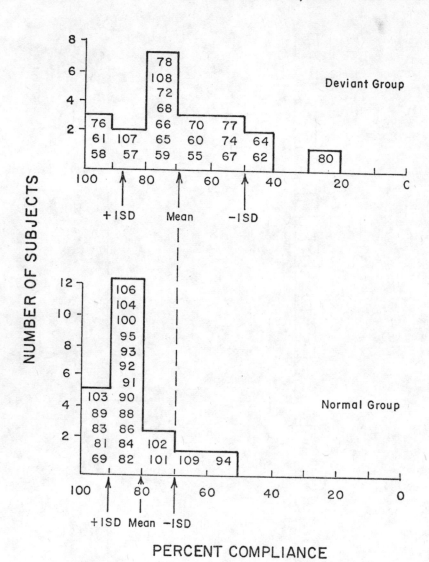

FIGURE 5. Subject distribution for percent compliance category.

6, this volume), who arbitrarily designated a child as deviant on a given variable if he scored beyond one standard deviation above the mean of a normative sample. The standard deviation was on the side of the mean representing deviant or unacceptable behavior for normal subjects.

In the present report, this standard deviation measure of deviance was used to specify the number of variables on which each deviant boy scored beyond one standard deviation (broken line Figures 2 through 5) of the normal group mean. An examination of Figures 2 through 5 shows that five of the deviant subjects (e.g., subject 57) failed to fall beyond one standard deviation of the normal group on any of the four variables; that seven deviant subjects (e.g., subject 55) fell beyond one standard deviation of the normal group mean on one variable; and that nine deviant subjects fell beyond the standard deviation criterion on two or more variables. Because 6 of the 21 normal subjects (e.g., subject 94) also fell above one standard deviation of their group mean on one variable, it was unclear whether exceeding the criterion on one variable was sufficient to characterize the seven deviant subjects who did so as different from normal. Four of these deviant subjects behaved quite unacceptably (subjects 55, 62, 74 on Percent Compliance; subject 72 on Deviant Category behavior) on the variable that exceeded the criterion and it was possible that parents referred them for help on this basis. The remaining three of these subjects, together with the five who did not exceed the criterion on any of the four variables, did not appear different from the normal subjects.

Behavior rates over the course of the study. Deviant and normal boys were not observed in random order; the deviant subjects' data were collected in December through February and the normal subjects' data were collected during the subsequent period of time between February and May. This failure to randomize order of data collection for the two groups could have provided two alternative interpretations of the data. One was that the differences between groups could have been due to a tendency for boys in general to behave in a progressively more acceptable manner over the months of December through June. To check this possibility, the means for Annoying, Desirable, and Percent Compliance (averaged over four observations for each child) were examined over the period of data collection. This examination indicated that within each group and over both groups there were no apparent systematic trends in the data as a function of the period of time during which data were obtained. An explanation of the differences between groups solely in terms of data collection order seemed less plausible, although it was impossible by this method to determine the extent to which such possible order effects may have contributed to between-groups variability.

A second explanation of the results was that there was instrument decay, i.e., a systematic change over time in the scoring of behavior which resulted from changes in interpretation of the scoring codes by the observers, or from changes in observer reliability. Here, there were data only on the topic of reliability changes to counter this interpretation. Examination of the observer agreement scores over the period of data collection revealed no systematic trends in agreement scores.

DISCUSSION

The purpose of this paper was to compare the behavior of parent-referred deviant and normal boys at home in the company of their families. The major findings were that deviant boys generally produced a higher rate of behaviors which were potentially bothersome or disruptive (Annoying Category) but were not physically aggressive or destructive acts. The latter behaviors (Deviant Category) occurred at very low rates in both groups. However, a significantly greater number of the deviant boys emitted these physically aggressive or destructive behaviors during the observation periods.

With respect to more acceptable behaviors, the deviant boys produced relatively lower rates of Desirable Category behaviors, and a relatively smaller percentage of Compliance, although there were no differences between groups in the actual frequency with which they complied.

Differences between parents in the two groups in the frequency and types of commands and requests also emerged. Compared to parents of normal children, parents of deviant children tended to give more overall commands, and a significantly greater proportion of these commands were posed in a threatening, angry, humiliating, or nagging manner. Contrary to the expectation that parents of deviant boys would need to repeat their commands more often, no differences between groups were found in the relative proportion of use of such repetitions. Finally, it was found that parent command rates in the deviant group were strongly associated with the children's disruptive behavior, but there was no such relationship in the normal group.

These results suggested that the deviant children's parents were providing more frequent supervision of their boys. However, the data did not indicate the direction of the relationship between the degree of parent supervision and child deviance. Thus, it was uncertain whether the deviant children needed more supervision because their behavior was more unacceptable, or behaved more unacceptably because they were being supervised more often and in a more negative manner than were the normal children.

The present results agreed in general with those of previous studies in which there was close correspondence between obsrvation codes and the behaviors used to classify deviant and normal children, and in which observation and classification settings were similar. For example, Lobitz and Johnson's (1974) home observation data showed that, compared to normal subjects, clinic-referred problem-behavior children emitted a significantly greater proportion of deviant behaviors and a significantly lesser proportion of positive or acceptable behaviors. Parents of these problem children issued a significantly larger proportion of commands and responded to their children with a greater proportion of negative consequences than did parents of normal children. The similarities between the Lobitz and Johnson results and the present ones occurred despite differences in behavior codes, selection of subjects, operationalization of deviant behavior, and data reduction.* The present findings also were congruent with those obtained in classroom comparisons of normal and deviant children using observational procedures (e.g., Werry & Quay, 1969; Nelson, 1971). These comparisons have shown that deviant children emitted significantly more deviant behavior and significantly less prosocial or appropriate on-task behavior than did normal children.

Some caution seemed warranted in the interpretation of the present results. One source of difficulty was methodological, in that the order of data collection for the two groups was not randomized, nor were the groups perfectly matched on several possibly relevant variables such as socioeconomic level, number of children in the family, or number of intact (two-parent) families. Although it seemed likely that order effects per se were not responsible for differences between groups, such effects may have contributed to the group differences. With respect to the problem of matching, there were significant differences between the groups in the number of intact families. Furthermore, it appeared that

---

* The authors would like to caution the reader regarding the specificity of our data. Although the present results agree in general with those of other observational studies, particular rates and percentages of desirable and undesirable behaviors can best be conceptualized as peculiar to our time sampling system, definition of behavior codes, and method of subject selection and setting, and should not be used as a base for comparison when different methodological conditions occur.

boys in mother-only families tended to be among the most disruptive in the deviant group. If there existed a general tendency for boys with single mothers to behave poorly compared to boys from intact families irrespective of the labels given them, then differences in the groups could have been due to failure to match on the intact family variable rather than to accurate parent identification of problem children.

The above methodological problems would appear to be of greatest concern if one were focusing mainly on statistical differences between groups. However, there appeared to be a great deal of overlap between groups when the dependent variables were considered either separately or in combination. This overlap suggested that some caution be used when interpreting group differences, since approximately half of the deviant boys appeared no different from the normal ones in the behaviors measured. Similar results were obtained by Lobitz and Johnson (1974), who emphasized the importance of learning why children who seemed to behave similarly were labeled differently. These authors suggested that, in addition to child behavior, other factors which may precipitate child referral—such as parent psychopathology, marital discord, parent tolerance levels, and parent expectations—should be examined. One study which addressed itself specifically to this issue was done by Shepherd et al. (1966), who compared the parents of clinic-referred and nonreferred children. In their report, the children in the two groups were matched on a number of variables such as age and sex as well as for type and severity of symptomatology. The question of interest was why parents of children with the same symptoms did or did not refer their children for professional help. The authors found that mothers of the clinic-referred children worried significantly more about their children, were more puzzled and helpless about coping with them, and were more irritated and exasperated by their children's behaviors. This variable, the degree of parent tolerance for deviance, has been emphasized by a number of other authors (e.g., Connors, 1970; Lapouse and Monk, 1958; Wolf, 1967) and may be an important determinant of whether or not children develop into reasonably well-adjusted adults (Lapouse and Monk, 1958). If parent tolerance is an important determinant of later adjustment, then the identification and treatment of low-tolerance parents whose children do not appear to differ from normals may be as important as identification and treatment of referred children who do differ from normals.

Despite the findings that many deviant children were not measurably different from normals, it should be noted that approximately half of the children labeled deviant did differ from the nonreferred children. Yet all except one of these young deviant children had never been previously referred by their parents for help with their behavior problems. Apparently, a substantial proportion of the parents discriminated that their children were different from other children although the boys had not yet been labeled deviant by professionals. One important qualification of previous statements was based on the necessity for exercising caution in concluding that parents were mislabeling their children because referred children did not appear to differ from normals as measured by behavioral observation. There was the possibility that the observation system did not detect the behaviors that concerned the parents because either the spectrum of observed behaviors was too narrow, the observation system was insensitive to certain characteristics of the disturbing behaviors such as intensity or duration, or the family was reactive to being observed (i.e., the behavior during observation was atypical). These deficiencies would apply to other studies as well.

With respect to group differences between normal and deviant boys, it appears that these can best be expressed as a difference in rates of the types of behaviors sampled. The tendency toward higher rates of unacceptable or aversive behaviors in the deviant boys, the tendency for their parents to emit more commands in a negative manner, and the relatively greater association between parents' commands and children's disruptive behavior in the deviant group, all support Patterson's (Patterson et al., 1972) coercion hypothesis, which predicts that as parents become more negative, children become more negative and vice versa, in a reciprocal escalation of the use of aversive events to control each other's behavior. This hypothesis is representative of the more recently accepted interactive model of child deviance. Proponents of this model do not assume that parent behaviors and attitudes are the major cause of child deviance as in the earlier parent causation model, but rather that child behavior can be equally important as a determinant of parent attitudes and behavior (Gewirtz, 1969).

REFERENCES

BERNAL, M. E., and NORTH, J. A.: Scoring system for home and school, Revision X. Unpublished manuscript, 1972. May be obtained from the senior author at the Department of Psychology, U. of Denver, Denver, Colo. 80210.

CONNORS, C. K.: Symptom patterns in hyperkinetic, neurotic, and normal children. *Child Devel.*, 41, 667-682, 1970.

GEWIRTZ, J. L.: Levels of conceptual analysis in environmental-infant interaction research. *Merrill-Palmer Quarterly*, 15, 7-47, 1969.

LAPOUSE, R., and MONK, M.: An epidemiologic study of behavior characteristics in children. *Amer. J. Public Health and the Nation's Health*, 48, 1134-1144, 1958.

LOBITZ, G. K., and JOHNSON, S. M.: Normal versus deviant children: A multi-method comparison. Paper presented at the Sixth Banff International Conference on Behavior Modification, 1974.

NELSON, C. M.: Techniques for screening conduct-disturbed children. *Exceptional Children*, 37, 501-507, 1971.

PATTERSON, G. R., COBB, J. A., and RAY, R. S.: A social engineering technology for retraining the families of aggressive boys. In: H. Adams and L. Unikel (Eds.), *Georgia Symposium in Experimental Clinical Psychology*, Vol. II. Springfield, Ill.: Charles C Thomas, 1972.

SHEPHERD, M., OPPENHEIM, A. N., and MITCHELL, S.: Childhood behavior disorders and the child guidance clinic: An epidemiological study. *J. Child Psychol. and Psychiat.*, 7, 39-52, 1966.

SPEER, D. C.: Behavior problem checklist (Peterson-Quay): Baseline data from parents of child guidance and nonclinic children. *J. Consult. and Clin. Psychol.*, 36, 221-228, 1971.

WERRY, J. S., and QUAY, H. C.: Observing the classroom behavior of elementary school children. *Exceptional Children*, 35, 461-470, 1969.

WODARSKI, J. S., and PEDI, S. J.: The comparison of behavior among "anti-social" and "normal" children in an open community agency. Paper presented at the Sixth Annual Meeting, The Association for the Advancement of Behavior Therapy; New York, Oct., 1972.

WOLFF, S.: Behavioral characteristics of primary school children referred to a psychiatric department. *Brit. J. Psychiat.*, 113, 885-893, 1967.

10

Mother-Child Interactions: A Comparison between Normal and Developmentally Delayed Groups

LEIF TERDAL, RUSSELL H. JACKSON,
and ANN M. GARNER

Current studies in behavior modification concerned with parent-child behavior patterns typically examine the effect of parental behavior upon child behavior. The usual assumption is that behavior patterns of a child are strengthened through parental reinforcement; those that are not reinforced by the parent are weakened. The influence of parent behavior on child behavior, in other words, is unilateral. The approach extends to clinical settings: parents may become the "mediators" through whom the therapist works to elicit change in target child behaviors (Tharp and Wetzel, 1969).

Bell (1964, 1968), on the other hand, has argued that in parent-child interaction data the results might well be viewed in terms of the child's effect upon the parent. Some researchers now reverse the traditional approach and treat the child's behavior as an independent variable and the parental behaviors as dependent variables. Osofsky (1971), for example, reports data on the impact of the child response classes of dependency, independence, and stubbornness upon parental behaviors. Yarrow, Waxler, and Scott (1971), investigating the impact of child characteristics on adult behaviors, find adult responses to individual children to be highly variable and to relate to child characteristics.

This study was supported by Health Services and Mental Health Administration, Maternal and Child Health Services Project #920.

As investigators and clinicians conceptualize parent-child interaction as a dyadic process, systematic observation of parent-child interactions becomes the principal means of data collection. The resultant data may be used not only for the evaluation of treatment programs but also for theoretical formulations and basic research about the socialization of the child. Such an approach, however, raises a number of important methodological questions.

A basic issue is the locus of observation. In a review of parent-child interaction studies, Lytton (1971) describes how distortion effects may be present both in naturalistic settings and in the standard laboratory situation, and compares data from behavior observation with data from interviews and paper-and-pencil measures. He concludes that the experimenter's dilemma consists of deciding which sort of distortion he is willing to tolerate, while doing his best to minimize it. A partial resolution of this dilemma is to be found in the Johnson and Lobitz (1974) recommendations to those conducting observation research in any setting: (1) Discover means of making the observer less obtrusive. (2) Broaden the range of measures used to investigate a given problem. (3) Make some of the confounding effects into the dependent variable. The problems involved in dealing with this issue can best be seen in observational studies in the home setting as compared with those in a laboratory setting.

Several recent investigations focus upon the systematic observation of parent-child interaction in the home (Wahl et al., 1974; and Johnson et al., 1973). From this systematic program of research there has emerged an attempt to develop normative data for deviant and nondeviant children in interaction with their families. The home was chosen as representing a natural setting for parent-child interaction. In spite of the many advantages of such a setting, some crucial methodological issues have confronted this research group: observer bias, subject reactivity, demand characteristics, response sets, the instrument decay (Johnson and Bolstad, 1973). The authors conclude that one cannot presume the validity of naturalistic observation without building in controls for these issues.

Standard laboratory situations, on the other hand, have their own advantages and disadvantages. While common sense suggests that home visits contribute information that might never be observed in the laboratory, little evidence is available to support the conclusion that this knowledge is a necessary condition for effective behavior change. For example, when deviant behavior cuts across all levels of responding, it is possible to develop efficient and effective treatment programs which occur totally in the standard laboratory environment (Hanf and Kling, 1974) and appear to generalize to the home environment. Furthermore, the structure which may be placed upon the family during an observation period in the home (cf., Wahl et al., 1974) may effectively transform the "naturalistic" home setting into a "standard situation."

When a standard laboratory situation is developed as a locus for parent-child interaction, certain aspects of the setting which were obscured in the naturalistic environment may become obvious and must be dealt with. For example, the task set for the dyad may be difficult or easy for the child; the child's problem-solving ability and cognitive style thus become important. Degree of maternal involvement in the task may also affect the interaction. These variables are examined by Campbell (1973), who uses a structured interaction situation to study mother-child pairs selected according to the child's cognitive style. She finds support for the view that degree of maternal involvement in a difficult task solution is determined in part by task difficulty and the child's ability to complete the tasks presented. Mothers of hyperactive children provided significantly more direct physical help, encouragement, and impulse-control, and more specific suggestions during the more difficult tasks. Apparently these mothers learned to structure tasks in response to their hyperactive children's inability to focus attention, control impulsivity, and persist. Such findings are consistent with those reported by Bee (1967), who found that parents of distractible and non-distractible children did not differ in amount of interaction, but did differ in interaction pattern.

The present study employs two standard laboratory situations, one unstructured (free play) and one structured (task). It seeks to fulfill the recommendations of Johnson described earlier (Johnson and Lobitz, 1974) by (1) keeping the observers unobtrusive and the child relatively unaware of their presence; (2) employing a broad range of measures including, in addition to direct behavior observation, paper-and-pencil measures and interviews assessing parent perceptions of the interaction; and (3) varying situations and instructions to parents.

The present study focuses on differences between the interactions of mothers with their developmentally delayed children and those of mothers with their normally developing children. Particular attention is paid to the question of gross behavior deficits on the part of the retarded child which result in impaired feedback to the mother, and which may consequently affect maternal behavior significantly. Such behavior deficits typically appear over a wide variety of situations, so that the retarded child may encounter repeated failures and the mother may be exposed to repeated lack of feedback. The stress which this places upon parents is a commonly observed clinical phenomenon. The retarded child seems to present a "blurred" picture to the mother. She, in turn, is often uncertain how to interpret her child's behavior, and uncertain also as to whether the child is interpreting her demands appropriately. Thus, for retarded children, *most* situations—including interactions with the mother—can be conceptualized as "difficult task situations," analogous to the tasks used by Campbell.

Normally developing children without gross behavior deficits, on the other hand, encounter fewer difficulties and provide less impaired feedback to their mothers in a dyadic interaction. Their responses are more definitive and easier to read. For them, most situations—including interaction with the mother—can be conceptualized as the "less difficult" task situation of Campbell.

From these conceptualizations flow the following hypotheses: (1) In a dyadic interaction in either an unstructured or structured standard situation, the more delayed the retarded child the more inadequate will be the responses to maternal behavior when inadequacy is defined as no response or inappropriate response. (2) In a dyadic interaction in either an unstructured or structured standard situation, mothers of retarded children will be more directive than will mothers of normal children. (3) In a dyadic interaction in either an unstructured or structured standard situation, mothers of retarded children will respond more diffusely to their children, i.e., show a wider range of behavior to both positive and negative child responses.

The present investigation provides support for all three of these hypotheses, as well as additional information concerning the differences between retarded and normal children and their mothers in dyadic interaction.

METHOD

Each mother-child pair was observed and coded for a 15-minute period in a free play situation, and for a second 15-minute period in a task situation. In the free play session, the mother and child were introduced to a 9' x 12' carpeted playroom that contained a variety of toys and play materials to facilitate play and interaction. In this situation, the mother is not under instruction to elicit any particular sort of behavior; rather, she is instructed to ". . . think of it as a time at home when you could play with your child without being interrupted by another child, or a neighbor, or a phone call."

Following the play interaction session, each mother was asked to require her child to complete two or three tasks, such as picking up toys, solving a puzzle, and putting on shoes and socks. The tasks varied in complexity according to the age of the child. The task situation was designed to sample the parent-child interplay as the parent structured the task and responded to the varied responses from her child, as the child responded or failed to respond to the requirement.

Following the task session, each mother in the normal group was asked to complete a 15-item questionnaire* which was designed to elicit her perception of the two sessions along the same dimensions as those employed by the observers. A rating scale of 1 to 7 was used.

SUBJECTS

Forty normal children and 42 developmentally delayed children were observed interacting with their mothers. The normal comparison group comprised children from families of upper-lower and upper-middle class income who volunteered to participate in the study. The retarded group consisted of children who had been seen for a multidisciplinary evaluation at a University Affiliated Mental Retardation Center. They represented no particular diagnostic classification, but had all been referred because of suspected developmental delay.

The normal group included 23 girls and 17 boys. In order to assess changes over chronological age, they were divided into a two-to-four-year-old group (mean age: two years, eight months), a four-to-six-year-old group (mean age: four years, ten months), and a six-to-eight-year-old group (mean age: six years, eleven months). The retarded group ranged in age from two years to fifteen years, six months. They included 28 boys and 14 girls. For this study, they were grouped into three levels by mental age. Group one (or the low mental age group) consisted of 15 children with a mean mental age of two years, one month, a mean chronological age of four years, one month, and a mean I.Q. of 46. Group two (the mid mental age group) consisted of 12 children with a mean mental age of four years, zero months, a mean chronological age of six years, four months, and a mean I.Q. of 63. Group three (the high

---

* The 15-item questionnaire may be obtained from the authors at the University of Oregon Health Sciences Center, Portland, Oregon 97201.

mental age group) consisted of 15 children with a mean mental age of six years, nine months, a mean chronological age of nine years, four months, and a mean I.Q. of 71.

The mentally retarded children were grouped into three levels by mental age in order to assess changes in interaction patterns related to developmental levels. The normal children, grouped by chronological age, provided a point of comparison for the retarded children.

MEASURES OF PARENT-CHILD INTERACTION

The parent-child interactions were recorded using the response class matrix (Mash et al., 1973). For this procedure, two observers record the parent-child interaction simultaneously. One observer records the mother's responses as they occur in the context of specified antecedent behaviors of the child. At the same time, the second observer records the child's behavior in the context of specified antecedent behaviors of the mother. In either case the tally represents the intersection between the mother's behavior and the child's behavior. The observer coding the mother-child interaction (in which the mother's behaviors as consequent to the child's antecedent behaviors are tallied) records the following seven behavior classes of the mother: commands, command-questions, questions, praise, negative behaviors, interaction, and no response. Each of those behavior classes is recorded in the context of the following child antecedent behavior response classes: compliance, independent play, competing behavior, negative behavior, interaction (verbal or non-verbal), and no response. The observer coding the child's behaviors consequent to the mother's antecedent behaviors records the same classes. However, this observer records the child's behavior in terms of its relationship to the mother's behavior as antecedent. Recorders make one tally in a matrix cell every 15 seconds, recording only the last scorable behavior unit to occur during that interval. Inter-observer agreement measures for the individual behavior categories have ranged from 70% to 96% agreement.

BEHAVIORAL INDICES

In addition to the specific response class coded during the interaction, a number of indices are derived from the patterns of behavior recorded during a session. These include: Index of Mother's Directiveness (IMD), Mother's Interaction Efficiency (MIE), Child's Interaction Efficiency (CIE), Question Efficiency of Mother (QEM), Immediate Command

Efficiency of Mother (ICEM), and Long-term Command Efficiency of Mother (LCEM).

These indices are obtained as follows:

Index of Mother's Directiveness groups behavior tallies of commands and command questions and divides them by the total number of tallies representing mother's behaviors;

Mother's Interaction Efficiency indicates the proportion of interactive behaviors of the mother that are responded to by the child with the response class of either question or interaction;

Child's Interaction Efficiency provides a similar measure to MIE. The CIE measure indicates the proportion of interactive behaviors of the child that are responded to by the mother with response class of either interaction or question;

Question Efficiency provides a score for the proportion of questions given by the mother that are responded to by the child. It divides the number of tallies of compliance or interaction that immediately follow a question by the total number of responses on the part of the child to questions from the mother;

Immediate Command Efficiency is an index which gives the proportion of commands that are followed by compliance within the 15-second scoring interval;

Long-term Command Efficiency indicates the average number of 15-second interval units of compliance that follow a command.

RESULTS AND DISCUSSION

Mother-Child Behavior in the Unstructured
(Free Play) Situation

The free play session provides an opportunity to evaluate the child's responsiveness to such ordinary maternal behaviors as questions and interactions. From the presumption that retarded children respond inadequately to a range of cues, it follows that they would be relatively unresponsive to such maternal behaviors. The behavioral indices relevant to this point are Mother's Interaction Efficiency and Mother's Question Efficiency.

The Mother's Interaction Efficiency ratio takes into account the child responding with a question or interaction as consequent behaviors to interactions from the mother. The low M.A. group responded to interaction 48.7% of the time, the mid M.A. group responded to interaction 81.0% of the time, and the high M.A. group responded 80.0% of the time. This is in contrast to consistent high levels of mother interaction efficiency of 87.0%, 86.3%, and 90.3% for the three age groupings of the normal children. There is a significant ($p < 0.01$) difference for the MIE indices between the low M.A. group and the young normal comparison group. The low M.A. group also differed significantly from both the mid M.A. ($p < 0.01$) and the high M.A. retarded groups ($p < 0.05$). These data support the hypothesis that the more severely retarded children provide the least adequate response to maternal behaviors. Although the obtained differences were not significant between the mid and high M.A. groups and their comparison groups, the differences were in the predicted direction. The three normal groups did not differ significantly from each other.

The lack of responsiveness of the retarded children to interactive behavior from their mothers did not result in fewer interactions from the mothers to the retarded children. The mothers of the low M.A. group provided nearly as many interactions to their retarded children as did the mothers of the young comparison group. Specifically, 33.0% of the responses of the mothers of the low M.A. children were interactions as opposed to 34.0% of the responses from the mothers of the normal two-to-four-year-old group.

Furthermore, regardless of the responsiveness of the children to interactive responses from the mothers, the mothers were highly likely to respond to interactive responses from the child once they occurred. Over 85% of the interactive responses of each retarded group were responded to by their mothers. Equally high levels of responding were obtained by the children of the comparison groups. This finding would appear not to support the hypothesis of diffuse responding on the part of the mothers to retarded children's antecedent behaviors. However, one must question what impact the impaired responding from the retarded children has upon the mother's behavior.

Table 1 presents the distribution of interactive behaviors from the mothers across the six antecedent behaviors of the child. The table shows that, for all three age groupings of the normal children, 77% or more of the mother's interactive behaviors were in response to interactions by her child. In contrast, most notably within the low M.A. group, the interactive behaviors of the mother were nearly equally divided among three response classes: compliance, independent play, and interaction. In this sense, the interactive behaviors of the mothers, interpreted as consequents, were somewhat more diffusely spread over a range of child antecedent behaviors than was the case with the interac-

TABLE 1

Distribution of Mothers' Interactive Behaviors in
Relation to Child Behaviors

Child Antecedent Behaviors

Group	Compliance	Independent Play	Competing behavior	Negative	Interaction	No Response
Low M.A.	22.8	27.1	3.8	11.4	29.6	5.5
2-4 Normal	4.3	14.2	0.4	0.8	80.1	0.4
Mid M.A.	9.0	30.4	2.0	0.0	58.3	0.5
4-6 Normal	5.9	16.1	0.0	0.3	77.1	0.7
High M.A.	8.6	14.9	3.0	0.0	73.7	0.0
6-8 Normal	5.0	11.3	0.0	0.0	80.8	3.2

tive patterns among the normal child-mother pairs. This difference supports the hypothesis of more diffuse responding on the part of the parent to a variety of child antecedent behaviors for the low M.A. retarded group. This finding should be interpreted with caution, however. The low M.A. group showed relatively few interactive behaviors which limited the opportunity for their mothers to respond to interactions. For the mid M.A. group the effect was present in only one of the six child antecedent behaviors (independent play).

Question Efficiency ratios indicate the responsiveness of the child to questions asked by the mother. It is not required that a child respond verbally to a question. Acknowledgment by nod, gesture, or even compliance behaviors would contribute to question efficiency. Again, the low M.A. group was less responsive than the other groups, showing that the children of that group responded to 62% of the mother's questions as opposed to 74% for the mid M.A. group and 75% for the high M.A. group. These figures are in contrast to the consistent high levels of question efficiency obtained from the comparison groups. Specifically, the two-to-four-year-old control group showed responsiveness to 89% of the questions, and the four-to-six-year-old group and the six-to-eight-year-old group showed responsiveness levels of 86% and 84%, respectively. On this measure, the two-to-four-year-old comparison group differed significantly from the low M.A. group ($p < 0.01$), and the four-to-six-year-old comparison group differed significantly from the mid M.A. group ($p < 0.05$). Among the retarded groups, the low M.A. group differed significantly from both the mid and the high M.A. groups ($p <$

0.05). The three comparison groups did not differ significantly from each other.

It was anticipated that a deficit in responding on the part of the child would be countered by some effort on the part of the mother to control the situation. This by itself would reflect a complex relationship in which low responsiveness on the part of the child does not result in low interaction on the part of the mother, but rather in an increase in directive behaviors. This appears to be the case with the mid M.A. retarded group, whose mothers showed a directiveness index of .23 as compared to .14 for the four-to-six-year-old control group ($p < 0.05$). However, the difference is not statistically significant between the low M.A. group (directiveness index of .20) and the two-to-four-year-old comparison group (directiveness index of .15). The mothers of the low M.A. retarded children may have been somewhat inhibited regarding directiveness by the consistent low responsiveness of the low M.A. retarded children to commands. For example, the immediate command efficiency of the low M.A. group in the free play situation is only .46 as compared with an index of .71 for the young (age two to four) comparison group ($p < 0.01$). The lowered responsiveness of the low M.A. retarded group to both interactions and directives may have accounted for the mothers of the low M.A. group showing a relatively high rate of no-response behaviors in the play session (17.7% versus 10.8% for the young comparison group ($p < 0.05$). The impact of low responsiveness to commands is further discussed in the context of the task session.

Mother-Child Behaviors in the Structured (Task) Session

In the task session the mother is asked to have her child complete a series of specified tasks. Inadequate responding on the part of the child in the task session would be shown primarily by low command efficiency. Two measures bear directly on this variable. The Immediate Command Efficiency of the mother (ICEM) provides a ratio indicating the proportion of commands that were followed immediately by compliance, i.e., within a 15-second scoring unit. The Long-term Command Efficiency measure provides an index of the average number of compliance units—each representing 15 seconds—that follow a command. The low M.A. retarded group showed an Immediate Command Efficiency index of .41, the mid M.A. retarded group showed an index of .76, and the high M.A. retarded group produced a score of .68. These scores are in contrast to ratios of .65 for the young comparison group, and scores of .69

and .77, respectively, for the four-to-six-year-old and the six-to-eight-year-old comparison groups. The low M.A. group differed significantly from the young comparison group ($p < 0.05$), as well as from the mid and high M.A. retarded groups ($p < 0.01$). The other comparisons did not reach statistically significant levels. The Immediate Command Efficiency ratio of .69 for the four-to-six-year-old control group is consistent with the figure of .72 reported by Johnson, Wahl, et al. (1973) for four-to six-year-old normal children observed interacting in the home with their families.

Long-term Command Efficiency ratios were .64, 2.03, and 2.06, respectively, for the low M.A., mid M.A., and high M.A. groups. The comparison groups showed ratios of 1.85 for the two-to-four-year-old group, 2.94 for the four-to-six-year-old group, and 2.63 for the six-to-eight-year old olds. The low M.A. retarded group differed significantly from the young comparison group ($p < 0.01$), from the mid M.A. group ($p < 0.01$), and also from the high M.A. group ($p < 0.05$). The young comparison group (age two to four) differed significantly from the four-to-six-year-old group ($p < 0.05$).

The impact of lowered responsiveness to commands can be seen in the context of a directiveness ratio obtained from the mother's record. For the low M.A. group, the mother's directiveness index was .67, which indicates that nearly 70% of all the behaviors emitted by the mothers during that session were commands. The ratios were .39 and .35, respectively, for the mid M.A. and the high M.A. retarded groups. These figures are in contrast to ratios of .37 for the two-to-four-year-old comparison group, .26 for the four-to-six-year-old group, and .31 for the six-to-eight-year-old group. The mothers in this low M.A. retarded group differed significantly from the two-to-four comparison group ($p < 0.01$), as well as from the mothers in the two other retarded groups ($p < 0.01$). The mid M.A. retarded group differed significantly from the four-to-six-year-old comparison group ($p < 0.05$). Among the comparison groups, the young group differed significantly from the four-to-six-year-old normal group ($p < 0.05$); the other comparisons among the control groups were not significant ($p > 0.05$).

The finding of increased directiveness shown by the mothers of the retarded children is interpreted as direct support of the hypothesis that mothers respond to inadequate responding on the part of their children by increasing structure. In addition, the observations are consistent with Campbell's (1973) findings, discussed earlier.

The directionality of effect must be viewed, however, as an issue that

TABLE 2

Percent of Positive and Negative Maternal Consequences to
Noncompliant and Compliant Behaviors Among Mentally
Retarded and Normal Children

RETARDED			NORMAL		
	Positive	*Negative*		*Positive*	*Negative*
Low M.A.			2-4 Year Old		
Noncompliant	12.8	8.8	Noncompliant	7.6	5.7
Compliant	20.8	4.0	Compliant	43.6	0.5
Mid M.A.			4-6 Year Old		
Noncompliant	22.3	11.2	Noncompliant	8.9	11.8
Compliant	21.5	5.4	Compliant	37.3	2.4
High M.A.			6-8 Year Old		
Noncompliant	17.7	4.0	Noncompliant	5.3	5.3
Compliant	24.8	8.5	Compliant	28.5	1.1

is not resolved. It would be possible to view the finding as representing either lowered responsiveness to commands resulting in greater directiveness or greater directiveness resulting in lower responsiveness.

Table 2 provides data regarding the percentage of positive and negative maternal consequences to noncompliant and compliant behaviors among retarded and normal children. The data bear directly on the prediction that mothers of retarded children will provide poorly differentiated consequences to appropriate and inappropriate behaviors of the retarded children. Among all three mental age groupings, the mothers provided nearly as much positive behavior (praise or interaction) to noncompliant behaviors as they did to compliant behaviors. Among all three normal groups, the children were at least four times as likely to receive positive feedback for compliant rather than noncompliant behavior. A similar relationship was found with respect to negative feedback. The three groupings of retarded children received about as much negative feedback for compliant behavior as they did for noncompliant behavior. Among all three normal groups, the children were at least four times as likely to receive negative feedback for noncompliant behavior as for compliant behavior. This is interpreted as relating to the blurred input provided by retarded children. Their behavior may be more difficult to evaluate as representing compliance or approximation to compliance on the one hand, or as representing refusals or inability to comprehend instruction or inability to perform the task on the other hand. The mothers, not sure of what the children's behavior represents, respond somewhat diffusely to them. One would certainly expect that such a pattern of blurred input from the child and somewhat undifferentiated consequent behavior from the mother would continue to work against the child.

Maternal Rating and Interview

Following the interaction session, each of the mothers of the normal children was asked to fill out a questionnaire. A 7-point rating scale was used. The items corresponded to the behavioral categories that were coded during the sessions. In this way it was possible to examine the correspondence between maternal rating of behavior that occurred during the session and the independently recorded observations.

Of the 15 items on the scale, 5 relate closely to the behaviors reviewed in this study. To the item, "When you asked your child to do something, how often did he do it?" the mothers of the normal group in general rated their children as being responsive to commands. Eleven of the mothers rated their children as always complying (a rating of 1), fifteen mothers rated their children as nearly always complying (a score of 2), and thirteen gave their child a score of 3 or over. As a group, the mothers rated their children as compliant in the standard situation, and they were. Moreover, their rankings differentiated the children in terms of their scores on immediate command efficiency. The mean Immediate Command Efficiency score of the children whose mothers rated their response to commands as 1 (always) was .86 (they complied to 86% of the commands within a fifteen-second scoring unit). The scores of the children whose mothers indicated a rating of 2 was .77, and the scores of the children whose mothers rated them as 3 or over was .58 ($\chi^2 = 8.41$, 2 *df*, $p < 0.05$).

A similar relationship was observed in comparing maternal ratings to the item, "When your child did something other than what you asked him to, did you scold or punish him?" with observed frequency of *negative response* from mother to child as recorded in the task session. Twenty-five of the mothers responded with a rating of 7 (never), twelve indicated a rating in one of the remaining categories, but mostly in category 6 or 5, indicating some, but infrequent, use of scolding or punishment. As a group, the mothers of the normal children in fact used negative responses very seldom, and their ratings are in accord with that. Furthermore, the twenty-five mothers who indicated a rating of 7 had a mean frequency of less than one (.35) instance of negative response. The twelve mothers with ratings of 6, 5, or lower had a mean frequency of 1.5 negative responses, and a higher proportion of them had at least one instance of negative response than the mothers who indicated "never" ($\chi^2 = 4.5$, 1 *df*, $p < 0.05$).

There was, however, a less clear relationship between maternal ratings and other observations. For example, to the item, "When you asked your child a question, how often did he answer and start talking with you?" the mothers, as a group, rated their children as always or nearly always responding. While that was true for the group, the individual ratings did not necessarily correspond to the Question Efficiency scores of the children when compared individually. The same held for instances of observer and maternal ratings of *interaction* during the play session. Furthermore, the mothers, as a group, rated themselves high on the item, "When your child did what you asked of him, how often did you praise or reward him?" The average number of praises recorded for each mother-child pair was less than three. In addition, the mothers who indicated a rating of 1 (always) used no more praise than those who indicated a rating of 2, 3, or 4.

There may be a variety of reasons why some particular constructs show higher agreement than others between maternal ratings and independently coded observations. Possible factors are: ambiguity in the wording of items; differences in meaning attributed to an item by mothers and coders; differences in value attributed by mothers to the end points of the ratings—for example, one instance of praise following a series of tasks may be taken by one mother as representing "always" and by another as "seldom" or "never"; or errors in the coding process itself. At any rate, the concordance—or lack of concordance—between mothers' ratings and independently coded observations may vary from one behavioral category to another, as well as between different raters and coders. Presumably, if a mother is to learn to respond contingently to select response classes, it is essential for the mother and the therapist to attribute similar meaning to behaviors.

The mothers of the mentally retarded children were not given the questionnaire. They were interviewed, however, and it is our impression that many of them have considerable difficulty in labeling or describing the various nuances of their children's behavior. An initial methodology to study parental report of child behavior has been developed (Seitz and Jackson, 1974) and is to be the focus of further investigation.

Implications for Behavior Modification

Although the present study addresses itself to an analysis of differences in interaction patterns between normal and developmentally delayed children and their mothers, the results have implications for the practical techniques of behavior modification with retarded children.

1. If, as suggested by these results, the characteristic behavior of retarded children—including behavior deficits—appears across many different situations, then a standard laboratory setting may be entirely appropriate for dealing with the behavior. It may not be necessary to spend much time in the home.

2. If, as suggested by these results, there may be discrepancies between maternal report and observed behavior which interfere with the mother's capacity to deal with her child, these discrepancies should be attended to. This means that it is necessary to employ multiple measures of the interaction and to treat all measures, whether by trained coder or by mother, as valid in their own right. To assume that the observed behavior is "right" and any deviations from it "wrong" may be to ignore the cues to maternal readiness for intervention and thus to prejudice the therapeutic outcome.

3. If, as suggested by these results, the mother receives impaired and confusing feedback from her retarded child, she may need added support and assistance in order to carry through a program independently. It may not be enough to instruct her to consequate her child's behavior.

4. If, as suggested by these results, the retarded child finds most everyday situations difficult, and therefore presents a "blurred" picture to his or her mother, the mother will have special difficulty identifying the behaviors to be consequated. Parental uncertainty and confusion compound the child's diffuseness and again may require special attention.

REFERENCES

BEE, H. L.: Parent-child interaction and distractibility in 9-year-old children. *Merrill-Palmer Quarterly,* 13, 175-190, 1967.

BELL, R. Q.: Structuring parent-child interaction situations for direct observations. *Child Devel.,* 35, 1009-1020, 1964.

BELL, R. Q.: A reinterpretation of direction of effects in studies of socialization. *Psychol. Rev.,* 75, 81-95, 1968.

CAMPBELL, S. B.: Mother-child interaction in reflective, impulsive, and hyperactive children. *Devel. Psychol.,* 8, 341-349, 1974.

HANF, C., and KLING, J.: Facilitating parent-child interaction: A two-stage training model. Submitted for publication, 1973.

JOHNSON, S. M., and BOLSTAD, O. D.: Methodological issues in naturalistic observation; Some problems and solutions for field research. In: L. A. Hamerlynck, L. C.

Handy, and E. J. Mash (Eds.), *Behavior Change: Methodology, Concepts, and Practice*. Champaign, Ill.: Research Press, 1973. Pp. 7-67.

JOHNSON, S. M., and LOBITZ, G. K.: Parental manipulation of child behavior in home observations: A methodological concern. *J. Appl. Behav. Anal.*, 1974.

JOHNSON, S. M., WAHL, G., MARTIN, S., and JOHANSSON, S.: How deviant is the normal child? A behavioral analysis of the preschool child and his family. In: R. D. Rubin, J. P. Brady, and J. D. Henderson (Eds.), *Advances in Behavior Therapy*, Vol. 4, New York: Academic Press, 1973. Pp. 37-54.

LYTTON, H.: Observation studies of parent-child interaction: A methodological review. *Child Devel.*, 42, 651-684, 1971.

MASH, E. J., TERDAL, L. G., and ANDERSON, K.: The response-class matrix: A procedure for recording parent-child interactions. *J. Consult. and Clin. Psychol.*, 40, 163-164, 1973.

OSOFSKY, J. D.: Children's influence upon parental behavior: An attempt to define the relationship with the use of laboratory tasks. *Genet. Psychol. Monographs*, 83, 147-169, 1971.

SEITZ, S., and JACKSON, R. H.: Behavioral projectives: The child as a stimulus. Unpublished manuscript, 1974.

THARP, R. G., and WETZEL, R. J.: *Behavior Modification in the Natural Environment*. New York: Academic Press, 1969.

WAHL, G., JOHNSON, S. M., JOHANSSON, S., and MARTIN, S.: An operant analysis of child-family interaction. *Behav. Ther.*, 5, 64-78, 1974.

YARROW, M. R., WAXLER, C. Z., and SCOTT, P. M.: Child effects on adult behavior. *Devel. Psychol.*, 5, 300-311, 1971.

Section III

PROBLEMS AND PERSPECTIVES

Commentary

Since the late 1960's the literature has been reminding us that the "whoopee" stage of development in behavior modification is past. Gerald Patterson, the major spokesman for this announcement, presents his argument again without remorse for our simplistic formulations and prescriptions of the past. The powerful and personally attractive conception of "accentuating the positive and eliminating the negative" to deal with disturbing behavior remains, but with realistic predictions of the necessary but insufficient conditions such a procedure represents.

Refinements of theoretical base suggested by the data dictate the formulation of the family as a social system—a system with reciprocity as the core to understanding and intervention. Reciprocity not only requires us to account for all members of the system, but brings the principles of negative reinforcement and punishment, stimulus control and chaining, and schedules of reinforcement into the framework and technology of behavior modification with families. This section offers the reader evidence of the level of development of the theoretical and technological work for applied behavioral analysis with families. The evidence is impressive in relation to the relatively short history, but sobering with regard to the methodological issues as well as the prospects for immediate widespread clinical application.

The methodological questions or issues interact and differentially affect the theory and technology. Of obvious concern in any scientific activity is the problem of the sample size and representativeness. Observer influence or reactivity as well as reliability of the data continue to attenuate results. Generalizations of effects (well discussed in the prior section) across situations, behaviors, and time remain problems. Component analysis of procedures in intervention and the influence of competing conditions—marital problems, for example—are discussed but still

265

unanswered. All in all, the methodological problems are precisely identified, with technological issues generally intensified. The reader should have a "whoopee" response in small type. How can we extend such clinical procedures to the community and simultaneously refine the process? Frances Horowitz has suggested the agricultural research station model for behavioral science. The Joe Cobb Family Intervention Clinic is the first; let's hope Patterson et al. can assist in the development of others.

The papers by Corson and Benassi and Larson exemplify the extension of the family-system concept to clinical applications. Benassi and Larson describe the focusing of attention upon the child's role in determining parent behavior. Corson accounts for the system concept with his discussion and data on the mutual control system of the family. He details a strategy for clinical work utilizing (a) contracts for duties and privileges, (b) systematic parental attention, and (c) a method for systematizing positive and negative reinforcement.

Control and permutations of the concept are well illustrated in all papers of this section. Patterson points out the linkage and interaction between family members which can lead to a self-destructive spiral unless the countercontrol of family members is redefined for adaptive chains. Peterson invokes overcontrol and provides several arguments for a careful examination of goal setting and intervention procedures. In general, the papers can be said to lead to the recognition that a major aspect of a family intervention is that it is unnatural to the "normal-natural" behaviors of the family members. They behave the way they do because of their history of learning in the context of the family environment. Some of their individual control/countercontrol behaviors may be weak or overreactive to health, but they are *functional*. Consequently, any intervention is "unnatural" to the system and the clinician must approach the problem family with clear, concise goals and prescriptions and then ensure that the procedure is reinforceable for all members.

11

The Aggressive Child: Victim and Architect of a Coercive System

GERALD R. PATTERSON

Overview

The report describes a functional analysis of ongoing family interaction as it is found in the homes of aggressive and nonaggressive children. It was assumed that there were interdependencies holding between the behaviors of family members and those of the target child. Presumably, analyses of these serial dependencies would provide a base for understanding some of the determinants for both *inter-* and *intra-*subject variations in the performance of children's coercive behaviors.

The data were sampled on six-second time intervals. The primary focus of the analyses was upon the differences between nonproblem and aggressive children in their reactions to parental punishment. That analysis is described in the first section of the report.

The next stage of the investigation moved from fine-grained functional analysis of response events to larger social units. These larger units consisted of the role of father, mother, and older and younger

This study was supported by Grants MH 10822 and R01 MH 15985 from the NIMH Section on Crime and Delinquency. Computing assistance was obtained from the Health Sciences Computing Facility, UCLA, sponsored by NIH Grant FR-3.

This study was supported by Grants MH 10822 and R01 MH 15985 from the NIMH period. The interactions occurred primarily within weekly group meetings where the discussions dealt with an endless series of questions concerning measurement and intervention procedures. In a very real sense, the following contributors might well be thought of as co-authors: W. Bricker, J. Cobb, R. Conger, H. Hops, S. Johnson, R. Jones, A. Levine, R. Ray, J. Reid, D. Shaw, K. Skindrud, J. Straughan, R. Weiss, G. White, N. Wiltz, R. Ziller.

The writer is indebted to L. Rorer and E. Mash for their careful critiques of an earlier draft of this paper.

siblings as they related to the problem behaviors of the target child. The second section outlines some speculations concerning such findings and empirical interrelations. In general, it seemed that the identified deviant child both resided in, *and* contributed to, an aggressive system. It was assumed that each family member, but especially the deviant child, contributed to a spiraling increase in coercive performance. In such interchanges, the latter gave and received increasing amounts of aversive events and was thus both victim and architect of the system.

This general formulation, together with the supporting data, provides a means for conceptualizing the impact of treatment upon the family of an aggressive child. The third section outlines the changes *among family members* which accompanied a social-learning-based parent training program. All of the families had been referred for treatment because *one* or more children had been labeled as "aggressive." Within the present formulation, it would be expected that changing the aggressive behavior of the child might have been of only limited clinical utility unless accompanied by concomitant changes in other family members. Observation data comparing baseline, treatment, and 12-month follow-up were examined to determine to what extent the *family* changed.

COERCION

At the inception of the Project, it seemed reasonable to select children labeled as highly aggressive and to study only a limited set of responses such as "Hit." However, actual field observations in families (Reid, 1967) suggested that a large number of additional behaviors seemed to have functional characteristics similar to those noted for Hit. Eventually 16 "noxious" behaviors were identified which, a priori, seemed to occur with rather high frequency, for boys labeled as "aggressive": Command Negative, Cry, Disapproval, Dependency, Destructive, Humiliate, High Rate, Ignore, Non-Comply, Negativism, Tease, Physical Negative, Whine, and Yell. It was hypothesized that identified aggressive children would display higher rates for all 14 categories. Data were collected in the homes for 6 to 10 sessions using a 29-category code system described in Patterson, Ray, et al. (1969); studies of its psychometric properties were reviewed by Jones et al. (1975). The demographic characteristics of the samples were detailed in Patterson and Cobb (1973, pp. 165-168). The comparisons between the samples of 27 problem and 27 matched nonproblem boys showed that the expected differences for coercive behaviors were significant for 8 of the 14 behaviors (see Appendix A).

The field observations suggested that the boys employed a wide spectrum of behaviors in shaping and controlling family members. This general process of control-by-pain was labeled "coercion" (Patterson and Reid, 1970). The network of coercion hypotheses described by Patterson and Cobb (1971, 1973) detailed the means by which aversive behaviors serve as stimulus events in punishment and/or negative reinforcement arrangements. As shown in the laboratory study by Devine (1971), a normal preschool child, under negative reinforcement arrangements, will show significant changes in behavior in as few as *three* S-R-C (aversive stimulus-child response-removal of aversive stimulus) repetitions. For either punishment or negative reinforcement, an aversive stimulus is applied contingently and *repeatedly* to accelerate or decelerate behaviors exhibited by the other person. The impact of such contingencies is reflected in the accompanying alterations in probability of recurrence for the target response.

Presumably, as one member of a system applies pain control techniques, the victims will eventually learn, via modeling (Bandura, 1973) and/or reinforcing contingencies (Patterson et al., 1967), to *initiate* coercive interchanges. As the victims acquire coercive "skills," they will also be more likely to counter the coercive initiations of others by coercive measures of their own. This process produces extended interchanges in which *both* members of the dyad apply aversive stimuli. This would suggest that the persons most frequently victimized by the coercive child would eventually be shown to reciprocate at commensurate levels. In keeping with this notion, the analyses by Reid (1967) showed an average correlation of +.65 among family members in their exchanges of aversive stimuli.

The coercion hypothesis suggests that with training there are significant increases in both rate *and* intensities of coercive behaviors. In extended interchanges, where one or both persons employ aversive stimuli, if one member suddenly increases the intensity of the aversive behavior the other person is likely to terminate his or her attack. In this manner, high amplitude aggression is reinforced. Following such training, one member may adopt a consistently submissive stance. If not, then both members are likely to escalate in the rate and intensity of their coercive behaviors. Cairns (1972) and J. Knutson (personal communication) have noted such escalations in their laboratory investigations of pain-induced aggression. As one animal increased the vigor of its attack, the other reciprocated in kind. Toch (1969) provides anecdotal evidence for regular sequences of escalating violence characterizing individual policemen and criminals who had been involved in repeated aggravated assaults and homicides. Zimbardo (1969) provided anecdotal evidence for another form of escalation which occurred in the behavior of certain attackers even when dealing with passive victims. Although a formal analysis of escalating processes is badly needed, such a study will not be immediately forthcoming. The difficulty lies in the problem of defining "increasing intensity of aversive stimuli."

Aversive Behaviors

One of the key assumptions underlying all of the coercion hypotheses concerned the special status of some social behaviors as "aversive." Two types of studies were carried out to determine, empirically, the status of events identified, a priori, as noxious. One series sampled parents' perceptions of the entire 29 response categories in the code system, including those grouped, a priori, as noxious. The studies relied upon response definitions from the code system developed for the current project. The mothers of 20 normal preschool children (in Jones et al., 1975) and the mothers of 14 children referred for stealing rated each of the code categories on a nine-point scale of "pleasant-aversive." In both instances, all of the responses labeled a priori as noxious were also perceived as such by the mothers. In that there were few differences in mean values for the two samples, no formal comparisons were made of the ratings. In the study by Johnson et al. (1974), mothers of normal children rated the same code categories on a dimension of "normal-deviant." Again, the a priori classification agreed perfectly with the mothers' perceptions of deviancy.

The consensual validation data were supportive of the status of these events as "aversive." However, it would also seem useful to demonstrate that in interpersonal interaction the events *functioned* as aversive stimuli. Analyses of sequential dependencies found in family interaction showed that, when supplied contingently as a consequence for "Talk," these events served to suppress the probability that "Talk" would recur in the next time frame (Patterson and Cobb, 1971, p. 108).* In effect, when serving as consequences for *prosocial* behaviors, these events had some of the characteristics of "punishment." This response suppression

---

* In the analyses, the data for both the target response (Talk) and the consequences sampled the behavior of *all* family members. The analyses would provide a closer fit to the current problem if the target responses were based on all family members other than the deviant child and the consequences were provided only by the deviant child.

effect was obtained for data from both problem and nonproblem families.

Obviously not all consequences associated with response suppression would be thought of as punishers; for example, an analysis of the consequence for a mand would also demonstrate a "suppression" effect. In this sense, then, the suppression effect was a necessary, but not sufficient, characteristic required for status as an aversive event.

The findings from both mothers' ratings and the analyses of sequential dependencies found in social interaction agree in identifying the 14 responses as "aversive stimuli."

The Burst Phenomenon

Extensive experience in making field observations suggested that responses seemed to come in "bursts" (Patterson et al., 1967). Given the occurrence of one response, there seemed to be a significant increase in the probability that the same response would recur (persist) into the immediately following time interval. In the current report, a measure of this tendency served as the dependent variable in the search for variables which controlled its occurrence. The dependent variable consisted of the conditional probability that the noxious response (Rj) would occur at t_2, given its occurrence at t_1. The time intervals for these analyses were roughly six seconds.

The first hypothesis tested was that the sample of 27 aggressive boys, as compared to the matched sample of nonproblem boys, would have significantly higher conditional probability values $p(Rj_2/Rj_1)$ for each of 14 noxious responses and for three different classes of these behaviors: Social Aggression, Hostile, and Total Deviant. In keeping with the hypothesis, 5 of the 14 noxious responses showed significantly higher recurrence (duration) probabilities for the clinical sample. For these responses, once the problem child "began," he was more likely to continue being noxious. Ten of the responses showed substantial reductions following treatment. It is interesting to note that Cry, Dependency, Whine, and Yell were more likely to persist among *nonproblem* children. The "burst" phenomenon then is *not* a general *trait* of aggressive children, but is specific only to *certain* coercive responses.

In general, it was assumed that coercive behaviors of the problem child would be characterized by (a) shorter latency between bursts, and (b) more extended "bursts." The analyses summarized in Table 1 did not directly test these hypotheses, but were supportive of the general notions. One might conceive of at least three different determinants for

TABLE 1

Some Comparisons of Conditional Probabilities (Rj_2/Rj_1)
for Aggressive and Nonproblem Boys

Code Category		Baseline			Termination
		Nonproblem Boys, N = 27	Problem Boys, N = 27	"t"†	Problem Boys
		$p(Rj_2/Rj_1)$	$p(Rj_2/Rj_1)$		
Command					
Negative	(CN)	.000	.144	4.00*	.000
Cry	(CR)	.658	.594	0.74	.528
Disapproval	(DI)	.114	.203	3.78***	.116
Dependency	(DP)	.231	.225	0.95	.125
Destructive	(DE)	.182	.610	2.03*	.456
High Rate	(HR)	.281	.492	1.68	.386
Humiliate	(HU)	.000	.203	0.65	.152
Ignore	(IG)	.231	.100	0.14	.091
Non-Comply	(NC)	.158	.187	0.17	.181
Negativism	(NE)	.177	.284	2.75**	.163
Physical					
Negative	(PN)	.167	.225	1.06	.133
Tease	(TE)	.159	.255	1.77*	.255
Whine	(WH)	.379	.253	1.26	.189
Yell	(YE)	.254	.206	2.23*	.128
Social Aggression (Soc. Agg.)					
(PN & TE)		.171	.263	0.39	.247
Hostility	(HO)				
(DI, NE, HU, IG, WH)		.270	.334	2.67**	.254
Total Deviant	(TD)				
(all 14 Rjs)		.302	.388	1.31	.317

* p .05 (one-tailed);   ** p .01;   *** p .001.

† The "t" tests should be thought of as only suggestive. In that each child could contribute more than one event to the sample, it is unlikely that the assumption of independence of events would be tenable. The fact that one of the fundamental assumptions for parametric analyses has been violated means that one cannot really interpret the results.

the burst phenomenon: (1) The child's response may serve as a stimulus which sets the occasion for an immediate repetition of the same response. (2) There may be specific consequences provided by family members which serve to maintain a coercive response once it has been initiated. (3) In extended interactions, the behavior of the child and the family member may create *mutual*, or bilateral, effects, both of which maintain ongoing coercive behaviors.

The data from Table 1 could be construed as supportive for all three of these positions. The transactional alternative (3) seems to be highly relevant to clinicians; it was briefly explored in the report by Patterson (1974b). The major focus in the present report is upon the possibilities inherent in the second alternative. An earlier report (Patterson and Cobb, 1971) showed that there were indeed behavioral events whose function seemed to be that of maintaining ongoing behaviors. Although the analyses constituted a promising lead, the events which were of greatest clinical interest occurred at very low frequencies. In addition, there were several possible confounds in the pilot analyses.* As a next step, a search was made for classes of children's coercive behaviors which could serve as relatively "high rate" dependent variables in the continued search for maintaining stimuli. Two such classes, Hostile and Social Aggression, were identified in the investigation by Patterson and Cobb (1973). Members of each class differed in topography, but shared *common networks of initiating stimuli.* This is analogous to the approach advocated by Moyer (1973). His work with animals showed that different aggressive responses were under the control of different stimuli. He noted a limited number of response classes, each of which seemed to be under the control of different "elective" stimuli. He also hypothesized that different classes of responses might relate to different neural substrates.

In the next stage, Hostile and Social Aggression served as dependent variables in the search for networks of maintaining stimuli (Patterson, in preparation). That analysis showed that such networks did indeed exist for the clinical sample and to a lesser extent for nonproblem boys. For example, when a Hostile response occurred, there were certain reactions of family members which reliably increased the probability that another Hostile response was forthcoming. Family members of problem children were five times as likely to supply such consequences for Hostile behaviors as were their nonproblem counterparts. Similar findings obtained for Social Aggression.

Thus far, the data suggested that the "burst" phenomenon was partially related to the tendency of other family members to supply the coercive child with maintaining consequences. Given that "maintaining stimuli" existed and that they were to be found in greater supply for the aggressive children, it became understandable that "coercive bursts" were more likely to characterize their performance.

The punishment "paradox." Two analyses of sequential dependencies from interactions among members of problem families (Patterson, in

---

* See footnote, p. 270.

preparation; Patterson and Cobb, 1971) showed that the same class of consequences which effectively suppressed ongoing prosocial responses also served to *accelerate* coercive responses! This "punishment-acceleration" effect for problem individuals was also obtained in a study by Kopfstein (1972). His data described older, retarded children in an institutional setting. It is important to note that in all of the studies the focus was upon individuals labeled as "deviant."

If one assumes, as did Patterson and Cobb (1973), that negative reinforcement is a key mechanism in the maintenance of coercive responses, then perhaps this aspect of the burst phenomenon becomes more understandable.* Given an aversive antecedent (Aῑ) followed by the child's noxious response, a presentation of another aversive stimulus as a consequence would mean that the child was not reinforced. Given Aῑ and only a moderately aversive "punishment," then the aggressive child is likely to repeat or escalate the intensity of the coercive behaviors until the aversive stimuli are terminated. Presumably, the recurrence of coercive responses would be less likely if the "punishment" were intense. It seems that negative reinforcement arrangements may constitute a particularly severe context in which to test the effectiveness of punishing consequences. The Patterson and Cobb (1971) findings showed that those punishments found effective for other social behaviors may very well be found wanting when applied to coercive behaviors. The question at this point concerns the determinants of status as conditional punishers.

The current literature suggests two possible mechanisms relating to the effectiveness of aversive consequences: (1) The series of studies by Parke et al. (1970) showed that children whose prior history consisted of intermittent punishment were not later controlled as effectively by schedules of consistent punishment as were children whose prior history had been consistent punishment. Parke's findings suggest that parents who are inconsistent in their use of punishment may be less effective

---

* Assuming negative reinforcement to be a factor would imply the presence of aversive antecedents (Aῑ) for many of the coercive responses. A reanalysis of data from Patterson and Cobb (1973) showed this was in fact the case. Twenty-two percent of the coercive *initiations* of both the aggressive and nonaggressive boys were preceded by aversive behaviors of other family members. The finding for the clinical sample (Patterson, in preparation) that many of the aversive antecedents which control the responses also served to accelerate them when presented as consequences strongly implicates the mechanism of negative reinforcement as a key factor in understanding "bursts."

It is of interest to note that the two samples did differ in p (Total Deviant/Aῑ). The conditional probabilities were .382 for the clinical sample and .277 for the nonproblem sample.

even when they later become consistent. (2) The review of laboratory findings by Solomon (1964) showed that the frequency of the CS-UCS pairings and the intensity of the UCS were significant parameters determining the effectiveness of the conditioned punisher in controlling behavior. That paradigm would suggest that parents of problem children may less often back up their threats by withdrawal of reinforcement than do parents of nonproblem children, e.g., loss of privileges, grounding, Time Out, loss of allowance, loss of dessert for evening meal, etc. In keeping with this formulation, our clinical experience suggested that parents of problem children are *more likely* to apply very intense spankings or physical assault (UCS). However, these consequences are not necessarily paired with a "warning" or "threat" nor are they introduced for the majority of the child's coercive behaviors. The majority of their punishments seem to consist of threats and imprecations which are seldom "backed up."

Neither set of speculations about conditioning histories was tested in the present analysis. It is assumed, however, that one or both would differentially describe the histories of punishing behavior for parents of aggressive and nonaggressive boys. Presumably, the effects of such histories would be reflected in the differential responsiveness of the boys to parental punishment. The data in Table 2 summarize the outcome of a functional analysis of the impact of punishment upon coercive behaviors for samples of both aggressive and normal families. The dependent variables consisted of the coercive classes, Hostile and Social Aggression. In the current analysis, baseline data were used to calculate conditional probabilities for the immediate (six seconds) recurrence or persistence of any member of the coercive class, given either aversive ($C\bar{i}$) or non-aversive (Ci) consequences, dispersed by any of the following family members: older siblings, parents, and younger siblings.*

The data showed a complex interaction among agent status, class of consequence, and response class. However, for both samples and both response classes, there were *marked* acceleration effects when the siblings

---

* The consequences classified as positive included the following code categories: Approve, Attend, Comply, Indulge, Laugh, Play, Physical Positive, Touch, and Talk. This a priori grouping was also used in the Taplin (1974) analyses, but is slightly different than that used by Shaw (1971) who did not include Touch. Sallows (1972) used Approval, Laugh, Play, and Positive, but substituted Work for Attend, Comply, Indulge, Touch, and Talk.

The classification of aversive consequences used in the current study included all the categories used by Taplin (1974) in his grouping of aversive consequences but also added Dependency, Cry, Whine, and Negativism. (The latter constituted only 4.6% of the consequences provided by deviant behaviors by normal families.)

TABLE 2

Conditional Probabilities that Noxious Behaviors
Will Persist as a Function of Consequences

Consequences by Agents	Normal Families			Aggressive Families		
	N events	$p(Rj_2/Rj_1-Ci)$	$p(Ci/Rj)$ noxious	N events	$p(Rj_2/Rj_1-Ci)$	$p(Ci/Rj)$ noxious
HOSTILE						
Aversive						
Parent	62	.23	.28	141	.41	.30
Older sibling	9	.33	.29	68	.60	.32
Younger sibling	16	.25	.39	43	.35	.36
Nonaversive						
Parent	158	.32		333	.26	
Older sibling	22	.09		120	.35	
Younger sibling	25	.16		92	.15	
Base Rate						
Parent	220	.29		474	.31	
Older sibling	31	.16		188	.44	
Younger sibling	41	.20		135	.22	
Total	292	.26	.30	797	.32	.32
SOCIAL AGGRESSION						
Aversive						
Parent	25	.12	.56	55	.29	.53
Older sibling	6	.33	.40	41	.29	.48
Younger sibling	28	.14	.34	83	.32	.47
Nonaversive						
Parent	20	.30		48	.29	
Older sibling	9	.00		45	.18	
Younger sibling	19	.16		94	.24	
Base Rate						
Parent	45	.20		103	.29	
Older sibling	15	.13		86	.23	
Younger sibling	47	.15		177	.28	
Total	107	.17	.55	366	.27	.49

attempted to punish the problem child's coercive behavior. The consistency of these findings for seven of the eight comparisons suggested that siblings were consistently ineffective when attempting to punish coercive behaviors for the high rate problem child.

The findings for parents of nonproblem children stand in marked contrast to the general findings for siblings. When they provided aversive consequences for either Hostile or Social Aggression behaviors, the

TABLE 3

Parents' Aversive Consequence as Accelerators
p (Rj$_2$/Rj$_1$ → Ci) for Coercive Behaviors

| | Child Behaviors | | | |
| Status of Parental Consequences | Hostile | | Social Aggression | |
	Nonproblem Sample	Problem Sample	Nonproblem Sample	Problem Sample
Aversive	.23	.41	.12	.29
Nonaversive	.32	.26	.30	.29

effect was a *slight suppression in the coercive responses*. In the case of Hostile, the suppression was reflected in the contrast between the conditional probability value of .23 as compared to the base rate value (for parents) of .29. The comparable figures for the Social Aggression data were .12 and .20, respectively. The consequences previously shown to be effective in suppressing "Talk" for both problem and nonproblem families (Patterson and Cobb, 1971) were also effective in suppressing coercive child behaviors when used by parents of nonproblem children. The data in Table 3 summarize the key findings (from Table 2).

Given that the parent provided a nonpunishing consequence, there was little difference between response classes or samples; for example, there was better than one chance in four that the target child would persist in that behavior. Also, as shown in Table 2, the *proportion* of coercive behaviors punished did not differ markedly for the two samples. However, given punishment as a consequence, there was a marked difference in the child's reaction to it. Regardless of response class, the problem children were approximately *twice as likely as normals to persist in their behaviors when punished*. Parental punishment served to accelerate ongoing coercive behavior.

The implications of these findings for designing treatment strategies and for measuring their effect will be considered at a later point. At a more general level, the punishment-acceleration effects are of interest because they seem to relate to findings from several other areas of research. For example, Kuenstler (1970) and Bommarito (1964), cited by Sallows (1972), found that children labeled as "deviant" were less responsive to verbal punishment in conditioning tasks. Similarly, Hare (1968), Lykken (1957), and Schacter and Latane (1964) found that adults labeled as psychopaths conditioned less well to aversive stimuli than did other adults.

Several laboratory studies suggest that out-of-control children are less effectively controlled by garden variety social reinforcers dispensed by adults. The findings reviewed in Patterson (1969) have been replicated and extended by Herbert et al. (1973) and Walker and Buckley (1973). A relative lack of control for adult-dispensed social reinforcers has also been noted for adolescent delinquents in studies by Johns and Quay (1962) and Quay and Hunt (1965). However, as noted by Sarbin et al. (1965), such effects have not been obtained in several replication attempts for subjects in this age group.

Determinants of responsiveness to adult-dispensed social reinforcers have been investigated in a series of highly innovative studies by R. Cairns. A field study by Cairns and Paris (1971) showed that children from classrooms in which teachers "reinforced" non-contingently tended not to shape well in laboratory situations where adult-dispensed social reinforcers were given contingently. The laboratory study by Warren and Cairns (1972) showed that children first exposed to rich schedules of noncontingent "reinforcement" shaped less well on later trials when the arrangements were made contingent, as compared to children whose history had been contingent reinforcement. These findings are of great interest because Sallows' (1972) comparison of the ORI problem and nonproblem samples showed that parents of problem children provided much richer schedules of *positive* consequences for children's *coercive* behaviors than did parents of nonproblem children. These findings are in keeping with the hypothesis derived from Cairns' work to the effect that parents of problem children may be more noncontingent in their use of reinforcers.

The "remedy" would seem to be straightforward. The findings from the Warren and Cairns (1972) study would suggest that training parents to use consequences *contingently* should increase the child's responsiveness to adult-dispensed positive reinforcers. This effect was in fact obtained by Wahler (1967). When parents used both praise for prosocial behavior and Time Out for deviant behavior, the children's behavior came under control and their responsiveness to parental reinforcement increased. The latter was measured by a laboratory procedure.

These findings suggest that parental use of social reinforcers and social punishers in an inconsistent or noncontingent manner may create a situation in which the child may become increasingly *less* likely to be controlled by these consequences. Under such an aegis, the rates of coercive behaviors are likely to accelerate. While the empirical supports for these speculations are far from complete, they emphasize the need for training parents (a) to be more contingent in their use of social reinforcers; (b) to be more consistent in their use of punishment; and (c) early in treatment to use backup consequences for both positive reinforcers and punishers.

While social learning principles led the earlier therapists to stress *contingent* reinforcement, clinical experience led them eventually to supplement social reinforcement via contractual point systems which in turn earned powerful backup reinforcers. In like manner, most clinicians were eventually shaped by experience to train parents to back up scolding by withdrawing privileges which the child had long taken for granted. Presumably these more powerful arrangements reduce the probability that target children will accelerate their coercive behavior when the parents attempt to interfere. This being the case, then successful treatment should be accompanied by (a) reduced rates of coercive behaviors; (b) reduction in the conditional probability of the immediate recurrence of a coercive response $p\,(Rj_2/Rj_1)$; and (c) reduction in the conditional probabilities describing the punishment acceleration phenomenon $p\,(Rj_2/Rj_1 \rightarrow C\bar{\imath})$.

THE FAMILY AND THE COERCIVE CHILD

A Developmental Viewpoint

Bell's (1971) classic paper emphasized the bilateral effects which obtain for mother/child interactions by illustrating the role of the infant in *shaping the mother*. In that context, he reviewed studies which demonstrated the effect of "infant-crying" as an aversive stimulus in controlling mothering behaviors.

There is some reason to believe that such applications of pain control techniques by infants may be unlearned. An infant's screaming when cold or hungry would certainly seem to have survival value in that it provides a means by which the *infant trains* the parent in the necessary mothering skills. As noted by Eibl-Eibesfeldt (1974), complex coercive patterns such as temper tantrums are found in blind children and young primates as well.

It is assumed that by the age of two most children have made strides in substituting an impressive range of verbal and motor skills for the more primitive coercive responses which they formerly employed. There are a number of things parents might do to insure that infants would retain high rates of performance for coercive skills: (a) neglect to condition prosocial skills, e.g., seldom reinforce the use of language, or other self-help skills; (b) provide rich schedules of positive reinforcement for coercive behaviors (e.g., Sallows, 1972); (c) allow siblings to increase the frequency of aversive stimuli which are terminated when the target child uses coercive behaviors (e.g., Devine, 1971); (d) use punishment inconsistently for coercive behaviors; and/or (e) use weak conditioned punishers as consequences for coercion. Only a longitudinal study can provide data directly relevant to what this developmental process might be.

In the present context, it was assumed that the average three-year-old in our society has *learned* all of the 14 noxious behaviors identified by our code system. This early acquisition is facilitated by the ubiquitous presence of coercive models in the home, in the nursery school, and on television. For example, observations (Jones et al., 1975) in the homes of *normal families* showed that coercive behaviors occurred from a range of .02 to .50 responses per minute! Because the code sampled only dyads, these figures represent *minimal* estimates of the rates with which such aversive stimuli occurred. Presumably these events provide rich opportunities for vicarious learning for young children. Extensive observations from two nursery schools showed a range of 11 to 40 verbal or nonverbal attacks per session (Patterson et al., 1967)! In the review of studies evaluating the content of children's TV programs, Friedrich and Stein (1954) cited a study which showed an average of 25.1 aggressive episodes per hour for children's cartoons. For "adult" shows, there was a mean of five *violent* episodes per hour for shows presented on prime TV time. Most children surveyed were found to watch three to four hours of TV per day.

Children view the behaviors of coercive models and also note the consequences which accrue to these events (Bandura, 1973). They may also acquire these "skills" via their interactions as a victim of siblings and peers as shown by Patterson et al. (1967). First they learn to effectively counter the coercive behaviors of peers; then they learn to *initiate* aversive behaviors of their own. The reactions of their victims will provide the training necessary to shape yet more skill in the use of coercion. "Skill" in this context refers to whether or not the coercive behaviors are effective in shaping the ongoing social behaviors of peers and family members.

While most children have *learned* an impressive spectrum of coercive skills, they differ in the *rate with which they are performed*. Observation data collected in the field show large *intra*-individual as well as *inter*-individual variations in the rates with which coercive behaviors are performed. One function of a "theory" of aggression, if indeed one existed, would be to explain both of these variations in rate.

There are data which suggest a steady decline in performance rates for coercive behaviors from a high point in infancy down to more moderate levels at the age of school entrance. The laboratory-observation studies by Reynolds (1928) showed that the highest rates of negativistic-disruptive behaviors occurred before the age of two, followed by a steady decline through the age of four-and-a-half years. In the study by Patterson (1974a), home observation data were analyzed for small samples of three-year-old siblings of aggressive and nonaggressive boys. The mean Total Deviant score for the combined sibling sample of three-year-olds was .820 coercive responses per minute. This value was even higher than the mean of .750 responses per minute obtained for boys referred for treatment because of "aggressiveness" (Patterson, 1974c). The ages of the clinical sample ranged from 5 to 14. The comparable values for the four- and five-year-old siblings were .670 and .397, respectively. Hartup (1974) also noted a significant decrease in aggression for ages four through eight in his study of classroom behavior. Taken together, these findings suggest that the identified "aggressive" boy performs coercive behaviors at a level commensurate with a three- to four-year-old child. In this sense, he might be thought of as an exemplar of arrested socialization.

It is hypothesized that with increasing age certain coercive behaviors are no longer acceptable to parents. The behaviors then become the target for consistent tracking and punishment which in turn is accompanied by reductions in their rate. Data from the Patterson (1974a) study showed that two- and three-year-olds displayed the highest rates of Whine, Cry, Yell, and High Rate, as well as high rates for most other coercive behaviors. By age four, there were substantial reductions in Command Negative, Destructive, and Humiliate. By the age of five, most children used less Negativism, Non-Comply, and Physical Negative than did the younger siblings. Some behaviors such as Disapproval showed little changes in rates over these age ranges, presumably because they were "acceptable" to parents and received less punishment. Because of the small samples involved, these changes in "patterns" were at best only suggestive.

The changes in frequency patterns by age suggested the possibility that older children might display a progression in performance which reflects these developmental sequences. Those coercive behaviors which developmentally were "dropped" first (CN, DS, HU) might occur at the lowest rates in the older child. Those responses "dropped" later (NC, NE, PN) would occur at higher rates. The response, Disapproval, which was never really "dropped," would occur at the highest rate of all. Within this formulation, children who displayed a low rate response would display all of the higher rate responses as well. This transitivity reflects the fact that the parents have done little that is effective in training them and they display the full repertoire of the three-year-old's coercive behaviors. If parents "allowed" behaviors such as Humiliate to be performed, they would presumably allow the occurrence of all the less disapproved coercive behaviors as well.*

Two studies provided tests for the hypothesis that children's performance of coercive responses would be patterned in a transitive fashion. Patterson and Dawes (1975) showed that for eight coercive behaviors transitivity held across the sample of normal boys. The reproducibility coefficient was .91. This value was replicated for the sample of problem boys. The study by Patterson (1974a) showed that only a slight reordering of the same eight noxious responses produced consistent scalogram patterns for three-, four-, and five-year-old siblings as well. The findings strongly suggest that the performance of coercive behaviors may be a highly patterned enterprise even at an early age.

Parenting Skills

Using data from the Oregon Research Institute (ORI) samples, both Shaw (1971) and Sallows (1972) found parents of aggressive boys supplied more *positive* consequences for coercive behaviors than did parents of normal boys. Depending upon one's a priori classifications of "positive consequences," and the subject sample, the data show estimates ranging from 27% (Patterson et al., 1967) and 21% (Taplin, 1974; Sallows, 1972), up to 38% (Shaw, 1971) for problem families. The corresponding values for nonproblem families ranged from 30% (Shaw, 1971) up to 42% for younger normal children (Johnson et al., 1974). These findings suggest that the parents and the other family members provide sur-

---

* As a partial test of this hypothesis, parental ratings of aversiveness were correlated with the base rates with which 29 coded child behaviors actually occurred (Patterson, 1974a). The correlation obtained for one sample was —.36 ($df = 26$; $p < .05$) and for another, —.52 ($df = 27$; $p < .01$). The child behaviors rated most aversive tended to occur with the lowest frequency.

prisingly rich schedules of consequences which seem a priori to be positive reinforcers. Given that many of the antecedents were aversive (see footnote, page 274), then, these positive consequences could constitute *double* reinforcement, e.g., the removal of an aversive stimulus *plus* the presentation of a positive consequence.

Several aspects of Taplin's (1974) analysis of the ORI clinical sample showed that these schedules of parental positive consequences for coercive behaviors may not really play a crucial role in determining rates of behavior. His correlational analysis showed an across-subjects correlation of only .34 (N.S.) between the child's Total Deviant score during baseline and parental positive consequences provided for these behaviors. The cross-lag correlation between the baseline parental schedules and the child's Total Deviant score at termination was —.10 (N.S.). Furthermore, the data showed significant *decreases* in the child's deviant behavior during the first treatment probes; the data for parents showed *increases* in their schedules of positive consequation for deviant behaviors during the same time interval.

The functional analyses discussed earlier (Table 2) showed that the parents of problem children tended to employ aversive consequences which were less effective in controlling coercive behaviors. The implications of these findings for parental schedules are not clear. One might predict that agents using weak conditioned punishers would redouble their efforts. On the other hand, it is equally reasonable to believe that they would become extinguished and use them less. The comparative study by Sallows (1972) showed no differences between problem (23%) and nonproblem samples (22%). The figures were in close agreement with the 19% parental punishment for coercive behaviors for younger normals noted by Johnson et al. (1974). The current reanalysis of these schedules in Table 2 showed no substantial differences between samples. However, it was of interest to note that parents punished Social Aggression proportionately much more often than they did Hostility. The data also showed parental preferences were highly similar in terms of the *type* of punishing consequences used for the two samples. The relative frequencies were calculated for the occurrence of each of the 10 most likely parental punishments for boys' coercive behaviors. The rho for these data from the problem and nonproblem samples was +.85 ($df = 9$; $p < .01$). The termination data for the clinical sample showed *no* changes in parental punishment schedules (see Table 5).

These kinds of simplistic analyses suggest that parental *schedules* of consequences for coercive behaviors are probably *not* key variables.* It seems more likely the case that it is the *kinds* of reinforcement and punishment employed which are crucial. The earlier speculations (Patterson and Reid, 1970) about the determinants for these parental inconsistencies and noncontingencies remain without an empirical base. However, our understanding is becoming clearer about *what* it is that is missing in the behavior of some parents that relates to acceleration in children's performance of coercive behavior.

The System Is Disrupted

It is assumed that the parents' faulty application of reinforcing contingencies, both positive and aversive, is associated with high levels of coercive behaviors *among all family members*. It is within the matrix of a coercive system that the "aggressive children" are most likely to learn their skills.** For the ORI nonproblem sample, the mean Total Deviant scores among members was .276 responses per minute (S.D. of .171). Presumably, families displaying significantly greater coercion rates than this would be "high risk," e.g., more likely to produce a child labeled by the community as "aggressive." Given that a moderately coercive system produces a high rate coercive individual, it is assumed that this will lead in turn to the significant increases in mean rates of coercive behaviors among all members of the family. Reciprocity is a *descriptive* term for the process by which this occurs (Gouldner, 1960; Homans, 1961).

Research from a number of areas shows that within dyads there is an

---

* It should be noted in passing that the above notions about schedules of positive and aversive consequences may be overly simplistic when considered within an operant framework. As pointed out by Catania (1966), the prediction for the rate of particular responses requires information about the reinforcement schedules available for *concurrent* operants. The experimental work of Hernstein (1961) and Eckerman (1969) also emphasized the necessity to consider the reinforcement schedule for response A concurrently with the schedule available for response B in predicting the rate for either response. Presumably, rates of coercive behaviors for an individual child could be predicted only if one had information on the *relative* reinforcement schedules for the other responses under control of stimuli found in the same setting.

** Clinical observations (Patterson et al., 1973, p. 147) suggested one general exception to this hypothesis. Experience in working with a number of families showed that some of them had been very effective in raising several children. However, in the instance of the problem child, these "selective diffusion parents" neglected to apply contingencies which were already well known to them. The reasons for the omission were varied—e.g., the child was diagnosed as retarded or minimally brain damaged, the child had a history of prolonged illness, both parents were not working and felt "guilty about this child."

equity in the exchange of "positive" and "aversive" stimuli. These findings hold among family members (Reid, 1967), across married couples (Patterson, Weiss, and Hops, 1975), or in small groups in laboratory settings (Bales, 1953; Ray, 1970). Manipulating the behavior of one member of a dyad produces corresponding changes in the behavior of the other (Rosenfeld, 1966).

The study by Patterson et al. (1967) described one means by which a noncoercive victim could learn to perform coercive behaviors and contribute to an equity in the exchange of aversive stimuli. As the victim counters coercive attacks with aversive behaviors of his own, they will often "work" in that the attack is terminated. Over trials the "victim" will increase the number of aversive-counterattacks and coercive initiations. These increases contribute a small portion toward an equity between attacker and former victim in their exchange of aversive behaviors. However, the major contribution to equity is more likely found at a more molecular level (see footnote, page 275). Within a disrupted system, when a family member presented an aversive behavior the conditional probability was .38 (see footnote, page 274) that the problem child would respond in kind. With training, the "experienced" victim becomes more likely to respond in kind. This would mean periodic *extended* aversive interchanges. These "dyadic bursts" of coercive behaviors are thought to be the major determinants for the reciprocity correlation cited earlier.

Although an extremely passive parent may serve as an excellent victim for the development of high rates of more advanced coercive skills, it is assumed that the "best" victims would be siblings close in age or younger. Presumably, they would be most likely to provide reinforcement for coercive behaviors. This was borne out in the large-scale survey by Rutter et al. (1970) which showed that highly aggressive boys tended to be the middle child and were less likely to be the only or the youngest. On the average, the aggressive child in the ORI clinical sample tended to be the second born. Anderson (1969) showed that children referred for treatment as "aggressive" also tended to be middle, while "neurotics" tended to be firstborn. She also cites several additional studies which replicated these findings for aggressive children.

Data from the study by Arnold et al. (1975) showed that the Total Deviant scores for the problem child correlated +.74 $(df = 26; p < .001)$ with the mean score for sibling(s). The differences in mean levels for the scores were not significant. The reciprocity correlations between target child and father were .76 $(df = 22; p < .001)$ for the clinical

TABLE 4

Mean Rates of Coercive Behaviors for Family
Agents Across Two Samples

Family Members	Nonproblem Sample			Problem Sample			"t" test
	Mean	S.D.	N	Mean	S.D.	N	
			Total Deviant Per Minute				
Deviant boys	.277	.359	27	.661	.641	27	2.78**
Younger siblings	.453	.295	16	.650	.460	20	1.49
Older siblings	.177	.164	16	.425	.448	20	2.30*
Mothers	.267	.189	28	.505	.360	27	3.64**
Fathers	.230	.235	19	.318	.273	19	1.36
			Approval Responses Per Minute				
All family members	.056	.039	27	.025	.018	27	3.88***

* $p < .05$; ** $p < .01$; *** $p < .001$.

sample and .38 ($df = 19$; $p > .05$) for the nonproblem sample. The finding of covariations in coercion levels for child and parents was in keeping with the findings obtained by Johnson et al. (1974). However, the ORI data for mothers and children did not support Johnson's findings. The correlations were .16 ($df = 32$; $p > .05$) for the deviant sample and .25 ($df = 27$; $p > .05$) for the normal sample. A scatter plot for these data suggested the regression to be nonlinear, but calculating the epsilon did not improve the estimates of covariation. These intercorrelations among family members only partially supported the notion of equitable exchanges among all family members in rates of coercive behaviors. The data suggest that the role of mother may, in some sense, be inequitable vis-à-vis the target child. The regression slope suggested that the mean rates for mothers leveled off at a certain point such that further increases in rates for target child were not accompanied by corresponding increased rates for mothers.

The second hypothesis about the "disrupted family system" required that all family agents in the clinical sample display higher coercion rates than their counterparts from the nonproblem families. Table 4 summarizes the mean performance levels among family members from normal and deviant samples.

The comparisons of the mean values for the two samples showed that indeed all members from deviant families performed coercive be-

FIGURE 1

Child-Family Interactions

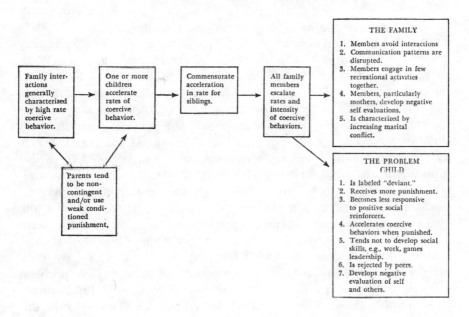

THE FAMILY

1. Members avoid interactions
2. Communication patterns are disrupted.
3. Members engage in few recreational activities together.
4. Members, particularly mothers, develop negative self evaluations.
5. Is characterized by increasing marital conflict.

Family interactions generally characterized by high rate coercive behavior.

One or more children accelerate rates of coercive behavior.

Commensurate acceleration in rate for siblings.

All family members escalate rates and intensity of coercive behaviors.

Parents tend to be non-contingent and/or use weak conditioned punishment,

THE PROBLEM CHILD

1. Is labeled "deviant."
2. Receives more punishment.
3. Becomes less responsive to positive social reinforcers.
4. Accelerates coercive behaviors when punished.
5. Tends not to develop social skills, e.g., work, games leadership.
6. Is rejected by peers.
7. Develops negative evaluation of self and others.

haviors at higher rates than did their normal family counterparts. In keeping with the hypothesis, the differences were significant for the target child, the older siblings, and the mothers. However, these differences were not significant for fathers or younger siblings. These data offer partial support for the notion that the entire system is disrupted.

Some further speculations. It is assumed that as the family becomes involved in using pain control techniques, several critical mechanisms become disrupted. (1) Attempts to *negotiate* behavior changes with other family members are likely to be accompanied by aversive stimuli. The other member responds to the aversive stimulus rather than the problem, and negotiations are effectively sidetracked (Patterson et al., 1975). (2) Presumably, a similar aversive quality would be found in their general attempts to communicate with each other. Even attempts to be supportive are accompanied by qualifications and criticisms. It came as a surprise in our clinical work to find that both parents *and* children often had to be *taught* to be reinforcing to each other! Clinically, much of the communication disruptions seem analogous to those described by

Haley (1963) and Minuchin (1974). (3) In keeping with this, Johnson et al. (1974) noted a significant correlation between degree of marital satisfaction and the observed rates of the target child's deviant behavior. (4) Families who use high rates of pain control techniques should eventually simply learn to avoid each other as much as possible. The data for distressed married couples showed that they engaged in significantly fewer shared recreational activities than did nondistressed couples (Weiss et al., 1973). It is not clear, of course, in such relations as to what is cause and what is effect. It is the writer's hypothesis that exchanging high rates of aversive stimuli *produces* these other phenomena as concomitants. As yet, there are no data which can provide a test for such a notion. But the limited findings available suggest that, at the very least, disruptions in problem solving, avoidance of social interaction, disruptions in communications, and marital dissatisfaction are concomitants for social systems involved in high rate exchanges of aversive stimuli. (5) It would come as no surprise then to discover that the mothers and fathers of extremely aggressive children referred for treatment tend to have negative evaluations of themselves (Lobitz and Johnson, 1974; Muller and Gottlieb, 1974). Several studies have compared parents of aggressive children to parents of nonaggressive problem children. They found high MMPI scores for Hysteria and Psychopathic Deviate, while low scores for Masculinity/Femininity consistently differentiated mothers of aggressive children (Anderson, 1969; Hanvik and Byrum, 1959; Wolking et al., 1967). The Hysteria scale also differentiated fathers (Anderson, 1969; Butcher, 1966; Wolking et al., 1967). The data in Appendix B summarize the comparable MMPI findings from mothers and fathers of the ORI clinical sample. The findings for fathers were in keeping with those from the Anderson (1969) study. Fathers of aggressive boys show little elevation in profile and clinically seem but little different from fathers of normal boys. However, a steady attrition in self-esteem seems to characterize the mothers of these boys. Data from both the Anderson (1969) and ORI sample showed a general elevation on almost all clinical scales. Both studies showed higher scores on the Depression scale than was the case for the normal samples. The ORI clinical sample showed larger elevations on the Psychopathic Deviate, Masculinity/Femininity, Schizophrenic, and Mania scales than was the case for either the normal samples or Anderson's (1969) sample of mothers of aggressive children.

Figure 1 summarizes the sequence as it is assumed to occur.

In terms of sheer amount of punishment, the sample of identified aggressive children received approximately *three times* as much (1277 aversive Cis versus 378, Table 2) as did their nonproblem compatriots. As shown by Shaw (1971), and Taplin (1974), he even gets punished at higher rates when he is behaving appropriately! It is also our clinical impression that he is retarded in the development of many basic social skills, e.g., how to initiate a conversation, how to reinforce peers, sibs, or parents, how to assume a leadership role. Studies have shown that aggressive boys have significantly lower social status as measured by peer sociometric data (Moore, 1967). Many of these boys also experience academic failure (Semier et al., 1967).

The study by Lobitz and Johnson (1974) showed significantly fewer positive social behaviors for these children. In keeping with this, the data from Appendix A showed nonsignificant tendencies for the aggressive boy to give others fewer physical positives, compliances, and laughs. These omissions in his behavior could lead to a situation in which other persons perceive him as nonattractive and react to him accordingly. For example, Rosenfeld (1966) found a correlation of .70 between frequency of "head nods" and ratings of attractiveness checked about female speaker.

Our clinical impression is that the identified problem child also receives many negative verbal evaluations by others. Certainly many intake interviews are initially characterized by a verbal assault upon the child, who sits with eyes downcast as he listens to this oft heard recital. All of these "inputs" taken together, an accurate perception by the problem child of his social reality *should* lead him to believe he is not treated as well as other boys. Given the consistency of negative inputs from the home and school, one would expect him to perceive his peers, parents, siblings, and teachers in a "negative" light. His concept of himself would also tend to be negative. While Coopersmith (1967) failed to find a significant correlation between low self-esteem and aggressiveness for a sample of normal children, our structured interviews with conduct-problem children strongly suggest that these boys tend to see themselves, their parents, siblings, peers, and friends in a negative way.

INTERVENTION PROCEDURES

Based upon the preceding formulation, it was assumed that the key component required to aid the child and restore the system to equilibrium was training in "parenting skills."* Furthermore, it was assumed that any nonpsychotic or nonretarded parent could learn child management skills. Therefore, parents were trained to (a) observe and keep records; (b) use effective punishment (withdrawal of reinforcers) for coercive behaviors; and (c) use more effective social/nonsocial reinforcers for prosocial behaviors.

As the rates of deviant child behavior were reduced, it was expected that the parents would apply the same principles and procedures to other members of their families. In effect, there should be significant reductions in the rates of coercive behaviors for the entire family. These changes would in turn be accompanied by alterations in self-esteem, communication disruptions, feelings of anger, and the other accompaniments of coercive systems.

For some, the contingencies for maintaining parenting *performance* seem "built in." If the new parental practices are effective, they will produce reduction in rates of the child's coercive behavior. This arrangement would constitute *negative reinforcement* for the performance of these parental skills. As some parents increase their use of positive reinforcers for prosocial behaviors, the child reciprocates in kind. Given that both of these mechanisms are operative, then the system should maintain the changes brought about by treatment.

To test these notions, several years were spent in pilot testing of treatment and evaluation procedures tailored for families of aggressive boys (Patterson, Ray, and Shaw, 1968). Then 27 families of conduct-problem children were treated, using the procedures developed earlier. Observation data were collected during baseline and treatment, and for a 12-month follow-up, to provide a basis for testing the following hypotheses: (1) The target child will display significant reductions in rates of coercive behavior as measured by both observers and by parents. (2) After treatment, *parental* aversive consequences made contingent upon coercive behaviors will suppress these responses to the degree found for parents of the nonproblem children. (3) There will be significant re-

---

* It would indeed be tempting to make the statement that teaching parenting skills is either necessary and/or sufficient as a treatment. However, in that some parents already have the skills but simply need encouragement in their performance, one can hardly claim "necessary" as a condition. In addition, our clinical experience suggests that just focusing upon child management skills would be sufficient treatment for only about a third of the disrupted families encountered. Many of them require additional skills training in the resolution of severe marital conflicts, depression, and a variety of other problems. This being the case, one can hardly say that training in child management skills is a *sufficient* condition for effective treatment.

ductions in the rates of coercive behaviors for siblings, mothers, and fathers. (4) There will be a lower proportion of positive consequences provided by parents for the child's coercive responses.

The initial referrals for treatment came from professionals working in the community. The cases required intervention with both the schools and the children's parents. Clinical experience in these two settings showed the treatment effects to be entirely setting-specific. These impressions were corroborated by studies such as Wahler's (1969). It became necessary, then, to simultaneously develop *two* intervention procedures, one for the home and one for the classroom. In either case, however, the emphasis was upon training agents found in the settings to modify the coercive behaviors.

A brief summary of the sample, the intervention procedures, and the criterion measures is given in the sections which follow.

Sample

During the period from January 1968 through June 1972, 35 families were referred by community agencies such as the Juvenile Court, schools, and mental hygiene clinics to the Social Learning Project at the Oregon Research Institute. They were referred for treatment because at least one boy between the ages of 5 and 15 in each family had been identified as a severe "conduct problem." At intake, the referring adults claimed that 50% of the boys exhibited problems in *both* the home and the school settings, and the remainder were problems in one setting or the other. Of those accepted for treatment, home observations showed 59% were socially aggressive (Total Deviant score $\geq$ .450 per minute). Some of these also performed low base rate asocial behaviors and were disruptive in school. Of the 11 remaining, the parent data (PDR) showed 6 of them performed low base rate asocial behaviors such as fire setting, stealing, and truancy. Of the 5 remaining cases, 2 displayed serious problems in classroom adjustment. By the criterion measures employed in the study, 3 cases that were accepted for treatment had been mislabeled. In spite of the referral complaints, their level of deviant behavior was not above normal levels in either setting.

The parents' descriptions, plus reports from community agencies, indicated that most of the cases had long-term histories of conduct problems. Many had already received alternate forms of treatment. The intake evaluation, plus diagnostic records from other community agencies, served to exclude most of the families containing *severely* retarded, *acutely* psychotic, or *severely* brain-damaged members.

The sample contained 8 father-absent families. Five of the children had been diagnosed as minimally brain damaged, or hyperkinetic; during baseline they were on medication such as Dexedrine or Ritalin. The sample contained a disproportionate number from the lower socioeconomic levels. The details of the demographic data were presented in an earlier report (Patterson and Cobb, 1973, pp .165-169).

Of the 35 referrals, 8 families dropped out after baseline data were collected. The 27 families who remained in training for longer than four weeks comprised the treated group. At termination, one family moved to another community; two more moved part way through follow-up. Four families refused to participate in the follow-up study; three others dropped out of the study before follow-up was completed.

Treatment in the Home

Five staff members (G. Patterson, J. Cobb, R. Ray, D. Shaw, and K. Skindrud) trained the majority of the parents. Five "trainees" (V. Devine, B. Martin, H. Walter, G. White, and N. Wiltz), supervised by the staff, also worked on the project for a year or less.

A general outline of the treatment procedures used for these families has been presented in Patterson et al. (1968, 1973). A manual (Patterson, Reid, et al., 1975) and a film (Reid and Patterson, 1974) provide more detailed descriptions of these clinical procedures.

All treated families received at least one month's training, which included the following: (1) The parents were required to study a programmed text on social-learning-based child management techniques which included *Living with Children* (Patterson and Gullion, 1968) or *Families* (Patterson, 1971) depending on the educational level of the parents. (2) They then learned to carefully define, track, and record a series of targeted deviant and/or prosocial child behaviors. They were monitored frequently by telephone during all stages of this training. (3) They were then assigned to a parent training group, where modeling and role playing procedures were used to illustrate appropriate techniques. (4) They learned to construct contracts which specified contingencies for a list of problem behaviors occurring at home and/or at school.

Where necessary, training sessions were conducted in the home, with the experimenters modeling the desired parenting skills. The contracts carefully specified the withdrawal of reinforcers accompanying point losses for deviant behaviors. The consistent use of the backup punishers presumably served to strengthen (CS-UCS) the parents' verbal request that the child terminate his coercive behavior. In like manner, the parents were carefully instructed in techniques for providing points *and* social reinforcers contingent upon desired social behavior. Daily telephone calls emphasized the importance of being consistent and contingent in using reinforcement and punishment.

Baseline data were collected for 6 to 10 days prior to treatment, following the reading of the programmed text, at the 4th and 8th weeks of treatment, and at termination. Usually the clinician and the family decided together when it was feasible to terminate. Following a decision to terminate, all criterion data were collected and then again at months 1 through 6, and at months 8, 10, and 12. At any time during follow-up, either the clinicians or the parents could initiate arrangements for additional "booster shot" training.

Intervention in the Classroom

Fourteen of the boys were identified by their teachers as displaying high rate disruptive behaviors; in some instances this included academic failure. Many had already been dropped from school or were placed on a limited time schedule. Because many of the teachers involved ranged from apathetic to antithetical about learning behavior modification skills, it was necessary to develop procedures which functioned effectively but at *low response cost to the teacher*. The treatment procedures for the classroom were described in detail in Patterson, Cobb, and Ray (1972), Patterson, Shaw, and Ebner (1969), and Ray et al (1970).

The classroom intervention procedures had the following characteristics: (1) The experimenters served as behavior managers and brought the disruptive classroom behavior under control during the first week or two of intervention. (2) In these classroom sessions, the child received signals from a "work box" placed on his desk. The signals were *contingent* upon his displaying nondisruptive behaviors, or "survival skills." The work box was eventually faded to a "work card" for recording points. (3) The backup reinforcers earned by the points consisted of such "natural" consequences as additional recess time, movies, or story reading which were *shared with the peer group*. From the beginning (Patterson, 1965), it was assumed that peer-group involvement was a key feature in classroom intervention. Experimental tests by Walker and Buckley (1972) and by Wolf et al. (1970) also suggest that earning reinforcers for peers may be a key component in this procedure. (4) In cases worked with during 1971 and 1972, contracts were negotiated with the family and the school personnel so that the child brought his work card to the parents each day and was given positive consequences for desired behaviors and aversive consequences for disruptive behaviors. The contracting procedures were based on prior work of investigators such as Homme et al. (1970) and Stuart (1971). (5) When the program was running smoothly and required only a few moments of "bookkeeping time" each day, it was turned over to the teacher. (6) For those children lacking academic skills, the parents were trained and supervised as remedial teachers. A procedure for training the parents as remedial agents, innovated by Skindrud (1972b), was introduced in 1971. This general approach to classroom intervention has been considerably improved and subjected to further intensive investigation by Hops et al. (1973).

Baseline observations were collected for a minimum of five sessions in the classroom, and then during treatment and at termination. During each session, the target child was sampled, together with each of the normal peers. Observation data were also collected for a 6- to 12-month follow-up, by which time all of the target children had moved to new classrooms.

Criterion Measures

Evaluation of family intervention. The observation procedures described in Patterson et al. (1969) were designed primarily to describe the noxious behaviors displayed among family members; to a lesser extent the code also sampled prosocial behaviors. Six to ten baseline observations were made in each home prior to intervention.

For each session, the observer went to the home at about dinner time and made two five-minute observations on each family member in a prearranged, random order. This produced a sequential account of each target subject's behavior and the reaction of other family members to him, described in terms of one or more of the 29 behavior categories. A portable interval-timing device signaled the observer every 30 seconds, at which time she shifted to the next line on the protocol sheet. With practice, an observer could record five reactions of the target subject and five reactions of the family members on each line. In the discussions which follow, many of the variables will be expressed as "rate per minute." Within the present context, it should be understood that the upper limit for such expressions would be approximately ten responses per minute for any given subject.

During intervention, observational "probes" were carried out. Each probe consisted of two consecutive observation sessions (days) during which the referred child was observed for 20 minutes and each of the other family members for 5 minutes. Probes were introduced immediately following the parents' reading of the programmed text, after 4 and 8 weeks of intervention, and at termination. During follow-up, two probe sessions were carried out for each of the first 6 months and for months 8, 10, and 12.

The same five observers collected the data for the entire study. In order to guard against the decay in reliability demonstrated by Reid (1970), biweekly observer training sessions were held and biweekly reliability checks were carried out in the homes. The agreement between pairs of observers was calculated by dividing total agreements by total agreements plus disagreements for each 30-second segment. The event-by-event analysis required agreement for category *and* sequence. The analysis for the data used in the present report showed an average agreement of 74.2%. The ability of observers to agree upon coding antecedents plus coercive behaviors (Ai-Rj) and coercive behaviors plus consequences (Rj-Ci) was investigated by Patterson (1974b). The data showed a median observer agreement of 56.5% for Ai-Rj events, and 59.5% for Rj-Ci units.

The earlier series of methodological studies on the problems associated with the use of the code were summarized in Patterson et al. (1973, pp. 156-165). A more extensive discussion of such problems as observer reliability, reactivity to observer presence, observer drift, code complexity, and stability of event estimation are to be found in Jones et al. (1975). To conserve space, no attempt will be made to summarize these materials here.

Earlier studies utilizing relatively inexperienced observers had found substantial biasing in their data collection. For this reason, in the current project, during 1968, two uninformed "calibrating" observers were employed at regular intervals. The analysis of these data by Skindrud (1973) showed that giving *experienced,* well-trained observers information about treatment states did not produce a significant biasing effect. Laboratory (Skindrud, 1972a) and nonlaboratory (Kent, 1972, dissertation in preparation) studies also showed no biasing for well-trained observers. In both of these studies, observers were given information which it seemed, a priori, would bias their recording. Because of these replicated findings, no effort was made later in the series to keep observers uninformed.

Two criterion variables were used to evaluate treatment. One was based upon observers' data; the second, on parents' daily reports of symptom occurrences. The observation data provided rates (per minute) for 14 noxious responses. This criterion score was labeled "Total Deviant" (TD) and consisted of the following: Command Negative, Cry, Destructive, Dependent, Disapproval, High Rate, Humiliate, Ignore, Non-Comply, Negativism, Tease, Whine, Yell, and Physical Negative. Estimates of the Total Deviant score based upon three to five observation sessions were correlated with estimates made a week later using a comparable number of sessions. The test-retest reliability correlation (uncorrected) was .78 ($p < .01$; $df = 26$). The validity data summarized in Jones et al. (1975) showed that this score correlated significantly with various parental ratings of aggressiveness for their boys.

The deviant families in the current sample were carefully matched for SES level, father presence-absence, number of children, and age of the "target" child with 27 families who had not sought treatment (see Patterson and Cobb, 1973, for details on matching). The latter were paid for 6 to 10 baseline observations in their homes. The mean TD score for this sample was .277. Using an extension of the same code system, Johnson et al. (1974) also observed a sample of 33 younger boys and girls from predominantly middle-class homes. The mean Total Deviant behavior score was .314 responses per minute (S.D. of .282).

An examination of the distributions of scores for the ORI clinical and nonproblem samples suggested that a score of .45 was maximally efficient in discriminating between the two samples. Scores falling at, or below, this Total Deviant score were identified as "within the normal range."

For the second criterion, the parents were asked during the intake interview whether or not each behavior from a list of "symptoms" (Patterson, 1964) was of sufficient concern for them to wish to change it. This Parent Daily Report (PDR) criterion was first introduced for case #24; the parents collected data for only one week of baseline and at termination. Beginning with case #32, these data were collected on each occasion that the observers went to the home during baseline, treatment, and follow-up. After each session, the parents were given a list containing the most easily observed and defined problems previously identified by them. They were asked to indicate the occurrence, or non-occurrence, of each of these events during *that* day for the time up to, and including, the observation session.

To determine the test-retest reliability, the mean proportion of PDR symptoms for the first week of baseline was correlated with the comparable score for the second week of baseline. The Pearson product moment correlation (uncorrected) was .60 ($df = 16$; $p < .01$). For the subjects in the present sample, the mean frequency of PDR symptoms for baseline correlated .69 ($df = 14$; $p < .01$) with the Total Deviant scores obtained from the baseline observations. These findings suggest modest convergence between these two measures of Conduct Problem behaviors.

Evaluation of classroom intervention. Behavior was sampled in both group and individual academic work situations. Observations were also made for some settings of special concern to the teacher, e.g., the physical education class.

The details of the data coding system were described in Patterson, Ray, et al. (1969) and Patterson, Cobb, and Ray (1972, pp. 187-194). The final code contained 19 behaviors (target child) and 19 reactions (peers or teacher). The target subject was observed at 15-second intervals for 12 minutes, and then randomly selected peers were observed in the same manner for 6 minutes. A minimum of five sessions of baseline data were collected for each child. On the average, about three-and-a-half hours of actual data recording were obtained for baseline, another five hours during intervention, and about two-and-a-half hours during follow-up.

The dependent variable used to test hypotheses about changes in classroom behavior consisted of a summary score "Inappropriate Behavior" (IB). This included the specific behaviors: Noisy, Physical Negative, Not Attend, and Self-Stimulation.

The reliability of observers for the present report was based upon the sum of their agreements divided by the total number of events recorded. The data collected in 21 sessions for 11 subjects and peers produced an 84.5% agreement for coding subject behavior (Patterson et al., 1972).

To determine the stability of the Inappropriate Behavior (IB) score, the first and second halves of the baseline data for the problem children were correlated. The Spearman-Brown correction correlation of .61 ($df = 13$; $p < .05$) suggested that even five or six baseline sessions provided minimally stable estimates. Cobb (1972) found a significant correlation between IB scores and achievement test scores for both fourth- and first-grade children. Patterson et al. (1972) showed that children referred for disruptive classroom behavior displayed significantly higher IB scores than did the "nonproblem" peers from the same classroom. Taken together, these studies showed the IB scores to be a minimally reliable and valid measure of performance skills relevant for adjustment in the classroom setting.

To facilitate the interpretation of changes in scores, the mean and S.D. were calculated for the normal peers from the 14 classrooms involved in the present study. The mean value of .247 (S.D. of .196) was comparable to the mean of .23 obtained by Werry and Quay (1969) when observing nonproblem children. Inspection of the distributions of scores for the ORI normal and deviant samples suggested a score $\geq .31$ as defining the lower limit for "normal." It was hypothesized that at the close of intervention, the IB scores for the problem boys should fall within the normal range.

TREATMENT OUTCOMES

Changes in the Problem Child

The major hypothesis concerned the increase in control of parental punishment for the target child's coercive behavior. However, for such a finding to be meaningful, it would require that it be accompanied by significant reductions in the target child's deviant behavior.

Reductions in coercive behaviors. Three measures of behavior change were used to assess the significance of changes in the child's coercive behaviors in the home: (1) Targeted Deviant child scores based upon home observation data that summed across the deviant behaviors for which the parents received specific training (the analyses and the details for individual Ss were reported in Patterson, 1975, 1974d). (2) Total Deviant scores based upon home observation data for 14 noxious responses (the analyses of the details for individual Ss were reported in Patterson, 1974c). (3) Parent Daily Report including data obtained from parents' daily reports of symptom behaviors (the details of the analyses were reported in Patterson, 1975, 1974d). The score was expressed as the average proportion of symptoms which occurred.

For the school, the single criterion score was Inappropriate Behaviors. It included the proportion of time intervals in which the child was engaged in Inappropriate classroom behaviors (the details for individual subjects were reported in Patterson, 1974c). The score described the proportion of time intervals in which Inappropriate Behaviors occurred. The mean scores for each of these criteria during baseline, termination, and follow-up, together with the results from the ANOVAS for repeated measures, are summarized in Appendix C.

The analyses showed significant improvement on all four criteria measuring changes in the two settings. These changes were produced at an average cost of 31.5 hours of professional time for the family training programs and 28.6 hours for the classroom intervention. During the 12 months of follow-up, an average of 1.9 hours of professional time was invested in "booster shot" training. Due to the fact that 11 families failed to provide complete follow-up data, these findings must be considered to be only suggestive. However, these findings do replicate the data from the earlier pilot studies for both the family intervention (Patterson, Ray, and Shaw, 1968) and the classroom intervention (Patterson, Shaw, and Ebner, 1969) procedures.

In both settings, approximately two-thirds to three-fourths of the boys, depending upon which criterion was used, showed major reductions from baseline performance levels in their performance of coercive behaviors. These changes were both clinically and statistically significant.*

Pre- and post-ratings by parents for a subset of the sample showed the mothers' perceptions of the child became significantly more positive as measured on four different personality dimensions (Patterson and Cobb, 1973, p. 193). Using rating scales of the type traditionally employed in evaluating "child therapy" showed that following termination, 100% of the parents felt the child had improved. A majority also felt the child was "happier" and that the whole family was better adjusted (Patterson and Reid, 1973).

Two small-scale comparative studies were carried out; each used 12 different families from the sample described in the current report. A waiting list control study by Wiltz and Patterson (1974) showed that five weeks of parent training produced significant decreases in observed rates of targeted deviant child behavior. No changes were observed for the control families. A placebo study described by Walter and Gilmore (1973) showed significant reductions for the experimental group in both Total Deviant and Parent Daily Report scores. Aggressive boys whose parents met leaderless placebo groups showed nonsignificant *increases* in both criterion measures. A limited attempt by Eyberg and Johnson (1974) to replicate some features of the family intervention procedures

---

* As shown in Appendix C, the data from both settings showed a steady increase from baseline to follow-up in the number of subjects who functioned within the ranges arbitrarily defined as "normal." A careful analysis of the follow-up data (Reid and Patterson, in preparation) showed that the dropouts tended to be families (a) who had higher rates of deviant behavior during baseline, and (b) responded most dramatically to intervention. These trends in Appendix C towards increasing normality during follow-up do little more than reflect this selective factor in the dropouts.

produced significant changes in both observation and parent report data.

Although no detailed descriptions of the clinical procedures were available, intensive consultation partially overcame this difficulty. Ferber et al. (1974) attempted to replicate some features of the family intervention based on their reading of the published reports and a single consultation. Data showed improvement for three out of seven families at termination, a finding very close to that which obtained for the Eyberg and Johnson study. No systematic follow-up data were collected.

In the present study, the effects of family intervention and classroom intervention were confounded in that effective treatment in the home *could have facilitated treatment* in the classroom. This possibility was tested in a classroom intervention study of disruptive children by Hett (1972). He compared three groups: (a) a placebo group (nondirective therapy); (b) a group in which the teachers were trained as behavior modifiers; and (c) a direct intervention group based upon most of the classroom treatment procedures used in the present report (excepting contracting and parents as remedial reading teachers). Both of the behavior modification groups showed significant increases for classroom Appropriate Behavior, while the placebo group did not. A further partial replication of the classroom direct intervention procedures was also reported by Walker and Buckley (1972).

For these kinds of families, the most convincing data for evaluating treatment outcome would be found in long-term follow-up data from the community agencies, including the juvenile court and mental health clinic. Such a retrospective study was begun in 1974 for 35 cases referred for treatment, 33 nonproblem families matched with the clinical sample, and 18 cases who dropped out prior to assessment. Table 5 summarizes the data only for those cases which were known to have been in the community for 12 months prior to the study *and* for 24 months following treatment. The data consist of the number of police contacts which involved "severe offenses." The classification was based upon the work of Sellin et al. (1964) and included: physical injury, theft, and property damage.

Interpretation of these findings must be severely limited because of the small samples and because there was no random assignment to treated and dropout samples. It is, however, of interest to note during follow-up, the treated group was doing better than they had during baseline. This is particularly meaningful in view of the expected increase in police offenses as a function of age. In fact, the treated group was functioning within the range of the normal group. The somewhat older (median

TABLE 5

Baseline and Follow-up Data for Police Contact
Involving Severe Offenses

Samples	N	Baseline 12 Months	N	0-12 Months	N	13-24 Months (accumulative)
				Percent of Ss with Severe Offenses *Follow-up*		
Treated	23	17	23	4	23	13
Dropout	8	62	8	37	8	62
Nonproblem	22	0	12	8	12	8

age 13 years) dropout group showed a consistently higher rate of serious offenses.*

Reductions in coercive "bursts." The earlier analyses (Table 1) showed that 7 of the 14 coercive responses exhibited significantly higher recurrence/persistence probability values for the problem than the non-problem families. It was predicted that, following treatment, these values would be comparable to levels displayed by nonproblem children. Table 1 summarizes the mean probability values for the treated sample at termination. The data showed *reductions* in the "burst" characteristics for 13 of the coercive responses. In fact, 8 of the responses (CN, CR, DP, IG, NE, PN, WH, YE) now showed values equal to or lower than the comparable baseline data for nonproblem children. The class of coercive responses, Hostile, was most affected. This is of some interest because this was the response class shown by Patterson and Cobb (1973) to be initiated *and* maintained (Patterson, in preparation) largely by aversive contacts with adults.

The boys' reactions to parental punishment were assumed to be crucial in determining the magnitude of the "burst" index. Presumably, the treatment program would give the parents more effective conditioned punishment to employ in their attempts to control coercive responses. Table 6 summarizes the values for $p(Rj_2/Rj \rightarrow Ci)$ calculated for baseline, termination, and follow-up. The dependent variables for the anal-

---

* Currently cases acceptable for treatment at the ORI Family Center are randomly assigned to experimental treatment (social learning) and community treatment groups. Community follow-up data for these cases will provide the basis for more definitive statements about the long-range utility of these procedures.

TABLE 6
Changes in Conditional Probabilities That Noxious Behavior Will Persist

Consequences	Baseline			Termination			Follow-up		
	N	p(Go)	% Ci noxious	N	p(Go)	% Ci noxious	N	p(Go)	% Ci noxious
Hostile p (Hostile$_2$/Hostile$_1$ →C$_1$)									
Aversive									
Parent	141	.41	30	62	.24	23	16	.12	26
Older sibling	68	.60	36	13	.15	39	8	.12	21
Younger sibling	43	.35	32	21	.10	36	5	.20	18
Nonaversive									
Parent	333	.26	70	128	.30	67	45	.09	74
Older sibling	120	.35	64	20	.30	61	29	.03	79
Younger sibling	92	.15	68	37	.08	64	22	.04	82
Total									
Parent	474	.31		190	.28		61	.10	
Older sibling	188	.44		83	.24		37	.05	
Younger sibling	135	.22		58	.10		27	.07	
Total	797	.32	.32	281	.24	.34	125	.08	.23
Social Aggression p (Soc Agg$_2$/Soc Agg$_1$ →C$_1$)									
Aversive									
Parent	55	.29	53	28	.18	55	13	.08	72
Older sibling	41	.29	48	18	.22	50	14	.29	78
Younger sibling	83	.32	47	30	.27	48	27	.30	68
Nonaversive									
Parent	48	.29		23	.35		5	00	
Older sibling	45	.18		18	.22		4	00	
Younger sibling	94	.24		32	.22		13	.15	
Total									
Parent	103	.29		51	.26		18	.06	
Older sibling	86	.23		36	.22		18	.22	
Younger sibling	177	.28		62	.24		40	.25	
Total	366	.27	.49	149	.24	.51	76	.20	.71

yses were the classes Hostile and Social Aggression. A comparable analysis for Total Deviant is summarized in Appendix D.

At termination, the data for both response classes showed the parent to be increasingly effective in using punishment to control coercive behavior. In fact, the conditional probability values closely approximated the values obtained for parents of nonproblem children (see Table 2). Status as an effective punishing agent increased during follow-up. Presumably, the parents continued to use backup punishment (withdrawal of reinforcement) and thus further enhanced the impact of the conditioned punishers employed. At follow-up, parents of problem children were even *more effective* than their counterparts from nonproblem families. The tenability of this attractive hypothesis is of course vitiated by the possibility of unknown factors operating in selecting the sample available for follow-up.

As a general characterization, the termination and follow-up data showed that even siblings were more effective in using punishment to control Hostile responses. There was, however, little change in their ability to handle Social Aggressive responses displayed by the problem child.

Changes Within the Family

Parental consequences. The parents were trained to either place deviant behaviors on extinction schedules or, if it were a targeted behavior, to immediately apply a punishment such as Time Out, loss of privileges, or points lost. Assuming the training to be effective, one might expect it to have some impact upon parental *schedules of consequences* provided for deviant behaviors. However, the data in Table 6 showed that while parents used *fewer* punishments at termination, they continued to punish the same *proportion* of coercive behaviors as they had at baseline. In addition, the training program particularly emphasized the importance of placing deviant behaviors on extinction schedules *for positive reinforcers.* For this reason, one would expect decreases in positive consequences provided by parents for coercive responses. Finally, it was assumed that the general emphasis on using punishment sparingly and contingently would be reflected in fewer accidental punishments noted by Shaw (1971), e.g., punishing prosocial behaviors.

For the present, it is assumed that these parental schedule variables were *not* determinants but rather *concomitants* of behavior change in treatment. Taplin (1974) tested these hypotheses with the data from the

ORI clinical sample of 27 treated cases. His definitions of coercive behaviors and of positive and aversive consequences were comparable to
those used in the present report (see footnote, page 275). When comparing baseline, termination, and follow-up data, he found a significant
reduction in the proportion of positive consequences provided for
deviant behaviors by the parents. The analysis of changes in the parents' use of aversive consequences for prosocial behavior was in the
predicted direction, but the findings were of only borderline significance.
These changes in consequence schedules were both in keeping with the
training program.

The treatment program required the participation of all fathers. In
keeping with this emphasis, Taplin also found significant increases in
the proportion of deviant behaviors punished by fathers, suggesting perhaps their increased involvement in dealing with the problem child.
However, the latter effects were short-lived, as shown in the nonsignificant
findings when comparing their baseline and follow-up performance.

Several reviewers, including the present writer (Patterson, 1973b, pp.
156-157), have suggested that training parents to reduce positive consequences for coercive behaviors would be followed by reductions in rates
for these behaviors. Analysis by Taplin (1974) showed that the hypothesis
may not be tenable. The analysis showed a nonsignificant correlation
between children's baseline Total Deviant behavior scores and the parents' schedules of positive consequences for these behaviors. A cross-lag
correlational analysis also showed no support for the hypothesis. Finally,
his data showed significant *reductions* for mean rates of the child's
Total Deviant behavior during the initial phases of treatment at which
point parental mean rates of positive consequences for these behaviors
were *increasing!*

Taplin's analyses are crucial in emphasizing that training parents to
alter the social behaviors which they provide as *consequences* may not,
in and of themselves, produce changes in the behaviors of the extremely
coercive child. Rather, it seems that it may first be necessary to teach
them to use more powerful non-social positive and aversive effective
consequences. This practice may in turn alter the status of the conditioned reinforcers which they typically employ. Taplin's data do not, of
course, directly test such alterations in responsiveness, but they are supportive of such a notion.

The family reduces its rate of coercive behavior. It was hypothesized
that as the behavior of the problem child was brought under control,
the coercive behaviors of all other family members would display com-

TABLE 7

Changes in the Family System

Family Members	N	Baseline	Termination	"t"	P value
Siblings†	27	.559	.387	3.78	.03
Mothers	27	.505	.410	1.08	n.s.
Fathers	18	.318	.194	1.31	n.s.

† Analysis for siblings taken from Arnold, Levine, Patterson (1975). The Total Deviant score was based upon the mean for all siblings.

mensurate reductions. Table 7 summarizes changes from baseline to termination in Total Deviant scores for siblings, mothers, and fathers. In keeping with the hypothesis, the data at termination showed reductions in Total Deviant scores for all family members. However, only the changes for siblings were significant. It is of some interest to note that at termination the fathers were performing coercive behaviors at rates *slightly lower* than for those which obtained for fathers of non-problem families (see Table 4). The mothers, however, remained more coercive at termination than mothers of nonproblem families.

The findings for family members only partially support the notion that the system changed as a function of treatment. The best that one can say is that *some* aspects of the system were altered. These general findings set further constraints upon our confidence in the likelihood of long-term adjustment for many of these cases. In keeping with this qualification, our community follow-up data showed that within two years of termination, seven boys in the clinical sample had been placed either in foster homes or in institutions. Needless to say, these findings emphasize the need for yet further innovations in our attempts to devise parent training programs.

DISCUSSION

The data supported the notion that many boys labeled as Conduct Problems do indeed perform disruptive behaviors at higher rates than their normal counterparts. In fact, the data suggest that they manipulate their immediate social environment in a manner characteristic of three- or four-year-old children. Aggressive boys tend to be members of aggressive families. Given a coercive response, the problem child is very likely to present a similar behavior in the next time frame. While nonproblem children also show a similar tendency, it is of a lesser magnitude. It was hypothesized that the main determinant for these differences in the performance of coercive bursts lay in the differential impact of parental punishment upon these behaviors. For problem children, parental punishment accelerates ongoing coercive behaviors. Comparable punishments employed by parents of nonproblem boys tended to suppress their occurrence. A number of studies have also raised the possibility that the extremely aggressive child may be less responsive than normal children to adult-dispensed social reinforcers. The "out-of-control" child seems to have three characteristics: (a) he displays significantly higher rates of coercive behaviors which tend to come in bursts; (b) he accelerates his coercive behaviors when presented with garden variety punishments; and (c) he is less responsive to adult approval.

These general findings relate well to the type of training programs provided for the parents. Here the emphasis was upon buttressing both parental social reinforcers and punishment in the context of contractual arrangements between child, parent, and school. The clinical findings showed that indeed most parents could be taught to perform these skills. While no formal analysis has been done, it is the writer's impression that for about a third of the families it is sufficient to adopt the *simplest* possible strategy, e.g., *teach the parent the specific skills for changing child behaviors*. Another third of the families seem to require much more—the teaching of negotiation skills and the partial resolution of marital conflicts and depression being the most common. Our attempts to develop such supplementary techniques are described in Patterson, Weiss, and Hops (1975). If these problems are not dealt with, we believe the long-term follow-up will show the treatment to have been ineffective. The remaining one-third seem to fail in spite of our best efforts.

Baseline, termination, and follow-up comparisons based upon the observation data showed significant changes in the behaviors of the problem child. Significant changes were also reflected in multiple criteria employed in evaluating the family intervention. The success rates varied as one moved from Targeted Deviant (75%) to measures of generalization such as Total Deviant (67%) or Parent Daily Report (70%). When using more global measures such as parental ratings, the success rates ranged from 80% to 100%. The follow-up data provided modest support for the notion that the changes persisted in both settings after treatment.

Our preliminary examination of the family as a system was rather cursory. The data did, however, clearly implicate one member of the family other than the identified problem child. The siblings of families in the clinical sample were shown to be significantly more coercive than those from nonproblem families. The data also showed significant reductions in these behaviors, changes which persisted during follow-up (Arnold et al., 1975).

The data for the involvement of parents were less clear-cut. The differences in coercion rates between parents of problem and nonproblem children were significant for mothers, but not for fathers. Neither parent showed significant reductions in rate during treatment. While the self-report data showed that the mothers described themselves as deviant, no data are available which showed these descriptions altered during treatment. Data were provided which showed significant changes in parental schedules of consequences for various behaviors of the problem child. However, it is not clear as to just what these changes mean.

One set of analyses does directly relate to the question of system changes. Patterson (1973a) showed significant changes in the status of stimuli provided by family members when comparing baseline to termination data for one child. At termination, there were fewer stimuli provided which facilitated the initiations for the child's coercive behaviors. These alterations varied as a function of role within the family. The stimuli provided by the younger sister were more affected than were those presented by the mother or father. The approach constitutes a powerful but very expensive mode of analysis.

What is needed are both further innovations and replications of existing techniques. The programmatic work currently underway by M. Bernal, S. Johnson, and R. Wahler relates to both of these issues. These investigators have innovated many of their own measurement and intervention procedures. However, a consensus of findings among the four groups would be strongly supportive for a *general* social learning approach to parent training.

A replication study is currently underway at ORI. The Joe Cobb Family Intervention Center, directed by Robert Conger, is providing service to families of carefully screened socially aggressive children. A detailed manual (Patterson, et al., 1975) has been prepared which describes the procedures used in this clinic. The criterion measures used in the earlier studies, as well as some new ones, will be used to evaluate the efficiency of the treatment for a large sample of families. Long-term community agency follow-up will also be carried out for cases treated by the social learning procedures, and for randomly selected cases referred back to community agencies for treatment by the means traditionally provided for such cases. Assuming the replication findings are supportive, then a series of studies will be carried out to determine which components, if any, are necessary for this treatment approach to be effective.

APPENDIX A

Comparisons of Problem and Nonproblem Boys for p (Rj)

Code Categories	Clinical Sample N = 27	Nonproblem Sample N = 27	"t"†
	Mean p(Rj) for Baseline Data		
	Coercive Behaviors		*One-tailed test*
Command Negative	.008	.002	2.09**
Cry	.019	.002	1.48
Disapproval	.135	.084	2.02**
Dependency	.007	.003	.90
Destructive	.031	.006	1.58
High Rate	.047	.014	1.09
Humiliate	.020	.001	2.82***
Ignore	.005	.004	.55
Non-Comply	.093	.050	2.00**
Negativism	.118	.025	2.91***
Physical Negative	.042	.009	2.55**
Tease	.050	.019	2.23**
Whine	.036	.041	.17
Yell	.058	.019	1.71*
	Noncoercive Behaviors		*Two-tailed test*
Approval	.017	.028	1.75
Attend	1.413	1.348	.69
Command	.048	.039	.70
Comply	.233	.184	1.16
Laugh	.081	.111	1.19
Normative	1.557	1.546	.40
No response	.072	.055	1.28
Play	1.290	1.358	.51
Physical Positive	.040	.014	1.34
Receive	.056	.031	1.30
Self-Stimulation	.232	.111	2.04*
Talk	1.545	1.562	.61
Touch	.017	.011	1.09
Work	.642	.820	1.06

† Data were subjected to an arc sine transformation.
* p .05; ** p .01; *** p .001.

Appendix B

Parental Self-Report Data

	Mothers				Fathers			
				Mean MMPI Scores				
MMPI[1] *Sample*	*Normal Sample*[2]	*Normal Sample*[3]	*Anderson's Clinical Sample*[4]	*ORI Clinical Sample N = 35*	*Normal Sample*[2]	*Normal Sample*[3]	*Anderson's Clinical Sample*[4]	*ORI Clinical Sample N = 21*
?	2.7	1.3			3.6	3.0	50	
L	4.1	3.7	50	4.3	3.7	4.0	50	5.2
F	2.9	2.5	50	6.2	3.1	3.6	50	4.7
K	16.9	16.9	59	13.7	16.7	16.1	61	16.1
HS	53	52	52	54	53	52	52	54
D	51	52	57	57	51	53	51	51
HY	56	56	59	59	56	56	60	58
PD	54	53	56	62	55	56	57	55
Mf	49	49	47	59	58	57	57	57
Pa	52	54	56	58	52	52	53	53
Pt	57	51	55	60	52	52	52	56
Sc	54	52	54	60	51	52	51	55
Ma	49	48	45	53	51	53	53	55
Si	—	—	51	57	—	—	48	51

[1] All clinical scales K corrected.
[2] Based upon 50 nonproblem families matched for families referred to the Child Psychiatry Service at Iowa Psychopathic Hospital (Goodstein and Rawley, 1961).
[3] Based upon sample of nonproblem families matched with a sample referred to child outpatient clinic for treatment (Liverant, 1959).
[4] Data from 29 families referred for treatment because of aggressive child (Anderson, 1969).

Appendix C

Behavior Changes for Problem Children in Two Settings

Criterion Variables	Baseline				Intervention					Follow-up			
	N	BL_1	BL_2	% S's† within normal range	Termination	% S's change ≥ 30 of baseline	% S's within normal range	F	N	Six months	N	Twelve months	% S's within normal range
Family Intervention													
Targeted	27	.371	.478		.190	74		4.31**	18	.188	16	.170	
Total Deviant	27	.704	.793	41	.402	67	55	5.15**	19	.360	17	.403	70
Parent's Daily Report	17	.616	.637		.327	67	67	15.85**	12	.403	10	.233	
Classroom Intervention													
Inappropriate behavior	14	.406	.439	22	.233	71	50	4.15***	10	.264	10	.220	80

* $p < .05$;   ** $p < .01$;
*** $p < .001$.
† See sections on evaluation of intervention for definitions of "normal range."

APPENDIX D

Changes in p(Total Deviant$_2$/Total Deviant$_1$) as a Function of Type of Consequence and Agent

Type Consequences and Agents	Nonproblem Sample			Baseline			$p(TL_2/TD_1)$ Termination			Follow-up		
	N	p(Go)	% Ci noxious	N	p(Go)	% Ci noxious	N	p(Go)	% Ci noxious	N	p(Go)	% Ci noxious
Aversive												
Parent	252	.36	40	689	.50	62	275	.35	43	137	.26	43
Older Sib	41	.46	31	275	.58	43	58	.31	41	69	.39	39
Younger Sib	85	.30	40	313	.41	42	119	.32	31	94	.45	41
Nonaversive												
Parent	380	.32	60	1100	.34	38	353	.32	57	185	.11	57
Older Sib	85	.11	69	355	.29	57	81	.27	59	104	.09	61
Younger Sib	128	.16	60	427	.20	58	166	.16	69	134	.14	59
Total												
Parent	632	.30		1789	.39		628	.32		312	.19	
Older Sib	126	.22		630	.42		139	.28		173	.21	
Younger Sib	213	.22		740	.29		285	.23		228	.27	
Sum	971			3159			1052			713		
Mean		.302	.389		.39	.404		.334	.429		.234	.421

REFERENCES

ANDERSON, L. M.: Personality characteristics of parents of neurotic, aggressive, and normal preadolescent boys. *J. Clin. and Consult. Psychol.*, 33, 575-581, 1969.

ARNOLD, J., LEVINE, A., and PATTERSON, G. R.: Changes in sibling behavior following family interaction. Submitted to *J. Clin. and Consult. Psychol.*, 1975.

BALES, R. F.: The equilibrium problem in small groups. In: T. Parsons, R. Bales, and E. Skils (Eds.), *Working Papers in the Theory of Action*. New York: Free Press, 1953. Pp. 111-162.

BANDURA, A.: *Aggression: A Social Learning Analysis*. Englewood Cliffs, N. J.: Prentice-Hall, 1973.

BELL, R. Q.: Stimulus control or caretaker behavior by offspring. *Develop. Psychol.*, 4, 63-72, 1971.

BOMMARITO, J.: Conditioning by mild verbal punishment as a prediction of adjustment in kindergarten. Unpublished doctoral dissertation, Wayne State University, 1964.

BUTCHER, J. N.: MMPI characteristics of externalizing and internalizing boys and their parents. Paper read at the "First Conference on Research Developments in the Use of the MMPI," Minneapolis, Minnesota, 1966.

CAIRNS, R. B.: Fighting and punishment from a developmental perspective. *Nebraska Symposium*, U. of Nebraska Press, 1972. Pp. 59-125.

CAIRNS, R. B., and PARIS, S. G.: Informational determinants of social reinforcement effectiveness among retarded children. *Amer. J. Ment. Retard.*, 76, 361-369, 1971.

CATANIA, C. A.: Concurrent operants. In: W. Honig (Ed.), *Operant Behavior: Areas of Research and Application*. New York: Appleton-Century-Crofts, 1966. Pp. 213-270.

COBB, J. A.: The relationship of discrete classroom behaviors to fourth-grade achievement. *J. Ed. Psychol.*, 63, 74-80, 1972.

COOPERSMITH, S.: *The Antecedents of Self-Esteem*. San Francisco: W. H. Freeman, 1967.

DEVINE, V. T.: The coercion process: A laboratory analogue. Unpublished doctoral thesis, State U. of New York at Stony Brook, 1971.

ECKERMAN, C.: Probability of reinforcement and the development of stimulus control. *J. Exper. Anal. Behav.*, 12, 551-559, 1969.

EIBL-EIBESFELT, L.: Ethological approaches to violence. In: J. DeWitt and W. Hartup (Eds.), *Determinants and Origins of Aggressive Behavior*. The Hague, Netherlands: Mouton Press, 1974.

EYBERG, S. M., and JOHNSON, S. M.: Multiple assessment of behavior modification with families. *J. Consult. and Clin. Psychol.*, 42, 594-606, 1974.

FERBER, H., KEELEY, S., and SCHEMBERG, K.: Training parents in behavior modification: Outcome of problems encountered in a program after Patterson's work. *Behav. Ther.*, 5, 415-419, 1974.

FRIEDRICH, L. K., and STEIN, A. H.: Aggressive and prosocial television programs and the natural behavior of preschool children. *Monographs of the Society for Research in Child Development*, 19, No. 2, 1954.

GOODSTEIN, L. D., and RAWLEY, V. N.: A further study of MMPI differences between parents of disturbed and non-disturbed children. *J. Consult. Psychol.*, 25, 460, 1961.

GOULDNER, A. W.: The norm of reciprocity: A preliminary statement. *Amer. Sociol. Rev.*, 25, 161-178, 1960.

HALEY, J.: *Strategies of Psychotherapy*. New York: Grune and Stratton, 1963.

HANVIK, L., and BYRUM, M.: The MMPI profiles of parents of child psychiatric patients. *J. Clin. Psychol.*, 15, 427-431, 1959.

HARE, R. D.: Psychopathology, autonomic function and the orienting response. *J. Abnorm. Psychol.*, 73, Monogr. Suppl. #3, 1968.

HARTUP, W. W.: Aggression in childhood: Developmental perspectives. *Amer. Psychol.*, 29, 336-341, 1974.

HERBERT, E. W., PINKSTON, E. M., HAYDEN, M. L., SAJWAJ, T. E., PINKSTON, S., CORDUA, G., and JACKSON, C.: Adverse effects of differential parental attention. *J. Appl. Behav. Anal.*, 6, 15-30, 1973.

HERNSTEIN, R. J.: Relative and absolute strength of response as a function of frequency of development. *J. Exper. Anal. Behav.*, 4, 267-272, 1961.

HETT, G. G.: The modification and maintenance of attending behavior for second, third and fourth grade children. Unpublished doctoral dissertation, U. of Oregon, 1972.

HOMANS, G. C.: *Social Behavior: Its Elementary Forms*. New York: Harcourt, Brace & World, 1961.

HOMME, L., CSANZI, A., GONZALES, M., and RECHS, J.: *How to Use Contingency Contracting in the Classroom*. Champaign, Ill.: Research Press, 1970.

HOPS, H., WALKER, H., and HUTTON, S.: CLASS program for acting-out children: Contingencies for learning academic and social skills. Center at Oregon for Research in the Behavioral Education of the Handicapped, U. of Oregon, March 1973.

JOHNS, J., and QUAY, H.: The effect of social reward on verbal conditioning in psychopathic and neurotic military offenders. *J. Consult. Psychol.*, 26, 217-220, 1962.

JOHNSON, S. M., WAHL, G., MARTIN, S., and JOHANSSEN, S. How deviant is the normal child: A behavioral analysis of the preschool child and his family. In: R. D. Rubin, J. P. Brady, and J. D. Henderson (Eds.), *Advances in Behavior Therapy*, Vol. 4. New York: Academic Press, 1974.

JONES, R. R., REID, J. B., and PATTERSON, G. R.: Naturalistic observations in clinical assessment. In: P. McReynolds (Ed.), *Advances in Psychological Assessment*. Vol. 3. San Francisco: Jossey-Bass, 1975. Pp. 42-95.

KOPFSTEIN, D.: The effects of accelerating and decelerating consequences on the social behavior of trainable retarded children. *Child Devel.*, 43, 800-809, 1972.

KUENSTLER, W. H.: Differential effects of positive and negative reinforcement on juvenile delinquents and Sunday school students. Unpublished doctoral dissertation, U. of Houston, 1970.

LIVERANT, S.: MMPI differences between parents of disturbed and non-disturbed children. *J. Clin. Psychol.*, 23, 256-260, 1959.

LOBITZ, G., and JOHNSON, S.: Normal versus deviant children: A multi-method comparison. Unpublished paper, U. of Oregon, 1974.

LYKKEN, D. J.: A study of anxiety in the sociopathic personality. *J. Abnorm. and Soc. Psychol.*, 55, 6-10, 1957.

MINUCHIN, S.: *Families and Family Therapy*. Cambridge, Mass.: Harvard U. Press, 1974.

MOORE, S.: Correlates of peer acceptance in nursery school children. *Young Children*, 22, 281-297, 1967.

MOYER, K. E.: The physiological inhibition of hostile behavior. In: J. F. Knutson (Ed.), *The Control of Aggression: Implications from Basic Research*. Chicago: Aldine, 1973. Pp. 9-40.

MULLER, W. H., and GOTTLIEB, F.: Predicting behavioral treatment out in disturbed children: A preliminary report of the responsivity index of parents (RIP). *Behav. Ther.*, 5, 210-214, 1974.

PARKE, R. D., DEUR, J. L., and SAIVIN, D.: The intermittent punishment effect in humans: Conditioning or adaptation. *Psychonomic Science*, 18, 193-194, 1970.

PATTERSON, G. R.: An empirical approach to the classification of disturbed children. *J. Clin. Psychol.*, 20, 326-337, 1964.

PATTERSON, G. R.: An application of conditioning techniques to the control of a hyperactive child. In: L. P. Ullmann and L. Krasner (Eds.), *Case Studies in Behavior Modification.* New York: Holt, Rinehart, & Winston, 1965. Pp. 370-375.

PATTERSON, G. R.: Behavioral techniques based upon social learning: An additional base for developing behavior modification technologies. In: C. M. Franks (Ed.), *Behavior Therapy: Appraisal and Status.* New York: McGraw-Hill, 1969. Pp. 341-374.

PATTERSON, G. R.: *Families: Applications of Social Learning to Family Life.* Champaign, Ill.: Research Press, 1971.

PATTERSON, G. R.: Changes in status of family members as controlling stimuli: A basis for describing treatment process. In: L. A. Hamerlynck, L. C. Handy, and E. Mash (Eds.), *Behavior Change: Methodology, Concepts and Practice.* Champaign, Ill.: Research Press, 1973. Pp. 169-191. (a)

PATTERSON, G. R.: Programming the families of aggressive boys. In: C. Thoresen (Ed.), *Behavior Modification in Education.* 72nd Yearbook. National Society for the Study of Education, 1973. Pp. 154-192. (b)

PATTERSON, G. R.: The aggressive child: An exemplar of arrested socialization. Oregon Research Institute, unpublished manuscript. Submitted to *J. Abnorm. Child Psychol.*, 1974. (a)

PATTERSON, G. R.: A basis for identifying stimuli which control behavior in natural settings. *Child Devel.*, 1974, 45, 900-911. (b)

PATTERSON, G. R.: Interventions for boys with conduct problems: Multiple settings, treatments, and criteria. *J. Consult. and Clin. Psychol.*, 42, 471-481, 1974. (c)

PATTERSON, G. R.: Multiple evaluations of a parent training program. In: T. Thompson & W. S. Dockens, III (Eds.), *Applications of Behavior Modification.* New York: Academic Press, 1975. Pp. 299-322.

PATTERSON, G. R.: Retraining of aggressive boys by their parents: Review of recent literature and follow-up evaluation. In: F. Lowry (Ed.), Symposium on the Seriously Disturbed Preschool Child, *Canad. Psychiat. Assn. J.*, 19, 142-161, 1974. (d)

PATTERSON, G. R., and COBB, J. A.: A dyadic analysis of "aggressive" behaviors. In: J. P. Hill (Ed.), *Minnesota Symposia on Child Psychology*, Vol. 5. Minneapolis: U. of Minnesota Press, 1971. Pp. 72-129.

PATTERSON, G. R., and COBB, J. A.: Stimulus control for classes of noxious behaviors. In: J. F. Knutson (Ed.), *The Control of Aggression: Implications from Basic Research.* Chicago: Aldine, 1973. Pp. 144-199.

PATTERSON, G. R., COBB, J. A., and RAY, R. S.: Direct intervention in the classroom: A set of procedures for the aggressive child. In: F. Clark, D. Evans, and L. Hamerlynck (Eds.), *Implementing Behavioral Programs for Schools and Clinics.* Champaign, Ill.: Research Press, 1972. Pp. 151-201.

PATTERSON, G. R., and DAWES, R. M.: A Guttman scale of children's coercive behaviors. *J. Consult. and Clin. Psychol.*, 1975, 43 (4), 584. See NAPS Document #74323 for 7 pages of supplementary material. Order from Microfiche Publications, 440 Park Avenue S., New York, N. Y. 10016. Remit in advance $1.50 for microfiche or $5.00 for photocopies up to 30 pages. Make checks payable to Microfiche Publications.

PATTERSON, G. R., and GULLION, M. E.: *Living with Children: New Methods for Parents and Teachers.* Champaign, Ill.: Research Press, 1968.

PATTERSON, G. R., LITTMAN, R. A., and BRICKER, W.: Assertive behavior in children: A step toward a theory of aggression. *Monographs of the Society for Research in Child Development*, 32, No. 5, 1967.

PATTERSON, G. R., RAY, R. S., and SHAW, D. A.: Direct intervention in families of deviant children. *Oregon Res. Inst. Res. Bull.*, 8, No. 9, 1968.

PATTERSON, G. R., RAY, R. S., SHAW, D. A., and COBB, J. A.: Manual for coding of family interactions, 1969 revision. Document #01234. Order from ASIS/NAPS, c/o Microfiche Publications, 440 Park Avenue S., New York, N. Y. 10016. Remit in advance $5.45 for photocopies, and $1.50 for microfiche. Make checks payable to Microfiche Publications.

PATTERSON, G. R., and REID, J. B.: Reciprocity and coercion: Two facets of social systems. In: C. Neuringer and J. D. Michael (Eds.), *Behavior Modification in Clinical Psychology*. New York: Appleton-Century-Crofts, 1970. Pp. 133-177.

PATTERSON, G. R., and REID, J. B.: Intervention for families of aggressive boys: A replication study. *Behav. Res. and Ther.*, 11, 383-394, 1973.

PATTERSON, G. R., REID, J. B., JONES, R. R., and CONGER, R. E.: *A Social Learning Approach to Family Intervention. Vol. 1. Families with Aggressive Children.* Eugene, Ore.: Castelia Publishing Co., 1975.

PATTERSON, G. R., SHAW, D. A., and EBNER, M. J.: Teachers, peers, and parents as agents of change in the classroom. In: F. A. M. Benson (Ed.), *Modifying Deviant Social Behaviors in Various Classroom Settings* Eugene, Ore.: U. of Oregon Press, 1969. No. 1. Pp. 13-47.

PATTERSON, G. R., WEISS, R. L., and HOPS, H.: Training of marital skills: Some problems and concepts. In: H. Leitenberg (Ed.), *Handbook of Operant Techniques*. Englewood Cliffs, N. J.: Prentice-Hall, Inc., 1975. Pp. 483-523.

QUAY, H. C., and HUNT, W.: Psychopathology, neuroticism, and verbal conditions: a replication and extension. *J. Consult. Psychol.*, 29, 283, 1965.

RAY, R. S.: The relation of interaction, attitude similarity, and interpersonal attraction: A study of reciprocity in the small group. Unpublished doctoral dissertation, U. of Oregon, 1970.

RAY, R. S., SHAW, D. A., and COBB, J. A. The work box: An innovation in teaching attentional behavior. *School Counselor*, 18, 15-35, 1970.

REID, J. B.: Reciprocity in family interaction. Unpublished doctoral dissertation, U. of Oregon, 1967.

REID, J. B.: Reliability assessment of observation data: A possible methodological problem. *Child Devel.*, 41, 1143-1150, 1970.

REID, J. B., and PATTERSON, G. R.: *A Social Learning Approach to Family Therapy.* 16mm film. Champaign, Ill.: Research Press, 1974.

REYNOLDS, M. M.: Negativism of preschool children: An observational and experimental study. *Contributions to Education*, No. 288, Bureau of Publications. New York: Teachers College, Columbia U., 1928.

ROSENFELD, H. M.: Approval-seeking and approval-inducing functions of verbal and non-verbal responses in the dyad. *J. Pers. and Soc. Psychol.*, 4, 597-605, 1965.

RUTTER, M., TIZARD, J., and WHITMORE, R.: *Education, Health and Behavior.* New York: Wiley, 1970.

SALLOWS, G.: Comparative responsiveness of normal and deviant children to naturally occurring consequences. Unpublished doctoral dissertation, U. of Oregon, 1972.

SARBIN, T., ALLEN, V., and RUTHERFORD, E. Social reinforcement, socialization and chronic delinquency. *Brit. J. Soc. and Clin. Psychol.*, 4, 179-184, 1965.

SCHACTER, S., and LATANE, B.: Crime, cognitions and the autonomic nervous system. In: D. Levine (Ed.), *Nebraska Symposium on Motivation.* U. of Nebraska Press, 1964. Pp. 221-273.

SELLIN, T., THORSTEN, D., and WOLFGANG, M. E.: *The Measurement of Delinquency.* New York: Wiley, 1964.

SEMIER, I., ERON, L., MEYERSON, L., and WILLIAMS, J.: Relationship of aggression in third grade children to certain pupil characteristics. *Psychol. in the Schools,* 4, 85-88, 1967.

SHAW, D.: Family maintenance schedules for deviant behaviors. Unpublished doctoral dissertation, U. of Oregon, 1971.

SKINDRUD, K. D.: An evaluation of observer bias in experimental-field studies of social interaction. Unpublished doctoral dissertation, U. of Oregon, 1972. (a)

SKINDRUD, K. D.: Generalization of treatment effects from home to school settings. Unpublished manuscript, Oregon Res. Inst., 1972. (b)

SKINDRUD, K. D.: Field evaluation of observer bias under overt and covert monitoring. In: L. A. Hamerlynck, L. C. Handy, and E. J. Mash (Eds.), *Behavior Change: Methodology Concepts and Practice.* Champaign, Ill.: Research Press, 1973. Pp. 97-118.

SOLOMON, R. L.: Punishment. *Amer. Psychol.,* 19, 239-253, 1964.

STUART, R. B.: Behavioral contracting with families of delinquents. *J. Behav. Ther. and Exper. Psychiat.,* 2, 1-11, 1971.

TAPLIN, P.: Changes in parental consequation as a function of intervention. Unpublished doctoral thesis, U. of Wisconsin, 1974.

TOCH, H.: *Violent Men.* Chicago: Aldine, 1969.

WAHLER, R. G.: Behavior therapy with oppositional children: Attempts to increase their parents' reinforcement value. Paper presented at the Southeastern Psychological Association, Atlanta, Ga., April 1967.

WAHLER, R. G.: Setting generality, some specific and general effects of child behavior therapy. *J. Appl. Behav. Anal.,* 2, 239-246, 1969.

WALKER, H., and BUCKLEY, N. K.: Programming generalization and maintenance of treatment effects across time and across settings. *J. Appl. Behav. Anal.,* 5, 209-224, 1972.

WALKER, H. M., and BUCKLEY, N. K.: Teacher attention to appropriate and inappropriate classroom behavior: An individual case study. *Exceptional Children,* 5, 5-11, 1973.

WALTER, H., and GILMORE, S. K.: Placebo versus social learning effects in parent training procedures designed to alter the behaviors of aggressive boys. *Behav. Ther.,* 4, 361-377, 1973.

WARREN, V. and CAIRNS, R.: Social reinforcement satiation. An outcome of frequency of ambiguity. *J. Except. Child Psychol.,* 13, 249-260, 1972.

WEISS, R. L., HOPS, H., and PATTERSON, G. R.: A framework for conceptualizing marital conflict, a technology for altering it, some data for evaluating it. In: L. A. Hamerlynck. L. C. Handy, and E. J. Mash (Eds.), *Behavior Change: Methodology, Concepts and Practice.* Champaign, Ill.: Research Press, 1973. Pp. 309-342.

WERRY, J. S., and QUAY, H.: Observing the classroom behavior of the elementary school children. *Exceptional Children,* 35, 461-470, 1969.

WILTZ, N. A., and PATTERSON, G. R.: An evaluation of parent training procedures designed to alter inappropriate aggressive behavior of boys. *Behav. Ther.,* 5, 215-221, 1974.

WOLF, M., HANLEY, E., KING, L., LACHOWICZ, J., and GILES, D.: The timer-game: A variable interval contingency for the management of out-of-seat behavior. *Exceptional Children,* 37, 113-118, 1970.

WOLKING, W. D., DUNTEMAN, G. H., and BAILY, J. D.: Multivariate analyses of parents' MMPIs based on psychiatric diagnosis of their children. *J. Consult. Psychol.,* 31, 521-524, 1967.

ZIMBARDO, P. G.: The human choice: Individuation, reason, and order versus deindividuation, impulses and chaos. *Nebraska Symposium on Motivation,* U. of Nebraska Press, 17, 237-307, 1969.

12

Families as Mutual Control Systems: Optimization by Systematization of Reinforcement

JOHN A. CORSON

Skinner (1961) has noted that all social organizations can be characterized as mutual control systems, with control being exercised upon, as well as being exercised by, each member of an organization.

Individuals can be seen as members of many mutual control systems, including their families, their occupations, and the various levels of the society in which they live. Within each of these systems, the individual's behavior is controlled by a characteristic set of categories, sources, and schedules of reinforcement.* These reinforcement features vary from system to system.

In this context, development from infancy to adulthood can easily be seen as involving a progression through various types of mutual control systems and various levels of participation in each control system. Furthermore, any mutual control system can be characterized by a more or less concise contract which sets forth the privileges, responsibilities, and reinforcement contingencies for each member of the system. The laws in adult society can be seen as components of an explicit contract, and in some occupational systems the contracts are also explicit; however, these explicit contracts are relatively rare at other levels of society. In fact most other systems, including the family, demand infer-

---

* Instead of the term "reinforcement" I would have preferred to use the term "incentive stimulus" throughout; however, the probable lack of familiarity of most readers with incentive theory was the reason for this choice. Incentive theory is used in this paper to deal with interactions between parental attention and self-esteem and is described in detail by Bindra (1974).

ences on the part of their members about the nature of an implied contract.

The implied nature of most contracts can be seen as a source of confusion about privilege and responsibility and, in turn, as a source of many developmental problems. The case has been made that some of the problems of adolescence are due to the increasing ambiguity of the adolescent's changing role (privileges and responsibilities) in the family as he or she progresses toward adulthood. It is my opinion that the occurrence of these problems can be decreased, and the eventual transfer into other control systems facilitated, if the family members develop an explicit contract (and modify the contract as expectations change) instead of relying on an implied contract which is often inconsistent.

A number of attempts to reach this general objective have been based on Skinner's plan (1948, 1971) for the redesign of society. This plan involves careful management of positive reinforcement (reward or "good things") and minimum use of negative reinforcement (threat of, or delivery of, punishment or "bad things"). We now have a large body of data with which to evaluate the impact of these procedures. The results with the very early phases of development and with regressed and retarded populations are most encouraging (Kazdin and Bootzin, 1972; Atthowe, 1973). On the other hand, the results with later phases or higher levels of development and with subjects who are not retarded or regressed are not as encouraging. Among the problems encountered in the use of such programs with relatively normal populations (in both therapeutic and commune settings) are: (a) high administrative costs of positive reinforcement schemes; (b) the eventual necessity of the use of powerful negative reinforcers to prevent system failure (Kinkade, 1973); and (c) an obvious mismatch problem (or sequencing failure) when a person leaving such a program reenters the real world, as it now is, and not yet redesigned in accord with Skinner's plan.

An essential aspect of the mismatch is the difference between the reinforcement schedules typical of the two settings. As mentioned earlier, the Skinnerian system carefully manages and makes maximum use of positive reinforcement and attempts to make minimal use of negative reinforcement. On the other hand, the schedules of reinforcement in the real world, as it is now, can be characterized as follows: (1) Salient positive reinforcement is usually unreliable and/or separated from salient positively reinforceable behavior by long intervals (i.e., is on variable high-ratio or long-interval schedules). (2) Salient negative reinforcement is usually reliable and/or separated from salient negatively reinforceable behavior by short intervals (i.e., is on fixed low-ratio or short-interval schedules). Skinner's remarks (1961, p. 542; 1971, p. 57) indicate that he would agree with this characterization of the present reinforcement schedules in the real world. On the assumption that this characterization is accurate, one can argue that both educational and remedial systems should be organized in an attempt to facilitate the individual's transition to this state of affairs.

An important objective of these educational and remedial systems should be the development in the individual of the concept of self as an agent who is capable of contracting with other agents for the operation of mutual control systems. The basic idea underlying this objective has been put forth by Skinner and others; it is that for a human being the optimal mode, or level, of participation in a mutual control system ranges from informed and consenting participation in system operation to active participation in system design and evolution. It is clear that, in order to reach this level of participation, one must develop: (a) some understanding of the mutuality of control in all systems; (b) the concept of the examinable, negotiable, and relatively arbitrary nature of contracts (or objectives and details of operation of control systems); and (c) an impression of oneself as an active agent in the examination and selection of the desired form of contractual arrangement for the mutual control systems in which one participates. (These notions touch on many important issues, such as questions regarding determinism versus freedom of choice and the presumed existential states of "object" and "being"; however, I will ignore these in order to make clear the operational details of my position and proposals.) An additional objective of these educational and remedial systems should be the development of self-esteem or a positive "self theory" (Epstein, 1973). While this is closely related to the development of the concept of the self as an agent capable of contracting with other agents, it can also be seen as involving a very different set of features.

"Self theory" can be seen as a summary term for many of the effects of an individual's reinforcement history. In terms of incentive theory (Bindra, 1974), the development of self-esteem or the status of self theory can be seen as having several major stages. Parental attention becomes a strong conditioned incentive stimulus as a result of the infant's learning the correlation between parental attention and various unconditioned incentive stimuli (e.g., food, warmth, etc.). The relationship between parental attention and the many unconditioned incentive stimuli could also have powerful effects on certain social and verbal stimuli. For example, messages in the "You're OK" category (see Harris, 1967, for elaboration of "OK" terminology and Bandura, 1969, for a discussion of social learning theory) would become conditioned appetitive incentive stimuli because they are so frequently correlated with delivery of unconditioned appetitive incentive stimuli; and messages in the "You're not OK" category would become conditioned aversive incentive stimuli because they are correlated with unconditioned aversive incentive stimuli (e.g., pain, deprivation, etc.). It seems that the course of development of the conditioned incentive power of parental attention determines the success or failure of its later subdivision (or discrimination) into positive and negative qualities, as well as the success or failure of the eventual transfer to nonparents of the conditioned incentive power of various qualities of attention; in other words it lays the foundation for later responses to social reinforcement.

In summary, I have argued that: (a) families are mutual control systems; (b) the family system should be leveled or sequenced so that the older children can transfer successfully to the control systems of the adult world; (c) the children should see themselves as capable of evaluating and influencing the operation of the systems in which they participate; (d) development of self-esteem or a positive self theory, and later responses to social reinforcement, are profoundly influenced by the experience of children with parental attention. On the basis of these ideas a strategy has been developed to assist families in optimizing the participation of their children in society's mutual control systems. This can be seen as being either a prophylactic or an optimizing strategy for "normal families"; it promotes a wealth-sharing team concept and gives a greater and more explicit control role to children than is typical in North American society.

The primary components of this strategy are (a) a specific family-unit contract regarding duties and privileges of all members, (b) a method for systematizing parental attention, and (c) a method of systematizing, monitoring, and matching positive and negative reinforcement ("rewards" and "punishments" in parental language) to the real-world schedules.

The specific methods used to implement this program with five normal families will now be described briefly. We will leave out various important steps regarding baseline procedures, operationalization, and parent training (in part because these varied from family to family), and will only touch on the general features of the program.

First, whenever possible, the family was gathered together and the general idea of the family unit as a team was discussed. The importance was stressed of all members knowing their privileges and responsibilities and of refraining from behaviors which are detrimental to themselves or to other members of the family. The contract was developed as follows:

1. The parents, as superordinate members of the family team, were asked to list the responsibilities and privileges of each member of the family.
2. The parents were asked to list any behaviors of any members of the family (including themselves) which bothered them or other members of the family.
3. Both the parents and the children were asked to list the "rewards" and "punishments" currently used in the family.
4. These lists were discussed and edited in collaboration with the family and formed the basis of the contract.

It was understood that the parents' responsibilities would include earning funds, preparing most meals, and being systematic and self-controlled in monitoring behavior and in delivering rewards and punishments. They would also have the role of leaders and primary decision-makers in the family and would be evenhanded in discussing problems and progress as well as in reconsidering contract details at regular intervals. It was also understood that the children, as developing members of the team, would have certain of their behaviors monitored by the parents and that some of their usual rewards and punishments would be delivered in accord with the results shown on the monitoring chart. Throughout, the complex mutuality of control within the family team was stressed, as was the obligation of all members (a) to be aware of the necessity for changes in the contract (e.g., to permit increases in responsibility and changes in privilege to growing children), and (b) to take an active role in considering and discussing possible changes.

Parental attention was partially systematized by means of a very simple procedure. Every morning at breakfast, for the five days of the working week, one child was in a separate room (such as a den) with the father alone, without siblings or mother being present. This lasted for about 45 minutes and in a two-child family this would occur every other day. On alternate days, the other child was in the separate room with the father and the first child was in the kitchen with the mother. This can be seen as programmed parental attention which is not contingent upon bad or good behavior of the children. This attention was paired with a part of the daily ritual to insure its occurrence, and was intended to partially satisfy the children's urge for individual parental attention.

The technique for systematizing punishment and reward was more complex. A chart (graph paper) was taped to the wall of the kitchen and the days of the month were blocked out on it. Each incident of detrimental ("unacceptable") behavior was immediately entered on the chart in the form of the first letter of the descriptive term (e.g., a tantrum was denoted by a T, hitting by an H, etc.); periods without unacceptable behavior were entered in the form of a G. The marks for unacceptable behavior were entered at the time the behavior occurred and the G's were entered during a review session the following morning. The maximum possible number of G's was two; these were given when a child had indulged in no unacceptable behaviors on the previous day and implied that the child had met all responsibilities. If a child indulged in an unacceptable behavior one time on the previous day he got only one G, and if unacceptable behavior occurred two or more times he got no G's. The parents were instructed to complete the morning review session quickly after giving praise for G's, but then to have a general discussion with the child over breakfast. This discussion was to be unrelated to unacceptable behavior and was to be used as a specific time for the child to receive individual attention.

Superimposed on this system was a second system of rewards and punishments; since all of these families had typically made use of physical punishment in the form of spanks, and all but one had made use of "reward" in the form of money or allowance, these features were incorporated into the system.

A spank was administered when a child had indulged in three consecutive incidents of the same category of unacceptable behavior, or five incidents of any category. The spank was administered immediately after the final mark was obtained; as mentioned above, the chart entries were made when each incident of unacceptable behavior occurred. It was stressed to the parents that children should be told of the mark being put on their chart and that this announcement (or the spank when necessary) should be the end of the attention gained by them for the unacceptable behavior. (However, in cases where children continued to be dangerous, destructive, or intensely disruptive they were removed, isolated, and ignored for a "time-out" period of five minutes. This turned out to be rarely necessary, as the entry of a mark on the chart generally ended such behavior.)

Each spank was denoted on the chart with an asterisk and after a spank the children started anew, in the sense that the next single un-acceptable behavior was the beginning of a new series. The children also started with a clean slate each morning, in the sense that marks for unacceptable behavior from the previous day were not counted toward a spank on the subsequent day. However, all of the marks did have a long-term consequence—each Saturday morning the previous week's behavior was reviewed with the children and, in all families which had previously used "allowance," the marks were assigned monetary values to match existing allowance rates. For example, in some families each G earned the child 10 cents (maximum week's total—$1.40) and each unacceptable behavior subtracted 5 cents from the total (in all cases the minimum was set at zero rather than having a child incur a debt for a particularly bad week). There was one family which had not previously used monetary incentives, but had instead used family outings; for example, bowling on Saturday afternoons had previously been with-held when the child had been "bad." In this family we systematized the delivery of various types of family outings in a similar manner to that used for money in the other families.

Note that the reinforcers were delivered in accord with the real-world schedules mentioned earlier, with negative reinforcers on a low-ratio, short-interval schedule and with certain salient positive reinforcers on a high-ratio, long-interval schedule. Note also that this scheme is quite different from the typical "token economy" approach (e.g., Atthowe, 1973).

Table 1 shows some of the data from these five normal families. In all cases daily occurrences of physical punishment were monitored by the parents for a four-week baseline period prior to the onset of the program, and this is compared with the frequency of physical punish-ment during the program: on this index the program has resulted in a clear improvement in all cases. There were other indications, which varied from family to family, of a more desirable level of function in all five families.

Applications of this program have also been made with a number of relatively troubled families.

The first troubled family presented itself to us with a behavioral problem in their seven-year-old boy. This boy was the older of two children, residing with his family in a suburban middle-class home. He was doing average work in school, although his intelligence was superior. The behavior of the child in the home was characterized by long periods of normal behavior interspersed, every day, with periods of

TABLE 1

Some Effects of the Use of Behavior-Control Technique in Five Normal Families

Family	Number of boys (ages)	Number of girls (ages)	Mean Weekly Number of Physical Punishments per Child During:			Mean Weekly Number for the Most Recent Month of:		Total duration of chart use	Modification to chart procedure described in text
			the month before the start of chart use	the last week of the second month of chart use	the most recent month of chart use	Bad marks	Good marks		
1	2 (9, 8)	1 (5)	2	1	.1	6	7	31 mo.	Maximum number of G = 1 per day.
2	2 (10, 7)	1 (4)	2	0	.1	6	7	10 mo.	maximum number of G = 1 per day.
3	1 (5½)		7	1	.25	6	14	8 mo.	G is given at the time of occurrence of certain target behaviors (maximum of 5 G's per day) if child gets more G's than bad marks he earns a family outing (e.g., bowling).
4	1 (8)	1 (6)	4	1	.5	10	9	4 mo.	G = 5 cents, bad marks = 2 cents.
5	2 (4½) Twins	1 (5½)	21	0	.25	10	9	4 mo.	Chart is discussed in evening before prayers; G = 5 cents, bad marks = 1 cent.

intense disruptive behavior. His disruptive behavior included the following: severe tantrums in which the child would destroy furniture, draperies, his sister's belongings, etc.; incidents of apparently unprovoked verbal and physical abuse of his younger sister; incidents of making of very loud noises and creating various disturbances when the other family members preferred quiet, including in church and in the middle of the night. The parents had tried to deal with the child in various ways before bringing him to us with a tearful plea for help. Conversation with the parents and child suggested the following: (1) The child's self theory was poor or "not OK" as reflected in word counts, in good and bad categories, in response to the request "tell me about yourself." (2) The child felt guilty about his behavior, and the parents confessed that they had frequently resorted to guilt-producing statements in an attempt to control the child's behavior. (3) Reports from both the parents and the child on what happened before and after his misbehaviors indicated that he was reinforced by parental attention and that he very rarely received parental attention which was not contingent on bad behavior. Some of the results of the application of this program are shown in Figure 1. The parents reported that the disruptive behaviors occurring after approximately the sixth week were much less prolonged and less disturbing to the other members of the family. A follow-up 15 months after institution of the system showed that the boy's frequency of disruptive behavior has remained at the level shown in the final four weeks covered in Figure 1. However, his parents report that certain disruptive behaviors no longer occur (e.g., tantrums involving destruction of furniture and the sister's belongings, and physical abuse of the sister) and that the remaining disruptive behaviors are relatively mild and brief.

It should also be noted that, according to parents' reports, the boy's behavior outside of the home and with his schoolmates, while not a target problem, has markedly improved since the institution of this system. This suggests that his new style of behavior has generalized to the extent that it is now shown in the absence of the programmed scheme of rewards and punishments. His school grades have also improved.

Finally, his self-theory, as reflected by the content of his self-references, has shifted to the point where bad references are hardly ever present and neutral and good references predominate (a standardized self-theory measure for children was not used here).

The program has also been used with three child-battering parents

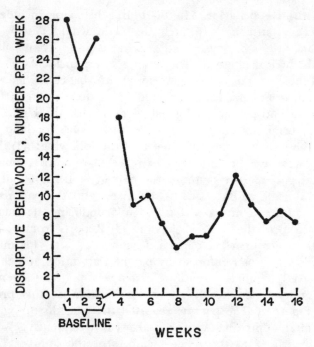

FIGURE 1. Disruptive behavior of a seven-year-old boy over a 16-week period.

in two family settings. In the first family (three boys) the average number of beatings per child was about 19 per week during the baseline period. One of the boys was brain damaged and this may have resulted from those beatings. (The parents admitted that some of the beatings were closed fist assaults above the neck.) By the time this system had been in effect for six weeks the frequency of physical intervention had dropped to one per week per child and severity had decreased to a less dangerous level (according to reports from both parents). The family has stayed on this program and we receive periodic reports which show that they are stabilized at this level; more importantly, there has been no further damage to any of the children which can be detected by our evaluations (see Figure 2).

In the second family (two girls and one boy) the mother was beating the oldest daughter from 6 to 16 times per week during the baseline period. When the system had been in effect for six weeks, the average frequency of physical intervention had dropped to below 1 beating per

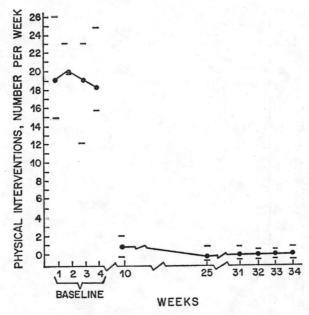

FIGURE 2. Median (Range shown in brackets) number of
physical interventions (Father or mother to three sons)
over a 34-week period.

week, and again, according to the mother, the severity of these interventions was reduced to a far less dangerous level (see Figure 3).

DISCUSSION

The basic method of assessment in all cases was the entry of the letters on the chart. However, in the first child-battering family the parents reported separately on each other's behavior, and in the family with the single child-battering parent there were two methods of record keeping which permitted a cross check. (Future applications will involve recording of family meetings and observers in the home.)

There is some evidence that the effect of this program outlasts the use of the monitoring and systematization methods. One of the normal families (the second shown in Table 1) was periodically observed before, during, and after use of the program. These observations suggest that behavior patterns developed in all family members during use of the program (for 11 months) have continued for at least a year since

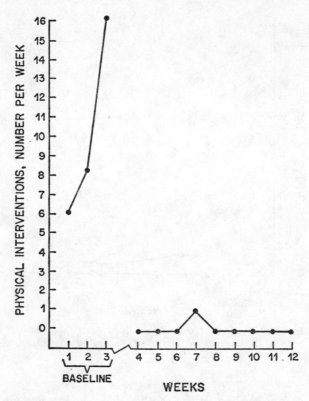

FIGURE 3. Physical interventions (mother to five-year-old daughter) over a 12-week period.

termination; for example, while the mean weekly physical punishments per child prior to the program was 2, there were no physical punishments during the post-program observation period.

There is also some evidence that the effect of this program generalizes to other settings, the most dramatic being in school grades and changes in other behaviors outside the home of the seven-year-old boy and of the children of the first child-battering family.

It is clear, in the family of the seven-year-old boy and in the two child-battering families, that a most important aspect of the program was the control of the behavior of the parents. For example, systematization of parental attention given to the disruptive seven-year-old boy may well have been the basis for the change found in this case. In the child-battering families it seems that control of parental mood swings and

resulting behavioral outbursts may have been an important result of
the use of this program.

Turning to consideration of the self theory, we have no evidence,
aside from that on the seven-year-old boy, concerning the status of the
children's self theory. (There is some indication from self-reports that
the mother of the second child-battering family experienced an improvement in her own self-theory during the use of this program.) We plan,
in future applications, to do more careful assessment of self theory of all
members of the family and also to include the assessment of other
dependent variables (such as contracting skills) related to the assumptions
set forth in the introduction to this report.

It is important to note the differences between this program and the
most popular format in which Skinner's plan has been applied. This
difference seems to be that of matching the reinforcement contingencies
to those which apparently prevail in the "real world."* Recently, this
objective of matching, sequencing, or programming generalization has
received attention from workers concerned with the therapeutic applications of programs based on the Skinnerian plan discussed earlier in this
paper. A review of the progress in this area (Kazdin and Bootzin, 1972)
suggests that further work on this problem is badly needed.

Among the other aspects of this program which may be of value are
the following: low cost in time of administration; a team approach to
negotiable contracts which implies the expectation of good behavior and
removes the necessity of rewarding each episode of good behavior; and
the control of parental attention which, in some cases, such as that of the
seven-year-old boy, seems to be a very difficult reinforcer to manage
properly.

We are currently conducting a study of the separate impact of each
of the components of the program described here.

---

* This program also answers some of Skinner's complaints about punishment by
(a) depersonalizing punishment and by (b) making punishment events "information-
ally strong."

REFERENCES

ATTHOWE, J. M., JR.: Token economies come of age. *Behav. Ther.,* 4, 646-654, 1973.

BANDURA, A.: *Principles of Behavior Modification.* New York: Holt, Rinehart and
Winston, 1969.

BINDRA, D.: A motivational view of learning, performance, and behavior modification.
Psychol. Rev., 81, 199-213, 1974. (Some aspects of this position were discussed by
Bindra in *Psychol., Rev.,* 75, 1968.)

EPSTEIN, S.: The self-concept revisited: or a theory of a theory. *Amer. Psychol.,* 28, 404-416, 1973.

HARRIS, T. A.: *I'm OK—You're OK. A Practical Guide to Transactional Analysis.* New York: Harper & Row, 1967.

KAZDIN, A. E., and BOOTZIN, R. R.: The token economy: An evaluative review. *J. Appl. Behav. Anal.,* 5, 343-372, 1972.

KINKADE, K.: *A Walden-Two Experiment: The First Five Years of Twin Oaks Community.* New York: William Morrow, 1973.

SKINNER, B. F.: *Walden Two.* New York: Macmillan, 1948.

SKINNER, B. F.: The design of cultures. *Daedalus,* Summer, 534-546, 1961.

SKINNER, B. F.: *Beyond Freedom and Dignity.* New York: Knopf, 1971.

13

Modification of Family Interaction with the Child as the Behavior-Change Agent

VICTOR A. BENASSI

and

KATHRYN M. LARSON

Studies of behavior modification and analysis in home settings have proliferated in recent years. Much of this work has been concerned with demonstrating that a behavioral approach to family problems is both feasible and effective (e.g., Bernal, 1971; Patterson et al., 1973), while some of it has dealt specifically with the effects of a variable (e.g., Christophersen et al., 1972; Herbert et al., 1973) or the validation of a particular approach to family intervention (e.g., the work of Patterson and his associates). It is not within the scope of this paper to review the literature on the topic of behavior modification in the home. Rather, the objective is to discuss, and present data on, what has been a neglected variable in this area of research—*the child*. Any attempt to understand the interactions that occur in families must include the contributions of the child to the development and maintenance of those interactions. This view, of course, has important implications for those who design behavior-change strategies.

The Child's Role in Family Interaction

On a common sense level, nearly all would agree that children control their parents' behavior through the presentation of antecedent and

The authors thank Barbara Benassi, Virginia Binder, Robert Kapche, Alan Lowenthal, and Elliott Nelson for their helpful comments on this manuscript.

consequent stimuli contingent upon certain parent behaviors (cf. Patterson, 1971, 52-53, 79). For example, Seymour wants to stay up past 9:00, his prescribed bedtime. When put to bed he begins to cry feverishly (aversive antecedent stimulus). His father ignores him for a while but finally tells him to be quiet. Seymour does not comply, and after several minutes of crying and yelling his father permits him to stay up for another half hour. Seymour stops crying and the father has been negatively reinforced for emitting the behavior which terminated the aversive antecedent event. The reciprocal nature of this hypothetical situation is obvious—Seymour's and his father's behaviors have been altered as a result of their interaction. A plethora of other examples could be described. However, no purpose is served in relying on such cases when a literature exists which supports the thesis offered in this paper. The areas drawn upon are diverse, including theories of socialization, observational research, and scattered behavior modification papers.

The traditional view of parent-child interactions has been that the child is a tabula rasa upon which the parents write. Lytton (1971) pointed out that "studies of parent-child interaction have in the past usually been based on the assumption that parents' behavior is the antecedent and children's personality the consequent . . ." (679). Similarly, Bell (1971) stated that "most investigators have only considered the child an object on which parental actions are registered, rather than a participant in a social system, stimulating as well as being stimulated by the other" (63). Gewirtz (1961), Stott (1966), Wenar and Wenar (1963), Kogan and Wimberger (1966), and Kogan et al. (1969) have made similar statements. Although these writers have been largely concerned with the development of social behaviors in families containing young children or infants, their comments are relevant nonetheless.

Contrary to the traditional view, each of the above writers believes that a reciprocal relationship accurately describes the nature of family behavior patterns. Lytton (1971) concluded that the traditional model of socialization is too narrow and needs to include the contribution to the family system made by the child. An example of the limitations of the traditional model will cement Lytton's point. Bell (1968) has pointed out that most parent-child research has involved correlations between parent and child characteristics. However, a correlation coefficient provides no information about the *direction* of the socialization effect. Bell suggested that researchers have found it more parsimonious to interpret these correlations as reflecting a parent-to-child effect. Contrary to this position, much of the extant literature may be interpreted in terms of child effects on parents. It should be noted that there is a difficulty in verifying or disproving Bell's contention when most of the research is correlational. An alternative would involve the manipulation of some aspect of a child's behavior to determine its effect on parental behavior. In the current literature, the child's behavior is seldom the independent variable or the parent's behavior the dependent variable. An exception to this general neglect concerns some data analyzed by Bell (1971). He demonstrated the role that young children's smiles and vocalizations played in determining their mothers' interactions with them.

Bell's (1971) model of family interaction is bidirectional. It attempts to explain interaction in terms of stimulus effects of all participants constituting a social system. A similar model of dyadic interaction was developed by Patterson and Reid (1970). They state that " 'Reciprocity' describes dyadic interaction in which the persons A and B reinforce each other, at an equitable rate. In this interaction, positive reinforcers maintain the behavior of both persons. 'Coercion' . . . refers to interaction in which aversive stimuli control the behavior of one person and positive reinforcers maintain the behavior of the other" (133). It is clear that the coercion hypothesis describes what was occurring in the situation presented at the beginning of this section. The child's behavior was positively reinforced when the father said that he could stay awake for another half hour. In addition, the father's compliant response terminated an aversive event, namely, crying. Patterson and Reid's model has sufficient generality to provide for fuller analyses of most, if not all, family interactions. These analyses should lead behavior modifiers in the direction of developing more comprehensive home intervention programs, programs which include the child as a change agent. Although some workers have used children to change parent behavior, the available reports are generally of a nonexperimental nature, so that it is difficult to assess the effectiveness of these efforts (see below).

Further support for the "reciprocal" view of family interaction comes from observational research. Kogan et al. (1969) made sequential observations of mother-child interaction patterns. This experimental approach permitted the authors to determine what mother and child behaviors occurred concurrently. Based on this kind of analysis it follows that a behavior modifier may be able to alter parent target behaviors by training a child to emit a behavior other than the one which was correlated with a parent target behavior. Larson (1973) collected some preliminary data using a similar approach. Multiple measurements of parent (as well as child) behaviors were made. A record was also kept of what antecedent and consequent events were associated with the occurrence of particular behaviors. It is only one step further to attempt to change a behavior by altering antecedents and consequences. This type of methodology has been more fully developed by Ray and his associates (e.g., Ray and Ray, 1972). Their model provides a powerful tool to the behavior modifier in his attempt to understand a family network and, if necessary, to produce changes in it.

In summary, both common sense and a substantial body of research indicate that parents and children control each other's behavior. Heretofore, behavior modifiers have stressed the parents' role in shaping and maintaining their childrens' behavior, and published papers reflect this fact. There have been, however, several efforts to train children to modify parent behavior. The discussion in the following section summarizes that work and, hopefully, will serve as an impetus for further systematic investigation into this area of applied behavior modification.

Training Children as Change Agents

There is an experimental literature on the use of children as behavior modifiers. Surratt et al. (1969) showed that a fifth-grade student successfully engineered change in four fourth-graders. Likewise, Winett et al. (1970) used second-grade students to dispense tokens to peers when the teacher was occupied elsewhere. Farris et al. (1968) have demonstrated that students between the ages of eight and twelve were successfully taught principles of behavior in an academic classroom. In an institutional setting for delinquents, Buehler et al. (1966) recognized that it was not a question of whether the children influenced each other's behavior. Rather, the issue was one of finding ways of structuring the interpersonal environment so that the influence was beneficial to the members of the institution. Thus, as shown in the above examples, children have been successfully taught to alter the behavior of others. The remainder of this paper will focus on work which bears directly on its theme—child-directed behavior change of parents.

Alvord (1973) published a manual for parents which described a home-based token system for the whole family. A section on "Child Manages Parents" is included. Alvord states: "Parents should be included in the Home Token Economy as a means of furthering their use of the Home Token Economy and of making the children feel that the parents are also involved." At this time, no experimental evidence on the Home Token Economy is known to the authors.

Patterson and Reid (1970) briefly mention a case in which siblings were taught to reinforce their mother for emitting operants such as smiling and laughing. Although they found that the children were initially quite mechanical in the dispensing of social reinforcers, improvements came in time. Once again, however, no experimental data were presented concerning this intervention.

A recent paper has discussed direct attempts to teach children to modify their parents' behavior (Gray et al., 1974). At the first contact, parents were asked to permit the authors to work with their child. The parents were not initially told that their children were to shape them. One case was described in which a girl's mother was not consistent in having meals on time nor did she wash and iron clothes. The girl was trained to shape these behaviors through the administration of contingent consequences. The new gains maintained over a more than one year follow-up. Data were not presented on this case.

The present authors have been studying methods of training children to modify parent behavior. The ultimate objective is to develop behavior-change strategies which include all family members. However, until sufficient data are collected on child-directed programs the focus will remain limited. The emphasis of the discussion is on method. The data gathered to date are still preliminary. Those, and new, data will be made public after an entire replication of the procedures has been carried out. Also, a reliability study of trained home observers and of child-monitored observations will be made.

Children have become involved in the project as a result of initial contact with parents. The parents are told that the therapists will be working with the children. A program for altering parent behavior is developed only if indicated by the information obtained from the initial phases of the program. A typical program is developed in the following sequence:

1. Contact with parents; they state their reasons for seeking consultation.
2. Contact with child.
3. Administration of checklists to determine type and severity of problem areas.
4. Therapist's decision if child-initiated intervention is appropriate.
5. If appropriate, trained observers begin making home observations two or three times weekly.
6. Concurrently, target behaviors are defined and intervention strategies are developed. This is done in a clinic setting.

7. Children are given instructions to follow through with parent(s).
8. Modification of a program is made after observer- and child-collected data are inspected.

Information concerning the nature of family interactions is initially obtained from behavior checklists administered to parents and children and from verbal reports. More specific data are subsequently collected by home observations. Based on these combined sources, parent target behaviors are selected. The intervention phase involves giving the children instructions to carry out while at home. Continued home observations by trained observers and by the children determine the effectiveness of a program.

For experimental purposes, a multiple baseline design is employed. The frequencies of several target behaviors are measured, with a contingency being applied to each at different points in time. If the behaviors change in rate after consequences have been applied to them, that is support for the effectiveness of the intervention. For example, in one family two daughters (ages 12 and 13) independently recorded the frequency of three of their parents' behaviors—yelling (father), smoking (mother), and spending time with daughters (father). Over a period of eight weeks a contingency was attached to occurrence of each of these behaviors. The findings indicated some evidence that the parents' knowledge that their behavior was being recorded (contingency initiated by children) was sufficient to alter the frequency of the target behaviors.

The authors believe that the model of family interaction and the approach to family intervention discussed in this paper offer a new direction to the behavior modifier. The family is a social system, and each member of that system plays a vital part in determining the types and quality of behavior of every other member. It seems only logical to conclude that programs to restructure family interaction should include all family members, not just parents as has been generally the case.

REFERENCES

ALVORD, J. R.: *Home Token Economy.* Champaign, Ill.: Research Press, 1973.
BELL, R. Q.: A reinterpretation of the direction of effects in studies of socialization. *Psychol. Rev.,* 75, 81-95, 1968.
BELL, R. Q.: Stimulus control of parent or caretaker behavior by offspring. *Devel. Psychol.,* 4, 63-72, 1971.
BERNAL, M. E.: Training parents in child management. In: R. H. Bradfield (Ed.), *Behavioral Modification in Learning Disabilities.* San Rafael, Calif.: Academic Therapy Publications, 1971.

BUEHLER, R. E., PATTERSON, G. R., and FURNISS, J. M.: The reinforcement of behavior in institutional settings. *Behav. Res. and Ther.*, 4, 157-167, 1966.

CHRISTOPHERSEN, E. R., ARNOLD, C. M., HILL, D. W., and QUILICH, H. R.: The home point system: Token reinforcement procedures for application by parents of children with behavior problems. *J. Appl. Behav. Anal.*, 5, 485-497, 1972.

FARRIS, H. E., KENT, N. D., and HENDERSON, D. E.: Teaching behavioral science in the elementary and junior high school. Unpublished paper, 1968.

GEWIRTZ, J. L.: A learning analysis of the effects of normal stimulation, privation, and deprivation on the acquisition of social motivation and attachment. In: B. M. Moss (Ed.), *Determinants of Infant Behavior.* New York: Wiley, 1961.

GRAY, F., GRAUBARD, P. S., and ROSENBERG, H.: Little brother is changing you. *Psychol. Today*, 7, 42-46, 1974.

HERBERT, E. W., PINKSTON, E. M., HAYDEN, M. L., SAJWAJ, T. E., PINKSTON, S., CORDUA, G., and JACKSON, C.: Adverse effects of differential parental attention. *J. Appl. Behav. Anal.*, 6, 15-30, 1973.

KOGAN, K. L., and WIMBERGER, H. C.. An approach to defining mother-child interaction styles. *Perceptual and Motor Skills*, 23, 1171-1177, 1966.

KOGAN, K. L., WIMBERGER, H. C., and BOBBITT, R. A.: Analysis of mother-child interaction in young mental retardates. *Child Devel.*, 40, 799-812, 1969.

LARSON, K. M.: Unpublished data, 1973.

LYTTON, H.: Observational studies of parent-child interaction: A methodological review. *Child. Devel.*, 42, 651-684, 1971.

PATTERSON, G. R.: *Families: Applications of Social Learning to Family Life.* Champaign, Ill.: Research Press, 1971.

PATTERSON, G. R., COBB, J. A., and RAY, R. S.: A social engineering technology for retraining the families of aggressive boys. In: H. E. Adams and I. P. Unikel (Eds.), *Issues and Trends in Behavior Therapy.* Springfield, Ill.: Charles C Thomas, 1973.

PATTERSON, G. R., and REID, J. B.: Reciprocity and coercion: Two facets of social systems. In: C. Neuringer and J. L. Michael (Eds), *Behavior Modification in Clinical Psychology.* New York: Appleton-Century-Crofts, 1970.

RAY, R. D., and RAY, M. R.: Behavioral contingency analysis: A method for the description and analysis of ecological behaviors. Paper presented at the Southeastern Psychological Association Meeting, Atlanta, Georgia, April, 1972.

STOTT, D. H.: *Studies of Troublesome Children.* New York: Humanities Press, 1966.

SURRATT, P. R., ULRICH, R., and HAWKINS, R. P.: An elementary student as a behavioral engineer. *J. Appl. Behav. Anal.*, 2, 85-92, 1969.

WENAR, C., and WENAR, S. C.: The short-term prospective model, the illusion of time, and the tabula rasa child. *Child Devel.*, 34, 697-708, 1963.

WINETT, R. A., RICHARDS, C. S., KRASNER, L., and KRASNER, M.: Child monitored token reading program. Unpublished manuscript, 1970.

14

Power, Programming, and Punishment: Could We Be Overcontrolling Our Children?

ROBERT F. PETERSON

Behavioral control is an emotional topic for many people. Most in our society see control as a negative word. Control implies a lack of freedom, of choice, of spontaneity, and of creativity. The word connotes aversive and punitive practices. It suggests getting people to act in ways they do not want to act. Few people want their behavior controlled.

On the other hand some control is O.K. To control one's environment seems desirable. It is important to keep out the cold, to eliminate disease, and to harness the power of a giant river. Control of our physical environment seems more acceptable.

Control may be conceptualized in several ways. The determinist assumes people are always being controlled. The controlling agents are the physical and social environments within which we live. Control may be the result of conscious planning by another person or the result of haphazard interactions. If one assumes behavior is lawful, one assumes it is controlled.

An assumption about behavior, however, is not the same as the ability to control behavior. Nevertheless, this ability is increasing. Since the early 60's a vast body of literature has been accumulated demonstrating how behavior can be controlled. We have learned a great deal about how to change behavior—particularly the behavior of children.

Positive Versus Negative Control

It has been argued that the problem of control really centers around the type of control employed. The solution involves turning from the frequent use of aversive, negative, and punishing consequences to the use of

The author expresses his thanks to Linda Whitney Peterson for her helpful criticisms of this manuscript.

reinforcing consequences. This argument suggests that there is no problem of control per se; it is merely a problem of the better use of consequences. It has also been stated that it may be possible, for example, to raise a child without ever having to use punishment. From a personal point of view I would love to know how to do that. I find it impossible to raise my own child without resorting to punishment. Perhaps programming is the answer. If we ultimately knew enough about stimulus control we could guide children from response to response. Learning would be errorless—as Terrace (1963) has demonstrated in other species. The obvious counterargument to this proposal is that no adult has enough control over the environment to arrange stimuli in such a fashion. Few would want to have such control. During a recent visit to the University of Nevada, Terrace argued that error-free learning may not be desirable from an emotional viewpoint. Individuals may need occasional failure to develop the stability needed to cope with the stress of an unprogrammed environment.

Behaviorists have also attempted to cope with concern over control by talking about the reciprocal relationship between individual and environment. Consider, for example, the now traditional cartoon of the rat in the Skinner box speaking to another rat, saying, "Boy have I got this psychologist under control. Every time I press this lever he has to put in another pellet." In other words, the control was considered reciprocal. This reciprocity also existed between parent and child. If a parent wished his son to play more cooperatively with his sister, the parent would control this behavior by praising examples of desirable play. The child in turn controlled Dad's praise with the type of response he displayed when playing. Some people have argued that this conceptualization diffused the issue of control in behavior. For many years this explanation seemed satisfactory but now it is difficult to be comforted by it. Instead, there appear to be circumstances where control could be and is a serious problem.

Why Reciprocal Notions of Control Are Unsatisfactory

The reciprocal notion of control seems unsatisfactory because any two individuals may not be equal in terms of the number of skills, responses, and alternatives they can bring to bear on each other's behavior. How much influence one person has over another could be defined as power. Interpersonal power is apparently a function of the number of different ways that one person can influence another, i.e., the number of potential reinforcers, punishers, and other stimuli that can be utilized. It seems clear that if we look at the rat in the Skinner box, the psychologist shaping the rat's behavior has many more alternatives available than does the rat. The same is true when we think of the interaction between an adult and a child. The adult can influence the child through physical force, through contingencies, through complex verbalizations and lines of reasoning, and through command over many physical assets, particularly money. The child may have considerably less at his or her disposal. For these reasons the reciprocal explanation of control and counter-control does not appear to resolve the issue.

If few people want their behavior controlled, then control must be bad. If control is bad, then overcontrol must be worse. What then, is overcontrol? One feature of overcontrol concerns the specification of behavior. Particularly important is the frequency with which specification occurs. Parents obviously specify more behaviors for their children than children ever specify for their parents. While there may be a reciprocal interaction between the two where the response of one does influence the other, that is a separate issue from the specification of which behavior an individual will perform. For example, a parent may order a child to pick up his dirty clothing and put it in the laundry. There are few children who have ordered their parents to leave dirty clothing strung around the house (if they tried they wouldn't get away with it). Thus overcontrol seems to occur when there is a high frequency of social S^D's for a behavior. These S^D's tend to occur when there are no particular consequences motivating the individual to carry out that behavior. Repeated specification of the same response ("Brush your teeth, John") is usually called nagging.

Let us consider other kinds of control. Earlier it was noted that people seem to be less concerned about control over the physical environment than control by the social environment. This lack of concern seems to extend to being controlled by the physical environment. The physical environment does seem to be a great deal more consistent in influencing our behavior; there are no exceptions to the law of gravity. People, however, are not nearly so consistent. Ferster (1967), in an excellent paper on behavioral control, has made a distinction between what he calls "arbitrary" and "natural" reinforcement. He points out that it may be better for a child to go outside without a coat and feel cold than have his parent tell him beforehand to wear his coat. If the child has not been outside and experienced the cold, he is not motivated to wear his coat. Some people react to such specification as if it's aversive. This reaction does not exist if mother says nothing and the child goes out and gets cold. It is important, however, to consider motives for behavioral control. In this case the child's mother may be seriously concerned that her son will become ill, or she may be worried that she will be forced to care for a sick child when she does not have time to do so. Thus it seems important to examine who benefits when one person attempts to alter the behavior of another. Overcontrol may occur when these benefits are grossly unequal.

To carry this point further, there is a controversy currently in the literature about how behavior modifiers should operate in classroom situations. Given a disruptive class, should they try to reduce disruptive behaviors in the classroom or should they ignore such problems and try to improve academic performance? Increased academic performance is likely to be incompatible with disruptive behavior. It is interesting to note that, given these two alternatives, teachers are the most immediate beneficiaries of a program involving the control of disruptions. There may be little skill gained by the children in becoming less disruptive. They may, of course, obtain different reinforcers for being less disruptive, but they may not receive a net increase in reinforcement, assuming a loss of peer attention for disruptive behavior. On the other hand, it is the children who gain the most in a program designed to increase academic skill. It would seem that the examination of issues like this one is important in determining the direction and future for techniques of behavioral control.

Programming Behavior

One technique that has been useful in controlling behavior is programming. Programming involves selecting a terminal behavior, breaking the behavior down into smaller bits, evaluating entering behavior, and finding sufficient motivation to move the individual toward the terminal behavior. The problem with programming, from a control point of view, is that one individual has specified the behavior for another individual. This may be without any particular negotiation on the part of the second individual. Children in the classroom may have no interest in learning to subtract. Such a deficit, however, does not stop us from trying to educate them. Teachers run into problems of resistance in learning simply because the students have little motivation to proceed through the program. The benefits may not be apparent to the learners. Again we come to the problem of specifying a behavior when the history of the person is not such as to motivate him to action.

The Behavioral Model for Dealing with Children

Let us examine the basic model that is most often utilized in working with children. Tharp and Wetzel, in *Behavior Modification in the*

Natural Environment (1969), have described this model as involving three people: a child, a parent or adult, and a therapist. The first is termed a "target"—the person with the problem behavior; the second, a "mediator"—the person with control over the target's reinforcers; and the third, the "consultant"—the person with the knowledge of how to control or change the target. It should be noted that the child does not seek change; it is an adult who seeks change in the child's behavior. (Parenthetically, how many of us would like to be known as a target? Does anything good ever happen to a target?)

Contrast this model with the model employed when an adult has a problem. Aside from the obviously psychotic and others referred by the courts, adults often seek out a therapist when their behavior is intolerable to them. Some do seek assistance when forced by another person in their environment. Thus the adult model includes the consultant and the target but not the mediator. Adult treatment is not based on the notion that one adult (the mediator) will be taught to change the behavior of another (although some marital cases may be the exception to this statement). In family situations a wife may come to a therapist because she thinks her husband is a problem, her husband may seek help because he thinks she is a problem, but most often people come to therapists because they find themselves unhappy, unable to achieve certain ends, or not functioning well in their environment. There is a sharp contrast between those who come to a therapist because *they* want to change *their own* behavior and the mother or father who brings a child to a therapist because they want the *child's* behavior changed. These are two different motivational situations and we must deal with them differently. The adults are motivated to change something about their life and their situation. The child may not be at all motivated to change. Thus, behavioral procedures have relied on external agents to specify the behavior to be altered, and we have taught this agent how to impose consequences in order to bring about new behavior.

The use of external agents to change responses is only one method for modifying children's problems. In a recent paper, Hively and Duncan (1972) elaborate two other models for controlling behavior. They point out that programs may involve "self" management, "other" management, and "reciprocal" management. Self management involves a situation where the individuals making the response choose new responses they would like to make, begin to record their own behavior, place contingencies or other motivational devices on themselves, and attempt to bring about the specified change. In this model there may be no interaction with another social agent over the problem. If therapist-client interaction occurs, it may only involve an exchange of information as to how to maximize the change.

The second category, other management, typically concerns two or more people. One person chooses the behavior that the other should display, sets up contingencies and motivational circumstances that will bring about those behaviors, and waits for the behaviors to appear. This is obviously the method used most often in the behavioral treatment of children and has already been discussed.

In the third kind of control, reciprocal management, two persons mutually determine which behaviors to change, both record responses and negotiate the motivational circumstances which might bring about change. It should be noted that this kind of reciprocal management is clearly different from the notion of reciprocal control discussed earlier. In no case did the rat and the psychologist discuss which behaviors each of them should display, or mutually record and jointly determine the motivational circumstances used.

What are the implications of these three models for the overcontrol of behavior? One implication is that high frequency specification of behavior is part of other management. A second implication suggests that overcontrol could be the result of a lack of balance between self, other, and reciprocal management. It is obvious that a person could engage in too much other-management. Whether this is true of self and reciprocal management is not certain. It is possible that a parent could become so skilled at self-management that a child's behavior could be even more controlled by a parent than through the direct approach of other-management.

Overcontrol in the abstract is not nearly as interesting as overcontrol exemplified by specific instances. Let us consider some examples.

A family sits down to dinner. The mother takes plates out of the cupboard, places them on the counter top, and fills them with portions of food which has been cooking on the stove. One of the family rules is that the children must eat all the food on their plates before they may have dessert. Mother has specified a contingency and the amount of behavior that must be displayed, in this case the amount of food that must be eaten. While mother may be reinforced by the amount and type of food her children eat—she does not consider their reinforcers in this regard. It would be better if the children were allowed to determine how much food they would eat before dessert is allowed. Some parents might be concerned that the children would choose little nutritious food and immediately call for dessert. However, some minimal amounts and types of food could be agreed upon in negotiation with the children. Another solution might involve specifying that the amount of dessert allowed would be proportional to the amount of other foods eaten prior to dessert.

A second example illustrates a different problem of control. Some years ago Allen and Harris (1966) published a study about a little girl who scratched herself. This behavior became so severe that the girl frequently bled and was covered with scabs. No physiological reasons for this behavior had been found. Allen and Harris noted that the interactions of this child with her mother were characterized by few reinforcers from the mother, much criticism, and a high frequency of commands to engage in various behaviors. A reinforcement program was developed which specified (1) that the little girl was to be reinforced by her mother at brief intervals for periods of not scratching, and (2) that criticism was to cease. If she went through an entire day without scratching, she was allowed to go to the store and buy an item for her Barbie doll. The child would be allowed to choose the item. This program was very successful for several weeks. The scratching was drastically reduced. One day the mother called Ms. Allen and Ms. Harris and indicated that the child had scratched herself severely and the program had fallen apart. The parents had become disillusioned, the father had spanked the child, and they were ready to abandon the program. Careful questioning by Ms. Allen and Ms. Harris revealed that the child had not scratched during the day and had been taken to the store to buy a Barbie-doll item. However, the item that the child selected was too costly and the mother told the child she could not have it. The following evening the girl resumed scratching. In this particular circumstance, not only had the contract with the child been broken, but control had been taken away from the youngster.

This mother controlled her child by commanding, specifying, and criticizing. The child controlled mother's behavior by scratching. When mother changed her form of control the child changed also. But when the child's opportunity to control a valuable reinforcer was taken from her, she went back to her earlier method of managing her mother.

The importance of control has been illustrated in studies of other species as well. Joffe, Rawson, and Mulick (1973) tested the effects of two environments on the emotional responses of rats. One environment was a contingent environment. Here the animals controlled the delivery of food, water, and light. The second environment was identical, but the animals could not control these conditions. The experimenters decided when food, water, and light would be available. Subsequently, the animals were tested for fear responses in an open field situation. The authors recorded urination and defecation. The animals raised in the environment where they controlled the presentation of light, water, and food were judged to be less emotional than those raised where control was held by the experimenters. Such findings provoke questions about how much and what kind of control is needed to insure that all organisms, particularly humans, develop into independent, well functioning adults.

Some Alternatives to Overcontrol

Given that problems in the overcontrol of behavior exist, how can they be resolved? Perhaps more important, how can they be prevented? What can we tell parents that will increase the joy of rearing children, as well as the pleasure of being a child? How can we increase the chances of bringing effective, useful new members into our complex society?

One currently popular psychologist, Thomas Gordon, has discussed several child-rearing methods which deserve attention. Gordon's book *Parent Effectiveness Training* (1970) is certainly not written from a behavioral point of view. It does, however, have a great deal to say about the control of children's behavior. Gordon suggests that in any parent-child conflict, it is important to determine "who's got the problem"—in other words, who is not being reinforced. If Johnny is unhappy because he did not make the Little League, that is Johnny's problem. On the other hand, consider Bill, who goes into his closet before school and puts on a red shirt and orange pants. He likes it. His mother (who happens to be an interior decorator) does not see such a combination as beautiful. In this case, the parent owns the problem, not the child. Mother is not being reinforced. It is clear that Bill's choice will cause no one harm and may have few negative consequences for him. His mother, however, may try to influence this behavior by criticizing his choice of clothing and suggesting that other colors be worn. The question is, should she? How much control should be used?

Gordon suggests three methods for controlling children's behaviors. With the first method the parent simply specifies what the child should do. If the child does not want to go to a church picnic, the parents simply say "you will—or else!" Compliance is either forced upon the child or the child is rewarded for going. The second method is used when the child has a solution to the problem. For example, Jill can't find her old coat. She wants to wear her new coat out to play. It is muddy outside. Jill's dad, however, doesn't like this alternative. Yet he gives in rather than go through a long argument with her. Using these two approaches the parent either gets his way or the child her way. One wins and one loses. Having employed both methods Gordon quotes one parent as saying, "I try to be permissive with my children until they get so bad I can't stand them. Then I have to change and start using my authority until I get so strict I can't stand myself" (p. 11).

According to *Parent Effectiveness Training,* there is a better way of living with children. This better way suggests that parents learn two procedures—active listening and "I" statements. Active listening is Rogerian reflection. The child presents a problem and the parent reflects back feelings. For example, a child says, "Boy do I have a lousy teacher this year. I don't like her. She's an old grouch." The parent says, "It sounds like you're really disappointed with your teacher." And the child says, "I sure am." Gordon argues that active listening when carried far enough allows children to achieve insight into their problems—an argument that we have heard for many years from more traditionally oriented therapists.

"I" statements involve a parental communication of feelings. This communication describes the parent's reactions to a problem. There should be no criticism, implied or otherwise, of another individual in an "I" statement. The opposite of the "I" statement is the "You" statement. "You" statements contain punitive and critical remarks about the child. The differences can be seen in the following situation. A parent arrives home and finds a messy house. The parent who is skilled at making "I" statements says, "I get very unhappy when I have to live in a messy house." In contrast a "You" statement might be, "You are very thoughtless. You have made this house a mess. Why can't you be more careful?" The use of both active listening and "I" statements can be seen in this final example: Father: "I'm upset about the supper dishes being left in the sink. Didn't we agree you would get them done right after dinner?" Jan: "I felt so tired after dinner because I stayed up until 3:00 a.m. doing that term paper." Father: "You didn't feel like doing the dishes right after dinner?" Jan: "No, so I took a nap until 10:30. I will do them before I go to bed, O.K.?" Father: "O.K. by me" (p. 137).

What has this approach to do with control and overcontrol? First, active listening does not involve a specification of what the child should do. The parent acts as an interested listener. It is an inexpensive form of traditional psychotherapy, where the child is allowed to control the direction of the conversation. Second, "I" statements decrease the possibility of parental overcontrol. They also do not specify the behavior for the child but do indicate when a parent is not reinforced. "I" statements appear to be a gentle communication of how an individual is affected by a situation. They appear to give feedback without producing the emotional responses which hinder a change in behavior.

Gordon's approach is not immune to criticism. "I" statements, for example, may only be effective ways of changing responses if the child is sensitive to and cares about a parent's feelings. If he or she does not care, there would be little motivation to change. However, research which would tell us how to develop such sensitivity would undoubtedly be worth pursuing.

Behaviorists have been leery about therapists who see talking to children as the basic treatment technique. Parents who "reason" with their children and seldom apply consequences often have unmanageable offspring. Nevertheless, Gordon's approach deserves examination. Studies are needed which would suggest when these methods might be used and how much change they can produce. If investigations support them, useful techniques for reducing overcontrol may be added to our repertoires.

Some Environmental Alternatives to Overcontrol

One method of controlling behavior is to employ antecedent and setting conditions to influence the probability of a given response. Antecedent and setting conditions include the physical, social, and historical circumstances surrounding the behaving organism. Interestingly, this area has not been subjected to intense study by those in applied behavior analysis. Instead, studies have tended to focus on the effects of response consequences. A brief survey of the *Journal of Applied Behavior Analysis* will substantiate this point.

The importance of setting factors was personally impressed on me several years ago when Grover Whitehurst and I began some research on generalized imitation (Peterson and Whitehurst, 1971). Generalized imitation involves the continued performance of imitative responses even though the child is never reinforced for them.

Whitehurst and I used a number of methods in an attempt to get nursery school children to stop imitating simple motor responses. We reinforced them for wrong responses and for no response, eliminated requests to imitate, and generally employed a variety of reinforcement contingencies to strengthen other kinds of behaviors—all to no avail. Ultimately we found that these very durable imitative behaviors could be decreased if the experimenter simply left the room after demonstrating the response and returned a few seconds later. In his absence an observer scored the child's behavior through a one-way glass. When a reversal was performed and the experimenter remained in the room after demonstrating the response, generalized imitation returned to its former high level. Thus the presence of the experimenter was a setting condition. It was not a consequence produced by the child's behavior. Yet it turned out to be a powerful controller of the child's actions.

There are obviously thousands of setting conditions that may influence responding. The wise parent has used them for many years. For example, a mother takes the family car in for servicing. There is a one-hour wait. The mother provides the child with games and books in order to reduce the frequency of whining, pestering, and other unhappy behaviors.

More than ten years ago Skinner delivered a talk to a group at the University of Washington. A student asked him how he would train a young child to stop banging on the family piano. Skinner suggested that it would be folly to develop a reinforcement program to keep a toddler from hitting the piano keys. He pointed out that many years had been spent developing the piano into a reinforcing device. A better solution was to change the physical environment. Lock the piano.

Research demonstrations on how the physical environment might be altered in order to change the frequency and topography of children's behavior are sorely needed. It could be argued that psychologists have not spent nearly enough time analyzing those aspects of the environment that may make a response more or less likely without considering consequences applied by social agents. This information could reduce the need for control, particularly punitive control emanating from people. The mother whose only dishes are of fine china may be much more likely to punish a child for getting his own bowl of cereal than the mother who keeps a supply of plastic bowls on hand. Reduced discomfort on the part of the mother is another possible benefit.

In the previously mentioned book, *Parent Effectiveness Training*, the author asks what physical changes you would make in your home if you learned that a partially paralyzed parent was to come and live with you. Many families would probably go to a great deal of trouble to simplify the home environment for such a person. Interestingly enough, parents don't seem as interested in making similar changes for individuals handicapped by size and lack of skill because they are children. Investigations such as those by Sommer (1969) on the effects of physical space on behavior, and recent studies on other aspects of the child's environment such as play materials (Quilitch and Risley, 1973), point to encouraging trends in this direction.

Natural Consequences as a Solution to Overcontrol

In an earlier part of this paper I discussed some of the differences between arbitrary versus natural consequences. This distinction may also be conceptualized as one between physical and social consequences, particularly since many social consequences for behavior are based on an arbitrary standard. Overcontrol might be reduced by allowing the child to experience more natural consequences. These consequences would act as motivation for new behavior. This seems like a better alternative than trying to get the child to respond through parental admonition. Experience still seems to be one of the best, although not necessarily the most efficient, teachers. The educational value of natural consequences may be seen in the following story told by one of my neighbors.

The neighbor's son and a friend wanted to take two horses and ride up into the hills of the Sierra Nevadas a short distance away. Father and son had been there often. However, Dad felt that the boy's horse, although he was a gentle animal, was nevertheless unpredictable. The child argued and argued with his dad that he should be allowed to go. Dad was hesitant but ultimately gave in. A few hours later, the child came back with his friend. They were both riding the same horse. The boy explained that his horse had been scared by a quail, thrown him, and run off. The child was very upset. While Dad prepared to go and look for the runaway horse, the boy searched for, found, and captured the errant animal. He demonstrated a newfound respect and caution regarding the behavior of horses. He had learned an important lesson. Fatherly lectures could not have made the point as well as an unpredictable environment.

The importance of natural consequences cannot be overestimated. It is true, however, that there are some natural consequences we cannot allow our child to experience. We cannot allow a three-year-old, for example, to run into the street and experience the natural consequence of being struck by a car—he may get to experience little else. Nevertheless, it may be important to study the use of natural consequences just as much as more arbitrary social consequences. Might natural consequences maintain the behavior better than arbitrary or social consequences? The former are certainly more durable and pervasive than the latter.

The Professional's Responsibility in Developing Programs for Children

Another alternative which may prevent overcontrol is to counsel parents against its use. Some years ago, a psychologist I know was approached by the parents of a preadolescent boy who were concerned because the child was not interested in activities they believed important to his development. They had encouraged him to join the Boy Scouts, take swimming lessons, play a musical instrument, and join a bowling team, yet were upset because their son did not want to do any of these things. The parents hoped the psychologist would teach them how to motivate their son to engage in some of these activities. The psychologist met with the parents and subsequently with the child alone. The child indicated that he was not particularly interested in any of the organizations his folks suggested. He enjoyed playing with the neighbor kids. He was not ready for the structured groups his parents felt important. From talking with the parents the psychologist learned that the boy was not otherwise a serious problem either at home or at school. Ultimately it was suggested that the parents stop urging the boy to join various groups and allow him to play as he pleased. The psychologist reiterated that the child was not a behavior problem. When the child heard of the therapist's suggestions, he was overjoyed. The psychologist had made a friend for life.

Other Management

Teaching children techniques of other management may also reduce control problems between parent and child. Knowledge and practice in reinforcement and punishment on the part of children should increase their ability to cope with overcontrol. Gray et al. (1974) recently reported success in teaching children from a special education class how to change undesirable teacher behavior. Learning to identify good teacher behaviors and give positive or negative feedback apparently transformed some children from deviant to delightful. In addition, teachers changed from controlling to considerate. Thus overcontrol may be diminished as children learn better ways of influencing adults.

Self Management

An additional alternative which may reduce overcontrol involves encouraging children to learn self management skills. Children who can determine which of their own behaviors are in need of change, obtain data on responses, identify conditions which influence the behaviors, and alter their frequency would have taken a giant step toward maturity and independence. While few research reports cover the range of self management skills mentioned, an increasing number of investigations are examining the effects of self-enforced performance standards (Bandura and Perloff, 1967; Lovitt and Curtiss, 1969; Glynn, 1960; Felixbrod and O'Leary, 1973), self-administered reinforcement (Bandura and Perloff, 1967), self government (Fixsen, Phillips, and Wolf, 1973), self reporting (Fixsen, Phillips, and Wolf, 1972), self evaluation (Kaufman and O'Leary, 1972), and self recording (Broden, Hall, and Mitts, 1971).

Reciprocal Management Skills

Reciprocal behavioral management holds considerable promise. Agreements between an adult and child to count behaviors and give mutual feedback must be negotiated in order to work. A cautionary note seems in order here. Many psychologists within the behavioral approach have employed contracts in order to carefully specify responses and consequences. A contract in itself does not guarantee reciprocal management. Many contracts between child and adult describe the behavior the child is to display and the reinforcers which the adult will then deliver. Such an arrangement involves other-management rather than reciprocal management. A reciprocal program allows each member of the pair to manage consequences for the other member of the pair. While this author has found few published studies involving children on the effects of reciprocal management, such an arrangement should also reduce tendencies toward behavioral overcontrol.

Hively and Duncan (1972) note in their fine paper that "warmth and trust may be closely related to . . . the frequencies of self, other and reciprocal management." They also speculate on the implications such procedures have for behavior maintenance. It does seem possible that self and reciprocal management programs have a better chance of maintaining behaviors over time and in different settings than programs based on other management. Tomorrow's research should begin to cast light on the likelihood of such an outcome.

In *Beyond Freedom and Dignity*, B. F. Skinner (1971) said: "If a scientific analysis can tell us how to change behavior, can it tell us what changes to make? This is a question about the behavior of those who do in fact propose and make changes." It is clear that behavior analysis is well into the "how" of behavior change. The "what" is before us. We must ask not only about the children whose behavior we propose to change but about the effects of our techniques and procedures on the adults with whom the children live. Hopefully, Pogo's dictum, "We have met the enemy and he is us," will change to, "We have seen control and have applied it to ourselves."

REFERENCES

ALLEN, K. E., and HARRIS, F. R.: Elimination of a child's excessive scratching by training the mother in reinforcement procedures. *Behav. Res. and Ther.*, 4, 79-84, 1966.

BANDURA, A., and PERLOFF, B.: Relative efficacy of self monitored and externally imposed reinforcement systems. *J. Pers. and Soc. Psychol.*, 7, 111-116, 1967.

BRODEN, M., HALL, R. V., and MITTS, B.: The effect of self-recording on the classroom behavior of two eighth-grade students. *J. Appl. Behav. Anal.*, 4, 191-200, 1971.

FELIXBROD, J. J., and O'LEARY, K. D.: Effects of reinforcement on children's academic behavior as a function of self determined and externally imposed contingencies. *J. Appl. Behav. Anal.*, 6, 241-250, 1973.

FERSTER, C. B.: Arbitrary and natural reinforcement. *Psychol. Record*, 17, 341-347, 1967.

FIXSEN, D. L., PHILLIPS, E. L., and WOLF, M. M.: Achievement Place: The reliability of self reporting and peer-reporting and their effects on behavior. *J. Appl. Behav. Anal.*, 5, 19-30, 1972.

FIXSEN, D. L., PHILLIPS, E. L., and WOLF, M. M.: Achievement Place: Experiments in self government with pre-delinquents. *J. Appl. Behav. Anal.*, 6, 31-47, 1973.

GLYNN, E. L.: Classroom applications of self determined reinforcement. *J. Appl. Behav. Anal.*, 3, 123-132, 1970.

GORDON, T.: *Parent Effectiveness Training.* New York: Peter H. Wyden, 1970.

GRAY, F., GRAUBARD, P. S., and ROSENBERG, H.: Little brother is changing you. *Psychol. Today*, 7, 42-46, 1974.

HIVELY, W., and DUNCAN, A. D.: Reciprocal and self-management in educational communities. Paper presented to the International Conference on Behavior Modification, Minneapolis, Minn., 1972.

JOFFE, J. M., RAWSON, R. A., and MULICK, J. A.: Control of their environment reduces emotionality in rats. *Science*, 180, 1383-1384, 1973.

KAUFMAN, K. F., and O'LEARY, K. D.: Reward, cost and self evaluation procedures for disruptive adolescents in a psychiatric hospital school. *J. Appl. Behav. Anal.*, 5, 293-309, 1972.

LOVITT, T. C., and CURTIS, K. A.: Academic response rate as a function of teacher and self-imposed contingencies.. *J. Appl. Behav. Anal.*, 2, 49-53, 1969.

PETERSON, R. F., and WHITEHURST, G. J.: A variable influencing the performance of generalized imitative behaviors. *J. Appl. Behav. Anal.*, 4, 1-9, 1971.

QUILITCH, H. R., & RISLEY, T. R.: Effects of play materials on social play. *J. Appl. Behav. Anal.*, 6, 573-578, 1973.

SKINNER, B. F.: *Beyond Freedom and Dignity.* New York: Knopf, 1971.

SOMMER, R.: *Personal Space: The Behavioral Basis of Design.* Englewood Cliffs, N. J.: Prentice-Hall, 1969.

TERRACE, H. S.: Discrimination learning with and without "errors." *J. Exper. Anal. of Behav.*, 6, 1-27, 1963.

THARP, R. G., and WETZEL, R. J.: *Behavior Modification in the Natural Environment.* New York: Academic Press, 1969.

INDEX